Democratic Theory Today

Democratic Theory Today

Challenges for the
21st Century

EDITED BY

April Carter and Geoffrey Stokes

Polity

First published in 2002 by Polity Press in association with Blackwell
Publishers Ltd.

Reprinted in 2007, 2008, 2009

Polity Press
65 Bridge Street
Cambridge CB2 1UR, UK

Polity Press
350 Main Street
Malden, MA 02148,USA

ISBN 978-0-7456-2194-4
ISBN 978-0-7456-2195-1 (pbk.)

A catalogue record for this book is available from the British Library.

Library of Congress Cataloging-in-Publication Data

Democratic theory today : challenges for the 21st century / edited by April
Carter and Geoffrey Stokes.
    p. cm.
    Includes bibliographical references and index.
    ISBN 978-0-7456-2194-4 – ISBN 978-0-7456-2195-1 (pb)
    1. Democracy. I. Carter, April. II. Stokes, Geoffrey.
JC423 .D4444 2001
321.8 – dc21

                                    2001037491

Typeset in 10 on 12pt Sabon
by Best-set Typesetter Ltd., Hong Kong
Printed in Great Britain by MPG Books Ltd, Bodmin, Cornwall

This book is printed on acid-free paper.

For further information on polity, please visit our website: http://www.polity.co.uk

Contents

Acknowledgements   vii
Contributors   viii

Introduction   1
April Carter and Geoffrey Stokes

Part I Challenges to Democracy

1 **Democracy and Citizenship**   23
   Geoffrey Stokes

2 **Democracy and Inequality**   52
   Harry Brighouse

3 **Democracy, Citizenship and Gender**   73
   Elizabeth Frazer

4 **Democracy and Group Rights**   97
   John Kane

5 **Democracy and Indigenous Self-determination**   121
   Michele Ivanitz

6 **Democracy and Nationalism**   149
   Margaret Canovan

Part II Theoretical Responses

7   Deliberative Democracy   173
    Mark Warren

8   Civil Society and Democracy   203
    Baogang He

9   Associative Democracy   228
    April Carter

10 Social Democracy   249
    Raymond Plant

11 Transnational Democracy   269
    Anthony McGrew

Index   295

Acknowledgements

Many people have helped bring this book to completion. The editors would like to thank the Department of Government at the University of Queensland for granting financial assistance towards the preparation of this book. We are also indebted to Karen Gillen and Karen La Rocca for their expertise in getting the manuscript ready for publication. Gratitude is due to Kate Feros for her valuable research assistance. Geoff Stokes would like to thank St Catherine's College, Oxford University and the Research School of Social Sciences, Australian National University for providing facilities and surroundings conducive to working on the book. David Held deserves a special mention for encouraging us to take up the project.

April Carter
Geoffrey Stokes

Contributors

Harry Brighouse is Professor of Philosophy at the University of Wisconsin, Madison, and Professor of Philosophy of Education at the Institute of Education, University of London. He has published many articles on political philosophy and education policy and is a frequent contributor to the bi-monthly US socialist magazine, *Against the Current*. He has recently published a book entitled *School Choice and Social Justice* (Oxford University Press, 2000).

April Carter is an Adjunct Associate Professor in the School of Political Science and International Studies, University of Queensland. Her books include *Authority and Democracy* (Routledge, 1979), *The Politics of Women's Rights* (Longman, 1988), *Peace Movements, International Protest and World Politics* (Longman, 1992) and *The Political Theory of Global Citizenship* (Routledge, 2001). She has co-edited (with Geoffrey Stokes) *Liberal Democracy and its Critics* (Polity, 1998) and written a number of articles on citizenship.

Margaret Canovan is Professor of Political Thought in the School of Politics, International Relations and the Environment at Keele University in England. She has published work on many aspects of political theory. Her books include *Hannah Arendt: A Reinterpretation of her Political Thought* (Cambridge University Press, 1992) and *Nationhood and Political Theory* (Edward Elgar, 1996). One of her principal interests at present is the relation between populism and democracy.

Elizabeth Frazer is Official Fellow and Tutor in Politics, New College, and Lecturer in Politics, Faculty of Social Studies, University of Oxford. She is the author of *Problems of Communitarian Politics* (Oxford University Press, 1999) and co-author (with N. Lacey) of *The Politics of Community* (Harvester/Wheatsheaf, 1993). She is currently working on ideas and ideals of public life, and questions regarding political education.

Baogang He is Associate Professor in the School of Government, University of Tasmania. He is the author of *The Democratisation of China* (Routledge, 1996), *The Democratic Implication of Civil Society in China* (Macmillan, 1997), and co-author (with Yingjie Guo) of *Nationalism, National Identity and Democratization in China* (Ashgate, 2000). He has co-translated several books into Chinese (including John Rawls's *A Theory of Justice*) and has published widely in English-language journals.

Michele Ivanitz is an ARC Senior Research Fellow in the Centre for Australian Public Sector Management and a lecturer in the School of Politics and Public Policy at Griffith University, Queensland. She has published articles in the *Australian Journal of Public Administration*, *Australian Aboriginal Studies* and *Accounting, Accountability and Performance*, as well as many chapters in books pertaining to indigenous politics. She has worked with indigenous communities on issues of self-determination and native title, as well as public sector programme and service devolution from government to Aboriginal jurisdictions in Canada and Australia. She is currently co-authoring a book on the management of indigenous policy in Australia.

John Kane is the Head of the School of Politics and Public Policy at Griffith University, Queensland. His articles have appeared in *Political Theory*, *NOMOS* and *Telos* and he has published many chapters in edited collections. He is co-editor (with Wayne Hudson) of *Rethinking Australian Citizenship* (Cambridge University Press, 2000) and author of *The Politics of Moral Capital* (Cambridge University Press, 2001).

Anthony McGrew is Professor of International Relations at the University of Southampton, England. He is co-editor (with P. G. Lewis et al.) of *Global Politics* (Polity, 1992), editor of *The Transformation of Democracy?* (Polity, 1997), co-author (with D. Held, D. Goldblatt and J. Perraton) of *Global Transformations* (Polity, 1999), co-editor (with D. Held) of *The Global Transformations Reader* (Polity, 2000), and co-editor (with D. Held) of *Governing the Global Polity* (Polity, 2001). He is currently engaged in research (both normative and empirical) into globalization and global governance.

Raymond Plant is Professor of European Political Thought at the University of Southampton. Prior to this, from 1994 to 2000, he was Master of St Catherine's College, University of Oxford. He has been a Labour member of the British House of Lords since 1992. His publications include *Community and Ideology* (Routledge, 1974), *Hegel* (2nd edn, Blackwell, 1983), *Citizenship, Rights and Socialism* (Fabian Society, 1988), *Conservative Capitalism in Britain and the USA* (co-authored with K. Hoover; Routledge, 1988), *Modern Political Thought* (Blackwell, 1991) and *Politics, Theology and History* (Cambridge University Press, 2001).

Geoffrey Stokes is Professor of Politics at Deakin University, Melbourne. He works in the areas of democratic theory, citizenship and Australian political thought. He is the author of *Popper: Philosophy, Politics and Scientific Method* (Polity, 1998) and has co-edited with April Carter *Liberal Democracy and its Critics* (Polity, 1998). He has also edited *Australian Political Ideas* (UNSW Press, 1994), *The Politics of Identity in Australia* (Cambridge University Press, 1997) and co-edited (with P. Chalk and K. Gillen) *Drugs and Democracy* (Melbourne University Press, 2000).

Mark E. Warren is Professor of Government at Georgetown University in Washington, DC, where he teaches political theory. He is editor of *Democracy and Trust* (Cambridge University Press, 1999) and author of *Nietzsche and Political Thought* (MIT Press, 1988). His most recent book is *Democracy and Association* (Princeton University Press, 2001).

Introduction

April Carter and Geoffrey Stokes

Since the end of the Cold War, few voices have queried the ideal of liberal democracy. Its values and institutions have now been accepted throughout most of the world as providing the only framework for achieving or maintaining genuine democracy. In the twenty-first century they provide the necessary starting point for any debate about democratic reforms.[1]

The features of the liberal democratic ideal model appear relatively straightforward. They include popular choice and governmental accountability to citizens through regular and fair elections that are contested by a number of parties. In addition, liberal democracy requires strong parliaments that can exercise control over governments and a framework of the rule of law. As a result of the historical evolution of institutions, liberal values that give priority to individual freedom have merged with the democratic emphasis on popular participation. For both liberals and democrats the provision of channels for free debate, freedom of association and political protest are essential. Constitutional and legal curbs on government policies aim to provide liberal safeguards against the oppression of minorities by the majority, but they may also have the democratic function of restraining elites from subverting the system.

With the apparent ascendance of liberal democracy, it is often forgotten that such a theoretical and institutional framework is not static but dynamic. There remain, for example, significant tensions between liberal and democratic values. In addition, liberal democracy, broadly understood, incorporates a range of traditions from both republicanism and liberalism. Where republicanism stresses an active role for citizens in governing, one major strand of liberalism sees governing as the prerogative of an elite, with citizens playing a primarily passive role as voters. Within liberal democratic theory there are debates about the extent of direct popular participation that is possible or desirable. There are also variations in the institutional forms of liberal democracy and the relative strength of liberal or democratic ideology between countries.

This book offers a critical assessment of liberal democratic theory and practice from a normative standpoint. It aims to expand the usual terms of debate to consider criticisms which can be made of the operation of existing liberal democracies from a variety of values and perspectives. In this connection, several chapters comment on different forms of inequality embedded in western societies and institutions. Various chapters also discuss theoretical approaches to citizenship and democracy that are intended both to overcome some present problems and to give greater effect to democratic and egalitarian goals. These arguments do not accept multi-party parliamentary systems as the end point of democracy, but neither do they reject liberal democratic institutions.

In advancing a series of critiques of liberal democracy today and suggesting possible ways forward, the book explores the challenges posed to liberal democratic institutions and values by significant global trends and new social movements. In particular, it discusses the implications of powerful tendencies in the capitalist economic context of liberal democracy, such as privatization and deregulation and the dominance of global market forces. Secondly, it explores the implications of other forms of globalization for democratic states. Thirdly, it examines the implications of the growing assertion of group identity and difference. The focus is primarily on western democracies, and draws on examples from Britain, the United States, Canada and Australia. But some of the chapters do encompass a wider comparative perspective, including examples from Europe, Asia and Africa. This is not, however, a book about democratization, but about how the difficulties assailing even the long-established liberal democracies give rise to new and distinct normative theoretical questions.

Challenges for Democracy

Despite the general agreement on the political benefits of liberal democracy, there is a widespread sense that its present institutions are not operating satisfactorily. First, it can be argued that they are unable to deliver reliably what citizens expect from any government, namely, a reasonable degree of social stability and economic security. These problems are exacerbated by the growing tendencies towards economic globalization and the accompanying impetus to put greater limits on government intervention in society and economy. It can also be argued that the liberal democracies are failing to fulfil their normative ideals such as maintaining liberal values and practices and providing democratic channels for people to have a say in their own collective destiny. Thirdly, liberal democracy does not take sufficient account of economic and social realities that inhibit individual fulfilment and the creation of a fully democratic society and polity. Some of these criticisms have often been made before, but they need restating in a way that responds to a changing world. Other criticisms arise out of recent awareness of the hidden injustices inflicted upon those denied full citizenship, and the inadequacy of earlier concepts of citizenship in the light of global trends.

A key problem seems to be the lack of civic engagement and widespread apathy about national politics.[2] Liberal theories of democracy assume that individuals identify themselves with a political community and have at least some minimal commitment to a shared public realm. In the richer western countries, however, such commitments appear to be in serious decline. Critical observations that individuals in an affluent society concentrate on consumerism and personal entertainment at the expense of social activity and politics arose in the 1950s in theories of 'mass society'.[3] During the 1980s, when home entertainment through television was complemented by videos and computers, concern about increased privatism and the deterioration of communal networks resurfaced. These themes were also the focus of Robert Putnam's studies of social capital which we consider below.[4]

Disquiet about loss of public spirit seems to be vindicated by the trend, most visible in the USA in the 1980s, for voters to demand tax cuts, which in practice bear most heavily on the poor and erode public services.[5] There is also evidence of a decline in traditional citizen activities. A Home Office report in November 1999 revealed that over two-thirds of those called for jury service in Britain applied for exemptions or simply failed to respond, and half of those available requested a postponement.[6] The data on electoral turnout in most western countries in the 1990s show that not only is voter turnout low, but that it is also declining.[7] This trend suggests a decreasing willingness to exercise the most basic democratic right, the vote. Such data indicate a widespread apathy about local and parliamentary politics, and, for many, a declining trust in liberal democratic governments.[8]

One of the areas of renewed debate concerns what counts as effective citizenship and how to promote it.[9] There is also growing awareness of the challenges to conventional notions of citizenship in a culturally diverse society, where people may have multiple identities and allegiances and where the possibility of global citizenship is on the agenda. In chapter 1 Geoffrey Stokes takes up these issues with reference to the theoretical and practical relationship between democracy and citizenship. He sets out a few of the key problems confronting liberal democracies and enquires into how they bear upon questions of citizenship. With a primary focus upon civic identity, Stokes then demonstrates how four normative models of democracy – liberal minimalism, civic republicanism, developmental democracy and deliberative democracy – entail different approaches to citizenship. It is argued that such models need to be evaluated in terms of their capacity not only to solve the practical problems of democratic institutions, but also to provide a basis for critique and transforming democracy, economy and society. Stokes contends further that deliberative forms of democratic citizenship may offer the best prospects for responding to these challenges.

Stokes's chapter also reminds us that some of the key questions about liberal democracy arise out of the fact that it is closely linked to the existence of a market economy. Liberalism focuses on individual autonomy and freedom, but liberal citizenship originally required independence based on property rights. Furthermore, parliamentary government and civil rights have arisen historically in countries that have strongly developed capitalist economies. For these reasons, many theorists have debated the connections between free markets and liberal democratic polities.[10] As socialists have always argued, however, market economies create major divisions between the rich and the poor. Even though the dynamics of capitalism tend to encourage rapid economic growth, and therefore to provide resources for better standards for all, the actual gap between the rich and the poor tends to widen. Moreover, the instability of capitalism subjects many – workers, businesses and farmers – to the mercy of market forces that could deprive them of their livelihoods.

The enormous differences in the conditions of the rich and the poor have also meant that, even after formal legal and political equality was achieved, the social and economic reality was gross inequality. Thus, socialists contended that formal civil and political rights were diminished by the lack of material resources to exercise them. The rich had effectively much more political power – even when workers had the vote – and the poor lacked the economic basis for becoming autonomous and effective citizens. Some liberals came to accept the moral and factual force of such socialist arguments, and supported trade union rights and experiments in worker ownership or control over their workplaces.[11] With the rise of social liberalism at the beginning of the twentieth century, civil and political rights became linked to some degree of economic security. After 1945, the implementation of progressive taxation and welfare state social security programmes extended further this 'socializing' trend in western liberal democracies.

In the 1970s, however, the evolution of the global economy, which weakened national state control of economies, and the parallel rise of neo-liberal economic and political ideology seriously damaged the older forms of social liberalism. There has been a striking rise in social inequality, especially in countries that have embraced neo-liberalism most enthusiastically. For example, a report on health in Great Britain early in December 1999 revealed that 'increasing inequality in income lifestyle, educational opportunities and jobs is resulting in thousands of extra deaths in the most deprived inner cities'.[12] A New Policy Institute report on poverty and social exclusion published a few days later claimed that, despite some improvements, especially in the level of employment, inequalities in health and education appeared by the end of 1998 to be getting worse in Britain.[13]

Harry Brighouse, who in chapter 2 documents growing inequality in the USA, Britain and Australia, starts from socialist and radical claims that material social and economic inequalities are incompatible with substantive political equality, as opposed to purely formal equality. Although he believes that in the long term a significant redistribution of wealth is required, he addresses these issues by deploying an internal critique of liberalism. Brighouse claims first that substantive political equality is a 'fundamental value of justice', but argues primarily from the liberal ideal that governments are bound to treat all their citizens with equal respect. This principle requires governments to promote substantive political equality, and Brighouse outlines three areas where political reform would assist in realizing this ideal: in electoral systems, campaign financing and political education.

Another challenge to liberal democracy's formal commitment to civic and political equality is posed by the continuing exclusion of women from full citizenship. Although women's rights became a political issue in the mid-nineteenth century, women only gained formal civic and political equality in stages during the twentieth century. The second wave of feminism, starting at the end of the 1960s, launched wide-ranging campaigns to secure women greater legal and economic rights. It also prompted a flourishing feminist scholarship that examined the roots of women's social and political inequality. Feminist political theory has often focused on the question of citizenship, arguing that women have been systematically excluded from the public realm and that, when belatedly included, they have been effectively marginalized as second-class citizens. The assumption embedded in early liberalism – that men participate in politics as head of the household – has continued to influence political culture, and therefore feminists have argued that democracy must be extended to the family and private relationships.[14] The social attitudes that denigrate women have often also been linked to extreme prejudice against men who do not conform to masculine, heterosexual roles or act as head of the family. The rise of the gay movement has challenged orthodox views about sexuality and social roles and the political exclusion of gay men and lesbians.

In chapter 3 Elizabeth Frazer addresses the inequalities experienced by both women and homosexuals. She draws on recent feminist social theory to address the topics of inequality and discrimination based on gender with reference to three main themes: inclusion, independence and voice. Like Brighouse, but for slightly different reasons, she argues that governments must be involved in transforming social relations of inequality. She examines critically the traditional ideal that citizens must be independent agents and argues instead for an understanding that citizens are social and interdependent beings. She also explores whether the principles of deliberative democracy can allow for all voices to be given a genuine hearing. Finally, Frazer broadens the discussion of gender to consider how sexuality provides a basis for public political contest.

Feminist and gay campaigns are not only a demand for equality but are often a form of identity politics that seeks public recognition for their particular identities and lifestyles. Both therefore contribute to the recent struggles for group rights within democracy. The politics of identity may take two main forms. The first is where ethnic, racial or other groups are discriminated against and they seek greater equality and inclusion (participation or representation) in liberal democratic politics. The second is where such groups aim to protect their culture against erosion and seek a separate way of life, or even rights to self-government. The lesser challenge comes from immigrant minorities within a dominant host culture. The more fundamental challenge to liberal democracy posed by the growth of identity politics comes from those groups asserting their right to a separate cultural or religious ethnic identity. Even more serious is the problem arising from larger ethnic groups with a territorial base demanding national autonomy or independence.

The growing assertion of religious or ethnic identity by minorities is due both to the increase in migration in a globalized world and to a new assertiveness among migrants, who are often no longer willing to be assimilated into the dominant culture. Some governments have responded with policies encouraging forms of multiculturalism, and such recognition of difference attempts to apply liberal principles. For example, where the Australian approach aims simply to encourage the recognition and retention of cultural difference, the North American version focuses more upon establishing regimes of affirmative action and encouraging positive discrimination for cultural minorities. Where the Australian policies operate as a form of integration into the host society, the North American ones tend to work against integration.[15]

Nonetheless, many liberals are uneasy about extending rights to groups. Such claims tend to contravene the original impetus of classical liberalism that opposed special privileges for groups such as the aristocracy and the church. Contemporary liberals fear that groups with distinct traditions might deny individuals true freedom of choice. Recognition of group rights also poses difficulties for democrats.

Encouraging religious schools of any sort promotes a sense of separate identity, but conceding the right to separate religious schools, for example, prevents a shared academic and civic education.[16] Encouraging the use of migrants' mother tongues may hamper their ability to become fluent in the mainstream language of politics, which is a major issue in relation to Spanish-speakers in the United States. Moreover, minority religious and cultural identities may raise serious questions about the civic and political equality of women. Cultures that expect women to remain secluded in domesticity exclude them from full political rights. Nonetheless, the attitudes of the dominant culture to the minorities in its midst often create greater difficulties. The intolerance of different beliefs and customs often shown by the majority of the host nation, and the prejudices which tend to exclude ethnic or racial minorities from proper representation in mainstream politics, pose a serious threat to both liberal and democratic principles that require respect for individuals and full political equality.

Distinguishing between liberal and democratic approaches, John Kane examines in chapter 4 the question of whether there are sufficient theoretical and practical grounds for claiming group rights. As background, he reviews the communitarian critique of liberalism which gives a rationale for the importance of community and the recognition of different identities. He also outlines different liberal attempts to accommodate group claims. Kane argues that a democratic perspective, with its stress on political equality, is more appropriate to assessing the case for group rights than liberalism. Nonetheless, it is important to clarify whether the goal is to give denigrated groups social respect, or whether the central issue is redistribution of resources. Kane argues that group rights are a more appropriate strategy to promote social respect. To achieve redistribution, however, Kane suggests that it may be necessary to revive leftist critical discourse based upon radical political economy.

A particularly compelling claim for group rights has come from indigenous peoples. These peoples, who, as a result of colonization, have often lost much or all of their land and had their livelihoods and cultures destroyed, began to make their voices heard politically in the 1960s and to achieve some political recognition of their demands by the 1980s and 1990s. One element in indigenous campaigns has been to demand those same political and social rights enjoyed by the majority population. For example, in one state of Australia, namely Queensland, Aborigines did not gain full voting rights until 1965, and at the Commonwealth level they did not gain full citizenship rights until 1967.[17] Indigenous people, whether living in cities or in remote areas, also suffer from significantly higher rates of unemployment, poverty, incarceration and ill health than other citizens. For example, where the unemployment rate for the total population of Australia in 1991 was 11.7 per cent, for indigenous people the rate was 30.8 per cent.[18] Regarding health, Burdon writes: 'Throughout Australia, for almost all disease categories, rates for Aborigines are worse than for other Australians: death rates are up to four times higher and life expectancy is up to twenty-one years less.'[19] Similar patterns are evident among indigenous communities elsewhere in the world.

The claims of indigenous peoples also pose a different kind of problem from those of other identity politics. As 'first nations' or 'first peoples', indigenous peoples have allegiances to place and community that take priority over the usual claims that the modern nation-state makes upon national allegiance and political obligation. Given the isolated regions in which many indigenous people live, and the serious inequalities they endure, they often seek forms of self-determination. Although they do not accept the sovereignty of the 'settler' nation, they rarely seek self-determination outside the boundaries of the nation-state. Often they draw on the resources of the nation-state to devise procedures for indigenous self-government within liberal democracies, such as in the Saami parliaments in Scandinavia, the new administrative unit of Nunavut in Canada or the arrangements for regional government in the Torres Strait Islands of Australia.

By contesting or sharing sovereignty, requiring constitutional recognition of first ownership of land and seeking public recognition of past wrongs, indigenous claims for special rights can be seen as contravening the political equality central to liberal democracy. Such criticisms have frequently been voiced by populists in Australia, who call for everyone to be treated equally.[20] The indigenous response, however, stresses that such measures are essential to reverse historical injustices.[21] Perhaps more important, such policies are crucial for simply ensuring the physical and cultural survival of indigenous groups.

Michele Ivanitz considers in chapter 5 whether the indigenous quest for self-determination can be accommodated within liberal democratic theory and practice. She reviews two key principles of democratic theory, namely, self-determination and political equality, and examines their relevance to indigenous politics in Australia and Canada. The chapter outlines the historical and cultural background to movements for indigenous self-determination, with a focus upon different concepts of property, sovereignty and political action. Ivanitz then provides case studies of how 'group rights' have been put into effect in Canada and Australia. She sketches various official forms of indigenous self-government established in the two countries, their implications for democratic theory and the consequences for indigenous people. Ivanitz's chapter demonstrates how, despite the wide differences in culture, liberal democracy can accept various programmes for indigenous self-determination without compromising core democratic principles. One problem for indigenous peoples, however, is that such regimes of self-determination have often not brought the socio-economic benefits they had envisaged.

Political recognition of identities and differences assume an even more potent form when they consolidate into nationalism. Nationalism, when it takes the form of demanding territorial political rights for those who identify themselves as a nation, can underpin liberal democracy, by providing a strong social basis for the polity. National pride can, however, turn into xenophobic rejection of strangers. Nationalists claiming to speak for the dominant group may seek to curb immigration, exclude non-nationals from democratic politics or even evict them from the country. The recent growth of right-wing populism in Western Europe reflects this tendency.[22] Where national conflict erupts between constituent groups of established states, it can be even more destructive, dividing a previously stable political society, inflaming memories of past wrongs and exacerbating current grievances. National minorities may seek more autonomy by trying to change the boundaries of the state.

Since the 1970s there has been a rise in regional nationalism in well-established western democracies, and demands for secession. In some cases devolving political powers or accepting secession may enhance the participation of people in the devolved region and increase their sense of control over their own future. But nationalist passions may inhibit cooperation on crucial policies which transcend regional borders, and lead to forms of social and political discrimination within the new 'nation'.

Margaret Canovan discusses the complex relations between democracy and nationalism by demonstrating in chapter 6 how they resist simple generalizations. She examines first how nationalism can either assist or threaten democracy, and then considers those aspects of democracy that either limit or facilitate its capacity to cope with nationalism. Canovan queries the attempts that have been made to distinguish neatly between 'civic' and 'ethnic' nationalism and the assumption that the former is more liberal than the latter. She also explores the relationship between nationalism and three interpretations of democracy: popular sovereignty, deliberative democracy and negotiated compromise. To show the complexities involved, Canovan draws upon the example of the Northern Ireland peace process undertaken in the late 1990s.

The revived awareness of ethnic identity and distinctiveness appears to be a response to the opposing trends towards a more economically and culturally uniform world under the pressure of multinational corporations and powerful media dominating channels of entertainment and information. Both tendencies – the revival of localized ethnic identity and global economic and cultural forces – are operating to weaken the established nation-state. Liberal democrats have always assumed that the boundaries of democracy were set by the boundaries of their state. Therefore the weakening of these boundaries and of the power of national governments constitutes a major threat to liberal democracy. If multinational corporations and the key finance markets determine most economic realities, then the right to vote for a national government no longer gives the citizen any effective influence on a range of crucial policies.

Democratic Responses

Political theorists have responded in a number of ways to these threats to liberal democracy. One critical postmodern approach is to shift radically the terms of discussion and query the very nature and function of democracy. Michel Foucault and those influenced by his work would argue that democratic theory is simply another 'regime of truth' facilitating the governing and disciplining of populations. Central tasks for those engaged in studies of 'governmentality' are to demonstrate how governments regulate individual and social conduct, and also to uncover possible practices of resistance.[23] On this view, for example, liberal citizenship rights are inherently limited, but they may have value in opposing the 'arbitrary impositions of governments'.[24] Although the contributors to this book examine deficiencies in existing liberal democracies, they are generally united in accepting the possibility of working through democratic institutions and of trying to realize liberal and democratic values. Despite the efforts of various theorists,[25] the relationship between the Foucauldian project and democratic theory tends to be ambiguous,[26] and it is therefore not pursued here.

One theory that seeks to draw out the implications of the liberal and democratic principles inherent in liberal democracy is deliberative democracy. This is one of the most influential and sophisticated contributions to democratic theory in recent years.[27] The theory of deliberative democracy recovers and reshapes the core ideal of reasoned public debate as the foundation for making political decisions. It is therefore also relevant to a new understanding of citizenship. By advocating greater opportunities for reasoned debate at all levels of politics, deliberative democracy not only encourages shifts in the institutional focus of citizenship activity, but also seeks to change our basic presuppositions about the nature of citizenship and the way in which it is to be practised. Another virtue of deliberative democracy is that it can be incorporated into other proposals for strengthening existing democracy, such as recognition of group rights, civil society and associative democracy. As Mark Warren points out in chapter 7, however, deliberation does not require participants in debate to discuss issues 'reasonably', nor is the aim that of achieving 'consensus'.

The most distinguished exponent of deliberative democracy is Jürgen Habermas, whose arguments arise out of his wider social theory. Warren's chapter, therefore, focuses on Habermas and provides a genetic account of how deliberative democracy relates to a wider theoretical position. Warren argues that deliberative democracy is becoming a credible alternative to liberal and republican approaches. Deliberative democracy shares certain features with earlier democratic theories, such as the requirements for an equal right to vote (power) and for a public process of deliberation (judgement). But republicans who stress deliberation envisage small unified communities, and liberals limit deliberation in larger and complex societies to elected representatives. Deliberative democracy is distinguished by its emphasis upon 'equal and effective opportunity to participate' in processes of will formation. In practice, this means that deliberation ought not to be left to political representatives and other elites, but encouraged more widely within society. That is, it should extend to associations that are part of civil society and to economic organizations. Warren concludes that deliberative democracy combines the radicalism of the democratic ideal with a strong sense of the complex realities of large-scale societies. It provides a strong normative and critical dimension to democratic theory, but one that is based upon much of what we already know and practise.

Since the 1980s, a number of democratic theorists have focused upon civil society as a means of revitalizing citizenship and democratic participation, and combating apathy within liberal democracy.[28] They argue that civil society, understood as comprising voluntary associations and organizations independent of direct control by the state, is crucial, not only for establishing democracies, but also for their consolidation and persistence. Theorists of civil society argue that it is not just political groups that are significant for empowering people and educating them to be responsible citizens. Social and cultural organizations are also important. This is the contention of Robert Putnam, who has undertaken empirical studies that compare societies where such organizations exist with those where they do not. His best-known findings arise from his long-term research into citizenship and democracy in regional governments in Italy, where some regions have much more efficient and honest government than others.[29] He concluded that the quality and effectiveness of the official institutions of democracy is strongly dependent upon the vitality of local communal groups. Organizations such as choral associations and sporting clubs tended to promote a greater sense of 'engagement, trust and reciprocity'.[30] Where this 'social capital' is strong, so too is popular commitment to the institutions of government. Although Putnam's insights have been subjected to strong criticism, he remains one of the more influential exponents of the case for civil society.[31]

A comprehensive overview of debates about civil society is given by Baogang He in chapter 8. He begins by considering the origins and various meanings of the term and the place of civil society in different theories of democracy. He also considers whether the faith placed in civil society as a means of democratization, for example by dissident intellectuals in Eastern Europe, has led its advocates to exaggerate its importance once parliamentary regimes are established. Finally, he examines a rather different function for civil society – namely, how it can contribute to resolving disputes that cross over territorial boundaries or that require their modification. By drawing upon recent examples from international politics, He suggests that where the nation-state is unable to resolve such conflicts, civil society organizations (national and international) can play a useful role. He argues that where this occurs, democracy is not diminished but enhanced.

Civil society is also central to associative democracy, but associative democrats go further and argue for devolving a range of functions now performed by the state to independent and voluntary bodies, drawing them into actual governance and providing channels for participatory democracy. The advocates of associative democracy see the focus on protest by many pressure groups and social movements as too negative. It is indeed arguable that there is a danger that some of the groups that operate outside the established political system will become increasingly alienated and that some may then reject the reasoned debate and non-violent forms of protest which are required by liberal democracy. Associative democrats suggest that campaign groups, such as Greenpeace, could also play positive roles in relation to government, for example by performing a recognized function such as monitoring standards of environmental quality.

Associative theorists also stress the pluralism and scale of contemporary western societies. Thus, they are sympathetic to the emphasis of deliberative democrats upon social complexity and the need for multiple sites of democratic deliberation. Indeed, Joshua Cohen, one of the main advocates of associative democracy, is also an exponent of deliberative democracy. Associative theorists note too that global forces are undermining the state – although Paul Hirst is critical of neo-liberal claims about the inevitability of economic globalization – and see a role for associations within global civil society.

Associative theorists also see their programme as a means of reducing economic inequalities, for example by increasing worker participation in industry and promoting the cooperative economy as an alternative to capitalist forms of management and finance. They further advocate an associative framework for administering welfare. Associative democracy can therefore be understood as an attempt to advance the goals of social democracy without the traditional emphasis on the state. Whether associative measures could achieve the multiple goals envisaged by their advocates is debatable. In chapter 9 April Carter addresses this question in the context of examining key arguments by Cohen and his co-author Joel Rogers, and by Hirst. She queries in particular whether an associative strategy could realize radical democracy and social justice within present social and economic realities.

The more traditional approach to reducing economic and social inequality and strengthening social citizenship is social democracy. The difficulty here, however, is that social democracy has usually relied upon state control over the economy, and the opportunities to continue this strategy have been severely constrained by global trends. The capacity of governments to provide health services and social welfare, and, even more fundamentally, their ability to provide and protect employment have been eroded since the 1970s. Even governments such as those in Germany and Sweden that are committed to robust programmes of social welfare and to protecting workers' rights have come under great pressure to retreat. The more radical forms of social democracy have required effective government controls over the economy and a major role for trade unions in businesses and in economic policy formulation. Now, however, there are increasing moves towards a more limited role for the state, the reduction of trade union power, and less generous welfare provision. This is one reason why associative democrats reject the previous models of social democracy and are also critical of reliance on state hierarchy. These tendencies also suggest the need to reformulate arguments for social democratic principles and policies.[32]

Raymond Plant reviews in chapter 10 the evolution of social democratic thought from its late nineteenth-century origins until today. He begins with the revisionist theory of Eduard Bernstein, who articulated the key principles of a social democracy to be achieved through parliamentary means, in opposition to Marxist analyses of capitalism and advocacy of revolutionary socialism. Plant then examines the second revisionist phase of social democracy in the 1950s, which questioned the necessity of extensive nationalization of the economy, and drew on Keynesian economics to elaborate an alternative social democratic strategy. A key advocate of this approach was C. A. R. Crosland. Plant next considers the challenges posed by the ideology of the new right and economic globalization to social democrats. He points out how the Third Way response to these challenges can be seen as either a continuation of social democracy or a departure from it. One conclusion to be drawn is that social democratic strategy has shifted decisively from a politics based on class to a politics based on a more inclusive concept of citizenship. Plant demonstrates that social democracy's emphasis on a moral critique of extreme market economic inequality, its commitment to social justice within a free market economy, and its belief in the autonomous role of politics are opposed to both Marxist and neo-liberal beliefs in the inevitable logic of global capitalism.

Where Plant focuses on moral and political challenges to neo-liberalism, other social democrats concentrate more on a critique of neo-liberal economic analysis and reject the inevitability of globalization. They question whether national governments, especially if they act cooperatively through international organizations, are really unable to control their own economies.[33] Since Sweden for long provided an ideal model of radical social democracy, its high unemployment rate in the 1990s seemed to confirm the difficulties of maintaining high levels of welfare and taxation and entrenching trade union rights in the global economy. It can be argued, however, that Swedish unemployment, which began to decline by the end of the 1990s, primarily reflected internal economic factors. Significantly, Sweden maintained generous welfare benefits to the unemployed and, although the gap between rich and poor grew in the 1990s, it remained one of the most equal countries in the OECD.[34] Furthermore, throughout most of Western Europe (except the UK) trade unions continued to shape labour contracts. Goran Therborn concludes:

'First-way social democracy still has room to manoeuvre in the world of globalization.'[35]

Social democrats seek to limit the impact of global trends. But another school of thought argues that although globalization can be a threat to national self-government, the weakening of the nation-state does not always mean a loss for democracy. In some cases, where states have agreed to international conventions enshrining a range of civil, political and social rights, it can be argued that a surrender of national sovereignty serves to give greater weight to liberal and democratic principles, which now have the force of international law. Social groups suffering discrimination, such as indigenous peoples, have appealed to international law to strengthen their claims against their own government. In addition, the more fluid political structures emerging in global society open up new arenas for democracy and citizenship.

The possibility of constructing global or transnational forms of governance, which are also responsive to democratic deliberation and control, is the question addressed by Anthony McGrew in chapter 11. He surveys the growing literature on this topic, examines communitarian, realist and radical criticisms, and argues strongly that there is a case for serious consideration of transnational democracy. McGrew identifies four distinct ideological approaches to transnational democracy – liberal internationalism, radical democratic pluralism, cosmopolitanism and deliberative democracy – and assesses their strengths and weaknesses. He concludes that cosmopolitan and deliberative theories of democracy complement each other. Furthermore, together, they provide 'the most sophisticated and persuasive arguments for democracy beyond borders' and constitute the most comprehensive attempts to reimagine democracy in this context.

Conclusion

This book surveys the current issues, the lines of tension and the possible directions of future developments in democratic theory. It has been stimulated in part by the apparent historical fact that liberal democracy has become the principal standard for evaluating national polities and politics within them. The emphasis is on *democratic* theory, and this is reflected in many of the chapters where liberal democracy is subject to criticism. The project of enlarging the democratic aspects of liberal democracy is integral to many of the analyses. A guiding assumption also is that democratic theory must have a normative dimension. Without this, democratic theory is reduced to empirical analysis whose role is simply that of explaining, and often implicitly validating, existing polities. One of the constant challenges for democratic theory therefore is to take account of the constraints of empirical 'reality', but resist closure based upon their alleged intransigence in political life.

On this argument, democratic theory provides not only the resources for critique of all forms of government, but also suggests various options for reform. For this reason, a commitment to *democratic* theory and the extension of citizenship practices requires us to explore their application to organizations and sites of conflict that are usually considered 'private'. Given that national and transnational corporations have an economic might that often translates into political power, there are good grounds for examining how they might be subject to at least a degree of democratic control. The democratic focus on equality and empowerment of all citizens may also require us to examine relations within other areas of private life, such as the family. Democratic theory therefore encourages us to examine the exercise of power at all levels. In so doing, democratic theory offers the promise of rethinking the conditions under which people can exercise greater autonomy and participate in shaping the decisions that affect their lives.

NOTES

1   On a cautionary note it should be said that similar triumphalist announcements were made after both the First and the Second World War. See H. B. Mayo, *An Introduction to Democratic Theory* (New York, Oxford University Press, 1960), pp. 20, 25–6.

2   Addressing this problem raises a number of other difficulties. Political apathy may sometimes be due to an authentic sense of powerlessness. In the past the fact that women seemed generally less interested in formal politics than men could be explained partly by their immersion in family responsibilities, but also by their lack of self-worth and low confidence in their ability to bring about change. Apathy may also be a response by the poor who lack empowerment. But, ironically, the impact of affluence in a capitalist consumer society can also erode the practice of citizenship by the comfortably off majority.

3   See Hannah Arendt, *The Human Condition* (Garden City, NY, Doubleday Anchor, 1959), pp. 38, 48, 53, 54, 196; C. Wright Mills, *The Power Elite* (New York, Oxford University Press, 1956); W. Kornhauser, *The Politics of Mass Society* (London, Routledge, 1960).

4   See also R. D. Putnam, *Bowling Alone: The Collapse and Revival of American Community* (New York, Simon and Schuster, 2000).

5   See J. K. Galbraith, *The Culture of Contentment* (London, Penguin, 1993).

6   *Independent*, 11 November 1999, p. 11. Although some people had good reasons for opting out of jury service, it remains an historically and politically important civic responsibility.

7   A. Lijphart, 'Unequal participation: Democracy's unresolved dilemma', *American Political Science Review* 91, 1 (1997): 6.

8   See 'Is there a crisis? (citizens report less trust in democratic governments)', *Economist*, 17 July 1999, pp. 49–50. For good discussions of such issues, see the essays in M. Warren (ed.), *Democracy and Trust* (Cambridge, Cambridge University Press, 1999).

9   See, e.g., G. Andrews (ed.), *Citizenship* (London, Lawrence and Wishart, 1991); E. Frazer (ed.), Special Issue on Political Education, *Oxford Review of Education* 25, 1 and 2 (1999); D. Oliver and D. Heater, *The Foundations of Citizenship* (London, Harvester/Wheatsheaf, 1994); G. Shafir (ed.), *The Citizenship Debates: A Reader* (Minneapolis, University of Minnesota Press, 1998).

10 See, e.g., G. A. Almond, 'Capitalism and democracy', *Political Science and Politics* 24, 3 (1991): 467–74; F. Bealey, 'Capitalism and democracy', *European Journal of Political Research* 23 (1993): 203–23; L. Diamond and M. Plattner (eds), *Capitalism, Socialism and Democracy Revisited* (Baltimore, Johns Hopkins University Press, 1993).

11 J. S. Mill, *On Socialism* (Amherst, NY, Prometheus Books, [1879] 1989).

12 *Independent*, 2 December 1999, p. 10.

13 *Guardian*, 8 December 1999, p. 14.

14 See C. Pateman, *The Disorder of Women: Democracy, Feminism and Political Theory* (Cambridge, Polity, 1989) and the discussion in B. Sullivan, 'Carole Pateman: Participatory democracy and feminism', in A. Carter and G. Stokes (eds), *Liberal Democracy and its Critics* (Cambridge, Polity, 1998), pp. 175–95.

15 J. Jupp, 'Immigration and national identity: Multiculturalism', in G. Stokes (ed.), *The Politics of Identity in Australia* (Melbourne, Cambridge University Press, 1997), p. 140.

16 In January 1998, the British Labour Government approved state funding for a Muslim school for the first time and for three Jewish schools. Since the Anglican and Roman Catholic Churches have a right to their own schools, the government correctly argued that this was an issue of fairness and non-discrimination (*Guardian*, 10 January, 1998, p. 7).

17 See J. Chesterman and B. Galligan, *Citizens Without Rights: Aborigines and Australian Citizenship* (Melbourne, Cambridge University Press, 1997).

18 See Appendices, in D. Horton (ed.), *The Encyclopaedia of Aboriginal Australia*, vol. 2 (Canberra, Aboriginal Studies Press, 1994), p. 1285.

19 J. Burden, 'Health: A holistic approach', in C. Bourke, E. Bourke and B. Edwards (eds), *Aboriginal Australia* (St Lucia, University of Queensland Press, 1994), p. 157.

20   The One Nation movement in Australia has recently made such claims. See G. Stokes 'One Nation and Australian populism', in M. Leach, G. Stokes and I. Ward (eds), *The Rise and Fall of One Nation* (St Lucia, University of Queensland Press, 2000), pp. 23–41.

21   These were the 'negative' grounds given for the High Court of Australia's rejection of the doctrine of *terra nullius* and their recognition of native title to land in the *Mabo* (1992) judgement. See R. H. Bartlett, *The Mabo Decision* (Sydney, Butterworths, 1993).

22   See H.-G. Betz and S. Immerfall (eds), *The New Politics of the Right: Neo-populist Parties and Movements in Established Democracies* (Houndsmill, Macmillan, 1998).

23   For select examples of studies in the governmentality tradition, see Graham Burchell, Colin Gordon and Peter Miller (eds), *The Foucault Effect: Studies in Governmentality* (London: Harvester/Wheatsheaf, 1991); Barry Hindess, *Discourses of Power: From Hobbes to Foucault* (Oxford, Blackwell, 1995); Barry Hindess, 'Representation ingrafted upon democracy?' *Democratization* 7, 2 (2000): 1–18.

24   Barry Hindess, 'Limits to citizenship', in W. Hudson and J. Kane (eds), *Rethinking Australian Citizenship* (Melbourne, Cambridge University Press, 2000), p. 73.

25   See e.g. William Connolly, *Identity/Difference: Democratic Negotiations of Political Paradox* (Ithaca, NY, Cornell University Press, 1991); W. Connolly, *The Augustinian Imperative: A Reflection on the Politics of Morality* (Newberry Park, Sage, 1993); W. Connolly, 'Beyond good and evil: The ethical sensibility of Michel Foucault', *Political Theory* 21, 3 (1993): 365–89; Jon Simon, *Foucault and the Political* (London, Routledge, 1995), pp. 116–25.

26   See L. McNay, 'Michel Foucault and agonistic democracy', in Carter and Stokes (eds), *Liberal Democracy and its Critics*, pp. 216–37.

27   See J. Bohman and W. Rehg (eds), *Deliberative Democracy: Essays on Reason and Politics* (Cambridge, MA, MIT Press, 1997); J. Elster (ed.), *Deliberative Democracy* (Cambridge, Cambridge University Press, 1998).

28   See J. L. Cohen and A. Arato, *Civil Society and Political Theory* (Cambridge, MA, MIT Press, 1992); R. Fine and S. Rai (eds), *Civil Society: Democratic Perspectives* (London, Frank Cass, 1997); J. A. Hall (ed.), *Civil Society: Theory, History, Comparison* (Cambridge, Polity, 1995); J. Keane, *Civil Society: Old Images, New Visions* (Stanford, Stanford University Press, 1998); M. Walzer (ed.), *Towards a Global Civil Society* (Providence, Berghahn Books, 1995).

29   R. D. Putnam, *Making Democracy Work: Civic Traditions in Modern Italy* (Princeton, Princeton University Press, 1993).

30   R. D. Putnam, 'What makes democracy work?' *IPA Review* 47, 1 (1994): 34.

31   See, for example, the essays in the special issue on Robert Putnam's *Making Democracy Work* in *Politics and Society* 24, 1 (1996).

32 See, for example, the essays in A. Gamble and T. Wright (eds), *The New Social Democracy* (Oxford, Blackwell, 1999).

33 The case for a continuing role for the state is argued by P. Hirst and G. Thompson in *Globalization in Question*, 2nd edn (Cambridge, Polity, 1999).

34 See Goran Therborn, 'Social democracy in one country', *Dissent*, Fall (2000): 59–65.

35 Ibid., p. 64.

Part I

Challenges to Democracy

1

Democracy and Citizenship

Geoffrey Stokes

Citizenship has become a major problem for liberal democracies. A growing disillusionment with electoral politics has accompanied declining participation in, and commitment to, liberal democratic institutions. At the same time, many groups that have suffered discrimination – women, gays, indigenous peoples and the disabled – have called both for full citizenship rights, and also 'special' rights appropriate to their distinctive needs or position in society. Against this background, since the 1980s, citizenship has become a major field of inquiry.[1] This chapter sketches a few of the main lines of thought related to citizenship and democracy.[2] The analysis raises questions about whether current theories of democratic citizenship provide sufficient resources for dealing with the problems in liberal democratic polities. A method for evaluating theories of democratic citizenship is thus proposed that focuses upon civic identity and the capacity for critique. This method is then used to evaluate four different normative models of democracy: liberal minimalism, civic republicanism, developmental democracy and deliberative democracy. It is argued that, on balance, deliberative democracy has the potential to provide a more comprehensive response to the challenges of participation, inclusion and critique confronting democracy and citizenship.

Citizenship as a Practical and Theoretical Problem

How one formulates a problem depends upon what value perspectives are adopted, and these may align with very different political purposes.

Citizenship, for example, may be understood in at least two ways, as a legal or administrative status and as a normative political concept or theory. Both understandings involve articulating a particular civic identity, as well as preferred political practices. Legal and administrative notions of civic identity primarily focus upon qualifications for citizenship and the codification of civic rights and obligations. The latter are usually determined by formal laws and regulations that reflect government policy, and generally operate to confirm the status quo. Normative conceptions of civic identity, while also indicating rights and obligations, are expressions of political possibility and imagination that transcend current practices. Furthermore, the normative concepts usually derive from democratic political theory.[3] The question 'What is the good citizen?' is therefore generally understood to mean 'What is the good citizen within a democracy?'[4] Nevertheless, normative conceptions of the democratic citizen may not always correspond to actual legal and administrative requirements. In many countries citizenship has been primarily a practice of political opposition and radical critique, oriented towards establishing or improving democratic norms, laws and institutions. Here, however, we shall consider briefly the challenges raised by 'democratic disenchantment', the politics of identity, and citizenship as critical practice within liberal representative democracies.

From the standpoint of government and political elites, the first problem with citizenship is a practical one, namely, that of a steady decline in those casting a vote in elections. On one view, this disenchantment with democracy, or 'civic deficit', is the result of citizens requiring much more of government and becoming radically disappointed when their demands are not delivered.[5] Such tendencies may have their sources in the growth of economic globalization, which has steadily undermined the sovereignty of nation-states and their capacities to control their affairs.[6] Where global markets and capitalism are dominant, the practical capacity and the normative claims of citizens to influence economic policy decisions are necessarily weakened.[7]

For liberal democratic governments, one of the proposed solutions to the problem of disenchantment is to revitalize liberal democratic citizenship. The practice of citizenship is supposed to supply a defence against the growth of authoritarianism and bolster governmental legitimacy. In this context, citizenship is often conceived as a method for promoting loyalty to the state that is not based upon nationalist sentiments or ethnicity. Such civic commitments and obligations to the larger political community are intended to help protect liberal democracy against racial or religious conflict and thus to reduce the scope for fragmentation of the nation. Accordingly, citizenship here is also a device for social control and assimilation. The argument is that strengthening a civic culture, in which citizens are more aware of their rights and responsibilities, will reinvigorate democracy. It is thought that such a political culture will insulate democracy from the threats of democratic disenchantment and ethnic conflict. Civic education is commonly proposed as an instrument for promoting citizenship values and enhancing democratic practices.[8] In this scenario, governments recognize that citizenship as a legal and administrative status is insufficient as a foundation for political loyalty or unity, and needs to be supported by programmes that encourage citizenship as a culture and practice. The question remains, however, what kinds of citizenship and democratic culture ought to be encouraged.

As for the problem of disenchantment, projects to revitalize citizenship may have little effect. Valuable as higher voter turnouts may be for enhancing the legitimacy of governments, voting by itself may not be a useful indicator of political participation or apathy. Citizens' interest and participation in politics may simply have shifted to such different sites as social movements or non-governmental organizations in civil society. It is also not clear that reviving national citizenship can have much impact on the processes of globalization. Achieving such an impact would require significant institutional change within the polity as well as reform to transnational institutions. The role of transnational corporations, which follow a political and economic logic of their own, severely limits the scope of government and hence the direct contribution that national citizens can make to economic decisions. Where national control over the economy has been greatly eroded, no amount of civic enhancement on its own will assist in restoring governmental legitimacy.

Two slightly different problems for governments emanate from the growth of the politics of identity.[9] First, there is the practical problem of how to deal with claims for recognition and rights from different cultural, ethnic and religious groups within liberal democracy. Where immigrants come from countries with little or no democratic culture, the problem arises of how to incorporate them into the society and polity. Second, even where immigration is not a central issue, in multi-ethnic states localist tendencies give priority to the maintenance of communities and ways of life based upon ethnicity, race or religion, and may give rise to conflicts. Here, issues of cultural and political autonomy such as self-government and even secession may become prominent. These claims upon local loyalty and culture can erode commitments to a wider democratic community and notions of a public good. The activism of women, gays, indigenous peoples and the disabled comprises another version of the politics of identity. The protagonists of this type of politics usually demand greater recognition, representation, more rights to resources, and reformed political procedures to allow them a more effective political voice. In practice, liberal democratic governments have responded by acknowledging a few of such claims and selectively granting various rights, such as women's rights and indigenous land rights.

One of the theoretical responses to such concerns has been to challenge the central normative ideal of a unitary citizen or civic identity that ought to have priority over other identities.[10] For those political theorists inspired by postmodern or post-structuralist ideas, there are few grounds for requiring citizens to have a unified identity with an overriding civic loyalty to the nation-state. It is argued that the differences in identity, culture and economic conditions under which many women, gays, indigenous peoples and disabled people live are so great that no universal normative theory can incorporate fairly their interests. Worse, such universalism is thought to 'suppress various particularistic identities'.[11] For some, liberal democracy is a regime that simply overrides difference, and citizenship has only a residual and limited protective value.[12] Nonetheless, deploying the concept of citizenship necessarily entails some conformity to a wider political culture and community. The main issues are where and how a polity sets the limits of conformity, and how it deals with those who do not want to conform.

A few of the writers above have attempted to revise democratic citizenship to take account of difference.[13] Critics more sympathetic to citizenship point to new assumptions that have to be made, namely, that there are multiple ways of being a citizen and multiple sites for civic action.[14] Although traditionally most emphasis is given to political citizenship, one can now speak of activities such as multicultural citizenship, ecological citizenship and global or cosmopolitan citizenship.[15] Such aspirations link up with an older critical tradition that rejects the governmental project of using citizenship as a means of regulation and assimilation. On this view, citizenship is a vital means for extending citizens' rights, claiming essential services from governments, and for resisting state incursions into citizens' lives. Citizenship practice may also be oriented towards protecting ecological resources and promoting national and global policies on the environment, peace or human rights. Accordingly, citizenship may be expressed in a variety of ways that only marginally touch upon the formal political institutions of liberal democracy. The new practices of citizenship may consciously aim to transform or even subvert these institutions. In liberal and social democracies, the issues of critique and transformation are significant elements of citizenship theory and practice.

These comments suggest a key question: to what extent do democratic theories have the potential to respond to these challenges? In evaluating democratic theories of citizenship, Aristotle offers a way forward. Just as he enquired into the nature of the 'good citizen',[16] so may we ask: what are the main features – capacities, competencies and values – required of the good democratic citizen? The main focus of this chapter will therefore be upon the problem of citizenship as a civic identity. Of particular concern, however, will be the capacity for critique and possible transformation of individual, society and polity. This criterion also prompts us to ask whether any of the democratic theories encourage critical reflection within and about democracy itself.

One of the inherent difficulties in this approach is that there are many ways of categorizing democratic theories. Following the precedents of C. B. Macpherson, David Held and Jürgen Habermas, I have chosen to use the device of a 'model' as a way of ordering the relations between democracy and citizenship.[17] Normative models offer a synthesis of arguments that serve to indicate the ideal relations between different components of a democratic theory. Such models specify the leading values, the ideal characteristics required of citizens, and recommend practical programmes for protecting or implementing values. Such a project necessarily involves historical and conceptual oversimplification and certain features overlap between the models. For example, in practice, liberal democracy may include elements of liberal minimalism, developmentalism and even deliberation. Nonetheless, the device of a model serves to isolate the key characteristics and normative principles of the main types of democratic theory and enables their systematic comparison.

Models of democratic theory vary according to the weight they give to different kinds of value and institution, as well as the nature and extent of citizenship participation. These elements are all reflected in the four models of democracy and citizenship considered below. They are (1) liberal minimalism, (2) civic republicanism, (3) developmental democracy and (4) deliberative democracy. The four models are selected because, arguably, they cover the principal traditions of democratic theory and citizenship, past and present. Although others have noted the main lines of these models, often under slightly different terminology, I have attempted here to draw out more clearly their implications for democratic citizenship.

Liberal Minimalism

Liberal minimalism is the generic term that encompasses protective theories of democracy and their ideas of citizenship. Although liberal minimalist models cover a variety of liberal democratic theories, they share a number of elements. The main internal aim and justification of theories of protective democracy is to protect individual citizens from arbitrary rule and oppression by government, as well as from infringements upon individual liberty from other citizens.[18] Democracy is an institutional instrument, based upon actual or implied contracts, for protecting the legal and political rights of individuals. In addition, all are united by their understanding of democracy as a procedure for choosing governments, and a preference for a minimal role for citizen participation. Democracy is not the highest value; it is simply a means to other political ends.

The liberal minimalist model of democracy involves establishing a constitutional framework (often involving a clear separation of powers), as well as laws and law enforcement mechanisms for the operation of representative and responsible government. These laws are also intended to provide the political and legal conditions for security and stability, as well as to protect the rights of individuals, such as rights to vote and the freedoms of speech and association. Voting also allows for the legitimation of governments by a form of popular consent. Generally, the theorists advocating protection require a minimal state but one capable of firm intervention where the laws are infringed. Placing limits on government serves to expand the space for personal freedom and especially the operations of markets. John Locke, the original protective theorist, argued for natural rights to 'life, liberty and estate [property]', which it is the purpose of government to secure.[19] Where individuals give 'tacit consent' to government, they are also obligated to obey its laws, but only as long as governments do not violate natural rights or go beyond their legitimate authority. Locke also provided arguments for individuals to claim a right of representation.

In the twentieth century, the liberal minimalist model was refined in slightly different ways by Max Weber and Joseph Schumpeter.[20] Both pointed to empirical evidence about the limits and possibilities for democratic politics that pressed democratic theory to become more 'realistic'. Central were the apparent ignorance of voters and their tendency to be swayed by emotional arguments. For both Weber and Schumpeter, elections were important for registering the views of citizens and for changing governments. Accordingly, democracy was best understood and practised as a means for choosing political elites who compete with each other for the people's vote. Similar features are evident in the pluralist theories of democracy developed, for example, in the early writings of Robert Dahl.[21] The main difference is that the pluralists focus less on individual citizens' relation to the state than on the role of factions, and participation in interest or pressure groups, such as business associations or trade unions. Pluralism therefore puts more stress on the importance of competitive political struggles between groups.

Liberal minimalist citizenship is founded upon the important normative principle of political equality that requires maintaining equal formal political rights among those considered to be citizens. The principle of each citizen being accorded only one vote in elections derives from the belief that neither wealth, power nor status should count before the law, nor in the ultimate exercise of democratic power, namely, voting. This anti-aristocratic principle of equal legal and political worth is central to the liberal minimalist. Equal citizenship is not an end in itself but an essential instrument for protection against oppression and injustice.

What is the good citizen?

The practice of good liberal democratic citizenship is largely confined to the requirement of voting in elections and possibly serving on juries. The main civic obligation is to obey the law, and sometimes assist in adjudicating it. The citizen's prime formal political task is to elect representatives who will form the government of the day. In this model, most citizens give up their power to govern to representatives and merely give periodic consent to governments formed by their representatives.[22] Where, in the early realist model, the good citizen is primarily a voter, in the pluralist version, good citizens are those who also cooperate with like-minded others to pursue their interests. For the twentieth-century realists, any more active forms of citizenship were considered dangerous, in that they were likely to threaten liberal political values or, at a minimum, result in poor policy-making. Because of their education and training, only the elites were sufficiently competent and able to rule, but these too had to be checked.

Citizen engagement in political deliberation before making judgements is important, but secondary as a source of legitimacy. Within liberal minimalist democracy, political decisions tend to be reached after limited debate and through the method of a majority vote. Although liberal minimalists advocate a citizen politics conducted through debate, such a politics tends to be oriented towards the assertion of one's individual political will and the pursuit of preconceived interests. Given the strong liberal distinction between public and private life, this model may also imply that men are more suited for civic participation, thus encouraging women to limit their civic commitments. Nevertheless, it is arguable that even women with heavy domestic responsibilities could meet the minimum requirements of voting once or twice every few years.

The liberal minimalist assumptions about civic capacities and practices are those of a market model in which human beings are understood as competitive individualists. These individuals – oriented largely to calculating and promoting their own self-interest – give priority to the pursuit of freedom and fulfilment in their private lives. Generally, individuals are regulated more by the threat of state sanction and punishment than by any cooperative impulses or social concerns. Nonetheless, in the public sphere the good liberal citizen will be prepared to discuss matters, make judgements and vote, or organize according to his or her perceived interests. Only a minority, however, will be prepared to undertake the task of managing the state. Although good citizens are simultaneously distrustful of the state and alert to its incursions into individual rights, they are generally politically passive. While Locke's theory of universal natural rights and his arguments for rebellion may give later liberal citizens the resources for the critique and transformation of governments, they are only to be activated under extreme circumstances.

The main site for citizen participation is within the nation-state and national government, but it also includes subordinate lower-level constituencies such as regional states within a federation, and local or municipal government. Although the pluralists appreciate the importance of participation in non-state groups in civil society, the main focus is upon their effect on government and state power. Although liberal democratic states may join with other states in international institutions such as the United Nations, the aims are primarily the minimal ones of securing mutual protection and the maintenance of stability within the system of states.

Liberal minimalism and civic deficit

For liberal minimalist theorists, citizen participation is valued instrumentally to the extent that it fosters the interests of stability, security and state administration. This project requires two levels of citizenship. Among the masses, citizenship is a way of maintaining regulation and control, and minimal participation is encouraged. Among political elites, participation and leadership is valued. At both levels, the liberal call for good citizenship is primarily an ethical appeal for individuals to be honest and upright and to refrain from always putting private self-interest above public interest. Yet, such a civic strategy conflicts somewhat with the more dominant liberal stress upon individualism. A similar problem confronts liberal democratic states that have called for an 'active citizenship'[23] to overcome apathy and loss of national integration. The fostering of 'active citizenship', however, has more in common with republican democracy.

Extending the reach and intensity of liberal minimalist citizenship would be impossible without changing the nature of liberal democracy or, at a minimum, provoking serious fractures within it. Globalization, for example, brings to prominence the conflict between economic liberalism and liberal human rights. Without a thoroughgoing stress on human rights, or extending its deliberative dimension, liberal minimalism is unable either to formulate effective critiques of governments or transform its theory of democracy. Indeed, in his liberal mode, Karl Popper argues that we have been 'unduly sceptical' of liberal democracies and that we ought to resist the tendency to devalue liberal democratic achievements.[24] At the heart of liberal minimalism is the contradiction that the more it encourages an active and critical democratic citizenship, the more it shifts the polity away from liberal values towards more democratic ones.

Civic Republicanism

Republicanism has its origins in the Athenian *polis* and in ancient Rome. A republican polity is defined by at least two elements: the importance given to the public interest or the common good (or the commonwealth), and a key role given to citizen participation in making political decisions. Typically, the latter process requires the use of reason and public deliberation. In this tradition, it is political community that makes the highest claims upon citizens and it is their political identity that is pre-eminent. Modern republicans share particular sets of rights and obligations with liberalism.[25] Like the liberal minimalists, republican citizens ought to have equal political and legal rights that enable them to pursue their private goals and their public roles. They also have a corresponding set of obligations that include obeying the law, paying taxes, performing jury service and, sometimes, military service.

We may distinguish between two different traditions of republicanism. Whereas civic republicanism grew out of the traditions of direct democracy in ancient Athens, protective republicanism corresponds to those more limited democratic forms of government associated with political traditions emanating from ancient Rome.[26] More recent civic republicans include Arendt, Barber and Oldfield, while the protective republicans include Sunstein and Pettit.[27] Unlike the civic republicans, the protectivists tend not to give the highest priority to democracy.[28] Nonetheless, much of the recent revival of republican thought is oriented towards overcoming the democratic deficiencies – low participation rates, lack of motivation and elitism – of liberal democracy. Because of its stronger democratic credentials and role for citizens, here we shall focus upon the civic republican tradition. On the Athenian model, for example, priority was given to direct citizen participation at all levels of government and administration in what is called direct democracy.

What is the good citizen?

The ideal republican citizen is one who is imbued with civic virtue, which means giving priority to the public (civic) good over one's private interests. This attitude and habit of civility is possibly the defining quality of the republican citizen. Central is the ability to maintain a critical and reflective distance from one's own interests and desires.[29] The good republican citizen is committed to making decisions after due deliberation with others, and tends not to resort to majority votes except as a last resort. In the Athenian version, republican citizenship was a distinctly political status and practice in which political participation was valued for its own sake.[30] Civic republicans generally reject the practice whereby citizens leave major political decisions to representative assemblies and envisage the role of a member of parliament to be more like that of a delegate. Citizenship is therefore a vital political activity for forming public opinion, as well as expressing the will of the people and sustaining checks upon it. Although the republican citizen has a range of rights and obligations, the latter are usually given greater prominence.[31]

Despite the original weight given to ownership of property as a qualification for citizenship, modern republicans seek to reduce differences in wealth and urge that all members of society ought to participate in the public sphere. Miller explains that the good republican citizen must be 'willing to take active steps to defend the rights of other members of the political community, and more generally to promote its common interests'.[32] In addition, the good republican citizen is obligated to play 'an active role in both the formal and informal arenas of politics'.[33] Yet, the citizen's political participation ought not simply to be oriented towards the liberal objectives of putting limits on governmental excess or corruption, or pursuing sectional interests, but 'as a way of expressing your commitment to the community'.[34]

For Oldfield, the republican citizen must have the capacities for autonomy, friendship and judgement. Individuals must be able to make 'authentic choices about the ways of life they wish to follow'.[35] Autonomous citizenship must also be based upon 'a particular form of moral bond' between individuals, which may be called friendship. Such bonds give the individuals the motivation to carry out the duties of citizenship. As citizens, however, individuals must also be able to make 'judgements about their identity and about the common purposes they wish to pursue'.[36] That is, they require the capacity and motivation to engage in rational deliberation with others. For Oldfield, the motivating force for civic action is 'political sentiment', which may be understood as a kind of 'reflective' patriotism.

Civic republicanism and civic deficit

Civic republicanism gives priority to political community, the use of reason in determining the public good and to the public realm over the private realm of life. Certainly, republicanism involves a strong critique of individualism and consumerism with their focus upon private interests and amusements. Civic republicans largely conceive democracy in non-instrumental terms and encourage participation of its citizens in public life as a way of expressing their commitment to the political community. Most civic republicans would presume that greater participation would increase political interest and knowledge. Thus active and informed citizenship is central to civic republicanism.

Identity politics raises difficulties for republicanism because republican citizenship, as a legal and administrative status, is necessarily exclusive. Oldfield explains: 'it is not a person's humanity that one is responding to, it is the fact that he or she is a fellow citizen, or a stranger.'[37] Giving priority to one's political community requires excluding those who are not part of it, for whatever reason. Recurring questions include: who may rightfully constitute the republican community? and what ought to be the criteria for granting citizenship?[38] Furthermore, for many civic republicans, an individual may be eligible for citizenship by birth, but will only gain the status of citizen by acting as one.[39] There are also problems with internal communities who do not meet either the ethnic or civic criteria for citizenship. Indigenous people in many countries have strong cultural and political commitments that do not fit easily into republican communities.

A key problem remains that of how citizens can decide what is the common good or in the public interest, or even whether this is possible. One widely held view is that most democratic polities now comprise so many different types of group, whose interests are not reconcilable, that determining a common good may be impossible, except perhaps for the most minimal commitment to the democratic process. In this regard, many feminists have criticized republicanism because of the emphasis it gives to the public sphere and the requirement for strong participation. Anne Phillips, however, is cautiously optimistic in suggesting that republicanism does provide an insecure resolution of 'that tension between insisting that different groups do have distinct and different interests and nonetheless projecting a vision of politics as something more than looking after yourself'.[40] The republican objective is to maintain a commitment to community and public good that is above the individual's private interests, but that does not sacrifice the individual. In the truly democratic republic, the broader democratic political culture must have precedence over local cultures that would threaten to erode it.

Active citizenship is a key element of civic republican democracy and offers the prospect of reducing democratic disenchantment. Yet, identity politics poses a special challenge for republicanism in that, historically, it has tended to restrict those who can become a citizen and participate in the public sphere. Since it is the common good of the republic and its civic identity that must prevail, republicanism has the potential for inflicting serious discrimination. The measures that are intended to bind a political community together, and thereby avoid the dilemmas of liberalism, bring their own difficulties. Nonetheless, under his revised neo-republican theory of citizenship, van Gunsteren argues that 'this type of citizenship demands no overarching or total claims of allegiance to the republic', but that where people do have to deal with their differences, they do so as citizens.[41] This republican possibility may only arise once citizens become aware of themselves as members of a 'community of fate'.

On the surface, republicanism encourages the use of reason and deliberation to make political decisions. These practices can allow for the criticism and transformation of internal political, social and economic arrangements within the republic. The priority given to maintaining the republican community, however, tends to rule out serious consideration of any options that would transform its basic character. Hence, republics can justifiably place strong restrictions on immigration and the award of citizenship. Because republican citizenship is confined within the national polity, republicanism may be hampered in its ability to respond democratically to major global issues that transcend the nation-state.[42] For these reasons, republican democracy does not fulfil its potential for critique.

Developmental Democracy

Those democratic theories designated as 'developmental' generally accept the political principles and institutions of liberal democracy as necessary, but not sufficient, for democracy to flourish.[43] Two other essential requirements are extensive individual participation in politics and the formation of strong communal bonds between individuals. Developmentalists consider political participation and deliberation to be a primary means of personal and intellectual development.[44] The developmental model of democracy is also more optimistic about the 'improvability' of citizens. Importantly, these writers see individual development occurring in association with others. They also espouse an interventionist conception of the democratic state that enables its members to fulfil themselves and their civic duties.

The developmentalists encompass those known as the 'new liberals' and various reformist socialists, liberal socialists and democratic socialists. The liberal developmentalist tradition begins with J. S. Mill and T. H. Green, and was elaborated in the twentieth century by L. T. Hobhouse, A. D. Lindsay, Ernest Barker, John Dewey and John Rawls.[45] Twentieth-century democratic socialists include G. D. H. Cole, Harold Laski and T. H. Marshall,[46] who drew upon similar values but extended the critique of capitalism and property.[47] There were, however, significant differences between Cole and Marshall. On the one hand, Cole's guild socialism advocated a retreat from using the state for socialist purposes and recommended citizen participation in a host of new functional and self-governing organizations and associations. On the other hand, Marshall envisaged an expansion of state power to fulfil a citizen's social rights to basic education and social welfare services. Certain developmental themes are also evident in the 'Third Way' rhetoric about 'reciprocity, equal opportunity and autonomy' in the British Labour Party.[48] The following discussion focuses primarily on the social liberals.

Although the state retains the instrumental role of establishing a system of law and enforcing justice, this is for the higher purpose of developing 'the capacities of the human personality in as many persons as possible to the greatest possible extent'.[49] The aim is not just to protect citizens from government, but to use governmental, or collective, resources to expand a citizen's freedom and enhance the overall condition of society. Concern for the common good lies at the heart of developmental democracy.[50] As citizens pursue the common good, they also transform themselves and become more autonomous. Democracy was pivotal in this process. J. S. Mill, for example, valued democracy as a means to self-improvement.[51] For others, democracy is an end in itself or way of life,[52] and not just a means to other ends. The developmentalists, however, did not confine citizenship to the formal political sphere of elections and voting. Few considered the act of voting to be especially educative.[53]

Later developmentalists came to stress the importance of citizens' rights to social justice as a means for facilitating political participation. In addition to the basic civil and political elements of citizenship, Marshall sees the historical emergence of a social element. By this, he means 'the whole range from the right to a modicum of economic welfare and security to the right to share to the full in the social heritage and to live the life of civilized being according to the standards prevailing in the society'.[54] The ideals of social citizenship register the reciprocal relationship between the individual and the democratic state. Marshall indicates the kinds of rights that the citizen ought to be able to claim from the state in order to have a suitable base from which to begin their self-development and become 'active citizens' in a democracy.[55] Put another way, without the proper resources supplied by education, health and social welfare, the poor are unlikely to be effective citizens in any of its meanings. Although Marshall was not writing in a normative sense, his concept of social citizenship has come to be used as an ideal against which the achievements of governments in meeting their obligations to their citizens can be assessed.[56]

The developmentalists often refer to compulsory membership of the state. In this way they recognize that some members of the state may have full political rights and others not.[57] Accordingly, two kinds of citizenship status are evident in the writings of many developmentalists. The first is citizenship as a formal or official status allowing one to exercise political rights such as the right to vote in elections. The second type recognizes that citizenship could also be exercised in social or economic or industrial spheres. Whereas in the political sphere governments are required to allocate formal citizens' rights to certain individuals, in social or economic spheres civic status may depend upon being a member of a workplace or organization or voluntary association.[58]

In addition to the usual domains of government and elections, developmental theorists stress the importance of participation in non-government, non-political or voluntary associations in what we now call civil society. Whereas many of these associations can assist in providing an 'education for democracy', they also constitute significant sites of democratic process in their own right.[59] In this regard, developmentalists have regularly recommended democratizing business corporations.[60] Overall, developmental citizenship can be exercised not only in elections for government, but also within voluntary associations or within the corporation, or internationally. For these reasons, developmentalism shares a great deal with the later associative democratic theory and the civil society theorists.[61]

What is the good citizen?

The good citizen participates in political activity wherever possible, at all levels within a polity.[62] Citizens will vote in elections, but also participate in the other non-political associations of civil society. While participation may include relatively unreflective political action such as casting an uninformed vote, it also ought to include participating in informed public discussion and debate. Here, the developmentalists favour political deliberation, which is a public activity requiring reflection, discussion and argument over a proposed course of action. Such activity encourages citizens to consider issues beyond those they would normally come across in their daily life. It is assumed that, as citizens become more active in their local communities, workplaces and churches, they will come into touch with wider national issues and so cast a more informed and responsible vote.

In addition to promoting the citizen's intellectual development, such activities encourage a wider consciousness of commonality and community.[63] Although citizens can pursue their own interests, one of their duties is to seek out the common good, which may also reach beyond their national community. The developmental citizen is urged to obey the law except in such cases where it may be needed to make the laws of the state accord more with its overall purpose of sustaining rights,[64] or where the disobedience can be justified with reference to some higher 'obligation' or principle of justice.[65] At whatever level the citizens participate, they will become more aware of themselves as members of a larger community united by the common good.

A major tendency among the developmental liberals is to conceive of the good citizen as one who exercises perceptive judgement.[66] A core assumption is that citizens have the capability to refine their judgements 'about what is in their interest'.[67] In particular, the good citizen in a developmental democracy ought to have the capacity for criticism and self-criticism. Here we find an overlap between the later developmental theorists and deliberative democracy, but the former tend to focus upon formal deliberation at the level of state and government. John Rawls's concept of public reason and his version of deliberative citizenship, for example, requires a certain level of self-reflection and distancing from the citizen's own beliefs and political position.[68] There are, however, certain limits. The good Rawlsian citizen would not pursue a 'comprehensive doctrine of truth', but is guided by 'an idea of the politically reasonable'.[69] Such requirements enable citizens to deliberate upon the common good. For William Galston, the aim is to foster those skills, values and virtues, such as the need to think critically, deemed essential to effective participation in democracy.[70] From a stronger social liberal/ social democratic perspective, however, Gutman and Thompson argue that this kind of deliberative democracy also requires citizens to 'enjoy basic opportunities that include adequate income and decent jobs'.[71]

Developmental democracy and civic deficits

Good developmental citizens are those who participate at all levels of politics and who transform themselves along the way. Providing for new types of social and economic rights also aims to facilitate greater participation. Yet, the recognition of new rights can be extended to other spheres, such as cultural and ecological rights. One problem with developmental democracy, however, is that it may be overly optimistic about how much participation is possible by the great mass of citizens. It is a commonplace that the pressures of life and work in modern societies may not allow sufficient time for the citizens to participate in the range of activities that the developmentalists envisage.

Developmental democratic theory provides a defence of broader schemes of state intervention to defend the larger community. Proposals for worker participation in industry, for example, create the new categories of industrial or economic citizen. Further innovations are possible, such as corporate citizenship, in which corporations would be encouraged to act like good corporate citizens, taking seriously their wider responsibilities to society. Such obligations would reach beyond the usual concerns with corporate ethics or corporate philanthropy, to include internal obligations to treat their workers according to certain standards, as well as external duties to avoid bringing social and ecological harm to communities. Thus the pursuit of profit would be qualified by a commitment to other civic obligations.

Given the developmentalists' concern to widen the range of sites for political participation, it could conceivably incorporate many of the claims of identity politics. There would appear to be few developmentalist reasons why, in principle, many of those who want recognition of their different identities could not be encouraged to make the most of their various talents. Kymlicka and others, for example, see liberalism as able to justify granting rights to certain kinds of cultural or ethnic group.[72] Although developmental democracy allows for the recognition of cultural differences, in principle, this is usually within the limits of perceptions of the common good. As with all concepts of the common good or public interest, however, this constraint is potentially oppressive. Developmentalism allows more extensive rights, but also stresses the importance of obligations to the larger community.

One of the strengths of citizenship in developmental democracy is the encouragement it gives to critique. When citizens engage in the process of reconciling their own private interests with the common good, it is thought that they can become not only reflective, but also critical and self-critical. By participating in democratic politics, and engaging in discussion, citizens can enlarge their horizons, and those of their community.[73] At the heart of the normative aspirations of developmental democracy is the idea that individuals and society need not remain as they are, and this would also apply to members of ethnic or religious communities. Nonetheless, there seem to be certain limits to critique. Fostering a civic outlook, in which one is critical of authority, will almost inevitably encourage criticism of the communities, families and cultures in which the critics live, so possibly undermining them.[74] Although personal transformation is vital for developmentalists, it is not clear that they envisage the possibility of fundamentally altering the liberal democratic polity or its economy.

Developmental theory is based upon an optimistic assessment of human capacities and conceives of citizens as they could become. This allows for criticism of the existing social and political order, and also, within certain limits, its transformation. Many of the claims of identity politics can be accommodated by developmental democracy, if only because it broadens the scope of citizenship status beyond that officially granted by the state. By extending the range of sites for exercising citizenship, developmental democratic theory also sets a broader agenda for democratic politics, both within and outside the nation-state. One weakness, however, is that whereas the developmentalists have a strong theory of participation, their theories of deliberation are somewhat limited. Nor is there any well-formulated notion of the common good or procedures for determining it.

Deliberative Democracy

Political deliberation has long played a role in theories of democratic legitimacy. It is only relatively recently, however, that liberal and critical theorists have attempted to formulate a distinctive theory and practice of deliberative democracy. Deliberative theorists argue that existing liberal democratic arrangements do not address sufficiently the various problems, including those of pluralism, inequality and complexity, that are a condition of contemporary society.[75] Such sentiments are implicit or explicit in the works of the critical theorists of deliberative democracy, Habermas and Cohen.[76]

At its most general, deliberative democracy 'refers to the idea that legitimate law-making issues from the public deliberation of citizens'.[77] Bohman and Rehg continue: 'As a normative account of legitimacy, deliberative politics evokes ideals of rational legislation, participatory politics and self-governance. . . . it presents an ideal of political autonomy based on the practical reasoning of citizens.'[78] The primary goal of deliberative democracy is to expand the use of deliberative reasoning among citizens and their representatives. The quality of this public deliberation is also a criterion for the legitimacy of democracy: the better the deliberation the more it can be said to be based upon the consent of the citizens, and the more legitimate the democracy. For Cohen, the outcomes of democratic deliberation are only legitimate 'if and only if they could be the object of a free and reasoned agreement among equals'.[79] In the Habermasian version, legitimacy can be based upon a version of the 'discourse principle' which allows for the impartial justification of morality and law: 'Only those actions are valid to which all affected persons could agree as participants in rational discourses.'[80] Accordingly, the ideal of deliberative democracy is premised upon a more radical form of political equality than that envisaged by liberal minimalism.

Although deliberative democracy is based upon a strong critique of other theories of democracy, it still draws on the values and institutions of republicanism, populism and liberalism. From republicanism it takes the idea of political participation and its orientation to the common good. In the deliberative version of populism, democracy is a way for citizens to exercise popular rule. It differs from republican theories in its scepticism about whether a single shared vision of the common good could ever be attained or effective in motivating citizens.[81] Nonetheless, deliberative democracy still allows for the formation of provisional notions of the common good by deliberation. From liberalism, deliberative democracy takes the values of individual political equality, autonomy and consent. Most deliberative theorists envisage democracy being conducted within a liberal constitutional framework and under the rule of law in which key rights are protected.[82]

Habermas is explicit in specifying that all those who have an interest in an issue ought to be allowed to engage in public debate to influence the decision. Here, political equality is given greater force than in liberalism and communitarian theories, and is not just limited to equality of voting. On the more generous view of deliberative citizenship, the citizenry would have to include those who were permanent residents and possibly even those often more marginal and temporary residents such as refugees and asylum seekers. For this reason too, a radical deliberative democracy allows for the concepts and practices of transnational citizenship, such as those embodied in the regional citizenship of the EU, as well as the global citizenship required by emerging institutions of global civil society and global democracy. A citizen of a deliberative democracy would therefore automatically have the status of a citizen of the world where the basic unit of reference is that of a common humanity.

Despite its diverse origins, deliberative democracy accepts that in modern liberal democratic states the people do not rule except indirectly through representatives. Habermas explains: 'Discourse theory has the success of deliberative politics depend not on a collectively acting citizenry but on the institutionalization of the corresponding procedures and conditions of communication.'[83] Because of this, it rejects an entirely instrumentalist and strategic approach to political decision-making. Accordingly, deliberative theorists also reject any elitist arguments on participation or arbitrary limitations on citizen engagement in the processes of public deliberation. Although deliberative democracy may be instrumentally effective, in the Habermasian version it is oriented to enhancing the processes of 'communicative action'.

For these reasons, deliberative democracy opposes the usual kinds of liberal politics that are based upon struggles to pursue predetermined interests that are consummated in decisions reached by aggregating votes and using the method of majority voting. Unlike liberal minimalism, deliberative democratic theory 'construes politics as aiming in part at the formation of preferences and convictions, not just at their articulation and aggregation'.[84] Bohman explains some of the procedural conditions for the implementation of public deliberation: 'The exchange of reasons takes place in a *discourse* in which participants strive to reach agreement solely on the basis of the better argument, free of coercion and open to all competent speakers.'[85]

What is the good citizen?

The ideal citizen in a deliberative democracy is an active one requiring many diverse capacities. Central is the ability to engage in dialogue and communication. Ideally, citizens do not form their preferences solely according to their previously established statuses, roles or identities. Citizens need to be able to exercise self-restraint in avoiding the immediate instrumental pursuit of their own self-interests. This quality would need to be accompanied by the capacity for critique and self-reflection. The good deliberative citizen would need the capability not only to formulate his or her own interests, but also to acquire an understanding of, and contribute to the formulation of the common or public good on a particular issue. As well as the ability to listen carefully to others, and open themselves to revisions of their earlier position and interests, citizens would need to have the moral strength to accept the decisions arrived at. Crucial too is the old liberal requirement that participants in public deliberation must be able to distinguish between arguments and the human beings who express them, and where the rejection of ideas does not entail the rejection of the person.[86] Bohman writes: 'Many different "self-governing capacities" are necessary if citizens are to participate effectively in public deliberation and dialogue, including understanding, imagining, valuing, desiring, storytelling, and the use of rhetoric and argumentation.'[87] All such self-governing characteristics are also those associated with the expression of political autonomy. But they also suggest some of the difficulties of implementing deliberative democracy. For these reasons, deliberative democratic theorists are alert to the material conditions and inequalities that impede proper deliberation and support measures to overcome them.

Deliberative democracy and civic deficit

Deliberative democracy of the radical kind is applicable to all kinds of organization. Cohen, for example, considers the secondary or voluntary associations of civil society as particularly important sites for practising, learning and expressing deliberative ideals.[88] For Habermas, deliberative citizenship would be applicable at any level of public politics where decisions need to be made, either within the nation-state or outside it. Accordingly, relevant organizations would include parties, parliaments, executives and judiciary within the nation-state, as well as the resolution of international issues between nation-states. Deliberative citizens would also operate through the many non-governmental organizations of global civil society that work to reform the policies of governments and transnational institutions. Since deliberation is not limited to institutions within the nation-state, deliberative reasoning would be required of citizens *and* their international representatives, whether these were governments or non-governmental institutions. Habermas, for example, sees state citizenship and world citizenship as forming a continuum.[89] Deliberative democracy may assist in the formation of a new ethical community of global citizens that would provide the overriding civic unity and principles of good citizenship that nation-states seem to have lost.

Habermas addresses a few of the problems raised by identity politics. He argues for a liberal immigration policy in, for example, the EU, partly on the grounds that immigrants will bring fresh and diverse perspectives on shared political constitutions. Habermas also claims that 'the democratic right to self-determination includes the right to preserve one's own *political* culture . . . but it does not include the right to self-assertion of a privileged *cultural* form of life'.[90] That is, democratic political values and institutions have priority over cultural values and communities, and a democratic civic identity has primacy over non-political cultural identities.[91] For Habermas, whatever the cultural forms of life, every citizen must be 'socialized into a common political culture'.[92] It also seems that this political culture may no longer have a foundation within the nation-state.

Radical deliberative democratic theory encourages citizenship participation on the widest scale at all levels (national and international), and all spheres (public and private), in democratic polities and beyond them. The normative ideals of deliberative democracy also put a premium on practical citizenship based upon extensive individual self-reflection. Although deliberative democracy begins from an analysis of the practical problems and characteristics of existing liberal democracies, it does not take them as unalterable. As citizens engage in public deliberation, they accept the possibility of change and reform at the level of both the individual and the institutions. Bohman writes: 'Out of this public expression of these problems and needs, some citizens begin to formulate new understandings of themselves and of institutions, all the while seeking to modify the current framework for deliberation.'[93] On this interpretation, deliberative democracy encourages citizens to be critical and self-critical, as well as allowing for the transformation of themselves, their institutions and their social contexts.

Numerous criticisms have been directed at deliberative democracy and I shall only raise two here concerning citizenship.[94] Arguably, the ideal capacities for citizenship vital to deliberative democracy represent a very high order of communicative standards that are often simply not readily available among large numbers of citizens. That is, the criteria for citizen deliberation may be too strong and so exclude large numbers of citizens who do not or cannot meet them, or who may have different cultural standards. Nonetheless, deliberative democrats such as John Dryzek, James Fishkin and John Uhr have devised various practical proposals for enhancing the quality of deliberation by citizens and legislative institutions.[95] Furthermore, what kinds of political context would be more conducive to deliberative democracy? Even where socio-economic and political conditions are relatively good, there remains the problem of how to encourage the kinds of civic identity best suited for public deliberation. For example, what sorts of civic education would need to be implemented to encourage the moral personality of the deliberative democrat?

Despite these problems, deliberative democracy seems to provide more of the theoretical resources needed to deal with the substantive problems of liberal democracies. Because deliberative democracy requires critique and self-critique it opens up a space for reflection upon entrenched views. Although deliberative values have civic priority, they are primarily procedural in character. As such, they allow for the widest possible participation – active citizenship – over a wide range of issues within and outside the nation-state. The concept of global citizenship alluded to by Habermas both offers a critical perspective on issues that reach beyond the borders of the nation-state and encourages practical political responses to globalization. Deliberative values also appear to provide a regulative ideal for managing many of the conflicts arising from identity politics.

Conclusion

As a valued legal *status*, citizenship may allow entry into a political community, command access to valuable resources and require the performance of certain obligations. Ideally, the granting of citizenship status enables the citizen to participate in determining the affairs and future of a community. Nonetheless, citizenship may be exercised inside and outside democracy, in affirmation or criticism of democracy, in formal political institutions or in civil society, in democratic or even undemocratic ways. *Democratic* citizenship, however, generally operates within the relatively familiar traditions, values and institutions oriented towards accountability, legitimacy and participation. Here, citizenship puts a premium upon the use of argument and discussion rather than physical force or violence, and the practice of criticism and critique is central. In this regard, each of the models offers diverse, though sometimes overlapping, accounts of an ideal civic identity, which rely, to varying degrees, upon criticism and critique. The models differ, however, according to how central the practice of critique is, its preferred scope, and the sites in which it can be exercised.

Under liberal minimalism, criticism and judgement are an essential part of individual political leadership in national politics, but they do not extend to critique and transformation of individuals or the liberal democratic system itself. The capacities of the liberal minimalist civic identity are far too restricted to adapt to the challenges discussed above. For civic republicans, participation, deliberation and criticism are encouraged in the public sphere on issues concerning the political community. With a few exceptions, however, the stress is upon defending the republic, not its criticism or transformation. Civic republicanism itself provides an important critique of liberal minimalism, but it remains primarily a normative aspiration and, unlike protective republicanism, it is only marginally grounded in current political realities. By contrast, developmental democratic theories have provided the rationale for many of the social and economic policies of twentieth-century democracies, especially through the extension of the welfare state. Developmental democratic theory acknowledges the necessary and recursive relationship between individual citizen and political community. The developmental democrats advocate participation and deliberation at all levels of the political community – local, national and international – in ways that are intended to encourage critical self-reflection. Furthermore, personal transformation is envisaged as a likely *outcome* of the process. Apart from a few of the social democrats, however, the possibility of criticism leading to radical transformation of polity, society or economy is limited.

For the radical deliberative democrats, critical self-reflection is essential at all levels of politics where deliberation is needed. This can occur alongside or within liberal democratic institutions. Deliberation itself creates a temporary discursive or dialogical community of citizens seeking to resolve issues that may arise out of more substantive communities and cultures. It would appear, however, that such discursive communities require personal transformation *before* one can participate properly. Another difficulty for deliberative democracy is that the skills required appear to be of a high order and there is little indication of how they may be encouraged. Although deliberative democracy, like civic republicanism, is a normative aspiration based upon theoretical critiques of liberal democracy and republicanism, its critical reach is far greater. Deliberative democracy is applicable in all sorts of political situations and allows for incremental institutional changes as well as more far-reaching ones. For these reasons, deliberative democracy seems to have a greater potential to respond, not only to the issues associated with democratic disenchantment in liberal democracy, but also to the challenges of identity politics and new social movements. Despite its shortcomings, there are good grounds for proposing that deliberative democratic theory offers the greater promise of renovating both the practice of democratic citizenship and democratic institutions.

NOTES

I would like to thank April Carter, John Dryzek, John Kane, Karen Gillen, Barry Hindess and Herman van Gunsteren who each made valuable comments on different versions of this chapter. Naturally, I remain responsible for any mistakes and misinterpretations.

1   See, e.g., J. Barbalet, *Citizenship* (Milton Keynes, Open University Press, 1988); R. Beiner (ed.), *Theorizing Citizenship* (Albany, SUNY Press, 1995); D. Heater, *Citizenship: The Civic Ideal in World History, Politics and Education* (London, Longman, 1990); W. Kymlicka and W. Norman, 'Return of the citizen: A survey of recent work on citizenship theory', *Ethics* 104 (1994): 352–81; G. Shafir (ed.), *The Citizenship Debates: A Reader* (Minneapolis, University of Minnesota Press, 1998); B. S. Turner, *Citizenship and Capitalism: The Debate over Reformism* (London, Allen and Unwin, 1986); B. S. Turner (ed.), *Citizenship and Social Theory* (Thousand Oaks, CA, Sage, 1993); B. van Steenbergen (ed.), *The Condition of Citizenship* (Thousand Oaks, CA, Sage, 1994); H. van Gunsteren, *A Theory of Citizenship* (Boulder, CO, Westview Press, 1998); U. Vogel and M. Moran (eds), *The Frontiers of Citizenship* (London, Macmillan, 1991); I. M. Young, 'Polity and group difference: A critique of the ideal of universal citizenship', *Ethics* 99 (1989): 250–74.
2   This concern is not new, as reading J. Bryce, *Hindrances to Good Citizenship* (New Brunswick, Transaction, 1993 [1909]) demonstrates.
3   Kymlicka and Norman suggest, however, that there is a need for an independent theory of citizenship that is not just a theory of democracy or justice. See their 'Return of the citizen', pp. 368 and 381.
4   In early republican theory and practice, citizens held a privileged political status based on having certain equal political and civil rights. But given the exclusion of women, the poor and slaves, for example, such citizenship was not exercised within a democracy.
5   P. Norris (ed.), *Critical Citizens: Global Support for Democratic Government* (Oxford, Oxford University Press, 1999).
6   See D. Held, *Democracy and the Global Order* (Cambridge, Polity, 1995), pp. 16–23.
7   R. Beiner, 'Why citizenship constitutes a theoretical problem in the last decade of the twentieth century', in R. Beiner (ed.), *Theorizing Citizenship* (Albany, SUNY Press, 1995), p. 1.
8   For the UK, see D. Heater, 'Citizenship: A remarkable case of sudden

interest', *Parliamentary Affairs* 44 (1991): 141–56; D. Oliver and D. Heater, *The Foundations of Citizenship* (London, Harvester/Wheatsheaf, 1994), pp. 123–6. For Australia, see Civics Expert Group, *Whereas the people . . . Civics and Citizenship Education* (Canberra, Australian Government Publishing Services, 1994), pp. 13–15.

9 See G. Stokes, 'An introduction to the politics of identity in Australia', in G. Stokes (ed.), *The Politics of Identity in Australia* (Melbourne: Cambridge University Press, 1997), pp. 1–20.

10 See, e.g., Young, 'Polity and group difference'; C. Mouffe, 'Radical democracy or liberal democracy?' *Socialist Review* 20, 2 (1990): 57–67, p. 64.

11 Beiner, 'Why citizenship constitutes a theoretical problem', p. 9.

12 See B. Hindess, 'Limits to citizenship', in W. Hudson and J. Kane (eds), *Rethinking Australian Citizenship* (Cambridge, Cambridge University Press, 2000), pp. 66–74.

13 E.g. E. Laclau and C. Mouffe, *Hegemony and Socialist Strategy: Towards a Radical Democratic Politics* (London, Verso, 1985); Mouffe, 'Radical democracy or liberal democracy?'; I. M. Young, *Justice and the Politics of Difference* (Princeton, Princeton University Press, 1990).

14 See W. Hudson, 'Differential citizenship', in Hudson and Kane (eds), *Rethinking Australian Citizenship*, pp. 15–25.

15 W. Kymlicka, *Multicultural Citizenship: A Liberal Theory of Minority Rights* (Oxford, Clarendon Press, 1995); B. van Steenbergen, 'Towards a global ecological citizen', in van Steenbergen (ed.), *The Condition of Citizenship*, pp. 141–52; G. Stokes, 'Global citizenship', in Hudson and Kane (eds), *Rethinking Australian Citizenship*, pp. 231–42.

16 Aristotle, *The Politics*, trans. T. A. Sinclair (Harmondsworth, Penguin, 1962), Book 3, p. 107.

17 E.g. C. B. Macpherson, *The Life and Times of Liberal Democracy* (Oxford, Oxford University Press, 1977); D. Held, *Models of Democracy*, 2nd edn (Cambridge, Polity, 1996); J. Habermas, 'Three normative models of democracy', in S. Benhabib (ed.), *Democracy and Difference: Contesting Boundaries of the Political* (Princeton, Princeton University Press, 1996), pp. 21–30. See also T. Janoski, *Citizenship and Civil Society* (Cambridge, Cambridge University Press, 1998), pp. 17–24 and 226–7, who uses three models similar to those used below.

18 Macpherson, *The Life and Times of Liberal Democracy*, p. 22; Held, *Models of Democracy*, p. 99.

19 J. Locke, *Second Treatise of Government* [1690], in C. Cohen (ed.), *Communism, Fascism and Democracy* (New York, Random House, 1962), p. 441.

20 See M. Weber, 'Politics as vocation', in H. H. Gerth and C. W. Mills (eds), *From Max Weber* (London, Routledge and Kegan Paul, 1948);

J. A. Schumpeter, *Capitalism, Socialism and Democracy*, 5th edn (London, Unwin, 1952).

21 R. Dahl, *A Preface to Democratic Theory* (Chicago, University of Chicago Press, 1956).

22 Held, *Models of Democracy*, pp. 83–4.

23 D. Oliver, 'Active citizenship in the 1990s', *Parliamentary Affairs* 44 (1991): 157–71; Civics Expert Group, *Whereas the people . . .*, pp. 6–7.

24 K. R. Popper, *Conjectures and Refutations*, 4th edn revised (London, Routledge, 1972), p. 372.

25 D. Miller, 'Bounded citizenship', in K. Hutchings and R. Dannreuther (eds), *Cosmopolitan Citizenship* (Houndsmill, Macmillan, 1999), p. 62.

26 Held, *Models of Democracy*, pp. 44–5.

27 H. Arendt, *The Human Condition* (Chicago, University of Chicago Press, 1958); B. Barber, *Strong Democracy* (Berkeley, University of California Press, 1984); A. Oldfield, *Citizenship and Community: Civic Republicanism and the Modern World* (London, Routledge, 1990); C. R. Sunstein, *The Partial Constitution* (Cambridge, MA, Harvard University Press, 1993); P. Pettit, *Republicanism: A Theory of Government and Freedom* (Oxford, Clarendon Press, 1997).

28 Pettit's republicanism, for example, does not regard democratic participation as a 'bedrock value'. See Pettit, *Republicanism*, p. 8.

29 See S. Burtt, 'The politics of virtue: A critique and a proposal', *American Political Science Review* 87, 2 (1993): pp. 361–2.

30 J. G. A. Pocock, 'The ideal of citizenship since classical times', in Shafir (ed.), *The Citizenship Debates*, pp. 31–41; p. 36.

31 See, e.g., M. Canovan, 'Republicanism', in D. Miller (ed.), *The Blackwell Encyclopedia of Political Thought* (Oxford, Blackwell, 1997), p. 434.

32 Miller, 'Bounded citizenship', p. 62.

33 Ibid., p. 63.

34 Ibid.

35 Oldfield, *Citizenship and Community*, p. 9.

36 Ibid., p. 148.

37 Ibid., p. 8.

38 See the discussion in R. Brubaker, *Citizenship and Nationhood in France and Germany* (Cambridge, MA, Harvard University Press, 1992).

39 Oldfield, *Citizenship and Community*, p. 159.

40 See A. Phillips, 'Feminism and republicanism: Is this a plausible alliance?', *Journal of Political Philosophy* 8, 2 (2000): p. 293.

41 See van Gunsteren, *A Theory of Citizenship*, pp. 26–7.

42 See A. Linklater, 'Cosmopolitan citizenship', in Hutchings and Dannreuther (eds), *Cosmopolitan Citizenship*, pp. 35–59.

43 In his article 'Democratic theory and self-transformation', *American*

Political Science Review 86, 1 (1992): pp. 8–23, Warren uses the term 'expansive democracy' to describe developmental democracy.

44 See G. E. Gaus, *The Modern Liberal Theory of Man* (London, Croom Helm, 1983), pp. 205–6.

45 On Rawls, see ibid., pp. 1–11.

46 While A. H. Halsey (in 'T. H. Marshall and ethical socialism', in M. Bulmer and A. M. Rees (eds), *Citizenship Today: The Contemporary Relevance of T. H. Marshall* (London, UCL Press, 1996), pp. 81–100) locates Marshall in the tradition of ethical socialism, M. Bulmer and A. M. Rees (in their 'Conclusion: Citizenship in the twenty-first century', in Bulmer and Rees (eds), *Citizenship Today*, p. 278) consider him to be a twentieth-century 'liberal democrat'.

47 The socialists also include R. H. Tawney and Anthony Crosland.

48 S. White, 'Rights and responsibilities: A social democratic perspective', in A. Gamble and T. Wright (eds), *The New Social Democracy* (Oxford, Blackwell, 1999), pp. 166–7.

49 E. Barker, *Principles of Social and Political Theory* (Oxford, Oxford University Press, 1951), p. 208.

50 L. T. Hobhouse, *Liberalism* (London, Oxford University Press, 1964), p. 70.

51 J. S. Mill, *Considerations On Representative Government* (Chicago, Henry Regnery, 1962), pp. 32–6.

52 J. Dewey, 'Creative democracy – The task before us', in D. Morris and I. Shapiro (eds), *John Dewey: The Political Writings* (Indianapolis, Hackett Publishing Company, [1939] 1993), pp. 241–2.

53 Gaus, *The Modern Liberal Theory of Man*, p. 209.

54 T. H. Marshall, *Citizenship and Social Class and Other Essays* (Cambridge, Cambridge University Press, 1950), p. 11.

55 Raymond Plant points out that Marshall did not envisage such rights as being claimable by individuals, 'but that the state had a general duty to provide collective services in the fields of health, education and welfare: he did not envisage that these would yield individual entitlements'. See R. Plant, 'Social rights and the reconstruction of welfare', in G. Andrews (ed.), *Citizenship* (London, Lawrence and Wishart, 1991), p. 57.

56 There has been much controversy over Marshall's work, including the claim that he encourages citizens to be passive recipients of welfare, that he focuses largely upon rights and not obligations, and that he does not sufficiently recognize the needs of women. Furthermore, there are other rights, such as ecological and cultural ones, that may, arguably, now be required for democratic citizenship, as well as domains other than the nation-state in which citizenship rights can be claimed.

57 T. H. Green, *Lectures on the Principles of Political Obligation* (New York, Longmans, 1931), p. 145; H. Laski, *Social Theory*, 2nd edn (London, Methuen, 1921), p. 456, repr. in M. Spahr, *Readings in Recent Political Philosophy* (New York, Macmillan, 1949).

58   Within the work of the developmentalists there are allusions to a conception of citizenship that extends beyond national boundaries. See, e.g., Green, *Lectures on the Principles of Political Obligation*, p. 145; Hobhouse, *Liberalism*, pp. 121–2; D. Held, *Democracy and the Global Order: From the Modern State to Cosmopolitan Governance* (Cambridge, Polity, 1995); D. Archibugi and D. Held, *Cosmopolitan Democracy: An Agenda for a New World Order* (Cambridge, Polity, 1995), pp. 12–15.

59   See, e.g., A. D. Lindsay, *The Essentials of Democracy*, 2nd edn (Oxford, Clarendon Press, 1935), p. 74.

60   Ibid., p. 66.

61   The associative democratic theorists tend to be more in the democratic socialist tradition of developmentalism. See April Carter's chapter on 'Associative democracy' and Baogang He's chapter on 'Civil society and democracy' in this volume.

62   J. Dewey, *The Public and its Problems* (Athens, OH, Swallow Press, 1927), p. 146.

63   Gaus, *The Modern Liberal Theory of Man*, pp. 206–9.

64   Green, *Lectures on the Principles of Political Obligation*, p. 147.

65   Barker, *Principles of Social and Political Theory*, pp. 224–5.

66   Burtt, 'The politics of virtue', p. 362. This writer is pessimistic about the prospects of encouraging American citizens to adopt such virtues.

67   D. F. Thompson, *The Democratic Citizen* (Cambridge, Cambridge University Press, 1970), p. 15.

68   The necessary political virtues of citizens are those of 'political cooperation, such as a sense of fairness and tolerance and a willingness to meet others half-way': J. Rawls, *The Law of Peoples* (Cambridge, MA, Harvard University Press, 1999), p. 15. On deliberation, see also J. Rawls, *Political Liberalism* (New York, Columbia University Press, 1996), pp. 212–54.

69   Rawls, *The Law of Peoples*, p. 132.

70   W. Galston, *Liberal Purposes* (Cambridge, Cambridge University Press, 1991), pp. 224–7. See also A. Gutman, *Democratic Education* (Princeton, NJ, Princeton University Press, 1987); S. Macedo, *Liberal Virtues: Citizenship, Virtue and Community* (Oxford, Oxford University Press, 1990).

71   A. Gutman and D. Thompson, *Democracy and Disagreement* (Cambridge, Belknap Press, 1996), p. 301.

72   See Kymlicka, *Multicultural Citizenship*.

73   For an astute critique of the transformative potential of democratic participation, see Warren, 'Democratic theory and self-transformation', pp. 13–16.

74   Kymlicka and Norman, 'The return of the citizen', p. 367.

75   J. Bohman, *Public Deliberation: Pluralism, Complexity and Democracy* (Cambridge, MA, MIT Press, 1996), p. 237.

76 See Habermas, 'Three normative models of democracy', pp. 21–30; J. Habermas, *Between Facts and Norms*, trans. W. Rehg (Cambridge, Polity, 1996), pp. 287–328; J. Cohen, 'Deliberation and democratic legitimacy', in J. Bohman and W. Rehg (eds), *Deliberative Democracy: Essays on Reason and Politics* (Cambridge, MA, MIT Press, 1997), pp. 67–91; J. Cohen, 'Procedure and substance in deliberative democracy', in Benhabib (ed.), *Democracy and Difference*, pp. 95–119.

77 J. Bohman and W. Rehg, 'Introduction', in Bohman and Rehg (eds), *Deliberative Democracy*, p. ix.

78 Ibid., p. ix.

79 Cohen, 'Deliberation and democratic legitimacy', p. 73.

80 Habermas, *Between Facts and Norms*, p. 459.

81 Bohman, *Public Deliberation*, p. 5.

82 Dryzek, however, sees the accommodation with liberalism as blunting the critical edge of deliberative democracy. See his *Deliberative Democracy and Beyond* (Oxford, Oxford University Press, 2000).

83 Habermas, 'Three normative models of democracy', p. 27.

84 Cohen, 'Deliberation and democratic legitimacy', p. 83.

85 Bohman, *Public Deliberation*, p. 7.

86 See the discussion in G. Stokes, *Popper* (Cambridge, Polity, 1998), pp. 61–5.

87 Bohman, *Public Deliberation*, p. 7.

88 Cohen, 'Procedure and substance in deliberative democracy', in Benhabib (ed.), *Democracy and Difference*, pp. 110–13.

89 Habermas, *Between Facts and Norms*, p. 515.

90 Ibid., p. 514.

91 Habermas offers the idea of 'constitutional patriotism' as a way of transcending the narrow 'motivating forces' of national political identities based upon ethnic community and culture. See his 'Citizenship and national identity', in *Between Facts and Norms*, pp. 500 and 514–15.

92 Ibid., p. 500.

93 Bohman, *Public Deliberation*, p. 198.

94 For other criticisms, see essays in Bohman and Rehg (eds), *Deliberative Democracy*; J. Elster (ed.), *Deliberative Democracy* (Cambridge, Cambridge University Press, 1998); R. E. Goodin, 'Democratic deliberation within', *Philosophy and Public Affairs* 29, 1 (2000): 81–109.

95 See also J. S. Dryzek, *Discursive Democracy* (Cambridge, Cambridge University Press, 1990); J. Fishkin, *Democracy and Deliberation: New Directions for Democratic Reforms* (New Haven, CT, Yale University Press, 1991); J. Fishkin, *The Voice of the People: Public Opinion and Democracy* (New Haven CT, Yale University Press, 1995); J. Uhr, *Deliberative Democracy in Australia: The Changing Place of Parliament* (Melbourne, Cambridge University Press, 1998).

2

Democracy and Inequality

Harry Brighouse

Radicals and socialists have long criticized capitalist democracies on the ground that the material reality of capitalism belies the promise of democracy. Citizens have equal formal political rights, but the economic inequalities generated and preserved by the operation of capitalist markets give the wealthy more resources to make use of their formal rights. Wealthy individuals and large corporations can contribute more to candidates and parties, and can have their views more widely disseminated in public. When their interests coincide, the wealth of the wealthy gives them more power collectively both in setting the political agenda and over policy outcomes. Capitalist democracies, in other words, preserve *formal* political equality, but deny *substantive* political equality.[1]

The difference between formal and substantive political equality is nicely brought out by John Rawls's distinction between the basic liberties and their worth:

[T]he basic liberties are specified by institutional rights and duties that entitle citizens to do various things, if they wish, and that forbid others to interfere. The basic liberties are a framework of legally protected paths and opportunities. Of course, ignorance and poverty, and the lack of material means generally, prevent people from exercising their rights and from taking advantage of these openings. But rather than counting these and similar obstacles as restricting a person's liberty, we count them as affecting the worth of liberty, that is, the usefulness to persons of their liberties.[2]

Liberties are formally equal when there are clear institutional guarantees and protection. They are substantively equal (in Rawls's terms, 'have equal worth') when individuals equally have the material means to make use of them. The radical criticism of capitalist democracies adopted here does not demand substantive equality for all liberties, just for those associated with participation in political decision-making.[3] It does not claim that material inequality is wrong *in principle*, then, but that *substantive* political inequality is wrong in principle, and that material inequality is wrong because, and in so far as, it inhibits the realization of this more fundamental ideal.

There are two rather obvious strategies for responding to this criticism. One is to claim that substantive political equality cannot be implemented in practice because no alternative economic system can serve it any better than capitalism. On this view capitalism secures as much as is feasible of what is valuable about democracy, and so is the best we can do. The second strategy is simply to deny the injustice of substantive political inequality. On this view, that capitalism leads to such inequalities does not impugn it. This response could be taken to vindicate capitalist inequalities; or it could suggest that the injustice of capitalism, though real, is independent of its effects on democracy.

I shall try to support the radical criticism, by arguing that substantive political equality is a fundamental value of justice. But I argue from the liberal principle that the government owes all its citizens equal respect. The argument, then, unlike the criticism it supports, is not radical. That the radical criticism of capitalist democracies can be given a liberal defence gives it wider appeal than it has often had, by showing that it does not presuppose radical premises.

Before presenting the argument it is worth looking at the extent of material inequality in some contemporary capitalist democracies. Take *income* inequality in the United States. According to the US Census bureau, in 1980 the top 5 per cent of households took in 15 per cent of the income. By 1993 the top 5 per cent took in 20 per cent of the income. Because it confers security and *generates* income, wealth is a better measure than income of how well-off people are. And wealth inequality in the USA is even worse: by 1993 the top 1 per cent held 39 per cent of national wealth, and over half the wealth was owned by just over 2 per cent of the population.[4]

Inequality is less extreme in most other capitalist democracies, especially because access to health care and education are less closely tied to income and wealth. But in Australia, in 1996–7, the worst paid 20 per cent received just 3.8 per cent of total income, whereas the best paid took 47.5 per cent. Lifestyle and life cycle factors affect income distribution, of course (young single households earn less than older, double-income households), but even the middle 20 per cent took just 15.2 per cent of the total.[5] In the UK, in 1994–5, 22 per cent of the population, including 4 million children, were living in poverty (less than half the mean income).

How do inequalities of income and wealth translate into substantive political inequalities? Today, obviously, not by affecting who gets to vote. Votes are usually equally distributed, roughly equally weighted and inalienable.[6] But four other important mechanisms give the wealthy more influence than others.

1. Wealthy individuals and large corporations have money to spend on political campaigning and lobbying. Even with strict campaign spending limits, wealthy individuals can contribute to parties, and to non-electoral political campaigns. In the USA, where expenditures are weakly regulated, candidates can spend unlimited amounts of their personal wealth on their campaigns: over two-thirds of US Senators are millionaires. Wealthy individuals can make large personal contributions to campaigns, and corporations can contribute large amounts through Political Action Committees. In 1998 it cost on average $1 million to win a seat in the House of Representatives, and in 1990 34 per cent of the money spent by Federal candidates was directly contributed by no more than 0.1 per cent of the voting age population.[7]

2. Inequalities of wealth frustrate substantive political equality indirectly. Because societies need the productive wealth they own, the wealthy bargain from a position of strength. In the USA state and local governments commonly provide tax breaks for corporations, in an attempt to dissuade them from moving to other states: several states even have government departments devoted to forging tax-exemption deals to attract corporations. Perhaps the most spectacular example of this mechanism working at the national level was the election of Mitterrand's socialist government in France in 1981. After winning a landslide on a strongly redistributivist programme, the socialist government faced a combination of capital flight and abnormally low investment, despite the introduction of reflationary policies. By 1983 the programme was abandoned.

3. The very terms of the political debate are circumscribed by the fact that everyone knows that the wealthy control vital productive assets. They need not exert their influence directly, because they control the agenda of political debate. This mechanism was nicely illustrated by the round of meetings and speeches in the City by UK Shadow Chan-

cellor Gordon Brown and Labour Leader Tony Blair during the two years prior to their victory in the 1997 General Election. For good reason, assuring a tiny minority of the business-friendly character of their policies took a high priority, because that minority wielded disproportionate power over the political agenda.

4. In capitalist societies the wealthy tend to be better educated, and so it is less burdensome for them to make accurate judgements about what political policies will serve their self-interest and about what would serve the common good. They have personal resources that give them better access to information and greater facility in processing it. This source of inequality is unlike the others, for it involves not the power of wealth as such, but the qualities that usually accompany it. Positions with wealth attached to them typically give people a sense of self-importance, a willingness to be assertive and a greater facility at manipulating and understanding information. The very wealthy gain most from this, but in societies with a more democratic public culture, such as the USA and Australia, the biggest inequality is probably between the middle classes and the very poor who, in many cases, completely lack the sense of social inclusion that is crucial to making effective engagement in politics a practical possibility.

Why Does Substantive Political Equality Matter?

The argument for substantive political equality starts with the liberal ideal that the government should treat all its citizens with equal respect. Much discussion of the government or the state treats it as an independent agent, which, though in some sense accountable to the citizenry, has its own ends and goals. To what extent this is true, of course, depends on the structure of social institutions. But morally, the state has no agency independent of the wills of its citizens. In a liberal society the state is an agency through which citizens deliver on their obligations to one another. It mediates the treatment of individuals by individuals, rather than acting as an independent agency. So the injunction that the state should treat its citizens with equal respect boils down to the claim that citizens should treat one another with equal respect through the state.

What does this claim amount to? Respect is a vague notion, so it is fruitful to start with a more personal context where we have clearer intuitions about what respect demands of us, and see whether our intuitions can be applied in the more impersonal context of the state. Think about how respect is expressed within a group of friends deciding where to eat. Each expresses respect, in part, by consulting all who wish to assert their views or preferences about where to go. If the expressed preferences of some are ignored, or if some in the group are not consulted, then whoever makes the decision can usually be seen as showing a degree of disrespect.[8] There are circumstances which excuse us from considering the preferences of our friends. If they are temporarily insane, for example, it is not disrespectful to neglect to consult them. But when they are in full command of their faculties and the decisions concern them, respect requires consultation and consideration of their preferences.

We must consult and consider the preferences of people in decisions that will affect them because to ignore their preferences is to treat them as if their own judgements about their own good has no significance. But that is only true if they are either incompetent or wicked. Neglecting their judgements, then, embodies a presumption that they are not worthy of our respect.

These considerations do not yet support democratic rights. Within intimate associations decision-makers can consult preferences by simply asking, and those who have been consulted can monitor directly whether their preferences were taken into account. We can even consider someone's preferences without consulting them, since they have often expressed those preferences previously. I know my wife's culinary preferences pretty well, and regularly consider them without consulting her. There is also, of course, both reasonable and unreasonable give and take in intimate contexts, and even quite unreasonable give and take is of no great social concern because the associations are in an important sense voluntary. So democracy is not a requirement of equal respect in such contexts.

But society-wide institutions differ in respects that support the idea of democracy. While for adults membership in intimate institutions is voluntary, membership in societies usually is not. The costs of immigration to the individual are typically high enough that the availability of emigration does not (contra Locke) render membership of one's own society voluntary.[9] Monitoring the consequences of actions by the individuals who perform them is not feasible at the society-wide level, and accurate assessment of whether and to what extent one's judgements are considered in decisions cannot be done informally, as it can in personal contexts. Formal mechanisms which can be publicly monitored are required. In particular, such mechanisms must guarantee the consultation and consideration of each individual's preferences in the process of determining social decisions.

It may be objected that the right to have one's interests considered is not identical with the right to be the person who determines what one's interests are and put them up for consideration. This is true. But my case rests not on the right to have one's interests considered, but on the right to have one's *judgements* considered. This is what is required by the duty of respect, at least in impersonal institutional contexts, because, as I have said, to neglect someone's own judgements about their individual interests or the interests we share with them is to presume them to be either incompetent or wicked. Democratic procedures are necessary to provide citizens with the guarantee that their own judgements will be operative. They are aimed at enabling persons who will be affected by decisions to proffer what they judge as their interests for consideration, to attempt to persuade others of their perception of the public good and, ultimately, to have, like all others, a *guaranteed* input into the decision itself. Any system of governance which depended on just some people to determine the interests of all those affected by social decisions, or which simply made available more influence over shared circumstances to some than to others would fail to implement a presumption of equal respect.

Before proceeding, one caveat is necessary. No guarantees are fail-safe, and different forms of democracy achieve the aim of guaranteeing everyone an input to different degrees: one of the central matters in the dispute about different voting systems is how well they guarantee input to all in different contexts. Furthermore, democracy is not the only value a just society should instantiate, and there may be trade-offs between democracy and other vital values. But the point remains that equal respect requires democratic institutions.

So far, we have an argument from equal respect to democracy. How does it support *substantive*, as opposed to merely formal, political equality? After all, the substantive inequalities generated by the workings of capitalist markets are not *deliberate* in any sense. They are simply a by-product of the workings of economic institutions which are designed for some purpose other than generating substantive political inequality, and which do not, in themselves, express disrespect for persons.

As a defence of substantive political inequality, this observation is unconvincing. Suppose that there are two friends: Dougal, who is poor, and Florence, who is extremely wealthy. While respect allows for a good deal of informal give and take in these contexts, it would be disrespectful of Florence to use whatever advantages flow from her wealth to influence the outcome of their collective projects. The reason that doing so would make her a bad friend is that she would be demonstrating a lack of respect for Dougal. Friendship is irrelevant in the impersonal context of decision-making at the level of the state, but respect is not, and it is quite plausible to think that using one's superior wealth to get one's own way in politics denies respect to one's fellow citizens. Thus, since in this context institutional guarantees are needed, inequalities of wealth should (at the very least) be prevented from translating into inequalities of political influence.

I have made a case for substantive political equality, understood simply as ensuring that inequalities of wealth do not have an impact on democratic outcomes. But the argument from presuming equal respect for our fellow citizens supports an even stronger principle, which I have elsewhere called equal availability of political influence.[10] Equal availability of political influence impugns the impact of unequal wealth on politics, but also impugns unequal influence resulting from the superior ability of some political agents to manipulate the flow and interpretation of information. Consider, again, the affective association, and suppose that when Florence and Dougal are deciding where to eat, Florence deliberately deprives Dougal of the information that there is a good Indian restaurant in town just in order to have him accede to her desire for Mexican food. In manipulating the information, she is, in the context, manipulating him in a way that fails to accord him respect. Similarly, when a party deliberately makes misleading claims to voters about the consequences of its policy recommendations in order to win elections, or distracts voters from policies by misleading negative campaigning or campaign techniques that seduce rather than inform or explain, it, and its backers, are thereby failing to grant them respect.

Nevertheless, two sources of unequal actual influence are, I think, prima facie acceptable, given the argument from equal respect. First, inequalities that result from public reason-giving seem acceptable. There is nothing disrespectful about offering sincere reasons for one's views and asking that those be considered by others. So the argument allows those who are better at persuasive public reason-giving to be more influential, as long as their influence is a consequence of their actual persuasion of others. This intuitively meshes well with equal availability of influence: once, for example, I have come rationally to accept someone else's reasons, they become my own reasons, so the influence I exercise when I vote according to those reasons is more clearly my own than that of my persuader.

Second, although this will be qualified later, unequal influence reflecting simply the extra effort one person has put into politics is, prima facie, acceptable. Citizens have the right to abstain from political activity, and even from voting: it would be perverse to object that those who participate have more influence than those who, with the same range of options, have chosen not to.

So far I have provided an argument for why substantive political inequalities are unjust. In the final section I shall sketch an account of what sorts of reforms would help to implement substantive political equality in contemporary capitalist democracies. But first it is important to respond to a series of objections to the principle of substantive political equality. These objections are that it is not feasible, that it does not promote genuine equality, that it undermines moral agency, and that maximin is superior to equality.

Objections to the Principle of Substantive Political Equality

The feasibility objection

The first objection does not claim that substantive political equality is, in principle, undesirable (though those who advance it do usually believe it to be in principle undesirable). Instead, it claims that political and economic arrangements designed to promote economic equality are in practice incompatible with substantive, and even formal, political equality.

Milton Friedman is a well-known exponent of this position, who claims 'that in particular, a society which is socialist cannot also be democratic, in the sense of guaranteeing individual freedom'. He adds that economic freedom is 'itself a component of freedom broadly understood, so economic freedom is also an end in itself. In the second place economic freedom is also an indispensable means toward the achievement of political freedom.' Individual freedom, then, understood roughly as the absence of coercion by other persons or groups of persons, is the basic value. Economic freedom is understood as freedom of contract: it is encroached upon by any government restrictions on the validity of contracts except when justified by bona fide concerns about externalities.[11] At one point Friedman defines political freedom in the same way he defines individual freedom (as 'the absence of coercion of a man by his fellow men'[12]), but the relevant part of the argument is his assertion that socialism would be incompatible with the freedom to political dissent. This is important because substantive political equality requires availability of the means, and not only the formal right, to dissent. Someone without the effective means to express her political views simply does not have substantive political rights.

Friedman argues by assuming that only two alternative sets of economic arrangements are available: free market capitalism (in which there are no restrictions on freedom of contract except those justified by externalities) and socialism (in which most essential productive resources are government-owned, and freedom of contract is restricted). Free market capitalism is incompatible with substantive political equality; therefore, Friedman claims, formal political equality is the best capitalism can give us. But socialism is not compatible with substantive political equality either, because the *government* controls the resources people need to use their political rights. So Friedman asks:

> How could the freedom to advocate capitalism be preserved and protected in a socialist society? In order for men to advocate anything, they must in the first place be able to earn a living. This already raises a problem in a socialist society, since all jobs are under the direct control of political authorities. It would take an act of self-denial . . . for a socialist government to permit its employees to advocate policies directly contrary to official doctrine.[13]

Substantive political equality requires that people can finance their dissent. But 'how could they raise the funds?' Since wealthy people in socialist societies will be deeply connected to officialdom, '[i]t strains credulity to imagine the socialist top brass financing such "subversive" activities'.[14] Political equality will not, then, be substantive. But, worse, it will not even be formal:

> In a free market society, it is enough to have the funds. The suppliers of paper are as willing to sell it to the *Daily Worker* as to the *Wall Street Journal*. In a socialist society, it would not be enough to have the funds. The hypothetical supporter of capitalism would have to persuade a government factory making paper to sell to him, the government printing press to print his pamphlets, a government post office to distribute them among the people, a government agency to rent him a hall in which to talk, and so on.[15]

What are we to make of this argument? While Friedman's characterization of Soviet bloc practices was fair, these were not the only ideological models of socialism, nor even the only practising models, at the time. Although certainly a more prominent view among socialists now than when Friedman was writing, the idea of market socialism dates to before the Second World War.[16] Market socialists are sensitive to the efficiency concerns and moral objections to government ownership, and argue that the government should place certain restrictions, designed to limit the emergence of material inequality, on capital and labour markets, but should retain private ownership of capital. The Scandinavian social democracies which represented the 'Third Way' at the time of Friedman's writing, had left industry almost entirely in private hands, but regulated capital and labour markets to limit inequality of outcome.[17] Many redistributive policies can lead to greater material equality without giving the government additional power or authority to frustrate the efforts of dissenters: for example, universal health care provision paid for through taxation; targeting greater educational resources at children from low-income households; and universal basic income grants.

Note also that Friedman's own claim that capitalist inequalities protect effective dissent over the long term is based on dubious assumptions. While it is true that the existence of extremely wealthy individuals can lower the coordination costs of a dissenting movement, the movement can only compete with the ideology of the status quo on anything like an equal basis if it is assumed that the preponderance of wealthy people who share an interest in maintaining the status quo are unable to coordinate their efforts to maintain it. Otherwise they collectively have far more access to the means of expression than the putative radical movement, which reflects not the persuasiveness of their ideas, or their numbers, but simply their disproportionate share of the wealth.

The inequality objection

Ronald Dworkin advances a series of objections to a view he calls 'equality of political influence'. I shall be concerned with only two of these, which are the most relevant to the slightly different principle I have advanced. The first is that equalizing political influence would actually be inegalitarian because it would require limits on individual spending on political campaigns. Because Dworkin sees unjust background inequalities of resources as the sole illegitimate external sources of inequality of influence, he disputes, in principle, the propriety of campaign contribution limits. He says:

> [Contribution limits] are of course appealing when these compensate for unjust differences in wealth. . . . But if resources were distributed equally, limits on campaign expenditure would be inegalitarian because they would prevent some people from tailoring their resources to fit

the lives they wanted though leaving others, who had less interest in politics, free to do so.[18]

Dworkin advocates a principle of equality of resources, and so does not defend the inequalities experienced in contemporary capitalist democracies. But equality of resources, according to Dworkin, does not imply equality of wealth throughout people's lives. His principle of equality of resources allows that someone who made bad gambles has far less wealth than someone who made good gambles. On his principle, some people will have much more money than others to spend on political campaigning regardless of how important politics is to them.[19]

More tellingly, Dworkin's response simply assumes that equality of resources is a more central value, and a more central element of the egalitarian ideal, than substantive political equality. We can, furthermore, give at least one reason for constraining campaign contributions within a regime of material equality. One of the reasons for favouring insulation from material inequalities is that the wealthy can accumulate power as a class, which they can in turn use to further their collective interests. Power, once concentrated, is hard to disperse, and can be used to accrue further advantages. This is obviously disturbing if those in whose hands power has concentrated are already materially favoured. But it is also disturbing if the powerful group comprises, for example, an alliance of religious fanatics.

Another reason for doubting the unfairness of limiting campaign contributions suggests a qualification to my earlier suggestion that inequalities of influence with their sources in unequal effort are acceptable. Dworkin says that this measure would single out the politically fervent and limit their ability to tailor their resources to fit the lives they want to lead. But attempting to do so recognizes the essential nature of politics: it is about exercising power over the conditions that shape our lives and the lives of others. In this, it is unlike many other pursuits, which although they may affect the lives of others do not aim essentially at that goal. Politics is not akin to ice-skating or listening to old-time radio shows. The purpose of limiting the ability of the politically fervent to tailor their resources to the life they want to lead is not to discriminate against them: it is to limit their ability to exercise disproportionate power over the lives of others. This allows the less fervent to be less constantly vigilant than they would otherwise have to be. They are enabled to focus their energy and attention on the lives they really want to lead, rather than having to lead lives which are less desirable to them in order to preserve the conditions in which they and future generations can continue to choose more desirable lives.

The agency objection

Dworkin also argues that implementing equality of political influence would violate a deep value of moral agency. Among the strategies for implementing equality of political influence which he considers is

> [teaching people] not to attempt to influence others . . . except in ways that do not rely on special advantages they might have, in experience or commitment or reputation, and also to attempt to resist being influenced by other people whose arguments might have special force traceable to such advantages.[20]

Such a strategy would, of course, be unlikely to succeed. But Dworkin claims that it would be objectionable even if it could work, because

> citizens should have as much scope for extending their moral life and experience into politics as possible. But people who accept equality of influence as a political constraint cannot treat their political lives as moral agency, because that constraint corrupts the cardinal premise of moral conviction: that only truth counts.[21]

He thinks that any measures implementing equality of political influence would violate this value of moral agency, and teaching people to try not to influence others would be particularly egregious since it would ask moral agents self-consciously to refuse to act on what they take to be the best reasons for acting.

There are two compelling replies to this objection. First, although morality requires us to promote the truth about morality, it does not require us to impose the truth regardless of whether others believe it. Morality limits what we may do to get others to believe the truth about morality: we must not manipulate or coerce them, or bypass their rationality. The rules governing the design of the institutions of political debate place morally appropriate external constraints on what citizens may do to influence one another, and hence allow them to pursue the truth without having to check themselves internally. Equal availability of political influence mandates structural measures that leave people free to pursue the truth as they see it without fear that they will be intimidating or manipulating others.

The second response is that substantive political equality is, and is seen by its advocates as, an element of the moral truth. Pursuing the truth, on this view, requires that we put our views on the table, but acknowledge that the views which others have advanced should be taken into account in the formation of the final policy. Thus, when they try to ensure that they do not have available to them more influence than others, they are indeed pursuing the truth as they see it, and therefore they *are* acting on what they take to be the best reasons for acting. The political egalitarian's concern with procedure does not conflict with, but is part of, her concern with the moral truth.

The maximin objection

Advocates of equality of some good face the objection that some other division than equality may be Pareto superior – that is, that some unequal distribution may make some people better off than under equality, while leaving no one worse off.[22] This objection is particularly biting if those who are worst off are among those who would be better off under a system which increased the total resources to be distributed. It seems very odd, if we care about the condition of the worst-off people, as egalitarians typically do, to want them to be worse off than they otherwise could be. This is why John Rawls, for example, does not advocate that income and wealth be distributed equally, but to the 'greatest advantage of the least advantaged'. David Estlund applies this objection to substantive political equality. What political egalitarians should seek, he says, is not equal, but maximin (the maximum amount to those with least), of availability of political influence.[23]

One response to this proposal is that political influence is essentially competitive: if one person has more then someone else necessarily has less.[24] So, unlike the case of wealth, where the total amount can be increased to the benefit of all by attaching inequality-producing incentives to certain tasks, maximin is equivalent to equality.

Estlund has recently denied this and devised a mechanism which, he claims, would increase the influence of the least influential by introducing inequality of influence. His Progressive Voucher scheme works as follows. Citizens are barred from spending money on political campaigns other than state-licensed vouchers, which can be redeemed by the campaign to which they donate it. While each voucher is worth the same amount (say $50) to the redeemer, for any citizen each voucher costs progressively more than the previous one: 'To buy one costs $50, to buy a second costs $87.50, a third, $153.13, a fourth, $267.97 and the fifth and final permissible voucher costs $468.95.'[25] If someone buys five vouchers on this scenario, she has paid $1,027.55, but her vouchers are worth only $250 to the campaign she chooses. The proceeds from the purchase of additional vouchers go into a general fund, which is divided by the number of voters and returned to each in the form a Singular Voucher, which they may now contribute to whatever campaigns they choose. The total input to the campaign can thus be raised above the level that campaign spending limits (aimed at enforcing equal spending) would have allowed.

The least influential, however, have more influence than under equality, only on the assumption that input, understood in terms of the amount of money spent in political campaigns, is equivalent to influence. As my focus on campaign contributions suggests, money is an important tool of influence. But it is far from the only tool, and it seems quite mistaken to equate campaign contributions with influence. People exert influence not only through campaigning but also by voting: campaigns try to influence people's votes via their views. The extent to which money helps us achieve this is a contingent matter, partly affected by the design of the system of deliberation.

The precise relationship between input (in Estlund's sense) and influence (in the sense we care about) is particularly hard to measure in the real world, because there is a wide spectrum of relationships between voters and their views. At one end, the voter has carefully and rationally thought out the issues involved, and has decided on the best candidate in the light of that reflection. At the other end the voter has heard a clever slogan which fits with her completely unconsidered prejudices, and votes with no further thought. It is reasonable to think that the rational voter's vote reflects just her influence, and no one else's, even if the election campaign is one in which there has been drastically unequal spending. If everyone voted like this, the only way to measure the distribution of influence would be by looking at the voting system: one-person, one-equally-weighted-vote would amount to equal availability of political influence regardless of the campaign finance regime. But there is an important sense in which the prejudiced voter is a vessel for the influence of those who have campaigned.

But let us assume, with Estlund, that unequal input improves the quality of decisions in the following way: unequal input leads to more input; more input ensures that there is a more widespread understanding of the relevant considerations; so all are more able to tie their voting behaviour to their genuine interests rather than their prejudices. Is this an instance of unequal influence? I think not. The fuller debate in this case has enabled people to vote according to their considered views rather than their prejudices – to better advance their true interests. Influence is no less equal than if the input had been equal but low, since it is no less the case that citizens are voting according to their considered views. Unequal input, *if it has the advantages assumed by Estlund*, does not exacerbate inequality of influence.

A second problem, however, is Estlund's assumption that the quantity of debate affects *positively* the quality of decisions, at least under favourable conditions.[26] To justify abandoning substantive political equality for substantive political maximin we need a description of a *reliable mechanism* which makes unequal influence work to the advantage of those with least relative to an equal distribution. But Estlund's progressive voucher scheme achieves this end only under favourable conditions. Under current conditions in the USA, where wealth is unequally shared and the rules governing campaign broadcasting do little to encourage a rational and deliberative political debate, there is every reason to believe that the scheme, while an improvement over the current campaign finance regime, would work to the disadvantage of the least powerful and the least advantaged, relative to a baseline of equality of influence.

Estlund therefore faces a dilemma: If conditions are strongly favourable to rational and deliberative debate, it is not clear that his voucher scheme would result in inequality of influence. If conditions discourage rational argument, resultant inequalities of influence would not be to the advantage of the least influential. So he does not seem to have justified a departure from substantive political equality. But it is worth saying that his intent, while antagonistic to strictly substantive political equality, is to implement a system in which political power is much more equitably shared than under contemporary circumstances.

What are the Specific Institutional Implications?

What kinds of institutional reform would be required to make political equality substantive? If the mechanisms I described in the first section of this chapter are correct, then capitalism as we know it is incompatible with substantive political equality; nothing short of a massive and irreversible redistribution of wealth in the direction of equality can ensure that no one has more influence over the agenda of public politics simply in virtue of their place in the distribution of wealth. Whether such a redistribution is compatible with the maintenance of some form of capitalism is beyond the scope of this chapter. But what is clear is that the kind of redistribution required is not on even the medium-term policy agendas of most capitalist democracies.

In the face of this it might be tempting to conclude that nothing can be done to make democratic rights more substantive. But some existing capitalist democracies depart from substantive political inequality further than others: institutional reforms within capitalism can make a difference. The capitalist democracy which departs furthest, in my view, is that in the USA, so I shall focus on deficiencies which could be corrected there. Feasible reforms fall into three categories, those pertaining to the electoral system, campaign funding and education.

Implications for the reform of electoral systems

Two aspects of the electoral system are particularly relevant to the distribution of political influence. First, the winner-takes-all system of electing representatives makes it disproportionately harder for parties with small minority viewpoints to achieve representation in elected bodies. Even if a third party were to get the votes of 10 per cent of the population, it could easily get none of the seats. That 10 per cent would be effectively denied representation in the legislative chamber, and would hence have less influence available to them than others. Since voters know this, even if a third party is on the ballot, it makes sense for them to vote for the lesser evil of the two candidates who have a realistic chance of winning; again, their influence is less than that of other citizens who do not face the same choice, and, furthermore, the result of the existing election artificially inflates the support for the major two parties in the mind of future voters, so that even if real support for the policies of the third party exceeded that of the second party, this fact would not be reflected in future results. Many states in the USA have ballot access laws which effectively keep third party candidates off the ballot, since it is often necessary to demonstrate a level of support across a whole state which might not be available to a candidate even if he or she could win a single constituency within that state.

A second aspect is rarely discussed: even within a winner-takes-all system, larger districts (constituencies) make for a more unequal distribution of political influence. The less immediately accessible an official is to his constituents, the more influence can be exerted on him by those with money, who, in turn, can and do often claim (spuriously) to be speaking on behalf of his constituents. In this regard it is worth noting that US Congressional Districts contain approximately seven times the number of constituents in a typical UK parliamentary seat.[27]

These considerations suggest two kinds of reform: the introduction of proportional systems of representation for elected state and federal offices;[28] and, in the most important levels of elected bodies, a much higher ratio of representatives to voters.

Implications for campaign financing

Private money is bound to affect elections. The focus in the USA has been on limiting contributions to campaigns. This could only be effective if limits were unreasonably low. Even at the existing figure of $1,000 per person per campaign in the USA, rich individuals can contribute the money required for a whole congressional seat. In 1998 Richard and Helen Has gave over $1 million to candidates in federal elections and Political Action Committees without violating campaign contribution limits, an amount that gives them substantially more influence than most Americans could aspire to.[29]

Other measures could help. Campaign spending should be limited to the threshold at which any campaign could be expected to reach all voters with its message. Even without providing public funding, such limits would come close to ensuring that no political candidate had an advantage over others just because of the superior wealth of her backers. Second, broadcast TV and radio channels should be required, as a condition of licensing, to provide a fixed amount of free advertising time to all registered political parties for each campaign. Many countries (not the USA) already regulate the broadcast media in this way. An urgent task, though, is to extend this regulation to cover the increasingly pervasive cable and satellite television providers. A third measure is to require parties that use free broadcasting time to participate in set-piece televised debates, the terms of which are set by an independent regulatory body. Such debates enable voters to make considered judgements as to the aims and reliability of the competitors in the election, without an unreasonable individual burden of investigation.

Implications for education

The connection between some public policy proposal and an individual's material interests is rarely clear-cut. If some have a much better understanding than others, they are in a better position to vote their own interests (and, for that matter, altruistically to vote someone else's interests), as well as being better able to manipulate the voting behaviour of others. Improved education for children who will be less well off, and especially educating them better in public policy matters, contributes to substantive political equality by helping to close the gap in political understanding that accompanies wealth inequalities. The trend of introducing citizenship education in European countries is a step in this direction.

Furthermore, the various mechanisms by which money can influence the outcomes of elections are often not directly visible, but are understandable. Improving transparency by teaching children the basic psychological techniques that are used and why they work, as well as improving their informal reasoning abilities, helps to lessen the impact of money on politics.

Conclusion

This chapter has argued that liberal democracy not only requires formal political equality but also substantive political equality, and that this entails rethinking our notions of equality of respect. The liberal argument from equal respect to democracy suggests that substantive political equality is an important, though not the only, value of justice; none of the objections to this thesis I have surveyed succeed. There are several mechanisms by which the material inequalities prevalent in capitalist societies undermine substantive political equality, and those material inequalities are therefore objectionable. Eliminating those material inequalities is, in my view, desirable both for the effect this would have on political equality, and for the effect it would have on the lives of those who do least well out of capitalism. But it is also quite far from the political agenda of most contemporary societies. I have outlined some alternative, indirect strategies for insulating politics from the effects of material inequality, so as to make political equality more substantive than it currently is. These reforms are feasible, and may even help to put more radical reform on the agenda. But they should not be seen as substitutes for more radical reform in the long term.

NOTES

1   Much of this criticism is inspired by Marx's writings on the Paris Commune; Lenin's pamphlets during the period preceding the 1917 revolution, and Rosa Luxemburg's commentary on the Russian revolution develop the criticism. See K. Marx, *The Civil War In France*, in R. C. Tucker (ed.), *The Marx-Engels Reader*, 2nd edn (New York, Norton, 1978); V. I. Lenin, *The State and Revolution* in *Collected Works*, vol. 25 (New York, Progress Publishers, 1955); R. Luxemburg, *The Russian Revolution and Leninism or Marxism?* (Ann Arbor, University of Michigan Press, 1961). More recently, see H. Draper, *The 'Dictatorship of the Proletariat' from Marx to Lenin* (New York, Monthly Review Press, 1987). For non-Marxist, or radical, versions

of the criticism, see C. D. Lummis, *Radical Democracy* (Ithaca, Cornell University Press, 1996) and J. Cohen and J. Rogers (eds), *Associations and Democracy* (London, Verso, 1995).

2 J. Rawls, *Political Liberalism* (New York, Columbia University Press, 1993), pp. 325–6.

3 Rawls's first principle of justice, the Liberty Principle, guarantees the basic liberties to all citizens formally, but singles out the 'political liberties' (those associated with democratic participation) as needing to be guaranteed 'fair value' (or equal worth). See *Political Liberalism*, p. 5. He explains what the fair value of the political liberties means at pp. 326–30, but provides very little argument for it.

4 Wealth here includes homes, automobiles, personal effects, boats, etc. and savings and stocks and shares. It does not include pension fund holdings. See E. Wolff, *Top Heavy: A Study of the Increasing Inequality of Wealth in America* (Washington, DC, Twentieth Century Fund, 1995), pp. 8–13.

5 See Australian Bureau of Statistics, *Australia Now: A Statistical Profile* (Canberra, ABS, 1999).

6 I leave aside the question of whether votes are really equally weighted in electoral systems which do not observe a proportionality principle. I also want to leave aside complexities raised by considering some second chambers, such as the US Senate and the British House of Lords.

7 For the price of a Congressional seat, see 'Mother Jones's Top 400', *Mother Jones* (Nov/Dec 1998). See also Frank Sorauf, *Inside Campaign Finance: Myths and Realities* (New York, Yale University Press, 1992), p. 51.

8 Considering a view or preference is, of course, consistent with deciding not to implement it.

9 Locke argued in his *Second Treatise of Government* (ch. 8, 'Of the Beginning of Political Societies') that a man can withdraw his tacit consent to the government of his country: 'he is at liberty to go and incorporate himself into any other Commonwealth, or to agree with others to begin a new one.' P. Laslett (ed.), *Locke: Two Treatises of Government* (Cambridge, Cambridge University Press, 1988), p. 349.

10 H. Brighouse, 'Egalitarianism and equal availability of political influence', *Journal of Political Philosophy* 4, 2 (June 1996): 118–41.

11 Even when externalities are involved, government restrictions are not necessarily justified. The externalities must be significant enough for the actual benefits of regulation to outweigh its costs; and the potential costs to the economy of the increase in governmental power must also be taken into account. See M. Friedman, *Capitalism and Freedom* (Chicago, IL, University of Chicago Press, 1962), pp. 30–2.

12 Ibid., p. 15.

13 Ibid., pp. 16–17. Friedman is, of course, being excessively kind here. Official Communist governments had, and the few that continue still

have, appalling records with respect to proponents of any version of socialism than the official one.

14 Ibid., p. 17.

15 Ibid., p. 18.

16 For recent versions, see J. Roemer, *A Future for Socialism* (Cambridge, MA, Harvard University Press, 1994); S. Bowles and H. Gintis et al., *Recasting Egalitarianism: New Rules for Communities, States and Markets* (London, Verso, 1998). Market socialism was developed in the 1920s by Oskar Lange. See O. Lange and F. M. Taylor, 'On the economic theory of socialism', in B. Lippincott (ed.), *On the Economic Theory of Socialism* (Minneapolis, University of Minnesota Press, 1938); and also H. D. Dickinson, *Economics of Socialism* (Oxford, Oxford University Press, 1939). These ideas were developed in Eastern Europe in the 1960s and 1970s. See, for example, W. Brus, *The Market in a Socialist Economy* (London, Routledge and Kegan Paul, 1972) and O. Sik, *The Third Way: Marxist-Leninist Theory and Modern Industrial Society* (London, Wildwood House, 1976).

17 G. Esping-Anderson, *Politics Against Markets: The Social Democratic Road to Power* (Princeton, Princeton University Press, 1985).

18 R. Dworkin, 'What is equality? Part 4', *University of San Francisco Law Review* 22 (1987): 1–30, p. 16.

19 I'm grateful to Dan Hausman for making this point. See R. Dworkin, 'What is equality? Part 2: Equality of resources', *Philosophy and Public Affairs* 10, 4 (1981): 283–345, for the account of equality of resources.

20 Dworkin, 'What is equality? Part 4', p. 16.

21 Ibid., p. 17.

22 'Pareto Optimality' is an economic concept to test, for example, the most satisfactory distribution of goods. A distribution is Pareto optimal when no one could be given more without someone being given less. It was formulated by Vilfredo Pareto, *Manuel d'économie politique* (Paris, Giard and Briere, 1909). Rawls's Difference Principle incorporates an adaptation of this principle; see J. Rawls, *A Theory of Justice* (Cambridge, MA, Harvard University Press, 1971), pp. 61–77.

23 D. Estlund, 'Political quality', *Social Philosophy and Policy* 17, 1 (2000): 127–60.

24 I make this response in 'Political equality in justice as fairness', *Philosophical Studies* 86 (1997): 155–84.

25 Estlund, 'Political quality', p. 154.

26 Ibid., p. 160.

27 In the UK, in the most recent review of constituency sizes, the target electorates were between 54,000 and 69,000 (the different principalities have different targets) (Parliamentary Boundary Commissions for England, Wales, Scotland and Northern Ireland, 4th Periodical Report). US House Districts have an average size of about 420,000

eligible voters (see Wisconsin Blue Book (Madison, WI, Legislative Reference Bureau, 1998), pp. 860 and 878). Thanks to David Boothroyd for pointing me to the UK information.

28   Proportional representation carries various disadvantages of which reformers should be aware. There is the risk that tiny parties which differ very little substantively will proliferate, potentially confusing voters and making the process of coalition building unnecessarily burdensome. Small parties can hold disproportionate power because no large party has an absolute majority. Pure proportional representation risks breaking the link between representatives and constituents (though this objection has little weight in the USA where constituencies are so large that representatives have little contact with constituents). Party List systems lend great power over candidate selection to party elites (though this effect is offset somewhat by the increased exit option available to dissident minorities within larger parties). A more proportional system could avoid some of these dangers by building in safeguards, such as requiring a 5 per cent threshold for representation, and by mixing single-member district seats with top-up seats selected by a list to ensure proportionality, as in the German system.

29   'Mother Jones's Top 400'.

3

Democracy, Citizenship and Gender

Elizabeth Frazer

In this chapter I first sketch in outline some of the key themes in debates about gender and democracy that have been conducted in liberal democratic polities during the closing decades of the twentieth century.

First, I look at theoretical and empirical analysis that explores processes of inclusion in and exclusion from democratic processes – from meaningful participation in policy formulation and decision-making. There are various criteria for inclusion or exclusion. Here, I am particularly concerned with 'gender' as such a ground or reason. If individuals have been unjustifiably excluded from full democratic citizenship on grounds of gender, the question arises how hitherto excluded individuals can be included. 'Inclusion' is by no means a simple matter of individuals entering settings and circles and institutions from which they were excluded before. For their presence changes or even disrupts the setting, and changes are hence required on the part of the incumbents.

Second, I look at the normative implications of unequal distributions of material and symbolic resources. Participation in democratic politics requires resources: time, money, skills. This has been recognized since democracy's inception. It has been presumed that only people who have economic means have the degree of disposable time necessary for participation in democratic forums. Further, unless people are economically self-sufficient they will lack the wherewithal to be truly dispassionate and independent in forming their views. Contradictorily, it has been argued that only economically independent property owners will have the right kind of long-term commitment to the state and its social order. On these and similar grounds dependent persons have found themselves excluded to a significant degree from democratic processes. But recently some theorists have taken issue with this contrast between independence and dependence, and have argued that in modern democratic societies citizens all are interdependent.

My third theme is 'voice'. It is a potential strength of democracy, as opposed to alternative forms of government such as autocracy or oligarchy, that many voices can speak and be heard, and make worthy contributions to decision-making. However, a preoccupation in recent theory is why this democratic promise is not realized. Critics emphasize the silencing of certain voices, the way others are unheard and unheeded. Social theorists argue that 'gender' itself is an explanation of the shape and structure of democratic processes, and explains a good deal about who is and who is not heard. Concomitantly, this gender system is the object of political conflict: it must be changed if the exclusionary and silencing structures of democracy are to be transformed.

Inclusion, interdependence and voice are all elements that contribute to my fourth and main subject – the politicization of sexuality. I take it that in writing about gender and democracy I am called on to write about more than 'sex differences' as conventionally conceived by political scientists – that is, differences between men's and women's rates and patterns of participation in politics – although these are undoubtedly relevant. I take 'gender' to be a theoretical term that links sex (male, female, neuter, hermaphrodite), sexuality (our capacity for the erotic life, which may or may not be directly connected with reproduction, and which encompasses, *inter alia*, individuals' constrained choices in erotic relationships), and systems of norms and rules (and the enactment of them) that govern 'being a man' and 'being a woman' in a particular society. How exactly these three aspects are linked is, of course, theoretically controversial.[1]

I take it, though, that 'masculinity' and 'femininity' in most societies and cultures (and perhaps in all societies and cultures) are both plural (there are many masculinities and femininities, including subversive and hybrid versions) and in flux (masculinities and femininities change over time, and are contested, violated, subverted and innovated). Such flux and multiplication, change and violation, mean that gender is inescapably politicized. Violating, stretching or subverting gender norms invite approbation from allies and censure from rivals (state actors are particularly important allies or rivals). Where this controversy is conducted publicly, or where state actors are involved, and demands for legislative, fiscal or cultural change are voiced, then gender and sexuality are fully political. That is to say, in the context of this volume, there is demand that democratic decisions and action are taken about sexuality.

Yet, of course, there is something of a strain here. Demands for gay rights or for rethinking standards of sexual morality might be thought to be unpromising matters for democratic decision-making precisely because the established framework of meanings of the normal and the abnormal or deviant, the reasonable and the unreasonable, are such that only a minority of citizens would vote for change. Sexual rights, like anti-racism, and democracy itself, are too precious to be put at the disposal of the *demos*.

My analysis in this chapter follows the line that there is more to democracy than majoritarianism. The theme of inclusion grounds the implication that the essence of a democratic polity is the continual nego-tiation of its boundaries and the continued effort on the part of com-mitted democrats to ensure that the voices of all are heard. That a referendum or plebiscite tomorrow would not usher in a period of sexual freedom and equality is not, then, an argument against democratic poli-tics, nor against the view that sexuality is a proper item on democratic political agendas.

Inclusion and Exclusion

Democracy, familiarly enough, has progressively come to imply the right-ness of universal suffrage (as the concept of the people, or *demos*, has been joined with ideals of equality and individual liberty). So, any bar-riers to participation, or any exclusions, have explicitly to be justified. Attempts at justifying unequal participation and power in democratic politics on grounds of sex or gender are not hard to find in the history of political thought. Numerous theories from classical to late modern times focus on women's alleged lack of rationality and reason, their lack of moral sense, their material dependence on men and their physical in-feriority, as compared to the rationality, reason, morality, self-sufficiency and physical and material strength with which male citizens are endowed. This contrastive analysis is enforced by arguments that patterns of sex difference are ontologically fundamental, materially necessary or divinely ordained.[2]

It is not just that femininity rules individuals out; a particular kind of masculinity rules people in. Thus, rights and duties that, on the face of it, in a conventional gender system should apply to adult men (the obvious example is military service) have been thought justifiably to be withheld from homosexual men.[3] Public policy in democratic societies can withhold privileges – for example, the social and material resources that legally and administratively accrue to married people – from gay men and lesbians.[4] Gay identities are accepted and acknowledged only in some circles in liberal democratic societies; and the question whether a gay man or a lesbian can properly act as a member of parliament or member of government, and how their sexual conduct has to be organized if they are so to do, is still controversial. The idea that the identity of a fully participating democratic citizen involves a particular social and gender identity still passes as a coherent one.

Of course, the coherence, social salience and social power of this idea is challenged and contested. In the course of such contest, gay people, like other minorities, may find barriers to their entering into or participating fully in public and governing circles. Such barriers include statements of preferences ('we don't want a gay or female MP'), the invocation of wider structures ('a gay or female candidate couldn't be elected in this constituency') or the identification of norms ('a gay or female person shouldn't hold public power'). These may be articulated as such, or not; they may take the form of formal or legal proscriptions, or operate informally. Political campaigns to oppose such exclusion have called for the explicit or legal proscription of this kind of discriminatory judgement.[5] Further, there have been demands for compensatory measures to secure for groups hitherto discriminated against a presence in the relevant public settings (workplaces, places of education, democratic forums) that is properly proportionate to their presence in the population. (This may not be literal mathematical proportion – there may of course be arguments for minority groups being overrepresented, mathematically speaking.[6])

So far, I have been discussing the ways in which gender operates to advantage or disadvantage individuals in political participation. Empirically, this begs the question of the extent to which, in the first place, people are unequally advantaged in their enjoyment of political power. Theoretically, it begs the question whether this is indeed a matter of 'gender'. The empirical question is, on the face of it, straightforward to answer. There can be no doubt that being female is associated with low levels or even the absence of participation. Recent international data show that men participate more; that is, they engage in more political acts, such as discussing politics, voting, attending meetings and so on, than women. They are present in legislatures and governments and the upper echelons of the bureaucracy in much greater numbers.[7] Of course, the pattern is not uniform: women participate in greater numbers in some forms of political engagement than in others; in some countries (notably the UK) the gender gap in rates of voting has closed.

More theoretically, feminist historians and political scientists have argued that women act politically in contexts and spaces that have tended not to be recognized as 'political' by mainstream analysts – because of the identification of politics with masculinity discussed above. Action in localities to build networks with the capacity for decision-making and protest has traditionally been dominated by women – although they are not always recognized.[8] Women have participated in social movements (such as feminism, campaigns for temperance, the green movement, anti-racism campaigns, etc.) to a greater extent than in other political organizations such as parties.[9] This is probably both because the issues are closer to women's diurnal concerns (given their position in the social structure) than matters of state and the party competition for the power to govern, and because, in any case, state circles and institutions have been closed to them, or open to them only in their capacity as wives, hostesses and the like. The most important social movements, as far as the concerns of this chapter go, are, of course, feminism and the gay movement. In both of these, despite the importance of demands for legislative reform in order to secure equality and freedom, a self-conscious rejection of conventional state-centred politics has been prominent. Party politics, the use of state power, and the conventional organization of pressure and influence are all thought to be suffused with gender and sex-biased ideas and ideals. Before meaningful intervention in and by state institutions is possible, it will be necessary to engage in cultural and social effort to secure the acceptance and legitimacy of genuine pluralism.

The opportunities and barriers considered so far are normative ideas of who ought to participate – these normative ideas are acted upon by individuals and groups with the power to exclude or include. But we must also consider another set of 'opportunities and barriers'. The distribution of material goods is both systematically related to gender norms, as we shall see, but also operates independently from such norms to condition relative participation rates.

When 'sex differences' data are disaggregated to compare women and men of similar age and stage in life (for instance, married men with young children and married women with young children), or when men and women with similar incomes and other material holdings are compared, it is clear that so-called 'sex differences' are to a great extent 'resources and burdens differences'.[10] Differences in resources and burdens, in turn, can be explained by sexual segregation and wage inequality in labour markets, and by the associated structure of sexually divided domestic labour. Conventional marriage and parenting are a threshold to men's participation in public life, because a female parenting partner (whether or not she is in waged work in the labour market) provides a range of goods and domestic services that free the man. Concomitantly, they are a barrier to the woman's participation, because she becomes time- if not money-poor. Notably, the result of those labour markets where there are more jobs for women than for men has not yet been a significant shift in the division of domestic labour – presumably because of a mixture of gender norms and skill distributions.[11] These explanations of inequality in the distribution of material goods are of course reinforced by continuing direct discrimination in employment both against women in general and against gay men and lesbians. This is a structural force in the distribution of goods.

A salient question is whether these patterns of distribution and deprivation are acceptable in democratic polities. Note that this is separate from the ethical and political question whether such unequal distributions and deprivation are acceptable on grounds of justice. The question is whether commitment to democratic politics as such adduces independent arguments for the unacceptability of such material inequalities. If material deprivation is grounds for the formal exclusion of people from democratic citizenship, or makes it practically impossible for them to participate, then the answer to this is 'yes'.

It can be seen from this very brief synopsis of relevant theoretical and empirical analysis that the relationships between 'family' or domestic life, markets for commodities such as labour and other goods, and 'public life' – membership of associations, participation in politics – are critical in the analysis and explanation of sex differences. These relationships have often been the starting point for social and political theory. Many theories of the proper conduct of government and politics begin by enquiring into the nature of relationships within households, and the conduct of inter- and extra-household exchange relationships.[12] Thus, constraints are set on what governments can do (they must not violate human rights, or interfere with civil association or private life), while also prescribing what governments must do (maintain the rule of law, defend the state, provide social security).

'Democracy' is a form of government which, *inter alia*, is said, on a number of grounds, to be superior to rival forms of government such as autocracy, oligarchy or anarchy.[13] It is more consistent with the equal status of individuals, as the voice of each, individually and in social and political groups, counts. It thus attributes to all individuals who participate the kind of capacity for autonomy and reason that is appropriate to one who is able to govern her- or himself and to participate collectively in the governance of all. It is more likely to result in responsible government which is both properly constrained and active – because there are clear and institutionalized ways in which the people and their representatives can challenge and question government, institutionalized means by which pressure can be brought to bear on government policy and a number of channels of oversight of government's administration and performance. It is a more efficient way of ensuring peaceful transitions of governmental power while leaving citizens free.

However, critics point out that democracy, both theoretically and practically, is underpinned by the separation of households from commodity markets and state or public power, by the associations between femininity and the domestic and masculinity and the public, and by the associated distribution of burdens and benefits. As we have seen, inequalities in participation are caused in part by material inequalities that, in turn, are structured by sexual divisions of labour, and the ideal of the independent, masculine, heterosexual citizen. That is, ideas of the proper scope of democratic government are conditioned by a gender system. This can be taken to mean that crucial aspects of that gender system are beyond the scope of democratic decision-making and governance.[14] Like other strands of political theory, most democratic theory – with the obvious exception of that which is explicitly critical of established sexual relations – presumes or states that sex and gender relations have a 'primordial' or 'natural' or 'given' status and character. They are the natural, social, non-political foundation on which democratic (and other) political systems are built.

Even if this were true, it would not warrant the inference that is often drawn that gender relations are exempt from political action and transformation. Relations between the sexes can and must be changed if democracy is to be realized. If commodity exchange and the goods and burdens of political power are to be equally shared, then domestic goods and burdens must also be equally shared. Apart from the view that gender relations are primordial and immutable, we can note other distinct approaches to the question. From one normative point of view, these matters should not be 'colonized' by government. It is absolutely crucial that there are social institutions and sites of personal and private life in which individuals can be absolutely free from the interference of other people and from government interference. 'The family' is pre-eminently such an institution – the main one to which this stricture applies.[15] This point of view is bolstered by liberal and libertarian suspicion of governmental power. Proponents argue that 'social problems' are constructed by interests which stand to gain from an expanded governmental sector getting involved in family life, parenting and so on. From a different point of view the issue is not the protection of private life from government interference; it is, rather, the degeneration of public life that follows from preoccupation with the minutiae of daily life, matters of reproduction and labour.[16] In response to this, others argue that family and household 'privacy' effectively underpins individual isolation and alienation from systems of social support. Governments have to be involved in reconstructing the associations and networks which mean that individuals have access to support and aid from outside their household or kin network. This is crucial if individuals are to escape from the personal oppression that is possible in these intimate and very intense settings. That is, if it is accepted that governments have any measure of responsibility for citizens' welfare, then the structure of 'private' relations cannot be beyond their ambit.[17]

Independence and Interdependence

The idea of 'citizen' has involved the idea of 'independence'.[18] Yet the public and private distinction which underpins liberal democratic polities operates, as we have seen, to justify unequal divisions of labour and rewards. Concomitantly, women have been relatively disadvantaged in employment. Even where they are not legally disbarred from property ownership, because of the structure of markets, the division of domestic labour and gender ideology, they own far less property than men. This means that women's citizenship status is undermined.

The critical response to this political structure has been well rehearsed. First, the so-called 'independence' of men is actually based on a hidden and denied but nevertheless necessary dependence – on kin, especially mothers and wives, on identification with other men, on associations, reciprocity and exchange.[19] Secondly, independence is not an unmixed good. It is both more plausible and more fruitful to base social theory on the facts of human relatedness and interdependence.[20] Theories of citizenship can and should start from the premise that men *and* women are social animals, that we are tied in complex and affect-laden relationships with kin and significant others, that we have needs that can only be met if we engage in generalized (not rigid) reciprocity. Such a line of thought certainly does not involve the rejection of the value of autonomy, meaning the capacity and practice of self-governance. But a condition of the attainment of autonomy is sustaining social and affective relationships.[21] Another way of putting this point is to emphasize that although 'dependence' has been, in many contexts, a synonym for 'subordination', and dependence does, indeed, mean 'insecurity' in many contemporary contexts,[22] the best way of addressing these ills is not to laud independence. The best way, rather, is to emphasize interdependence, to acknowledge our reciprocal needs.[23]

Another aspect of interdependence is our need for education and socialization before we can take up any social role whatsoever. Individuals need to be educated to participate as citizens – it is not a role that is 'natural' to persons of any gender.[24] Again, scholars find that some citizenship education materials and programmes have explicitly emphasized the masculine gender identity of citizens.[25] It is also a matter of concern whether educating people into citizenship is really possible if they are subject to authoritarian relations at work (as working-class people frequently are), at home (as in 'patriarchal' families), and in other organizations and associations like schools, churches and so on.[26] Another issue is that practice in citizenship requires opportunities for meaningful participation in democratic decisions. Obviously, the structure of political institutions matters here: there will be more opportunities where local government has powers and functions than where politics and administration are highly centralized; there will be more opportunities where government is open to exchanges with social organizations than where administration is highly professionalized or technocratic. For this reason, a good deal has been written about the importance of a properly democratically structured 'civil society' in an effective relationship with state power.[27]

Arguments about the democratic importance of civil society can be interpreted in part as arguments about who should be heard, who should be heeded, in public debate and political decision-making. This is a matter of 'who', both in the sense of 'which individuals? which persons?' and in the sense of 'which individuals organized how?' and 'which groups?' Voluntary associations such as social and special interest associations, cultural groups, churches, local organizations, voluntary projects and the like, and also political parties, are important for several reasons.[28] First, they are organizations to which people have a 'natural' social allegiance, organizations that draw people into social exhanges, mutuality and sociability. Secondly, they are places where people learn skills, and gain knowledge relevant to their role as citizens in democratic society – forming views on policy, framing demands and criticism of government, organizing meetings, campaigns, discussions, events, etc.[29]

Voice

The acceptance of the legitimacy of group participation (as opposed to just individuals' votes and party competition) in the democratic process does not settle the question of how relatively powerless or marginal groups are to get proper access to the debate. Proposals have been made to ensure that the relevant groups are always represented in policy discussions, or that legislative bodies should include representatives of all significant social groups in a locale (without their having to win places through the normal electoral process, which can, of course, disadvantage groups whose members are not geographically concentrated).[30] But doubts linger. Ensuring access to the debate for a group or an individual does not ensure that the more central and dominant members of the forum will listen or hear properly. It does not mean that the existing modes of conducting decision-making make it possible for new concerns to be adequately addressed or acted upon.

Questions regarding women's employment, education or cultural life can demand that very basic presumptions about social life and social identity have to be problematized – a kind of philosophical enterprise that is not consistent with the conventions of legislative debate. Derogatory jeering is a common enough response to 'metaphysics' or 'critique' in the academy, let alone in parliament. A common inference, then, is that something about the culture of parliaments has to change before the debate can go forward. By culture, I mean the interaction between informal modes of communication and conduct especially as these express or are conditioned by habits and beliefs about aesthetic matters (cuisine, music, entertainment, etc.) and morality (politeness, humour, deference, etc.). This is a very abstract way of talking about crucial matters such as how much decision-making is done in informal groups and where, who eats with whom and when, whether dominant modes of joke-telling are offensive for some members of the institution – the very practices that are often identified by minority or newcoming groups as the real barriers to their advancement and effectiveness within an institution. More formal frameworks are also important: the hours of work and time available for debate, the formal rules governing how debate is conducted and, of course, the constitutional and political issues – whether bureaucrats and others are properly responsive to changing social conditions and demands. Demands that the framework change are both harder to voice, harder to hear and harder to respond to and act upon than demands for changes within an existing framework.

Here, then, is one aspect of the idea of voice that has greatly exercised critical theorists of democracy: how are marginal and hitherto excluded voices to be properly heard?[31] Access is a precondition, but it is not sufficient. In the thinking of a number of feminist groups of the so-called 'second wave', transformed structures are key to liberation and true democracy. In many groups and circles a preference for consensus decision-making has been connected both with the idea that discussion and the sharing of experiences and understandings would lead to decisions about what to do, and with the idea that voting, competitive debate, speaking through the chair and the other paraphernalia of committees and legislatures in the Westminster and City Hall models were by their very nature and structure reactionary and unreceptive to the structure-breaking and identity-transforming aspirations of feminism.[32] However, the ideal of consensus decision-making can itself be criticized for concealing or suppressing dissent, and setting up very high and exclusionary boundaries to groups.[33] And in practice, of course, feminists and other radical groups have frequently engaged in quite orthodox political strategies and debates, although they tend to share with other critics of democracy misgivings about the way traditional theories and practices of democracy take participants' preferences as given, encourage unprincipled compromises or 'winner-take-all' outcomes and, as described above, rule out from the outset the articulation of views and desires which fundamentally question social identities and relationships.

'Dialogic' or 'deliberative' or 'discursive' democracy, by contrast, its proponents argue, put the quality of the debate at the centre of democratic theory.[34] The ideal is that rather than people coming into the forum with their preferences already formed, they allow their preferences to be formed by the debate with their fellows. (Of course, parliamentary systems embody this principle, although it is imperfectly realized and subverted by other aspects of the process.) The public nature of the democratic discussion itself forms a constraint on irrationality, intemperance and violence. However, critics wonder whether such a forum will really allow fundamental and structure-breaking views to be heard. Extra conditions to those set out by the 'deliberative democrats' include not only that all have the opportunity to speak, but that they are properly listened to and that they are able to speak in their own voice and that hearers will take the trouble to hear.[35] This entails relaxing the rules governing how people may speak in the forum, but, more difficult, requiring that participants learn to listen.

It is important to acknowledge that not only is listening difficult in itself, but that transparency in communication is an impossible ideal. The meanings of terms and utterances are not fixable, connotation is subject to flux, and meaning, in any case, is contestable.[36] So debate is not only debate about propositions and proposals, it is always about the meaning of interlocutors' utterances. Indeed, debate about the gaps between what is said, what is intended, the connotations of terms and the effort to change meaning is frequently the larger part of democratic political debate. Undoubtedly in a good deal of party political debate in democracies interlocutors routinely and wilfully misinterpret and misrepresent what their opponents have said and what they have thereby implied. The kind of practices of listening I sketch here would rule out of order such deliberate distortion. But it is increasingly unlikely that this 'interpretive' aspect of democratic discourse would cease to dominate. However, this only serves to underline the importance of open and concentrated listening, and a collective effort to clarify the range of meaning and interpretation immanent in the discussion.

The Politicization of Sexuality

We have seen that gender is important for democratic politics in at least two ways. First, it is an important dividing line of inequality in hold-ings of resources and therefore a significant barrier to democratic citi-zenship and participation. Secondly, it is itself the focus for democratic political effort and competition between those who wish for gender transformation and those who wish to maintain the status quo or some preferred older system. In this section I am going to discuss several ways in which gender has been contested in democratic politics. First, and most obviously, there have been political challenges to formal and legal exclusions of people from important social institutions on grounds of their gender or sexual identity. Secondly, I analyse the political con-struction of 'sexual harassment' and the argument that the harassment of women and gay people in public settings (both market and polity) is a crucial barrier to their full participation in democratic citizenship. This is both an indirect upshot of the fact that sexual harassment in the work-place can be an important mechanism for the maintenance of sexually segregated occupations, income inequalities and therefore deprivation of the kind of material resources necessary for equal citizenship participa-tion, and a direct upshot of harassment operating as a barrier to indi-viduals' political participation. Challenges to sexual harassment have been conducted both on an individual level, within organizations such as universities and workplaces, and also in state forums such as courts and legislatures. Third, an interesting aspect of these latter challenges, for my purposes, is the way they have represented a range of questions regarding the relevance of an individual's conduct in interpersonal rela-tions in domestic, friendship and sexual settings to her or his creden-tials as a representative, member of government, or protestor and challenger to political power. In these circumstances, the polite and euphemistic use of the term 'gender' has had to give way to a clearer discursive acknowledgement that what is at stake in many political argu-ments about gender is sexuality. Finally, I discuss the problem of the extent to which these contests are to be thought of as contests within democratic politics.

A key problem, it seems to me, and perhaps it is a perennial one, is that sexuality – sexual actions and relationships, identity as a being with the capacity for an erotic life – is one of those phenomena on the threshold of both public and private. While sexuality has long been an arena of life within which many have believed that freedom is important, it is not possible straightforwardly to say that our sexual lives are nobody's business but our own and those they directly involve.[37] On the other hand, one of the difficulties with campaigns about sexuality has been that they have involved speaking publicly about matters that have a private, even taboo, aspect. This means that protests against sexual coercion, for instance, sexualize the complainants, revealing their sexual being, and inviting comment and judgement on their sexual conduct and identity. A further paradox here is that social and political life is actually predicated on the public enactment and celebration of particular kinds of sexuality. Weddings and their surrounding paraphernalia are quintessentially public events; throughout social life all kinds of allusion to sexuality and eroticism are not only permitted but encouraged, while silence on these matters is in many contexts a sign of suspicion or deviance. One of the most significant aspects of 'sexual politics', then, is that it reveals the elusive nature of the boundary between public and private.[38]

Sexuality and public identity

One problem about this elusive boundary arises when we consider the campaigns and arguments about exclusion and citizenship. Citizenship is a theme that signals, as we have seen, social and political standing, participation in decision-making, and the rights and privileges of political membership and full state protection. In political and legal campaigns for rights in employment, public service and civil society, sexual minorities have explicitly argued that the goal here is full and equal citizenship status, secured by the proper enjoyment of social rights (in welfare and employment). Controversy arises, theoretically at least, when we consider the exact relation between sexuality as such and citizenship. In theories of democracy and related philosophy, as I have discussed, a particular sexual and gender identity has been understood to be a necessary condition for full citizenship and political participation. This being the case, then feminists, gay men and lesbians, and transsexuals can argue two ways. One is to say that sex and gender must be subtracted from citizenship; that citizenship is a role and identity that has no sex or gender element. The other is to argue that important aspects of citizenship in contemporary societies involve the recognition of individuals' cultural and social identities; that it is important that individuals are citizens as lesbians, or as women (or as heterosexual men).

From the point of view of democratic representation and government, this argument picks up an important and long-standing controversy.[39] On the one hand, it may be thought that representatives and governors need to be in some sense socially and culturally neutral – for they are called upon to consider and weigh up the interests of, and act for, individuals and groups with different religious, sexual, gender, marital, partisan, regional and so on ad infinitum ties. At its extreme this line of argument can find no fault in a parliament or government whose members all share some social identity – are all white middle- or upper-class men, say – as long as their behaviour in representing those different from themselves is correct. From another point of view, such an arrangement will always fall short of the democratic ideal. To begin with, it is symbolically important, in democratic polities, for political institutions to represent the society in the sense of containing a range of identities which exist in the society. It is practically important because citizens' and voters' allegiance to governing institutions is likely to be greater, given the importance of social identity for our sense of self, if people relevantly like them are selected for government. It is also important because, social identities being what they are, it has not proved to be the case that white men could be relied on to frame policy and organize institutions so as to favour people different from themselves. At its extreme, this line of argument can seem to suggest that every combination of identity and interest must be present in the forum (there must be at least one black Jewish disabled man, for example).[40] But this does not follow. Rather, what is needed is a range of social identities such that the practices of listening to 'other' voices, encountering and working with people different from oneself, attending to the range of difference in the society, are all part and parcel of the everyday work of and within the political institutions. According to this view, gay men and lesbians should indeed campaign for their presence in political society, as citizens, as representatives and governors, as gay men and lesbians – that is, as sexual beings. Only in this way is the crucial responsiveness of polity to society or government to people to be ensured. Only in this way can it be made even probable that newcomers to the society have a chance of being heard when they try to speak.

However, the implications of this view are that sexuality has a decidedly public aspect. The asexual view of citizenship will not do. It has to be acknowledged that, for instance, a gay man is in the public sphere as a gay man and, indeed, as whatever else he is socially. Now it would be unwise to imply that there is no problem here. For one thing, social identities can become onerous: always to be 'the woman' on the committee can be a burden. But the answer to this is not to revert to so-called neutrality ('I'm not a woman, I'm a person'), as many are tempted to do. The answer instead is to achieve a wide degree of plurality and difference in all committees and their equivalent, so that everyone can routinely bring their 'differences' to their work. This will fracture both the homogeneity of the original arrangements where white middle-class men (or their equivalent) had a monopoly in governing power, and the ossified arrangements for interest representation whereby there is always a woman on the committee but somehow she rarely prevails. A further problem is the one alluded to already: sexuality is widely thought to be a matter of personal choice which is nobody else's business, and a matter of intimate life which can and perhaps should remain invisible to others. As to the first, this is not difficult: one's choice of sexual identity – or if that is thought to be too strong and voluntarist a way of putting it, one's decisions about how to live sexually – is indeed a matter of freedom, with the usual constraints. That freedom is claimed in political campaigns such as feminism and gay rights. But the idea that one's sexual life is private in the sense of properly concealable is more difficult. An important aspect of democratic discussion is the understanding, if not the overt declaration, of one's identity. At the very least explicit concealment here is morally and democratically problematic.

This requirement of disclosure cannot, of course, hold in a world where certain sexual identities are a cause for censure, negative discrimination, persecution or worse. One of the features of sexual politics in the anglophone world at the start of the new century is the difficulty of distinguishing between individuals who keep their sexual identity secret for well-founded fear of discrimination or persecution, and those who keep their sexual identity secret and refuse to speak out for sexual liberation because of an archaic and repressed set of sexual attitudes and practices. The latter group is commonly censured as being hypocritical.

Nevertheless, it is not quite enough to say this. For one thing, as has been argued, 'sexual identity' is fluid across a life. It is therefore a lot to ask that for political purposes individuals must avow, or wholeheartedly present, an identity. Our identities are complex, and most of us rightly feel ambivalent about certain aspects of them. It may or may not be justified that sexuality is a particular source of ambivalence. Some theorists and activists have taken the view that sexuality is an aspect of life like any other and that it is politicized like any other in the sense that it is a ground for social and political status and acceptance. Accordingly, silence is a form of repression which will invariably have deleterious consequences. So the answer is openness and transparency about sexuality as about other aspects of social identity. Others doubt that such transparency is either possible or desirable. Perhaps in equal measure with, and perhaps more than, other aspects of our social identities like religion, culture, social class or gender, our sexuality is a source of inner and outer conflict, uncertainty and error. To require us to commit to an identity is to require too much. The particular connection between sexuality and taboo in most societies, between sexuality and the illicit, cannot be treated as an archaic state of affairs to be swept away with other forms of superstition.

I do not think the inference can be drawn here that all individuals, especially those in public life, must be fully open about their sexual relationships and identity. What can be concluded, though, is that the kind of lumpen heterosexuality and conventional marriage that is still, in many circles, the sine qua non of public acceptance has to be debunked. It is simply unacceptable that public figures have to live such lives. The concomitant of this must be the absence of such assumptions and requirements, and the full acceptance of sexual identities that are disclosed. But this is not the requirement of disclosure at the outset.

Sexual harassment

One of the most explosive issues in democratic politics at the turn of the century is sexual harassment; and disputes about sexual harassment shade into a wider and more complicated range of disputes about sexual behaviour and sexual character more generally. Sexual harassment in the workplace and other market and civil society settings undermines self-respect and confidence, as well as straightforwardly constituting a barrier to participation and presence. Thus it deprives people of some of the crucial social conditions that underpin citizenship.[41] Sexual harassment in public and political settings, of course, is a straightforward attack on people's citizenship and political standing.

Feminist and other critical responses have analysed at some length the nature of the harm in sexual harassment.[42] First, the unequal distribution of power to coerce sexually must give way to equally distributed rights to suggest the sexualization of a relationship, and the absolute right to refuse such sexualization if it is suggested by another. This means that in all kinds of social settings individuals have the right to present and to act in such a way that sexuality is unremarked and out of the frame. I deliberately do not say 'present and act non-sexually', as I think that gender and social identities do encompass sexuality. But to say this is not to say that sexuality is always, so to speak, remarkable.

This formulation leaves it an open question whether, when people are at work, for example, one might suggest a sexual relationship to another. It is an open question whether this counts as a boundary violation, whether offence is justifiably taken at such a context redefinition. Many critics have argued that attempts to bound sexuality are part and parcel of the privatization of sexuality, which has been part and parcel of denial of its political nature.[43] Binding and repression and privatization work perversely to allow dominant forms of sexuality to pass as 'neutral' – because they suppress talk and argument about sexuality. For this reason they also enable sexual harassment to count as 'normal', which has made for obvious difficulties in tackling it as a wrong or an offence. And it puts complainants who speak in public of sexual behaviour and actions in the wrong, as speaking sexually effectively sexualizes.

So the only course is to publicize sexuality, to discuss the power relations in sexual exchanges and the way these, like other power relations, can be exploited and abused. That complainants speak out about sexual harassment is of course a direct upshot of this move. But there is nothing to be gained theoretically or practically from ignoring the fact that a certain kind of privacy is lost here. This is not only the privacy of the harasser who, like other bullies, can rely on victims' shame at being attacked. It is also the privacy of the complainant who would cherish a social life that does not have to be described and analysed in public forums. And, further, it is the privacy of all sexual beings for whom sexuality is on the threshold of being indescribable. The difficulty here, of course, is that sexual relationships in public spaces and public contexts, using public resources – workplaces, state buildings – are at most only liminally private.

Character and sexual character

Since its inception, feminism has been concerned to address the gender asymmetry in sexuality. For women, character, morality and virtue have been identified overwhelmingly with sexual character, morality and virtue; while for men, sexual character has been (and in some cultural circles still is) seemingly irrelevant. Worse, in certain cultural circles the masculine sexual prowess that is necessary for social reputation puts women and men into a never-ending struggle in which women's sexual reputation is prize or casualty. Recent politics has seen a number of attempts at transforming established discourses and practices of sexual morality. These range from individualistic projects of self-exploration and realization, to egalitarian projects of mutuality, reciprocity and sharing between partners, to sexual practices that repudiate the ideals of 'couples' and 'relationships' altogether. What is shared in all these projects is the principle that sexual character and sexual action are relevant to public morality. A person's public persona is not independent of their sexual morality. But this makes sexual conduct a matter of public concern.

It would be unwise to argue that the explosion of sexual scandals in public life – sexual harassment charges against prominent individuals, revelations of extra-marital affairs, revelations of liaisons with prostitutes or strangers – is wholly different in kind from prurient and titillatory public interest in previous epochs. Rulers and other public figures are surrounded by an aura or mystique that begs to be punctured: this would be so whether the medium through which they are viewed were the palace gates or, as now, the press and broadcast media. (I'm not sure about this – but it would possibly continue to be so even in a fully realized democracy in which everyone reasonably felt they might at some time participate in ruling, in which all voices were heard in democratic debate.) Anyway, it is this register that is most dominant in media comment on recent controversies. But there is also present a more analytic strain of enquiry about whether and to what extent sexual character and sexual life is a relevant criterion by which to judge a public figure. The difficulty is that analysts get stuck going round and round the same vicious circle of arguing now that sexual privacy is an important good in contemporary societies (together, often, with the more consequentialist argument that if standards of sexual conduct are set too high, public life will be the loser, as this will act as such a powerful disincentive to public participation), and then that we rightly consider someone's sexual conduct is relevant to their character and trustworthiness in general, so sexuality cannot be entirely private.

A more promising line of analysis, in my view, is that limits must be put on the extent to which it is permissible to exploit what is essentially a public resource (political power and the material goods and appurtenances that go with it) for personal gain. Thus, using one's aura as a famous or prominent public figure to sexually exploit a person of much lower status or power looks the same as using one's contacts through public life in order to secure lucrative contracts or directorships.

Conclusion: Democracy and Sexuality

Sexual politics, campaigns for the rights and privileges of citizenship to be distributed without regard to sexual identity and for the barriers of sexual difference to be overcome, press up against the limits of democratic politics and are a crucial test of democratic values. In this chapter I have taken a view of 'democracy' as importantly discursive: debate matters. This does not imply a rosy and idealized view of reasoned consensus. The democratic debate about sexuality takes the form of conflict between warring parties, rather than consensual exchanges of views. Some parties question whether sexuality is a proper topic for public debate at all, and this adds to the sense of conflict. But the fact that 'debate' is unpleasant is not an argument against debate. Further, dialogue and debate take more forms than parliamentarianism. Sexual politics is likely for some time to come to take a carnival form, as one of the most pressing tasks is the visibility of people with oppositional sexual identities in public, the establishment of their presence, their rights to be there, and their rights to speak. Again, this in no sense undermines democracy.

Nevertheless, sexual politics is likely also for some time to come to seem to be something of a thorn in the side of democratic polity and society. Those who campaign in this area will continue to be seen to be discussing openly topics that, according to many, should be closed, and to be pushing at the limits of the democratic form of politics.

NOTES

1 Some relevant contributions are C. A. MacKinnon, *Feminism Unmodified: Discourses on Life and Law* (Cambridge, MA, Harvard University Press, 1987); R. W. Connell, *Gender and Power: Society, the Person and Sexual Politics* (Cambridge, Polity, 1987); J. Mansbridge, *Feminism and Democratic Community* (New York, Russell Sage Foundation Working Paper no. 25, 1992); J. Butler, *Bodies That Matter: On the Discursive Limits of 'Sex'* (London, Routledge, 1993); J. Butler, *Gender Trouble: Feminism and the Subversion of Identity* (New York, Routledge, 1990); H. L. Moore, *A Passion for Difference: Essays in Anthropology and Gender* (Cambridge, Polity, 1994); D. Cornell, *The Imaginary Domain: Abortion, Pornography and Sexual Harassment* (London, Routledge, 1995); V. Bryson, *Feminist Debates: Issues of Theory and Political Practice* (Basingstoke, Macmillan, 1999), pp. 46ff; J. Squires, *Gender in Political Theory* (Cambridge, Polity, 1999).

2   See for instance: C. Pateman, *The Disorder of Women: Democracy, Feminism and Political Theory* (Cambridge, Polity, 1989); M. L. Shanley and C. Pateman (eds), *Feminist Interpretations and Political Theory* (Cambridge, Polity, 1991); G. Lloyd, *The Man of Reason: 'Male' and 'Female' in Western Philosophy* (London, Methuen, 1984); D. Coole, *Women in Political Theory: From Ancient Misogyny to Contemporary Feminism*, 2nd edn (Hemel Hempstead, Harvester Wheatsheaf, 1993); E. Kennedy and S. Mendus (eds), *Women in Western Political Philosophy* (Brighton, Harvester, 1987); S. M. Okin, *Women in Western Political Thought* (London, Virago, 1980).

3   J. Butler, *Excitable Speech: A Politics of the Performative* (New York, Routledge, 1997), p. 105 calls these 'retractable zones of citizenship'.

4   I. M. Young, *Intersecting Voices: Dilemmas of Gender, Political Philosophy and Policy* (Princeton, NJ, Princeton University Press, 1997), pp. 102ff discusses the injustice of marriage.

5   Bryson, *Feminist Debates*, ch. 4; E. Frazer and N. Lacey, *The Politics of Community: A Feminist Critique of the Liberal Communitarian Debates* (Hemel Hempstead, Harvester, 1993), ch. 3. There is a large literature on anti-discrimination policy and law; many references are included in these two works.

6   A. Phillips, *Engendering Democracy* (Cambridge, Polity, 1991), pp. 60–91.

7   United Nations, Centre for Social Development and Humanitarian Affairs, *Women in Politics and Decision Making in the Late Twentieth Century: A United Nations Study* (Dordrecht, Martinus Nijhoff, 1992); United Nations, *From Nairobi to Bejing: Second Review and Appraisal of the Implementation of the Nairobi Looking-Forward Strategies for the Advancement of Women*, Report of the Secretary General, (New York, United Nations, 1995); United Nations, Division for the Advancement of Women, *Factsheet on Women in Government* (January 1996); United Nations, Division for the Advancement of Women, *Expert Group Meeting on Political Decision Making and Conflict Resolution: The Impact of Gender Difference*, Santo Domingo, October 1996 (Oslo, International Peace Research Institute, November 1996) – these and other UN reports provide invaluable statistics on women's role in government and public life worldwide; C. M. Mueller (ed.), *The Politics of the Gender Gap: The Social Construction of Political Influence* (London, Sage, 1988); J. Lovenduski and P. Norris (eds), *Gender and Party Politics* (London, Sage, 1993); R. Inglehart and P. Norris, 'Gender gaps in voting behaviour in global perspective' [http://www.ksg.harvard.edu/people/pnorris/articles.htm#Gender] (Paper prepared for Annual Meeting of the American Political Science Association, 1998).

8   N. A. Naples, *Community Activism and Feminist Politics: Organizing Across Race, Class and Gender* (New York, Routledge, 1998).

9   L. Weir, 'Limitations of new social movement analysis', *Studies in Political Economy* 40 (1993): 73–102; G. Kaplan, *Contemporary Western European Feminism* (London, UCL Press, 1992).

10   G. Parry, G. Moyser and N. Day, *Political Participation and Democracy in Britain* (Cambridge, Cambridge University Press, 1992).

11   O. Sullivan, 'Time coordination, the domestic division of labour and affective relations: Time use and the enjoyment of activities', *Sociology* 30, 1 (1996): 79–100; O. Sullivan, 'Time waits for no woman: An investigation of the gendered experience of domestic time', *Sociology* 31, 2 (1997): 221–39; A. Hochschild, *The Second Shift: Working Parents and the Revolution at Home* (London, Piatkus, 1990).

12   Notable examples include Aristotle, *The Politics*, trans. T. Sinclair (Harmondsworth, Penguin, 1962); G. W. F. Hegel, *Philosophy of Right*, trans. T. M. Knox (Oxford, Oxford University Press, 1967[1821]); and also the 'social contract theorists': T. Hobbes, *Leviathan* (1651); S. Pufendorf, *On the Duty of Man and Citizen According to Natural Law* (1672); J. Locke, *Two Treatises of Government* (1690); J-J. Rousseau, *The Social Contract* (1762) – see M. Lessnoff (ed.), *Social Contract Theory* (Oxford, Blackwell, 1990).

13   For discussion of all the following and more, see R. A. Dahl, *Democracy and its Critics* (New Haven, Yale University Press, 1989); B. Barry, *Democracy, Power and Justice: Essays in Political Theory* (Oxford, Clarendon Press, 1989); J. Dunn (ed.), *Democracy: The Unfinished Journey, 508BC to AD1993* (Oxford, Oxford University Press, 1992); D. Beetham (ed.), *Defining and Measuring Democracy* (London, Sage, 1994).

14   The most prominent proponent of this interpretation of democratic theory and practice is Carole Pateman, who argues that problems of gender and democracy can never be resolved unless the public–private distinction is dissolved. She argues that insofar as governments do regulate family life, they do so in order to shore up the conventional gender system. She emphasizes the need for genuine democratic relationships and arrangements to permeate all spheres of life – including the workplace, the site of production, and the household, the site of reproduction – instead of being a feature of 'public' life only. C. Pateman, *Participation and Democratic Theory* (Cambridge, Cambridge University Press, 1970); C. Pateman, *The Sexual Contract* (Cambridge, Polity Press, 1988); Pateman, *The Disorder of Women*; C. Pateman, *Democracy, Freedom and Special Rights*, The John C. Rees Memorial Lecture 1995 (Swansea, University of Wales, 1995); C. Pateman, 'Does sex matter to democracy? – A comment', *Scandinavian Political Studies* 13, 1 (1990): 57–63.

15   The worries about the 'colonization of the lifeworld' are articulated as such by J. Habermas, *Theory of Communicative Action, Volume 2. Lifeworld and System: A Critique of Functionalist Reason*, trans.

T. McCarthy (Cambridge, Polity, 1987); for criticism from a feminist perspective, see N. Fraser, 'What's critical about critical theory? The case of Habermas and gender', in S. Benhabib and D. Cornell (eds), *Feminism as Critique: Essays on the Politics of Gender in Late Capitalist Societies* (Cambridge, Polity, 1987), pp. 31–56. See also J. B. Elshtain, *Public Man, Private Woman: Women in Social and Political Thought* (Princeton, NJ, Princeton University Press, 1981); J. B. Elshtain, *Real Politics: At the Centre of Everyday Life* (Baltimore, Johns Hopkins University Press, 1997).

16 This point of view is most associated with Hannah Arendt, who argues that the sympathy and compassion that enter into deliberation and decision-making when minds are turned to such matters as poverty will subvert the rationality and sternness that is demanded when deciding matters of state. H. Arendt, *The Human Condition* (Chicago, University of Chicago Press, 1958); H. Arendt, *On Revolution* (Harmondsworth, Penguin, 1967), p. 112.

17 P. Gilbert, 'Family values and the nation state', in G. Jagger and C. Wright (eds), *Changing Family Values* (London, Routledge, 1999); Young, *Intersecting Voices*, p. 100; E. Frazer, *The Problems of Communitarian Politics: Unity and Conflict* (Oxford, Oxford University Press, 1999), ch. 6.

18 C. Pateman, 'Feminist critiques of the public/private dichotomy', and 'The patriarchal welfare state', in *The Disorder of Women*. The idea of independence has been re-linked to the idea of citizenship in recent discourses about the ill effects of dependency on the welfare state. N. Fraser and L. Gordon, 'A genealogy of dependency: Tracing a keyword of the US welfare state', in N. Fraser, *Justice Interruptus: Critical Reflections on the Postsocialist Condition* (New York, Routledge, 1997), pp. 121–50.

19 Cornell, *The Imaginary Domain*, p. 17; E. F. Kittay, 'Human dependency and Rawlsian equality', in D. T. Meyers (ed.), *Feminists Rethink the Self* (Boulder, CO, Westview Press, 1997).

20 C. Taylor, 'Atomism', in *Philosophy and the Human Sciences* (Cambridge, Cambridge University Press, 1985); V. Held, 'Mothering versus contract', in J. Mansbridge (ed.), *Beyond Self-Interest* (Chicago, University of Chicago Press, 1990); S. Benhabib, 'The generalised and concrete other', in *Situating the Self: Gender Community and Postmodernism in Contemporary Ethics* (Cambridge, Polity, 1992).

21 Cornell, *The Imaginary Domain*, especially pp. 4–8.

22 See N. Fraser, 'After the family wage: A postindustrial thought experiment' in *Justice Interruptns*, pp. 41–66; and Fraser and Gordon, 'A genealogy of dependency'.

23 Pateman, *Democracy, Freedom and Special Rights*, p. 18.

24 A. Gutmann, *Democratic Education* (Princeton, NJ, Princeton University Press, 1987); P. White, *Civic Virtues and Public Schooling:*

Educating Citizens for a Democratic Society (New York, Teachers' College Press, 1996); E. Callan, *Creating Citizens: Political Education and Liberal Democracy* (Oxford, Clarendon Press, 1997); E. Frazer (ed.), *Political Education: Oxford Review of Education, Special Issue* 25: 1, 2 (1999).

25 P. Brindle and M. Arnot, ' "England expects every man to do his duty": The gendering of the citizenship textbook 1940–1966', *Oxford Review of Education* 25: 1, 2 (1999): 103–24.

26 Pateman, *Participation and Democratic Theory*; H. Eckstein, 'Civic inclusion and its discontents', in *Regarding Politics: Essays in Political Theory, Stability and Change* (Berkeley, University of California Press, 1992); N. Rosenblum, 'Democratic character and community: The logic of congruence', *Journal of Political Philosophy* 2 (1994): 67–97.

27 J. Keane (ed.), *Civil Society and the State: New European Perspectives* (London, Verso, 1988); J. Keane, *Democracy and Civil Society: On the Predicament of European Socialism, the Prospects for Democracy, and the Problem of Controlling Social and Political Power* (London, Verso, 1988); C. Mouffe (ed.), *Dimensions of Radical Democracy* (London, Verso, 1992); C. Mouffe, *The Return of the Political* (London, Verso, 1993); J. Cohen and A. Arato, *Civil Society and Political Theory* (Cambridge, MA, MIT Press, 1992).

28 P. Hirst, *Associative Democracy: New Forms of Economic and Social Governance* (Cambridge, Polity, 1994). Voluntary organizations and the like are thought of as the repositories of 'social capital' – see P. Hall, 'Social capital in Britain', *British Journal of Political Science* 29 (1999): 417–61; A. Ware, *Citizens, Parties, and the State: A Reappraisal* (Cambridge, Polity, 1987).

29 On the educational importance of civil associations and (especially) churches, see S. Verba, K. L. Schlozman and H. E. Brady, *Voice and Equality: Civic Voluntarism in American Politics* (Cambridge, MA, Harvard University Press, 1995).

30 See, particularly, I. M. Young, *Justice and the Politics of Difference* (Princeton, NJ, Princeton University Press, 1990); see also W. Kymlicka, *Multicultural Citizenship: A Liberal Theory of Minority Rights* (Oxford, Clarendon Press, 1995), esp. ch. 7; A. Phillips, *Which Equalities Matter?* (Cambridge, Polity, 1999), esp. ch. 4.

31 There is a convergence here with another notable strand of political theory: that of exploring the relationship between justice and gender. Carol Gilligan argues that there are contrasting, and inconsistent, ways of framing questions about justice and what is right, about what one ought to do or what should be done. Gilligan identifies *dominant* conceptions of justice and received styles of ethical reasoning with a 'masculine' style, while in ethical dilemmas a 'feminine' style will go unheard – will be inaudible to all intents and purposes. It takes a special effort, a shift of standpoint, an acknowledgement of difference

and plurality in what are in any particular context established practices, to hear 'a different voice'. C. Gilligan, *In a Different Voice: Psychological Theory and Women's Development* (Cambridge, MA, Harvard University Press, 1982); see also A. Baier, 'The need for more than justice', in *Moral Prejudices: Essays on Ethics* (Cambridge, MA, Harvard University Press, 1994); S. M. Okin, 'Justice and gender', *Philosophy and Public Affairs* 16, 1 (1987): 42–72; S. M. Okin, 'Reason and feeling in thinking about justice', *Ethics* 99 (1989): 229–49.

32   Phillips, *Engendering Democracy*, ch. 5; A. Phillips, 'Must feminists give up on liberal democracy?', in *Democracy and Difference* (Cambridge, Polity, 1993).

33   Phillips, *Engendering Democracy*, ch. 5.

34   J. Cohen, 'Deliberation and democratic legitimacy', in A. Hamlin and P. Pettit (eds), *The Good Polity: Normative Analysis of the State* (Oxford, Basil Blackwell, 1989); J. Dryzek, *Discursive Democracy: Politics, Policy, and Science* (Cambridge, Cambridge University Press, 1990); J. Elster (ed.), *Deliberative Democracy* (Cambridge, Cambridge University Press, 1998).

35   I. M. Young, 'Communication and the other: Beyond deliberative democracy', in *Intersecting Voices*, pp. 60–74; J. Johnson, 'Arguing for deliberation: Some skeptical considerations', in Elster (ed.), *Deliberative Democracy*, pp. 161–84.

36   Butler, *Excitable Speech*, pp. 87–8.

37   Cornell, *The Imaginary Domain*, pp. 7–10, 168–70 for a clear programmatic statement of the relationship between sexuality and freedom.

38   N. Fraser, 'Sex, Lies and the Public Sphere', in *Justice Interruptus*, p. 99, makes the same point.

39   Phillips, *Engendering Democracy*, pp. 150ff; Young, *Justice and the Politics of Difference*, pp. 183ff.

40   Phillips, *Engendering Democracy*, pp. 150ff; Young, *Justice and the Politics of Difference*, pp. 183ff.

41   Cornell, *The Imaginary Domain*, pp. 167–227; Fraser, 'Sex, lies and the public sphere', pp. 99–120; T. Morrison (ed.), *Race-ing Justice, En-gendering Power: Essays on Anita Hill, Clarence Thomas and the Construction of Social Reality* (London, Chatto and Windus, 1993), p. xvi.

42   Cornell, *The Imaginary Domain*, pp. 167–227; Mackinnon, *Feminism Unmodified*, pp. 113–16; Frazer and Lacey, *Politics of Community*, pp. 88–91; M. Rubenstein, *The Dignity of Women at Work: A Report on the Problem of Sexual Harassment in the Member States of the European Communities* (Luxembourg, Office for Official Publications of the European Communities, 1998).

43   Cornell, *The Imaginary Domain*, p. 10.

4

Democracy and Group Rights

John Kane

Modern political theory seems, at least on the surface, to have outgrown its venerable preoccupation with class analysis versus individualism. New kinds of politics have arisen on new bases of theoretical concern: the politics of community, multicultural politics, the politics of difference and the politics of recognition or identity.

One topic that has emerged in this work is that of group rights, the debate over which has taken place largely within the context of modern critiques of liberalism. Before examining the implications of the idea for democratic theory, then, I must begin by outlining the challenge it represents to liberal thought. I will follow this with an examination of the kinds of right that are advocated for groups – making a distinction between those intended to protect cultures and those intended to promote greater democratic inclusion – and also the different kinds of group for which they are demanded. The differences between the liberal and democratic perspectives will be discussed and reasons given why the latter should be thought to give the better purchase on the issue of group rights. It will be argued that democrats, while always sympathetic to schemes for greater inclusion and equality of access to political processes, have reasons to be cautious, even sceptical, about strategies that affirm group identities, and that in fact they are often justifiably concerned to encourage democratic processes that de-emphasize the political salience of particular identities.

In the last section I will argue, however, that there is one identity issue that democrats can scarcely avoid and that some group theorists rely on without clearly addressing: this is the issue of a society's privileged elite.

The alleged dominance of this elite ensures that the liberal democratic state retains, despite its professed ideology, a specific identity that gives the exclusions of which the theorists speak much of their meaning and reality. But examination of this question reintroduces more traditional, political-economy forms of enquiry. I argue that these cannot be ignored if we are to be clear about democratic goals and how they might be politically attained in a globalizing world.

Critiques of Liberalism and Liberal Responses

The first of the critiques of liberalism which arguably gave purchase to the notion of group rights came from communitarian theorists. This group attacked the work of influential writers such as John Rawls and Robert Nozick who, for all their political differences, shared the traditional liberal view of human individuals. Individuals were conceptualized as 'atomistic' beings, 'unencumbered' by social connections, or even with intrinsic connections to their own valued projects.[1] Communitarians claimed that this autonomous, pre-social individual was an impossible metaphysical abstraction, one that ignored the way real human beings related to the communities and traditions that both formed them and provided the necessary context for their meaningful action. They argued that we do not exist as free individuals prior to community; rather, our communities are 'constitutive' of our very selves and therefore prior to individuality and to individual liberty.[2]

A more radical critique of liberal individualism by various postmodern writers was also influential. This work implied the virtual dissolution of the individual self within a fabric of determinative social relations; necessarily, social individuals were reduced to 'subject positions' within various 'language games', 'narratives' or 'discourses'. The importance of 'difference' was stressed, as was the allegedly radical incommensurability of the narratives and discourses in which human beings are embedded. Allegedly following from this was the impropriety of 'imperialistically' imposing the standards inherent in any one of these narratives (including supposedly universal standards of justice, truth and conduct) upon any of the others. Liberalism's universal ascription of the values of equality and individual rights could be seen as just this kind of difference-suppressing imperialism by a particular group – white, middle-class males who were the true bearers and beneficiaries of such values – on all others. This domination was deemed to constitute an injustice.[3]

Thus, both communitarians and postmodernists tended towards a similar view about what was needed to resist domination and correct injustice. Charles Taylor argued that different cultures in our midst should be granted not just toleration but rather a form of recognition based on at least a 'presumption of equal worth'.[4] Such a politics of recognition or difference seemed to imply a rejection of universal values that could be applied across cultures. Its intention was to validate and respect group differences instead of making them the basis for unwarranted exclusions, and to pursue affirmative action programmes to correct such exclusions.[5]

Partly in response to this work, there emerged, from within liberalism itself, further critiques that focused on the limits of the traditional value of tolerance. Three separate strands were distinguishable. The first took seriously the communitarian analysis and argued that liberal respect and liberal rights should be extended from individuals to the particular communities from which they came and which supported them in their being. To achieve this, it was argued, the state had to move beyond the essentially negative value of tolerance, even beyond the rule of non-discrimination, and on to 'multicultural affirmation'.[6]

A second variant criticized the inadequacy of the traditional liberal model of toleration when applied to multinational and multilingual polities. It argued that taking religious allegiance out of the public sphere and placing it into the private may have worked for ending religious conflict in the seventeenth century, but did not help answer questions as to which languages should be used in parliaments and courts, whether the public should fund education of an ethnic group in its mother tongue, whether powers should be devolved to regional minorities to give them greater control of their own affairs, and so on. Will Kymlicka argued that dealing with such questions required the attribution of group rights to national minorities, who would thereby gain some measure of cultural protection from the assimilative pressures of dominant cultures.[7]

Finally, a third strand of argument accused liberalism of violating the rule that underpinned its own doctrine of toleration, namely that which prescribed neutrality between different 'life choices' or 'ways of life'. Liberalism's scepticism about the possibility of making singular, rational judgements on value choices in general had resulted in an assertion of the only positive value that seemed open to it – the value of choice itself and, concomitantly, of the toleration of different choices. But critics argued that liberalism's insistence on individual autonomy itself implied a substantive, universal value commitment that liberals tried to impose on other groups. In other words, liberals, despite their scepticism, asserted a positive good or value – individual autonomy – that they prescriptively required to be respected across all 'ways of life'.[8]

One response of liberals to this charge was to admit its truth but to continue to assert autonomy as a (fundamentally non-rational) political commitment. Even Kymlicka stressed that the group rights he advocated should not be allowed to permit restriction by groups of the autonomy of their members; the liberty to choose – in this case to choose (or reject) one's cultural affiliations – remained the essential and inviolable liberal principle. An alternative response was to push for more thorough consistency, and to argue the desirability of tolerating even highly illiberal (that is, 'intolerable') beliefs, practices and ways of life. Such a strategy would make tolerance itself rather than individual liberty the fundamental value. Most liberals were highly resistant to this alternative, for obvious reasons.[9]

Given their ideological commitments, it is understandable that many liberals should tend to be suspicious of group rights, and that even those who argue for them should hedge them round with qualifications that reflected those same commitments. Liberalism does not easily concede that rights might or should be extended to collectivities, for to do so may jeopardize the rights of the individuals within them. For this reason some liberals reject group rights altogether. They argue that whatever moral significance may be attached to the preservation of cultures or ways of life, it is not strong enough to give rise to a collective right analogous to the individual rights that issue from the need to safeguard individual liberty and autonomy.[10]

Others expressed a larger fear, namely, that groups might use this concept to threaten the social order. These liberals were particularly worried about the mobilization of ideologically illiberal and often anti-liberal groups potentially able to dominate public debate and to use democratic processes to achieve 'unreasonable' ends. To them, the arguments of communitarians, multiculturalists and the proponents of recognition and difference seemed to play into the hands of these combatively divisive groups, providing them with justifications that heightened the danger of political instability and social fragmentation. These liberals therefore offered a different response to the phenomenon of group politics, christened with the name 'political liberalism', though described by some critics as a 'chastened liberalism'. In this theory, the traditional liberal concern with the tension between liberty and equality – whose reconciliation Rawls had presumed to effect in his *A Theory of Justice* – gave way to a concern with maintaining social order. It was argued that tolerating social and cultural diversity in the private sphere was one thing, but legally *affirming* particular identities quite another. The latter strategy meant sanctioning the entry of particular identities into the public sphere, a realm where people are supposed to enter not as representatives of groups but as individuals, and as 'reasonable' individuals at that. The effects of this intrusion on public debate and sensible policy formation were held to be inevitably detrimental.[11]

Political liberalism's solution was to narrow the boundaries of the political by depoliticizing identity. This was to be achieved by defining the realm of public reason in such a way that particular identities and allegiances, along with the troublesome claims and 'irrational' beliefs they import, would be excluded. Especially difficult controversies arising from conflicting value or belief positions would be removed from the political arena altogether and put into the hands of constitutional courts and judges for 'impartial' administration. This strategy of keeping differences out of the public arena was the exact opposite of that proposed by the politics of recognition and of differentiated citizenship, and it was attacked by some as undemocratic. And perhaps the old liberal mistrust of democracy *was* reasserting itself here. The trouble with giving people the right to choose is that they frequently choose according to their particular affiliations and prejudices, which is to say inconveniently, wrongly or irrationally – in a word, illiberally. Political liberalism's theoretical struggle with the rise of group politics has considerable significance, therefore, for anyone whose instincts are to argue for a *more* rather than a less democratic politics.[12]

This is a theme I will return to when discussing the attitude of democratic theory to the question of group rights. First, though, I must look briefly at the kinds of right that are commonly asserted, and also at the kinds of group on whose behalf they are asserted.

What Rights, Which Groups?

In the literature, various rights are claimed for various kinds of group, but on inspection they all appear to serve one or both of two different purposes. The first is the protection or preservation of a culture or cultural practice or, more broadly, way of life or identity. The second is to prevent or correct an unjust exclusion of, or discrimination against, a particular group.[13]

Protection and preservation might in some cases be held to require rights of recognition, as for example the legal recognition of religious marriages or of Aboriginal land rights. In other cases they may merely produce demands for exemptions for some groups from particular laws – as for example for Sikhs from the compulsory wearing of motor-cycle helmets. Rights aimed at preventing or correcting exclusions and discriminations, on the other hand, try to assist disadvantaged groups to gain more effective participation in society and polity. They might take the form of assistance rights – for example, the right to certain positions or offices provided by affirmative action policies – or representation rights – for example, the right to a certain number of parliamentary seats for a specified group.

We must note that the fact that these two purposes can be analytically distinguished does not mean that a particular claim may not serve both purposes. For example, language rights (the right to have one's own minority language used in education, on ballot papers or in courtroom procedures) may be argued as a temporary measure to permit immigrant communities time to adjust, or alternatively they might be advocated as a means for the permanent protection of a linguistic culture. In the latter case, the rights will serve both preservation and anti-discrimination functions, allowing members to maintain their culture without being unduly disadvantaged or excluded from the participatory rights and processes of the majority community. Demands for rights to full or partial self-government, too, are usually both preservative and anti-discriminatory in intention, though here the remedy is seen as greater separation from a dominating culture rather than greater inclusion.

What sort of groups, then, may want to lay claim to these various rights? So far, I have been talking mainly in terms of ethnically or linguistically defined cultural groups for whom preservation and protection functions have the clearest relevance. Because the question of ethnicity is addressed elsewhere in this volume, I do not want to treat it extensively here, though its relation to the issue of group rights makes some discussion unavoidable. Obviously, the customs, beliefs, languages and traditions of ethno-cultural groups constitute a heritage – what has been called a 'cultural patrimony' – that members may want to hand on, and a source of identity they may be concerned to preserve by means of rights-claims. A group may strive to defend its cultural existence because this is regarded as valuable in itself, or because it is under threat from other groups, or very often both. As cases from around the world demonstrate, the coexistence of several (or many) ethno-cultural groups within the boundaries of a single state creates the possibility[14] of stress and conflict if enduring political accommodations are not achieved. At the extreme end of a spectrum of malignant 'solutions' to problems of ethnic heterogeneity sits the obscenity of 'ethnic cleansing', but well short of this lie any number of strategies of discrimination, persecution, exclusion or forced assimilation. Such conflicts always revolve around the assertion of a culture's basic right to its existence, even if not its independence, the particular dynamics of any case being determined by local circumstances.

In multicultural (as opposed to multinational) politics, the 'cultures' in question are usually taken to be various immigrant groups which may experience exclusion from the political life of the dominant culture and/or are concerned to resist complete assimilation to that culture. Yet these are not the only groups that figure in the theoretical debates on group rights, and there is, as a result, some confusion in the literature. The politics of recognition, difference and multiculturalism are seldom clearly distinguished one from the other, and are usually taken to be about more or less the same thing because they all have something to do with 'identity'. But even in so-called multicultural politics, the discriminations targeted are often founded on 'identities' that have less to do with supposed cultural differences than with mere skin colour. The concerns of many black people in white society often have very little to do with defending some supposed 'ethnic' integrity and a great deal to do with overcoming barriers of racial discrimination. 'Ethnicity' is in fact frequently nothing more than a modern euphemism for 'race', and the problems of racism are not identical to (though in practice often inextricably mixed with) the problems of multicultural harmony and justice. The confusion of identity with cultural difference is apparent too in the case of other 'groups' that figure in the theoretical debates on group rights – gays, women, the poor, the disabled – which cannot remotely be considered 'ethno-cultural'. Much of the literature is actually less concerned with assigning rights for protection than with devising policies that will ensure adequate governmental representation of various groups and therefore (presumptively) of their interests: for example, the setting of quotas for women in parliamentary parties, or the drawing of electoral boundaries in ways liable to ensure that black candidates are elected. Even where the central issue is not the fairer distribution of social resources but rather the validation of an identity, as, say, in the case of homosexuals, the demand is not for protection of a particular 'culture'. Rather, it is for the old-fashioned liberal democratic right to be who one is, whatever that is, without suffering discrimination or victimization. The policies usually demanded are, therefore, not the assignment of special protective rights but the removal of overtly institutional discriminations, for example, bans on gays joining the military.

Care needs to be taken, then, when assessing the relevance and probable impact of proposals for group rights in any particular situation. The political goal (or goals) aimed at – for example, cultural protection or political inclusion – need to be established, as does, concomitantly, the specific nature of the group for which the rights are advocated. It is worth noting here that the most prominent liberal writers on group rights have mainly used the case of sub-national groups on which to found their arguments. This is certainly the case with Kymlicka's work, while Joseph Raz makes clear that his liberal multiculturalism is meant to apply only in states with large sub-national units. National groups are arguably the easiest case from a liberal point of view, since liberals, for all their suspicion of group rights, have never had any trouble accepting them at the level of the nation-state. But how readily arguments based on national cases can be applied to other kinds of group in different circumstances is debatable. Indeed, Kymlicka has said that immigrant groups have less of a claim for cultural protection than national minorities, and that public measures on their behalf should be a matter not of rights but of policy. Others take issue with him and argue that some groups, for example Muslims in western societies, need strong forms of recognition rights to combat the cultural stigmas and consequent disadvantages they suffer. Clearly, we should be cautious about making sweeping generalizations on the desirability or undesirability of group rights, and be prepared to look at cases and arguments on an individual and context-specific basis. With this caution in mind, we will examine the democratic perspective on the subject.[15]

Democracy and Group Rights

To speak of a democratic perspective on group rights as opposed to a liberal one is to presume that democracy is more than just a procedure for organizing liberal government. That democracy and liberalism have become conjoined in liberal democratic states correctly suggests an overlap of values, but should not blind us to the fact that they have partially separate and conflicting histories and represent distinct ideals. For example, where liberal theorists give priority to individual freedom, democratic theorists emphasize equality of a substantive kind, and tend to frown on social distinctions and hierarchies that diminish the value of some people's citizen rights and capacities. While liberal theorists look to private individual self-fulfilment, democratic theorists tend to stress the public good. Liberal individuals want only to be left alone to get on with their private lives, but democratic individuals demand an equal say in public decisions of importance to themselves, their lives, their communities, their world. Thus, while liberal theorists typically concern themselves with institutional devices to protect the individual from collective action, democratic theorists are more interested in structuring collective action to better reflect individual choices.

In fact, the democratic ideal is, in many ways, that of the staunch classical republican given an egalitarian twist. It demands an equal right to a say for all who are capable of exercising it, presumed to be anyone of sound mind and sufficient years. The various procedural rules for voting and decision-making in functioning democracies (e.g., majority rule) are intended to operationalize this right so that legitimate policy decisions can be generated. The democratic legitimacy of a decision-making process imposes an obligation on voters to accede even to policies they may abhor, and to defer to governments they may despise. Having an equal say means one's views have been heard and registered – an important component of esteem in people's lives – whether or not they are adopted by the collectivity. One's obligation to accede to an adverse legitimate result, however, does not diminish one's right to continue strenuously to oppose and try to change both policies and governors through peaceful democratic means. Indeed, an important part of the structure of liberal democracies is the institutionalization of permanent opposition.

The question here is whether a resolutely democratic perspective is a better place from which to examine the question of group rights than is a liberal one. I would argue that it is at least a more appropriate one, since democracy, unlike liberalism, has now a 'non-optional' character. This observation of Ian Shapiro's reminds us that democracy, for all its faults and problems, has no serious competitor as a source of political legitimacy in the modern world. 'Although few would openly assert that the state may require people to be liberal or conservative, or to belong to a particular (or indeed any) religion, few would deny that all are bound to accept the results of appropriately functioning democratic procedures.'[16] Thus groups may be free to reject liberalism and to fight in the democratic arena for illiberal aims, as many do, but they are increasingly less free to reject democracy itself.

In addition to this, democracy's central value – democratic equality – makes it predisposed to making sure that access to political processes is not limited by virtue of group or cultural affiliations. The difference between the liberal and democratic attitudes towards the state – object of suspicion versus arena of political action – is of relevance here. Liberalism, and particularly political liberalism, tries, as we saw, to defuse conflict by banishing problematic group differences and identities from the public realm into the private, there to be mutually tolerated. Democratic toleration, on the other hand, is the constant toleration of *public* dissent and of *public* opposition, provided this is kept within the channels of democratic order. This proviso observed, no views or positions can be ruled out of bounds on grounds of 'irrationality' or whatever. The republican democrat (as opposed to the liberal democrat) demands only that players of the democratic game be committed to equality of voice, continuing tolerance of dissent and opposition, and legitimate non-violent procedures. No voices and no identities, however troublesome, can or ought to be suppressed or forced from a public forum meant to provide a field where conflicts can be both played out and constrained within the bounds of peaceful order. This makes the democratic vision quite at odds with that of political liberalism, which imagines an ideal state that is a deliberative arena where only the 'rational' opinions and 'rational' discourse of 'rational' actors is permitted. Indeed, the democratic state is not an ideal one at all, but rather a forum of perpetual struggle, where, as Carl Schurz said, 'the forces of good have a free field as against the forces of evil, and in which the victories of virtue, of enlightenment, and of progress are not achieved by some power or agency outside the people, for their benefit, but *by* the people themselves'.[17]

Democrats also have a plausible response to liberal fears that welcoming closed and intolerant groups risks condoning and perhaps supporting their illiberal practices, including their tendency to exclusivity and internal coercion. The response is to point out the salutary effect of democratic practice and democratic constraints, particularly the requirement of toleration of dissent and opposition. This obligatory constraint is undoubtedly the one least congenial to some groups (and individuals), but people can scarcely argue for greater democratic inclusion without conceding the validity of democratic principles – including the perpetual right to dissent and oppose. It may be difficult in the long run for closed and undemocratic groups to deny the relevance of this tacit admission to their own internal affairs.

It might be expected, in the light of such considerations, that democratic theorists would have some sympathy for group rights arguments, or at least those that try to ensure greater inclusion of different groups and different voices in the political process. It is clear, in fact, that many of the concerns of those who argue group politics are essentially democratic, having to do with combating the de facto exclusions of people from genuine equality of status, voice and access to resources. Iris Young's proposal for 'differentiated citizenship', for example, is intended to remedy a situation in which some groups find themselves still treated as second-class citizens despite a formal granting of equal citizenship status. She concludes: 'The inclusion and participation of everyone in social and political institutions therefore sometimes requires the articulation of special rights that attend to group differences in order to undermine oppression and disadvantage.'[18] In other words, the differential treatment implicit in the granting of special rights to various groups is not intended to undermine democratic equality but, on the contrary, to realize it more fully.

Yet some democratic theorists, though naturally sympathetic to the aim of such recognition rights, are sceptical about them as a means. Elizabeth Kiss, for example, argues that democrats should indeed take serious note of the cultural, symbolic and other harms that are caused by misrecognitions (that is, by stigmatization of people on grounds of real or attributed identities): 'By focusing on how identity-based harms deprive people of opportunity, status, and voice, [democratic] accounts make respect for persons, not for cultures or identities, the centerpiece of their moral concern.'[19] But taking note of harms falls well short of 'recognition' of groups in any formal, legal sense. Such democrats are suspicious of rights based on identities, even when these aim at political inclusion and equality, partly because they may simultaneously affirm that identity as legitimate and thus perform a culturally protective or preservative function. The problem with doing this is that such identities are often created, at least in part, by the very processes that affect to use them as a basis for discrimination and exclusion.

Nancy Fraser has usefully pointed to the conundrums in this area. She argues that recognition is a hopeless strategy for a group with wholly redistributive aims (for example, an exploited working class), but concedes it may be valid for a culturally despised group demanding respect (for example, homosexuals): 'In the first case, the logic of the remedy is to put the group out of business as a group. In the second case, on the contrary, it is to valorize the group's "groupness" by recognizing its specificity.'[20] What the first case demands is not group affirmation, but the transformation of society and disappearance of the exploited class in the interests of justice. The problem with groups identified on grounds of colour or gender, however, is that *both* respect and redistribution are at stake. To pursue recognition rights as a redistributive remedy risks fixing and affirming gender and colour as relevant bases of distinction, whereas a transformative remedy would seek to dissolve gender and colour as politically salient categories for distributive purposes.

There are also other serious grounds for caution about the formalization of 'difference'. The politics of identity and recognition gain most of their moral purchase by asserting claims on behalf of groups that are marginalized, overlooked and discriminated against by dominant cultures. But identity politics can take a very vicious turn indeed when political leaders 'play the identity card' in times of instability and uncertainty. Vicious identity politics are inherently divisive and destabilizing of the good order that democratic politics both requires and is intended to promote. Democratic suspicion is not allayed by the fact that the allegedly 'primordial' identities brought into play are frequently of quite recent origin, the product of mythologizing or of sheer invention.[21] Democrats must be cautious about taking politicized identity claims at their makers' valuation, and should not accept their reifications of identity as causal explanations of political behaviour.[22] The equation of identity with unchangeable 'essence' worries democrats faced with demands for affirming and protecting cultural difference by means of recognition rights. Institutional affirmation usually requires the fixing of artificially and arbitrarily defined cultural boundaries with potentially oppressive consequences for those within.

Thus, while democrats generally seek to encourage greater participation of all in the political process, and enhanced representation for under-represented groups, they have reasons for resisting the formal attribution of group rights as a means to achieving this. Indeed, democrats often presume they are in the business not of formally recognizing and confirming group identities, but of de-emphasizing their political saliency for the sake of avoiding conflict. Here, however, democracy runs into some contradictions of its own, for its own processes can at times help confirm and solidify identities, providing a boost to the worst kind of identity politics.

The problem is that identities, though malleable, are not infinitely so. Postmodern writers who emphasize the 'social constructedness' of identity and the contingency of social reality often seem to operate on the tacit assumption that because things might be otherwise they could *easily* be otherwise, as though this were just a matter of seeing and choosing. But in fact identities, especially once they are politically mobilized, can be exceedingly obdurate. Though a democracy is supposed to provide a political sphere where conflicts, including cultural ones, can be played out, negotiated and managed without resort to violence, in situations of politically charged cultural differentiation competitive parties and free elections can easily encourage an ethnic mobilization that is anything but accommodating. Where ethnic identity (or any other form of group identity) is already highly politicized, party politics may serve only to exacerbate division and conflict in the absence of specific democratic strategies to transcend them. Jung and Shapiro have argued in their work on South Africa that democratic parties in countries where serious and potentially explosive divisions exist between groups must aim precisely at *not* being identified with any particular group.[23] In such situations, party policy and the institutional and electoral structure of the state should aim at defusing the political salience of identity difference. It was not without reason that Nelson Mandela and his African National

Congress were so adamantly opposed, in the negotiations leading up to a transition, to any institutionalization of group rights in the new, post-apartheid South Africa.

It is true, however, that if democracy itself carries dangers in certain political environments, it has also the potential to devise procedures that might not only avoid exacerbating dangerously hostile divisions but actually help to undercut them. Indeed, democrats have for some time been concerned that the organization of electoral and political institutions give incentives for leaders and parties to offer ideologies that appeal across culturally and ethnically divided groups rather than ones that mobilize specific identities, thereby de-emphasizing the political relevance of such identities.[24] Of course, such strategies become virtually impossible if the state itself forcefully, even aggressively, asserts a particular ethnocultural identity, for somewhere along the line the specified identity will have to be coercively enforced and protected in probably undemocratic ways. In such circumstances democrats would agree that other ethnicities within such a state have strong reasons to insist on the institutionalization of special rights for their defence. Kiss, for example, accepts this but adds that the onus should always be on those who would demand such rights to show how the granting of them would enhance democratic equality, especially when identity claims are at issue.[25] Her useful rule of thumb is that democrats ought to treat the claims of group politics with critical circumspection, discriminating carefully among the cases, eschewing those which threaten to diminish democratic values and welcoming those that promise to enhance them.

A Democratic Politics of Inclusion

A feasible democratic response to the claims of group rights theorists would seem to be as follows: a democratic state will work towards a better realization of its inclusive, egalitarian ideal by paying sympathetic attention to recognition claims, discerning whether cultural protection, greater inclusion or both are being sought, and devising appropriate responses and remedies. Where the democratic state itself asserts no identity beyond a thin civic one, there can no be obstacle, at least in principle, to striving for the wider inclusion of all citizens whatever their group affiliations. The democratic state will respect people's desires to maintain valued customs, languages and traditions, while understanding that a culturally plural society inevitably encounters innumerable problems of mutual accommodation. In seeking satisfactory solutions, it will not necessarily exclude the granting of some form of protective recognition rights in exceptional cases, but will be wary of such formal specifications of groups for all the reasons mentioned above. Certainly, a democratic state, with its egalitarian ethos, will be extremely reluctant to lend institutional support to groups that are themselves patently undemocratic or that are, however internally democratic themselves, hostile to the inclusive democratic processes of the larger state.[26] The egalitarian ideal must also be forever at odds with racism, sexism and any other ideology that promotes inequality, hatred and violent conflict. In combating such ideologies, the democratic state will generally be less interested in positively affirming difference, even where the intention is greater inclusion, than in reducing the *political* salience of group difference as a criterion of discrimination and exclusion.

Note, however, that the feasibility of this strategy is premised on the state itself neither asserting nor protecting any particular identity beyond the civic. If this were true, the exclusions and discriminations that defeat, in the short term, the state's democratic ethos could be put down to 'natural' human prejudice, or scapegoating in troubled times. The equalizing project would then seem possible, even if difficult, given better education, vigorous moral argument and the spread of secure prosperity. But the whole thing would be brought into serious question if the state itself turned out to be practising a form of identity politics, to be, in fact, implicitly culturally defined and thus the basis for at least some of the exclusions noted.

Historically, we know, this was the case with western liberal democratic nations despite an ideal of equal citizenship – of uniform civic identity – non-ethnically conceived. National identities, though important to the western states, were ideologically linked to a state-centred patriotism rather than to specific ethnic identities, unlike those of Eastern Europe and beyond.[27] Yet western nationalism always had some basis in an identity beyond the civic.[28] The democratizing states of the nineteenth century were generally founded, either implicitly or explicitly, on some strong, usually racial notion of cultural identity. This was, after all, the heyday of Social Darwinism, of the white man's burden, of manifest destiny, of the civilizing mission and of a frank belief in the 'facts' of race superiority and inferiority (and 'race' could be narrowly construed to mean a British or English race as opposed, for example, to the various 'wogs' across the channel).[29]

Moreover, white national identity, by subsuming various class identities within it, could be mobilized by the state to counter other political identities antithetical to its purposes. What is more, an extended democratic franchise played an important role in the state's ability to do this.

The industrializing nations of the nineteenth century were liberal and 'bourgeois', for liberalism was the ideology of a successful, propertied, mercantile and (in its day) revolutionary middle class. Liberalism's initial fear of democracy was at base a fear that an enfranchised, propertyless and envious majority would inevitably exercise its electoral power to dispossess the propertied minority. The birth of liberal democracy represented the triumph of a class that had learned to tame the democratic beast, to survive and thrive through control of a representative system which, because based on an extended suffrage, provided it with a solid basis of legitimacy. Marxists, of course, criticized bourgeois democratic nationalism precisely because it caused working men and women to identify more with 'their' nation than with an international proletarian class in whose victory alone, it was alleged, their real egalitarian interests lay. The economic-individualist values of bourgeois liberalism were thus everywhere underwritten by the creation of national communities that successfully competed as sites of solidarity and identity with other potential sites. Liberal individualism, despite its theoretical distrust of collectivism, actually pitted one form of collective identity, the national, against others, and racialism and xenophobia played a large part in its victory.[30]

Yet surely this *is* history. Times have changed, have they not, and changed radically? Western nationalisms are not as flagrant as even half a century ago, and the nation-state upon which nationalism rested is, we are constantly hearing, being reshaped by global and globalizing forces. Meanwhile, racial superiority arguments, despite the resurgence of extreme rightwing groups worldwide, do not play so convincingly as in the past. Similarly for the gender superiority arguments that ensured that racial-cultural dominance was also male dominance. There has been an undeniable sea-change in the dominant spirit of western self-consciousness. Pride and self-confidence have been dented, and Anglo-Europeans are not sure how to deal appropriately with cultures (and genders) they no longer automatically presume they have a right to dominate. Yet they are forced to confront the issue because racial and cultural heterogeneity is now part of almost everyone's life. In Europe, the outward flow of white imperialists and colonists in the nineteenth century was matched in the late twentieth by a reverse flow of the formerly colonized. Frequently, they have been invited in to undertake those menial tasks to which postwar prosperity made Anglo-European workers newly unsuited. In the United States, black people who were once securely if unjustly segregated have dispersed nationally in a huge internal migration, while formerly effectively excluded Puerto Ricans and Mexicans have entered, legally and illegally, in ever larger numbers. The challenge that this increased diversity presents to democratic societies has been an important stimulus to the modern theorizing on identity, difference and multiculturalism.

On the face of it, time and politics do indeed seem to be eroding not just the assumptions, but also some of the barriers to access set up by dominant groups. Nevertheless, many of the arguments about recognition and differentiated citizenship seem to imply that not all that much has changed beneath the surface – the liberal democratic state is still, apparently, dominated by much the same old elite. A democratic argument that we must, while paying attention to difference, be wary of enshrining it may miss the larger point that one difference remains *already* enshrined – that of the dominant group (or groups) whose interest the state, in the main, protects. Iris Young writes: 'In societies structured by group based privilege and disadvantage, political processes of procedural liberalism generally result in the dominance of the perspectives of privileged groups in political discussion and decision making.'[31] Young's traditional leftist argument is that the liberal ideology of formally equal citizenship disguises a continued hegemony, characterizing discriminations as unfortunate and contingent instances of all-too-human prejudice rather than as the result of systematic domination by a socially structured elite (or 'privileged groups').

But what exactly *is* the identity of the structured elite against which other identities are defined in order to be (at least partially) excluded? Is it a class defined by its relation to the ownership or control of property, or a technocratic elite with its hands on the modern levers of economic power, or a social-political elite exercising hegemonic political authority, or some connected constellation of these? How does this elite (of perhaps distinct but interdependent groups) define itself in order to identify members, non-members and potential members? What are its criteria for, and how does it effectively police the processes of, admission and exclusion in order continually to reproduce itself as a structured elite? How fluid and open or, alternatively, rigid and closed is its membership? How many different bases for discrimination are utilized by the elite (ethnicity, money, gender, etc.) and which of them are essential to its identity, which not? These are important questions for assessing the strategies suggested by group rights theorists more concerned with democratic inclusion than with cultural protection. Unless answers are given, it is difficult to say what an effective democratic practice of inclusion might be. If, for example, the claim is that elite economic control remains the real, hard nugget at the centre of liberal democratic society, then the politics of inclusion might choose one of two traditional strategies: a liberal democratic one or a radical democratic one (reflecting an old debate about the meaning and possibility of equality).

It is often claimed by group theorists that liberalism's covering illusion of universality, neutrality and equality have to be shattered to reveal the face of (white, male, heterosexual, class, etc.) privilege it conceals. This is to be done by noting group difference instead of ignoring it, privileging it instead of disprivileging it, honouring it instead of dishonouring it and finding the means to ensure the cultural, political and economic representation of excluded groups. As a strategy for democratic inclusion, this can be seen as aiming at either of two things: (a) securing a genuine equality of opportunity across groups (whether defined ethnically, socially or culturally) so that the elite becomes, in effect, multicultural; or, (b), claiming that the democratic revolution has been frustrated by a still-powerful elite and needs to be completed.

The politics of multiculturalism, differentiated citizenship and group rights are generally conducted as prescriptive exercises for liberal democratic states, but their strategic interventions, if they work at all, are unlikely to do so in a radically democratic direction. It is not just that one of the most enduring axioms of politics is that those with power seldom voluntarily relinquish it as a result of moral persuasion. It is that an entrenched elite can afford to give in on matters of group representation *within the elite* without relinquishing much. Even if liberal elites have, in the past, defined themselves in 'cultural' terms that included elements of race, religion and gender, their main defining feature as a hegemonic group is surely some form of economic and political control. That being so, they can, for the sake of increased legitimacy and however partially, drop their 'cultural' barriers to entry and tolerate a more variegated membership provided economic and political power are retained. This may be congenial enough to ideological liberals who emphasize equality of opportunity, but hardly to people who seek greater democratization of society where that is taken to mean a more inclusive and extensive democratic control of economic and social processes for redistributive purposes. Elites can often afford to be quite open and tolerant of difference, to welcome it as an exotic attraction or as a sign of their genuine liberalism, provided the basis of their privilege is not seriously endangered. They may even – with more sinister effect – tolerate or encourage group rights schemes aimed at cultural protection in the knowledge that any resentments generated are likely to create divisions among the lower strata of society, leaving the elite itself relatively untouched.

Radical democrats need to articulate group theory with some view of political economy that will show how the sort of democratization that leads to redistributive outcomes is possible. If this seems like a return to an outmoded form of political theorizing, we should note that one does not need to hold that all social cleavages are reducible to economic class, or that all group conflicts can be solved by greater social and economic equality, to appreciate the enduring structural relevance of political-economic factors. The thrust of at least some group theory is to seek democratically egalitarian goals within a new pluralist order, combining distributive equality with cultural diversity. In other words, the desire is to achieve a more equal distribution not just of incomes and resources but of cultural respect. But it is hard to find in this work any theoretical view of how an 'anarchic, oligarchic' international economy might lend itself to such political goals.[32]

This is only to say that the politics of democratic inclusion, at least for radical democrats, cannot be treated separately from a normative account of democratization as such, one that specifies precisely in what a politics of democratization is supposed to consist and how it may be politically advanced in the modern world.

Conclusion

The old left, whatever its shortcomings, at least had a clear idea of who the enemy was, and could devise its ameliorative or revolutionary political strategies accordingly. Of course, its concrete attempts at realizing its egalitarian dreams did not work out, and no doubt its experiences in the twentieth century have made the egalitarian goal seem hopelessly utopian in theory and frankly dystopian in outcome. Historical experience and capitalistic resilience have caused disillusion with and repudiation of so-called grand theory which attempted to understand the social-economic world comprehensively (that is, both empirically and normatively) for the sake of accomplishing radical political change.

This is understandable, and the lessons are for the most part salutary. The socialist revolutions of the twentieth century were *not* democratic revolutions, and that, for democrats, was precisely the problem. If they taught us anything they taught the unwisdom of imposing on people from above the theoretical solutions of an intellectual elite. From that point of view, the growing non-optionality of democracy today is a hopeful sign. The apparent movement of economic forces further away from democratic control, however, must worry radical democrats, which is why some attempt at a general theory of these still needs to be made. The work done on the politics of identity, multiculturalism and difference, though often important and enlightening, is too frequently divorced from questions of political economy that now seem, perhaps, too hard to tackle. This work often retains one feature of leftist critical discourse – the unveiling of ideological illusions, the exposure of forms of thought and attitude that both maintain and conceal exclusions, domination and injustice. But by and large it ignores the other feature of leftist thought – the economic and political context wherein these illusions are produced and reproduced, and wherein whatever possibilities that may exist for a more inclusive and polyglot democracy must lie.

NOTES

1 J. Paul (ed.), *Reading Nozick: Essays on Anarchy, State, and Utopia* (Totowa, NJ, Rowman and Littlefield, 1981); J. Rawls, *A Theory of Justice* (Cambridge, MA, Harvard University Press, 1972).

2 For communitarianism, see A. MacIntyre, *After Virtue: A Study in Moral Theory* (Notre Dame, IN, University of Notre Dame Press, 1984); M. Walzer, *Spheres of Justice: A Defence of Pluralism and Equality* (New York, Basic Books, 1983); M. J. Sandel, *Liberalism and its Critics* (New York, New York University Press, 1984); C. Taylor, 'What is human agency?', in T. Mischel (ed.), *The Self: Psychological and Philosophical Issues* (London, Blackwell, 1977), pp. 103–38; C. Taylor, *Multiculturalism and the Politics of Recognition* (Princeton, Princeton University Press, 1992).

3 See, for example, J-F. Lyotard, *The Postmodern Condition: A Report on Knowledge*, trans. G. Bennington and B. Massumi (Minneapolis, University of Minneapolis Press, 1997 [1976]); J-F. Lyotard, *Just Gaming*, trans. W. Godzich (Manchester, Manchester University Press, 1985); J-F. Lyotard, *The Differend: Phrases in Dispute*, trans. G. van den Abbeele (Minneapolis, University of Minneapolis Press, 1988); R. Rorty, *Contingency, Irony and Solidarity* (Cambridge, Cambridge University Press, 1989); R. Rorty, 'Human rights, rationality, and sentimentality', in S. Shute and S. Hurley (eds), *On Human Rights: The Oxford Amnesty Lectures 1993* (New York, Basic Books, 1993), pp. 111–34; J. Derrida, *Of Grammatology*, trans. G. C. Spivak (Baltimore, Johns Hopkins University Press, 1976); J. Derrida, *Specters of Marx: The State of the Debt, the Work of Mourning, and the New International*, trans. P. Kamuf (New York, Routledge, 1994); W. Corlett, *Community Without Unity: A Politics of Derridean Extravagance* (Durham, NC, Duke University Press, 1989).

4 Taylor, *Multiculturalism and the Politics of Recognition*, p. 72.

5 See I. M. Young, 'Polity and group difference: A critique of the ideal of universal citizenship', *Ethics* 99, 2 (1989): 250–74; I. M. Young, *Justice and the Politics of Difference* (Princeton, Princeton University Press, 1990); I. M. Young, 'Deferring group representation', in I. Shapiro and W. Kymlicka (eds), *Ethnicity and Group Rights* (New York, New York University Press, 1997); A. Honneth, *The Struggle for Recognition: The Moral Grammar of Social Conflicts*, trans. J.

Anderson (Cambridge, Polity, 1995). Though Young has drawn on the work of Derrida to defend her positions (in 'Deferring Group Representation'), there are also clear Marxist roots in her work (see, for example, 'Polity and group difference', p. 264). Indeed, a great deal of the new theoretical work continues to be haunted, in an unacknowledged way, by what Derrida has called the 'spectre of Marx'.

6   J. Raz, 'Multiculturalism: A liberal perspective', in *Ethics in the Public Domain: Essays in the Morality of Law and Politics* (Oxford, Clarendon Press, 1994), pp. 157–60.

7   W. Kymlicka, *Liberalism, Community and Culture* (Oxford, Oxford University Press, 1989); W. Kymlicka, 'The rights of minority cultures: Reply to Kukathas', *Political Theory* 20, 1 (1992): 140–6; W. Kymlicka, *Multicultural Citizenship* (Oxford, Clarendon Press, 1995).

8   R. Bellamy and M. Hollis, *Pluralism and Liberal Neutrality: A Liberal Theory of Minority Rights*. Special Issue of *Critical Review of International Social and Political Philosophy* 1, 3 (1999).

9   For autonomy as the fundamental commitment, see J. Rawls, 'The priority of right and ideas of the good', *Philosophy and Public Affairs* 17, 4 (1988): 251–76; J. Raz, *The Morality of Freedom* (Oxford, Clarendon Press, 1998); D. Fitzmaurice, 'Autonomy as a good: Liberalism, autonomy and toleration', *Journal of Political Philosophy* 1, 1 (1993): 1–16; Kymlicka, 'The rights of minority cultures', p. 142. For toleration as the basic value, see C. Kukathas, 'Are there any cultural rights?', *Political Theory* 20, 1 (1992): 105–39; C. Kukathas, 'Cultural toleration', in Shapiro and Kymlicka (eds), *Ethnicity and Group Rights*, pp. 69–104.

10   J. Narveson, 'Collective rights?', *Canadian Journal of Law and Jurisprudence* 4 (1991): 329–45.

11   On political liberalism, see J. Rawls, *Political Liberalism* (New York, Columbia University Press, 1993). Rawls now sought the organizing principles that would justly order a democratic society marked by 'reasonable pluralism'. For a critique, see J. C. Isaac, M. Filner and J. Bivens, 'American democracy and the New Christian Right: A critique of apolitical liberalism', in I. Shapiro and C. Hacker-Cordón (eds), *Democracy's Edges* (Cambridge, Cambridge University Press, 1999), pp. 222–64. See also W. J. Meyer, 'The politics of differentiated citizenship', in K. Slawner and M. E. Denham (eds), *Citizenship after Liberalism* (New York, Peter Lang Publishing, 1998); Meyer makes the point that, though liberalism is usually associated with quite modest commitments with regard to civic obligations and virtues, it in fact makes quite extraordinary demands of the individual; it demands, namely, that the things that matter most to individuals – their particular allegiances and values, the grievances they have that are associated with positions of social, cultural and economic

inequality – be excluded from the public realm where they must deal with one another purely as equal political citizens.

12 Rawls proposed a realm of public reason marked by an 'overlapping consensus' of all *reasonable* opposing 'comprehensive views' that people of different moral, philosophical and religious faiths might hold. This would then be a realm of shared reason, in which 'being reasonable' means not appealing to the 'whole truth' as different people see it, but only to such arguments as all would affirm as reasonable; see *Political Liberalism*, pp. 217–18. In this way debates over policy would be safely sanitized from the unreasonable demands of clamorous groups espousing separated and incompatible truths. Particular allegiances would be confined more thoroughly to the private realm – the realm of free and often 'irrational' choice – there to be subject only to the requirement of mutual tolerance. For a critique, see T. McCarthy, 'Kantian constructivism and reconstructivism: Rawls and Habermas in dialogue', *Ethics* 105 (October 1994): 44–63; Isaac et al., 'American democracy and the New Christian Right'.

13 Kymlicka distinguishes three forms of 'group-differentiated rights': self-government rights, polyethnic rights and special representation rights; see *Multicultural Citizenship*, pp. 26–33. J. T. Levy, on the other hand, distinguishes eight different categories of cultural rights claims: exemptions, assistance measures, self-government, external rules, internal rules, recognition/enforcement, representation and symbolic claims; see 'Classifying cultural rights', in Shapiro and Kymlicka (eds), *Ethnicity and Group Rights*, pp. 22–66. Valuable as these distinctions are, they can all be reordered according to whether they seek one or other of the two purposes noted here.

14 It should be stressed that this is always *possibility*, not certainty. 'Difference' may be made politically salient or it may not; see R. Brubaker, *Nationalism Reframed: Nationhood and the National Question in the New Europe* (Cambridge, Cambridge University Press, 1996), ch. 1.

15 Raz, 'Multiculturalism: A liberal perspective'; Kymlicka, *Multicultural Citizenship*, p. 250. On Muslim minorities, see J. Carens and M. Williams, 'Muslim minorities in liberal democracies: The politics of misrecognition', paper presented at the annual meeting of the American Political Science Association, Chicago, Illinois, 1–4 September 1996. On caution, see B. Parekh, 'Comment: Minority rights, majority values', in D. Miliband (ed.), *Reinventing the Left* (Cambridge, Polity, 1994).

16 I. Shapiro, *Democracy's Place* (Ithaca, Cornell University Press, 1996), p. 3. Shapiro notes that even many of the antidemocratic forces around often find it expedient to appeal to the democratic idiom, as when religious fundamentalists in America argue their legitimacy as representative of a *moral majority*.

17   Cited in A. Nevins, *The Statesmanship of the Civil War* (New York, Macmillan, 1962), p. 113.

18   Young, 'Polity and group difference', p. 251.

19   E. Kiss, 'Democracy and the politics of recognition', in Shapiro and Hacker-Cordón (eds), *Democracy's Edges*, pp. 193–209, p. 200.

20   N. Fraser, 'From redistribution to recognition? Dilemmas of justice in a "post-socialist" age', in C. Willett (ed.), *Theorizing Multiculturalism: A Guide to the Current Debate* (Malden, MA, Blackwell, 1998), pp. 19–49, p. 27.

21   See J. G. Kellas, *The Politics of Nationalism and Ethnicity* (London, Macmillan, 1991), pp. 27–8; E. Hobsbawm, *Nations and Nationalism since 1780: Programme, Myth, Reality* (Cambridge, Cambridge University Press, 1990). Hobsbawm has argued: 'history is the raw material for nationalist or ethnic or fundamentalist ideologies, as poppies are the raw material for heroin addiction. The past is an essential element, perhaps the essential element in these ideologies. If there is no suitable past, it can always be invented. Indeed, in the nature of things there is usually no entirely suitable past, because the phenomenon these ideologies claim to justify is not ancient or eternal but historically novel. . . . The past legitimises. The past gives a more glorious background to a present that doesn't have much to show for itself.' Lecture at the Central European University of Budapest, edited version, 'Nationalism thrives with history as handmaiden', *Australian (Higher Education Supplement)* (1 December 1993): 20–1.

22   C. Calhoun advises that identity be understood as a 'changeable product of collective action' and not as its stable underlying cause: 'The problem of identity in collective action', in J. Huber (ed.), *Macro-Micro Linkages in Sociology* (Newbury Park, CA, Sage, 1991), p. 59.

23   C. Jung and I. Shapiro, 'South Africa's negotiated transition: Democracy, opposition and the new constitutional order', in I. Shapiro, *Democracy's Place*, pp. 175–219. Generally, see I. Shapiro, 'Group aspirations and democratic politics', in Shapiro and Hacker-Cordón (eds), *Democracy's Edges*, pp. 210–21.

24   D. L. Horowitz, *Ethnic Groups in Conflict* (Berkeley, University of California Press, 1985); D. L. Horowitz, *A Democratic South Africa? Constitutional Engineering in a Divided Society* (Berkeley and Los Angeles, University of California Press, 1991).

25   Thus, in discussing the case of the Hungarian minority in present-day Romania, Kiss says it is understandable that members of a large national minority will demand protective rights when the highest law of the land, in this case the Romanian constitution, goes out of its way to deny their existence – a form, she says, of 'symbolic non-recognition'; see 'Democracy and the politics of recognition', p. 205.

26   Shapiro argues that this was the case with the White Right parties of South Africa in the interregnum period, which justified the state's

sidelining them in the negotiations; see 'Group aspirations and democratic politics'.

27 Kellas, *The Politics of Nationalism and Ethnicity*, pp. 30–2. It is for this reason that Brubaker argues that the Eastern European phenomenon of minority ethno-nationalism, which is a reactive product of state ethno-nationalism, can make no sense in a country like the United States with its non-ethnic ideal of equal citizenship; see *Nationalism Reframed*, p. 60 fn.

28 Even a liberal like J. S. Mill could argue that the free institutions of representative government would not work in a country of different 'nationalities', but rather required a substantial degree of homogeneity (characterized rather vaguely by Mill in terms of 'fellow-feeling' and a common language); see *Considerations on Representative Government* (New York, Bobbs-Merrill, 1958), p. 230.

29 Even a democratic nation like America whose founding ideology included a commitment to social heterogeneity and individual self-determination was marked by this form of ethnic exclusivity. Rogers Smith has persuasively argued that, in addition to the liberal and republican strands presumed traditionally to dominate United States political thought and history, there is a persistent strand of what he calls 'ascriptive Americanism', which assumed that citizenship rights should be differentially distributed among whites, African-Americans, Native Americans, Hispanic Americans, Jews, Catholics and others. Nor was this just a matter of unfortunate prejudice to be overcome in the course of time, but of national legislative enactment and legal enforcement; see 'Beyond Tocqueville, Myrdal, and Hartz: The multiple traditions in America', *American Political Science Review* 87, 3 (1993): 549–66. An Australian like myself finds this less surprising than most Americans seem to, since the federation of Australia, in 1901, was founded explicitly and proudly on a White Australia Policy; see J. Kane, 'Racialism, democracy and national identity: The legacies of White Australia', in G. Stokes (ed.), *The Politics of Identity in Australia* (Melbourne, Cambridge University Press, 1997), pp. 117–31.

30 See Meyer, 'The politics of differentiated citizenship'.

31 'Deferring group representation', p. 370. In 'Polity and group difference', p. 261, Young gives a long list of 'social groups' for which she wants special representation rights in order to overcome their political exclusion and oppression (the things that, in her view, *define* them as social groups). Taken together, they represent a majority of the population of the United States and include 'women, blacks, Native Americans, Chicanos, Puerto Ricans . . . Asian Americans, gay men, lesbians, working-class people, poor people, old people, and mentally and physically disabled people'. Who is most obviously missing here? White, propertied (Protestant?) males, of course, who are presumed still to be in essential control of the mechanisms of dominance and power.

32   Young argues that the 'social activities that most determine the status of individuals and groups are anarchic and oligarchic; economic life is not sufficiently under the control of citizens to affect the unequal status and treatment of groups'; see 'Polity and group difference', p. 251.

5

Democracy and Indigenous Self-determination

Michele Ivanitz

I believe that political theory is most fruitfully developed in applied contexts.[1]

One of the many challenges to liberal democratic theory and practice arises from indigenous peoples throughout the world.[2] Because of their status as 'first peoples', indigenous peoples have often made distinctive claims for self-government. In their resolute quest for self-determination, indigenous peoples have constantly stretched the boundaries of what would be acceptable to liberal democracy. Seeking to protect their cultures and ways of life, indigenous people question a number of primary assumptions about national sovereignty, political equality and even property. This chapter will review the relevant principles of liberal democracy and indicate how indigenous peoples have selectively adopted and altered them. The main liberal democratic principles to be considered with reference to indigenous peoples are self-determination and political equality. In the following section I briefly set out these principles and indicate the general problems that an indigenous politics of self-determination raises for them.

Self-determination and Political Equality

Self-determination is one of the key principles of liberal democracy, at the level both of the individual and of the group. Held writes of the strong theoretical links:

> The idea of democracy derives its power and significance . . . from the idea of self-determination; that is, from the notion that members of a political community – citizens – should be able to choose freely the conditions of their own association, and that their choices should constitute the ultimate legitimation of the form of and direction of their polity.[3]

The link between democracy and self-determination is evident within liberalism. For example, individuals are free only to the extent that they are autonomous moral agents capable of exercising influence or determining the course of their life.[4] This could not occur under the constraints of repressive or tyrannical governments. In this view, freedom consists in the exercise of autonomy and pursuing self-fulfilment.

During the late eighteenth century, the idea of self-determination was understood as the right of the subjects or citizens of a state to decide on their own government or system of government. Such sentiments were expressed in the United States with the American Declaration of Independence (1776) and in France with the French Declaration of the Rights of Man (1789). In 1919, US President Woodrow Wilson also advocated national self-determination as the governing principle for Europe after the First World War. The idea of self-determination included the possibility of national groups seceding from states or empires to establish their own national states. Such principles became the basis of modern nationalism. Self-determination was also understood as the right of a people or state to resist outside intervention in their affairs. Through the United Nations Charter and other instruments such as the International Covenant on Economic, Social and Cultural Rights and the International Covenant on Civil and Political Rights, self-determination became a part of international human rights law. But its meaning was drawn narrowly to include only states 'struggling for independence from colonial rule' and not those people who comprised those states, and who may have come into conflict with the state.[5] Indeed, neither the UN documents nor international law supports a right to secession.[6] Nor does international law support the rights of political minorities to claim self-determination.

Currently, self-determination is often regarded as one of a number of 'third generation' rights relevant to communities or peoples, rather than individuals.[7] It may take either an external or an internal form. Whereas the first 'external' form comprises radical, nationalist movements that seek secession, the other is more moderate and seeks autonomy within the nation-state. Accordingly, both the radical and moderate movements for self-determination have implications for national sovereignty.[8] Much discussion of self-determination, however, focuses upon the radical forms that seek secession from the nation-state and ignores the variety of indigenous forms that do not. One of the main questions here is: how do indigenous people pursue self-determination within liberal democracies?

Individual political equality is also a core principle of liberal democratic theory. The concept of formal equality begins from the premise that all people are of equal moral worth and that this requires each person to be given, at a minimum, equal legal and political rights. This means that every citizen 'is to be given equal status within the system of collective political authority'.[9] Furthermore, it does not simply mean that everyone is equal before the law and therefore ought to be treated equally, but it does require that 'everyone should have a place in the exercise of political authority', even if this is simply the opportunity to elect their governments.[10] These rights are individual rights. Indigenous movements for self-determination, however, usually strive to establish separate self-governing political institutions that give a primacy to the group. Such exercises of self-determination even extend to claiming constitutional recognition of the rights of indigenous people. Central among indigenous claims are those to group rights. Although on one view such reforms are a means for achieving political equality, indigenous institutions that exclude or discriminate against non-indigenous citizens clearly curtail the rights of the latter. One theoretical question is that of whether and how claims to group rights may be reconciled with the usual liberal democratic values that are based upon individual rights. This chapter does not deal with the conflict between group rights and the liberal democratic commitment to rights of individuals *within* indigenous groups. For such a discussion, see John Kane's chapter in this volume.[11] Certainly, indigenous peoples claim to have special needs and rights that other ethnic or cultural groups do not have. A key political question remains: how may indigenous rights be given political effect?

This chapter aims to shed light on these theoretical issues with reference to select case studies of the practice of indigenous self-determination in two liberal democracies, namely Australia and Canada. The focus is upon the descendants of those peoples, now often known as First Peoples, who inhabited Canada and Australia at the time of colonization by Britain. In both countries, indigenous peoples identify themselves as distinct groups and federal and regional (state and provincial) governments recognize these distinctions in their legal and administrative arrangements.

The pursuit of indigenous self-determination in liberal democracies such as Canada and Australia is, in part, expressed through institutional reform and agreements reached between indigenous groups and governments. Such agreements often seek to balance the collective rights of indigenous people with the individual rights of the rest of the population. The cases considered below demonstrate various practical exercises of self-determination within the confines of the liberal democratic state.[12] There are, however, major differences in the ways that self-determination is pursued and implemented in the two countries.

Historical Background: Australia and Canada

Prior to colonization by the British, indigenous peoples in Australia and Canada exercised their own systems of justice and law.[13] They conducted trade and entered into treaties with neighbouring tribes, and had complex systems of kinship and social structure.[14] They were, for all intents and purposes, sovereign entities. Following invasion and colonization by Europeans, indigenous people were often deprived of personal liberty and their very existence was threatened by disease and by official and unofficial violence against them. Many lost their lives in resisting the UK Crown's pursuit of territory for settlement. Although in Canada treaties and land 'surrenders' were negotiated with aboriginal people from 1680 to 1921, the terms of the agreements were not well understood by aboriginal signatories, who thought they were agreeing to a sharing of land with the Crown.[15] All eventually lost the freedom to exercise their status as self-determining peoples. The pursuit of autonomy and self-fulfilment was no longer relevant because life choices were dictated by settlers and colonists armed with guns and fencing wire, missionaries armed with the word of God and government ministers and officials armed with discriminatory policies. The scale of injustice and oppression was massive.

As a result of colonization and dispossession, indigenous people now suffer severe socio-economic disadvantages.[16] Indigenous infant mortality rates are therefore well below the national averages. When compared to the general population, indigenous people suffer higher rates of hypertension, stroke, cancer and respiratory ailments. Many indigenous communities suffer from high rates of alcohol and drug abuse and domestic violence is common. The death rate for indigenous Australians is three to six times that of the non-indigenous population. Unemployment rates are typically six times the national average, and average income distribution and education level attained are much lower than in the non-indigenous population.[17] In this environment of illness, poverty and lack of formal education it is a major achievement simply to stay alive and keep one's children healthy. Government policies contributed greatly to the current levels of indigenous disadvantage and it to these that we now turn.

Problems of policy

Despite the many differences of historical context and policy between Australia and Canada, there is general agreement that four broad policy frameworks were applied over roughly the same time periods: protection, segregation, assimilation and self-determination. During the 1960s, federal governments in both countries began formulating policies and programmes for full assimilation. These proposals, however, stimulated indigenous political leaders to mobilize against them and to support self-determination.

The early years of 'contact' in Australia and Canada were characterized by great conflict between indigenous people and the invaders. Nonetheless, during this time the indigenous people had the status of British subjects and the British home government regarded them as deserving to be protected from the assaults of settlers, merchants, fur traders, farmers and pastoralists. Such considerations led to policies of 'protection' being implemented in the colonies. Nonetheless, these principles and official directives were largely ignored by the colonists, and protection failed. The British government was too far away to control what was happening in the colonies and it could not offer even minimal protection to the indigenous people. Once the Canadian and Australian colonies achieved self-government in the latter part of the nineteenth century, attempts to protect indigenous people from outside became almost impossible.

The next period, from about 1900 until 1950, is broadly termed segregation. Indigenous people were seen as a dying race and all government could do was 'smooth the dying pillow'.[18] During this period, indigenous people were often forcibly relocated onto missions and reserves and vast numbers of children were removed from their families and sent to residential schools run by religious orders. In Australia, children were generally removed who were thought to have some non-indigenous ancestry. In Canada, children were removed regardless of ancestry. Because indigenous people were not considered to have the capacities for citizenship, they were often deprived of the vote in federal state and provincial parliaments. Such basic political rights were not awarded to all indigenous peoples until the 1960s in Australia[19] and Canada.[20]

By 1950 it became clear that indigenous people had not 'died out' and segregation policies were not working. Governments then decided that the only humane option was to encourage indigenous people to assimilate into the wider community. This approach had been discussed since the 1930s but it was not until the early 1950s that governments finally decided that assimilation into the mainstream population was to be the new objective of welfare measures. Paul Hasluck, a leading advocate of reform at the time, noted the main lines of the new policy:

> [W]e expect that, in the course of time, all persons of aboriginal blood ... will live in the same manner as white Australians do.... Full assimilation will mean that the aboriginal shares the hopes, the fears, the ambitions and the loyalties of all other Australians and draws from the Australian community all his social needs, spiritual as well as material. Whether biological assimilation goes hand-in-hand with cultural assimilation is a matter which time will reveal but my own guess would be that, if cultural assimilation occurs, mating will follow naturally.[21]

Assimilation policies remained in place in one form or another until indigenous people were recognized as full citizens. In Australia, the right to vote was granted to *all* indigenous people in the 1960s, but only after intense political pressure from indigenous people, human rights activists, church leaders and sympathetic political leaders.[22] The Australian constitutional referendum of 1967 allowed the federal government to take responsibility for aboriginal affairs and for Aborigines and Torres Straits Islanders to be counted in the census. For many Australians, this event represented the final step in recognizing the citizenship rights of the indigenous people.[23] The year 1967 marked a watershed in Australian Aboriginal politics as indigenous activists began to articulate publicly their demand for self-determination and specific indigenous rights, such as those to land. Under the Labor governments of 1972–5 and 1983–96, self-determination became official federal government policy in Australia.

A similar shift from assimilation to self-determination occurred in Canada. In 1968 the government of Prime Minister Pierre Trudeau was elected. Its early political rhetoric gave priority to the values of the 'just society' and 'participatory democracy', and stressed that it was time for disadvantaged groups to be fairly treated. The government acknowledged that existing policies designed to alleviate the disadvantaged state of aboriginal people had not been effective and the government undertook a year-long consultation process with Indian people across the country to get their views on policy changes that would achieve more positive outcomes.

As a consequence, in 1969, the government tabled the *Statement of the Government of Canada on Indian Policy*, known as the 'White Paper'.[24] This paper proposed the assimilation of aboriginal people by terminating all collective rights and special status and encouraging their rapid integration into the wider society. The rationale underlying the proposal for assimilation was that Canada had erred in maintaining a different status and special legal status for aboriginal people under the Indian Act.[25] Such laws and policies, it was claimed, had not only kept aboriginal people apart from, but also behind other Canadians. The White Paper proposed that Indians would relate to their governments as individuals, just as most other Canadians did, and as a collectivity they would function like other Canadian minorities.

Public deliberations on the White Paper elicited a less than sympathetic response from non-indigenous Canadians and outrage from aboriginal communities. Indians, for example, wanted economic and social recovery *without* losing their identity or organizations. Furthermore, aboriginal leaders rejected the federal government's policy assumption that they were simply another interest group, and began to insist their bands and tribal councils be treated as First Nations. For these reasons, the government decided to abandon their new policy and embark on a different course.

As assimilation policies are no longer considered appropriate in liberal democracies, the issue of self-determination has become more prominent for indigenous people. In addition, there remains the broader concern to provide greater freedom and social justice for all citizens, including indigenous citizens. Nonetheless, meeting demands for indigenous self-determination is not a simple process. The liberal democratic tradition and indigenous tribal philosophies represent two different world-views involving divergent values and theories about the nature of humankind and the good life. One is based on liberal values such as the right of the individual to own property and, within certain limits, gives primacy to individual rights over collective interests. The other world-view is based on non-ownership of property and the subordination of the individual to the collective. Nor is communication between the two cultures straightforward.[26] Their radically different notions of land and land 'ownership' also illustrate this point.

The problem of land

While liberal democracies value highly property ownership and the rights of the individual associated with ownership, indigenous concepts of land

and water broadly emphasize collective responsibility for the earth and its resources. Nor is physical proximity to land the only determinant of responsibility.[27] More important are the strong spiritual and socio-political obligations to particular geographic areas. These are generally maintained and exercised even when the physical occupation of these lands is diminished or absent.

This account generally holds true for indigenous people in both remote and urban contexts. When asked 'Where are you from?', an indigenous person living in a metropolitan area is likely to respond 'My country is X, but I live in Y'. A distinctive indigenous politics is also present in urban settings, and urban-based kin often play political roles in decisions that directly affect their distant 'home' communities. In metropolitan areas, however, the exercise of self-determination is approached differently and accommodation is made to include those who live away from their country. Self-determination is as important to those indigenous people who live in cities as it is to residents of remote areas.

Rather than ownership, stewardship of the land is central to indigenous practices. Stewardship entails performing certain obligations to land and kin. It is rooted in indigenous social structure whereby the social, economic, political and spiritual realms are embedded in kin relations and linked to particular geographic areas. Kin groups are also associated with particular political bodies and factions that lobby stridently for access to scarce resources. These relations, attachments and associations are embedded within specific sets of collective rights, obligations and fluid allegiances. At no time does private 'ownership' of land figure in an indigenous collective ideal. This is demonstrated in the language of Northern Tutchone elder Mary Hager when talking about the relationship between the physical person and the land:

> We do not walk *on* the land. We do not *own* the land. We are *of* the land. We are birthed from the land. We are part of the land, part of the water. Since we are part of the land and part of the water, we cannot own the land. That is like owning your Mummy! White men, they try to buy and sell the land. But they will never really own it. It is like owning the wind or the sky. I wonder if white men would ever try to own those too?[28]

It is also demonstrated by Mary Graham, a Kombumerri Elder whose traditional country lies in the heart of the Queensland Gold Coast. For Mary Graham, the individual is the repository of responsibilities rather than a claimant of rights. Rights can exist only in the measure to which each person fulfils his or her responsibilities towards others. There is no concept of *individual* claims to inalienable rights:

> We are very much group-oriented. Doesn't matter if people are remote or urban, we find our individuality within the group. The western individualistic thing is not too important. You [sic] are inextricably tied to a grid of other people. So if you want to be alone, you can forget it. Our social system is full of obligations. We are obliged to look after a large, extended network of relatives, we are obliged to look after the land and sacred sites, look after ceremonies. . . . The notion of individual rights is foreign, the notion of rights at all is a very new notion, a very western notion. We talk about responsibilities, not rights.[29]

The tensions between these two world-views have led to indigenous disenchantment with democracy.[30]

Failures of Liberal Democracy in Practice

Given their small numbers and relatively few votes, indigenous people have little impact upon the outcomes of elections and are thereby unable to exert much influence on governments. Partly for these reasons, indigenous people have had little or no representation in national or regional parliaments. Furthermore, if the capacity of indigenous people freely to exercise their vote is impaired by a lack of education, unemployment and ill-health, then for most practical purposes they have been excluded from democratic citizenship.[31] It is therefore arguable that indigenous people have less influence or control over political decisions that impact directly on their lives than most other groups in society. In particular, this includes the development and implementation of indigenous affairs policy. While governments no longer speak of 'protection' and 'assimilation', many of their policies continue to impede indigenous aspirations to self-determination.

With few exceptions, the policies of liberal democratic governments generally fail to recognize the existence of an indigenous politics based on kinship obligation and collective responsibilities. These types of politics significantly affect whether government policy will be carried out at the local level, for if policy is not relevant, there is little to compel people to implement it. Australian indigenous lawyer and land rights activist Noel Pearson argues:

> The objectives of the State, to resolve social problems, will not be achieved without effective community engagement. If it is to enable

communities and individuals, it must understand that good policy ideas and initiatives can be generated within the community. . . . the aboriginal affairs policies that the State has historically developed have almost invariably been moribund and have created the very problems we are seeking to resolve.[32]

Nevertheless, demands for the formulation and implementation of policy relevant to the needs and circumstances of indigenous people are based on claims to special political status, group rights and cultural uniqueness, all of which tend to contradict core values of liberal democracy.

Political equality is a central principle of liberal democracy, but it was not extended to indigenous people until relatively recently. Furthermore, the principles of *formal* political equality must be contrasted with those of *substantive* equality. Indigenous peoples communities require greater substantive equality as a means of reducing or eliminating disadvantage relative to the wider population. Substantive equality is important also for indigenous self-determination and the maintenance of a distinct identity as 'indigenous people'.

The perception that indigenous culture is no longer viable, held by many non-indigenous politicians and bureaucrats, contributes further to liberal democracy's failure to accommodate indigenous self-determination. In effect, white society generally has a romantic image of indigenous culture and assumes that once indigenous people come into contact with the modern world, they cease to have any distinctive or authentic culture. On this view, governments and their officials argue that contemporary indigenous peoples should be absorbed further into what they see as mainstream society. Hence indigenous claims for self-determination are not considered relevant.

The lack of significant opportunity to influence government, the continuing failure of policy and issues of substantive equality underlie demands for indigenous self-determination in liberal democracies. How have indigenous claims for self-determination been made within liberal democracies? And how do Canada and Australia accommodate these claims?

Indigenous Rights and Limits to Self-determination

On the face of it, Canada and Australia are very similar. Both are liberal democracies, governed under a version of the Westminster system, and both have written constitutions. In fact, the two countries operate on constitutional systems with legislative and policy processes that are different in many areas. These differences help shape indigenous politics and determine the possibilities available for mainstream and indigenous political leaders to reconceptualize self-determination within the liberal democratic state.

Canada: constitutional entrenchment of indigenous rights

Canada is a nation founded on what is referred to by Canadians as 'two solitudes': the English and the French. The anglophone majority has had to accommodate both solitudes and has acknowledged the right of the French Quebecois minority to govern itself within the Canadian state. This compromise has become critical to the continued viability of the country. Hence the accommodation of indigenous demands for self-determination, based on the primacy of the group, has not been a big leap to make for the majority non-aboriginal population. This accommodation is given political effect through constitutional entrenchment. Entrenchment means that the legislative authority of the British Crown is confined within key parameters through the constitutional recognition of aboriginal and treaty rights, constitutional affirmation of those rights and the constitutional recognition of land claims agreements as treaties.

In Canada, aboriginal title comes from the historic use and occupation of certain lands by aboriginal people,[33] the Royal Proclamation of 1763,[34] the common law[35] and section 91(24) of the Constitution Act 1867.[36] Aboriginal title was constitutionally entrenched in the Constitution Act 1982 after many years of litigation, negotiation and mediation between Canada's aboriginal leaders and the federal government. This entrenchment is based, in part, on the strength of fiduciary obligation between the Crown and aboriginal peoples, whereby the federal Crown must act in the interests of Indian people when dealing with Indian property and lands.[37] This trust-like relationship may also be linked to fiscal, political and jurisdictional responsibilities. It is also based on a long history of treaties between the two parties.[38]

Although aboriginal rights are created and recognized by the Constitution Act 1982, they are held by aboriginal peoples by reason of the fact that they were once independent, self-governing entities in possession of most of the lands now making up Canada. The rights set out in section 35 of the Act are protected through application of the Canadian Charter of Rights and Freedoms that is part of the Constitution Act 1982. In section 25 of the Charter substantive rights are not created nor is the position of aboriginal people enhanced by comparison to the wider

Canadian public. The purpose of section 25 is to ensure a balance is maintained between the protection of individual rights in the Charter and the collective rights held by aboriginal people.

To date, the Canadian courts have focused on the scope and nature of constitutionally protected rights in section 35. Questions have arisen such as whether this includes a right to self-government that includes the full administration of justice, civil and criminal. The limitations involved in applying section 35 are not clear. This is an issue in Canada, as the language of self-determination, when spoken in a liberal democratic context, has raised the spectre of separate institutions of law that are alien to Canadian legal traditions. Indigenous self-government as a manifestation of self-determination – of political autonomy within the nation-state – does not mean that the liberal democratic government has abrogated its responsibilities to non-indigenous people. Ministerial interventions are still possible.

Nonetheless, there is uncertainty over the extent to which aboriginal jurisdiction in areas such as child welfare and education extends to non-aboriginal people who reside on aboriginal lands. Such questions are now before the courts. Many in the larger populations fear that these 'foreign' laws and structures, made by those who are barely visible in the broader society and polity, will override liberal democratic institutions and 'they [aboriginal people] will take over the country'.[39]

Australia: Mabo, Wik and the Native Title Act

In Australia native title is not protected in the constitution and there is no history of treaties between the Crown and indigenous people. Furthermore, there is no clear source in law of fiduciary obligation between the Crown and indigenous Australians. These factors prohibit or greatly limit the recognition of indigenous claims for self-determination.

Native title to land was recognized formally in Australia in 1992 when the High Court delivered its judgment in the case of *Mabo* v. *the State of Queensland (No. 2)*. The High Court determined that particular indigenous property rights had pre-existed and survived the establishment of sovereignty in colonized lands. The *Mabo* judgment determined that indigenous people may hold native title to land by virtue of their having maintained a continuing connection with the land or waters, according to their traditional law or customs, and where this connection has continued to the present.

In 1996, the High Court of Australia brought down another important judgment on Aboriginal access to land on pastoral leases. In *Wik*

Peoples v. *Queensland* the High Court held that the granting of a pastoral lease did not necessarily extinguish native title.[40] Nevertheless, it also determined that where the rights of native title-holders were inconsistent with the rights of pastoralists, the rights of pastoralists would prevail.

Both decisions brought controversy, and federal Labor and Liberal National Party governments instigated institutional reforms to routinize key aspects of the decisions. Under Labor, the Native Title Act, 1993, established the Native Title Tribunal, to regulate the claiming of land by indigenous peoples following the *Mabo* decision. At the same time, the native title laws confirmed the validity of all land grants made to non-indigenous people or entities prior to the High Court's decision in *Mabo* and provided procedures for those wishing to undertake development of native title lands. In March 1996 the Liberal National Party coalition was elected to government and in September 1998 it amended the Native Title Act to ensure further that the rights of individual property-owners would prevail over native title rights.

Shortly thereafter indigenous political leaders requested a review of the amended Act by the United Nations Committee on the Elimination of All Forms of Racial Discrimination (CERD).[41] CERD found that Australia's native title laws represented the racially motivated impairment of indigenous rights. Further, the committee claimed that the more recent amendments impaired the possibility of achieving substantive equality by indigenous people. It observed that legal certainty for governments and third parties had been created at the expense of indigenous title.

CERD called upon the federal government to address these criticisms, and in February 2000 a Joint Parliamentary Committee undertook to examine the consistency of the amended Act with Australia's international obligations under the Convention. The record of debate indicates that members of the committee were unresponsive to CERD's concerns, since the wishes of the majority of the citizens had been carried out through democratic processes.[42] The final report of the committee rejected CERD's concerns outright.[43]

Self-determination and Political Autonomy

Any moves towards political autonomy have the potential to challenge national sovereignty and the prerogatives of government. Indigenous demands for self-determination, however, usually do not present a serious challenge to national sovereignty. For the most part, they bear little resemblance to those more radical, nationalist movements that seek secession. The exercise of indigenous self-determination is more an expression of internal political autonomy and has become a way of reducing disadvantage. In most cases, another level of government is created (or recognized) in which certain designated powers are handed over to indigenous governments from higher levels. Almost invariably, the political institutions are based upon various versions of representative democracy involving elections to governing bodies, which are rarely independent of state funding and accountability. The overall aim is to establish indigenous control over those policies and programmes that most concern them. The following case studies illustrate the implications of this for the state, for indigenous people and for the limits to autonomy.

Canada

In Canada indigenous political autonomy takes three main forms: regional agreements, self-governing territories and the Treaty Land Entitlements. Each will be considered below.

Regional agreements The policy on the Implementation of the Inherent Right and the Negotiation of Aboriginal Self-Government, 1995, is the most recent attempt by the Canadian government to rethink aboriginal politics and self-determination. The policy supports the principle that aboriginal people have an inherent right to self-governance based on the fact that sovereignty had not been ceded. This policy denotes an exercise in autonomy – as opposed to sovereignty – as aboriginal governments exercising these rights must operate within the legal framework of the Canadian Constitution and within powers exercised by other governments.[44] Implementing self-determination involves balancing group rights exercised by aboriginal governments with the individual rights exercised by the wider citizenry.[45] Because the scope and nature of section 35's constitutionally protected group rights are contested, public deliberation over the rights of the group and the rights of the individual continues.

Nevertheless, self-government negotiations based on the inherent right have proceeded more rapidly in northern Canada. The Gwich'in Tribal Council, the Inuvialuit Regional Corporation of the Beaufort Sea Coast and the Government of the Northwest Territories encapsulate self-government as expressed through the public government forum. This means that certain subject matters (such as curriculum development in education, community health and social assistance) will come under the heading of 'exclusive aboriginal jurisdiction' and will find expression through aboriginal institutions of governance. In areas of 'shared jurisdiction' the inherent right will be expressed through the already established institutions of governance. In these cases, both aboriginal *and* non-aboriginal political systems are used as vehicles to further indigenous demands for self-determination within the liberal democratic state.

While it is not a simple task to theorize the ideal relationship between group rights and individual rights, achieving a balance in practice is even more difficult. One of the major obstacles is the uncertainty experienced by the non-aboriginal population resident within the aboriginal jurisdiction. Key questions include the following: what happens to the liberal democratic rights of non-aboriginal residents on aboriginal lands? What may happen when non-aboriginal residents take issue with some aspect of the aboriginal system of governance? For example, in areas of child welfare and marital breakdown, do the rights of a non-aboriginal custodial parent carry the same weight as the collective rights of the aboriginal group of which the child is also a member? A related problem is that of how to protect the individual citizenship rights of all Canadians within the aboriginal collective. At the time of writing, there appears to be little protection given to non-aboriginal citizens under aboriginal governments. This has yet to be tested in the courts.

Self-governing territories – Nunavut Nunavut, meaning 'our land', has been a dream of Inuit leaders since the 1970s. When the Nunavut land claim was settled in 1993, the creation of a new territory, an Inuit territory, was realized by carving out those lands covered by the claim from the Northwest Territories. The agreement covers about one-fifth of Canada's land mass and a large marine area. The Nunavut Agreement provides a set of property rights that 'can move Inuit forward some distance on the road back to economic self-sufficiency'[46] and provides for joint Nunavut and federal government resource management boards.[47]

The new Nunavut Territory – created in 1999 – has a legislature that is elected by all its residents, regardless of ethnicity, and all citizens are able to stand for office. As Inuit make up 85 per cent of the population in the new territory, they will be able to play the major role in shaping a government that suits Inuit culture, traditions and goals. All public sector functions that were previously part of the government of the Northwest Territories have been transferred to Nunavut. While the seat of government has been moved to the High Arctic community of Iqaluit from its previously southern locale in Yellowknife, the usual institutions of liberal democratic governance will remain for the foreseeable future.

This new system has both its critics and its supporters. Whereas some claim that the institutions will evolve into ones that reflect more of the Inuit culture, others disagree. Expectations that Nunavut will bring about dramatic improvement in the socio-economic lives of its residents are very high throughout the central and eastern Arctic. Nunavut is primarily seen as a means to overcoming socio-economic disadvantage, rather than as entry into a difficult democratic process, and is viewed by many Inuit as a panacea for their socio-economic problems. The difficulties associated with a society oriented towards group values taking up and participating in the institutions of liberal democracy remain significant.

Treaty Land Entitlement Treaty Land Entitlement (TLE) is the phrase that describes the process of fulfilling outstanding treaty obligations on the part of the federal government to Indian bands – effectively the governments of Indian reserves – under the Indian Act 1985.[48] Significant monies are provided by the federal government to those Indian bands with rights under the Act to acquire additional reserve lands. Where land is not available, cash equivalents are paid into band development trust funds to be used for business enterprise. Entitlements to land exist only by virtue of the process instigated by the Crown in the late 1800s and do not contain self-government provisions per se.

Devolution policies are facilitated by, but exist outside of, TLE. These policies enable bands on reserves to gain control of programmes and services and the funds that go with them in areas of health, housing, education, economic development and business enterprise. Agreements are made between band governments and the federal and provincial governments. These agreements are then implemented through a range of aboriginal self-governing institutions. Bands also control their own policy development, within existing legislation.

The Peter Ballantyne Cree Nation (PBCN), for example, gained control over the development and delivery of programmes in services in education, health, housing, child welfare, economic development and business enterprise over a five-year period that commenced in 1990.[49] In addition, the band is now providing adequate services to the non-aboriginal population resident in the area. This devolution of political power combined with the acquisition of a significant amount of land and band development funding has enabled the PBCN to achieve a large measure of self-governance within the liberal democratic nation-state. These forms of indigenous political autonomy do not entail secession; they simply extend the theory and practice of shared or divided sovereignty that is characteristic of many liberal democratic polities.

Australia

The Aboriginal and Torres Strait Islander Commission The main vehicle for government-supported forms of self-determination in Australia is the Aboriginal and Torres Strait Islander Commission (ATSIC). ATSIC was created by the Commonwealth government through the enactment of the Aboriginal and Torres Strait Islander Act 1989. Previous indigenous affairs administrations had long attracted criticism for not addressing adequately the needs of indigenous Australians. ATSIC was originally designed to put into effect the principle of self-determination for Aboriginal and Torres Strait Islanders and is their peak elected representative body. At the same time, ATSIC functions virtually as a government department. The representative arm has dual accountability to both the Minister of Aboriginal Affairs and its Aboriginal and Islander constituents. By contrast, the administrative arm is accountable to the federal government, not to the elected representatives, and is legally required to serve the minister. This structure is unique in the Australian public sector, as it attempts to combine both representative and executive responsibilities.[50] ATSIC was also intended to be the main provider of policy advice to the minister.

ATSIC came into existence amid great controversy and debate in both Cabinet and Parliament. When then Minister for Aboriginal Affairs Gerry Hand first introduced the ATSIC bill in December 1987, the government was subjected to intense questioning about the public accountability in Aboriginal affairs and many revisions to the draft bill were required.[51] During the early years of its political evolution, it was widely thought that ATSIC's primary responsibility was to the indigenous community. Since 1989, the original vision has become somewhat clouded. The noted campaigner for Aboriginal rights, H. C. Coombs, argued that the most debilitating element in the present organizational structure is the misleading description of ATSIC as an indigenous body.[52] This criticism may be supported by reference to various debates and decisions on funding, elections and ATSIC's role in the provision of policy advice.

In theory, ATSIC's Board of Commissioners ought to have significant autonomy in making decisions about the budget, allocations and policy priorities for the coming year, as many of the functions previously performed by the Department of Aboriginal Affairs were transferred to ATSIC. In reality, the minister retains a significant degree of authority and takes an interventionist role. For example, in the 1996–7 budget cycle, the government made the decision to cut overall expenditure by 11 per cent and ATSIC's budget was reduced accordingly. The minister, however, also removed or 'quarantined' selected core programmes of ATSIC – such as the Community Development Employment Programme – from consideration by the commissioners as part of the budget reduction process. The minister, without consulting the commissioners, simply announced the quarantines in an ATSIC board meeting.[53] Then Chairperson of ATSIC, Lois O'Donohue, did not dispute that difficult financial times may call for difficult decisions on the part of government.[54] She did object, however, that the minister did not consult with the commissioners about the quarantines. Furthermore, she argued that, because little regard was paid to relative disadvantage and need, the burden of the government's decisions was not distributed equitably.

One characteristic of ATSIC that attracts political criticism from all sides is that kinship obligations and regional disputes tend to influence the allocation of funds at the commission level.[55] Substantial regional and socio-economic differences exist within the Aboriginal and Torres Strait Islander population and these have important implications for the distribution of funding and for policy and programme effectiveness. Nonetheless, the size of a region, both demographically and geographically, has little or no bearing on funding decisions made by ATSIC, which tend to reflect historical patterns established by political decisions early in the organization's history.[56] Hence, community members often accuse commissioners of not allocating enough money to their regions to achieve satisfactory service delivery outcomes. Critics in government point to the inappropriate allocations of existing funds. Both members of indigenous communities and the government accuse the ATSIC commissioners of patronage and nepotism. In turn, the commissioners have criticized government for not providing adequate levels of funding in the first place and for stripping away from them powers that would help advance self-determination.

Those who defend ATSIC say that billions of additional dollars are required to achieve better service delivery outcomes. Others claim that nepotism and favouritism among commissioners inhibit improvement, because the areas of greatest need may not receive funding. The Aboriginal Democrat Senator, Aden Ridgeway, argues that in some ways funding allocation has become based on personality.[57] Such expressions of indigenous politics do not appear to meet the standards of impartiality supposed to characterize decision-making in liberal democracies.

Criticism also extends to the relevance of democracy for ATSIC. The Board of Commissioners is an elected body, but the election process itself raises questions about the validity of a democratic process in the context of indigenous politics. Election results are determined more by indigenous politics that are based on extended family structures, kinship obligation and principles of reciprocity than they are by the right of each individual to vote. Due to the intense indigenous politics at local and regional levels, the results are often predetermined before voters go to the polls.[58] ATSIC elections also appear to have had a relatively low voter turnout over the years. Nonetheless, it is difficult to measure precisely actual turnout against numbers of registered voters because the number of registered indigenous voters is unknown and voting is not compulsory.[59]

An important innovation was to be ATSIC's primary role in the provision of policy advice to the Minister of Aboriginal Affairs. Yet, the Liberal National Party coalition government recently reinstated the Office of Indigenous Policy (OIP) – currently housed in the Department of Reconciliation and Aboriginal and Torres Strait Islander Affairs – as an alternative source of policy advice to ATSIC. Having a separate office to fulfil this function is not a new idea. Although ATSIC originally was to be the major provider of policy advice to the government, the Keating Labor government also wanted a broader base of advice and established an indigenous policy office in the department of Prime Minister and Cabinet. In effect, the Liberal National Party government has reactivated the earlier proposal in which ATSIC is to be just one of the organizations consulted about Aboriginal affairs. Some ATSIC commissioners fear that re-establishing the office foreshadows the 'mainstreaming' of ATSIC programmes, begun in the mid-1990s with indigenous health programmes. The goal here is to shift decision-making on funding allocations from the realm of indigenous politics to conventional government departments, and to reduce the influence of ATSIC in providing policy advice to the Minister of Aboriginal Affairs.

ATSIC was intended to be an innovative form of self-government that would provide Aboriginal and Torres Straits Islanders with a mechanism for exercising self-determination. It is now questionable as to whether it was a successful experiment with reference to either the goals of self-determination or representative democracy. Geoff Clark, Chairperson at the time of writing, argues that some serious rethinking about ATSIC's role needs to occur if the organization is to meet the aspirations of indigenous people.

This case study indicates a few of the practical complexities associated with the quest for indigenous self-determination within liberal democracy. Giving indigenous people control over policy and programme delivery hardly constitutes a radical departure from liberal democratic principles. Certainly, the increased political autonomy granted to ATSIC and less direct ministerial control may seem to be a reduction in national sovereignty. But when these characteristics are set against the retention of direct ministerial power over the legislation governing the body and its budget, indigenous political autonomy remains constrained and the issue of sovereignty is hardly significant. If ultimate accountability of the organization is to the minister, then it may be inappropriate to describe it as an example of self-determination.

What Do the Case Studies Show?

As we saw above, liberal democracy derives its power and significance from the idea of self-determination. Indigenous people in Australia and Canada have attempted to choose the form and direction of their government, not through radical secession from the state, but through achieving political autonomy within the state. National and regional governments in Canada and Australia have acknowledged, to varying degrees, that indigenous people have special needs and rights that other ethnic and cultural groups do not have. They have been recognized as First Peoples in law and, increasingly, in substantive practice.

The case studies also demonstrate that indigenous claims to self-determination can, within limits, be accommodated within liberal democratic states. Indigenous rights have been given political effect in liberal democracies through processes such as constitutional entrenchment and the reaching of formal agreements between government and indigenous groups that satisfy both. The capacity for liberal democracy to reshape its usual practices and accommodate indigenous claims is particularly evident in Canada.

The limits to indigenous self-determination in the liberal democratic state are determined not only by national and regional state politics and law, but also by the capacity of indigenous people themselves to put principles of political autonomy into action. Since the late 1960s, aboriginal Canadians have been struggling to achieve substantive equality, recognition of special rights and autonomy within the state. The courts have been the most successful mechanism whereby aboriginal people have secured collective rights, whereas land claims agreements are practical instruments that implement these rights.

The same degree of progress has yet to be made in Australia. Amendments to the Native Title Act and the response to the United Nations through CERD indicate a limited willingness by national and most state governments to recognize indigenous aspirations towards self-determination, other than through institutions under direct state control, such as ATSIC. Australian governments have resisted attempts to extend the principles and practice of liberal democracy. For example, the Minister for Aboriginal Affairs continues to exert direct authority over what was to be a representative body. Despite the legal and political recognition of some group rights, Australian governments also continue to address indigenous issues within a model of interest group politics. ATSIC's Board of Commissioners, however, tends to make decisions that are based more on the requirements of indigenous politics than those of the federal government, and this produces frequent political conflicts between the two. Furthermore, many indigenous leaders and communities view ATSIC with suspicion as not representing their interests or serving their needs. Nonetheless, moves towards indigenous self-determination in Australia are intensifying as indigenous people seek to publicize their concerns beyond the borders of the nation-state.

The Canadian examples also demonstrate that the process of granting special rights and of creating mechanisms to exercise those rights is not straightforward. Questions have arisen as to whether special rights can be granted to indigenous people without destroying the principles of equality of rights of all citizens underlying liberal democratic theory.[60] Fundamental questions, such as how to protect the rights of the non-indigenous majority, members of which happen to reside on indigenous lands, continue to provoke public and legal controversy.

Conclusion

As we have seen above, liberal democratic theory relies upon the principle of self-determination. Given its primary respect for the individual, however, liberal democratic theory finds great difficulty in recognizing forms of indigenous self-determination that incorporate group rights. Indigenous institutions of self-government may also infringe upon the key principle of political equality, as the indigenous group may be given rights that other non-indigenous people do not have. By seeking a devolution of political power to indigenous people, indigenous self-government also challenges the sovereignty of the nation-state. Overall, it would appear that there was little prospect of any theoretical or practical accommodation between liberal democracy and indigenous peoples. The liberal democratic and indigenous traditions represent two seemingly irreconcilable world-views.

In practice, however, there is a growing history of political accommodations, which have had varying degrees of success. The case studies presented in this chapter have demonstrated how various kinds of institution and government have been established in Australia and Canada to promote indigenous self-determination. It may be ventured that indigenous people have extended the principles and practice of liberal democracy. It is arguable that, by so doing, they have strengthened democratic principles such as tolerance of difference, and thereby enhanced the practice of political equality. In an era where there often seems to be no authoritative centre of political power, the indigenous challenge to national sovereignty is also marginal. Indeed, it may be argued that finding new ways of empowering indigenous citizens and encouraging their participation in self-government represents a positive achievement for liberal democracies.

The current problem, however, is not so much the infringement of key liberal democratic principles, but the incorporation of indigenous people within the liberal democratic institutions. We may recall that a major objective for indigenous people was to seek to influence the institutions by which they are governed and thus try to meet better the needs of their group. In many cases, these objectives have not been met. Many indigenous governments have found it difficult to deliver the outcomes needed to strengthen their communities. Although indigenous people now have a political voice and some even have their own forms of self-government, this has not always produced the desired results. In such cases, it may not be the political theory that needs revising, but the political practices.

NOTES

The author would like to thank April Carter, John Kane and Geoff Stokes for their helpful comments on earlier drafts of the paper. Nonetheless, any errors or misinterpretations remain my responsibility.

1 Ian Shapiro, *Democracy's Place* (Ithaca, Cornell University Press, 1996), p. 4.
2 Australians and Canadians use the terms 'indigenous' and 'aboriginal' in different contexts. For purposes of this chapter, the term 'indigenous' is used when discussing commonalities in both Australia and Canada. When referring specifically to the indigenous peoples of Australia, the terms 'Aborigines and Torres Straits Islanders' will be used. In the case of Canada, I will follow common practice there and use the term 'aboriginal' to refer to Indian and Inuit people.
3 D. Held, *Democracy and the Global Order: From the Modern State to Cosmopolitan Governance* (Cambridge, Polity, 1995), p. 145.
4 D. J. Manning, *Liberalism* (London, J. M. Dent and Sons, 1976), pp. 17–18.
5 Michael Freeman, 'Democracy and dynamite: The peoples' right to self-determination', *Political Studies* XLIV (1996): 748.
6 See discussion in Hurst Hannum, 'The specter of secession: Responding to claims for ethnic self-determination', *Foreign Affairs* 77, 2 (1998): 13–18.

7   J. Waldron, 'Rights', in R. E. Goodin and P. Pettit (eds), *A Companion to Contemporary Political Philosophy* (Oxford, Blackwell, 1995), p. 578.

8   A. Buchanan, 'Secession and nationalism', in R. E. Goodin and P. Pettit (eds), *A Companion to Contemporary Political Philosophy* (Oxford, Blackwell, 1995), p. 586.

9   A. Weale, *Democracy* (London, Macmillan Press, 1999), p. 54.

10 Ibid.

11 See also the discussion by Peter Jones in 'Human rights, group rights, and people's rights', *Human Rights Quarterly* 21, 1 (1999): 80–107.

12 There are numerous examples from Canada. The same range is not available from Australia, as this chapter discusses specific agreement processes as opposed to statements of reconciliation.

13 The early French explorers and fur traders were not part of a French colony and did not seek sovereignty or to replace indigenous systems of justice and law.

14 See R. M. Berndt and C. H. Berndt, *The World of the First Australians: Aboriginal Traditional Life: Past and Present* (Canberra, Aboriginal Studies Press, 1996) and R. B. Morrison and C. Roderick Wilson (eds), *Native Peoples: The Canadian Experience* (Toronto, McLelland and Stewart, 1995).

15 Canada has a long history of land 'surrenders' and treaties that precedes Confederation in 1867. Treaties that were negotiated post-1867 are referred to as numbered treaties, the last of which was signed in 1921. Under the Canadian Constitution, land claims agreements are also referred to as treaties.

16 There is an extensive literature documenting the details of colonization and dispossession. For example, see Berndt and Berndt, *The World of the First Australians*; H. Buckle, *From Wooden Ploughs to Welfare* (Montreal, McGill-Queen's University Press, 1992); S. Carter, *Lost Harvests* (Montreal, McGill-Queen's University Press, 1990); R. Kidd, *The Way We Civilise* (St Lucia, University of Queensland Press, 1997); P. Kulchyski (ed.), *Unjust Relations: Aboriginal Rights in Canadian Courts* (Toronto, Oxford University Press, 1984), pp. 1–20; Henry Reynolds, *Dispossession* (Sydney, Allen and Unwin, 1989); and C. Roderick Wilson and R. Bruce Morrison, 'Taking stock', in R. Bruce Morrison and C. Roderick Wilson (eds), *Native Peoples: The Canadian Experience* (Toronto, McClelland and Stewart Inc., 1995), pp. 607–31.

17 See, for example, Australian Bureau of Statistics, *The Health and Welfare of Australia's Aboriginal and Torres Strait Islander Peoples* (Canberra, Australian Government Publishing Service, 1997); S. Couzos and R. Murray, *Aboriginal Primary Health Care: An Evidence-Based Approach* (South Melbourne, Oxford University Press, 1999); J. S. Frideres, *Native People in Canada: Contemporary Conflicts*, 4th edn (Scarborough, Prentice-Hall, 1993); Government of

Canada, Department of Indian Affairs and Northern Development, *Basic Departmental Data* (Ottawa, Ministry of Supply and Services, various years).

18   See G. C. Bolton, 'Aborigines in social history: An overview', in R. M. Berndt (ed.), *Aboriginal Sites, Rights and Resource Development* (Perth, University of Western Australia Press, 1982), pp. 59–68; Paul Hasluck, *Native Welfare in Australia: Speeches and Addresses* (Perth, Paterson Brokenshaw 1953), p. 6.

19   See J. Chesterman and B. Galligan, *Citizens Without Rights* (Cambridge, Cambridge University Press, 1997).

20   Aboriginal people in Canada are defined under the Indian Act (RSC 1970, c. I-6), which sets out a complex system for registering Indians, administering their lands and regulating lives. Under the Act, to obtain treaty benefits Indians had to remain on reserves. To gain the right to vote, however, Indians had to leave the reserves. This remained in place until 1960 when all Indian people were granted voting rights.

21   Hasluck, *Native Welfare in Australia*, pp. 56–7.

22   See Chesterman and Galligan, *Citizens Without Rights*.

23   See B. Attwood and A. Markus, *The 1967 Referendum, or When Aborigines Didn't Get the Vote* (Canberra, Australian Institute of Aboriginal and Torres Strait Islander Studies, 1997); and 'Representation matters: The 1967 referendum and citizenship', in N. Peterson and W. Sanders (eds), *Citizenship and Indigenous Australians* (Cambridge, Cambridge University Press, 1998), pp. 118–40; A. C. Cairns, *Citizens Plus: Aboriginal Peoples and the Canadian State* (Vancouver, UBC Press, 2000); A. Davidson, *From Subject to Citizen* (Cambridge, Cambridge University Press, 1997), pp. 188–216.

24   Government of Canada, Department of Indian Affairs and Northern Development, *Statement of the Government of Canada on Indian Policy* (Ottawa, Queen's Printer, 1969).

25   See the Indian Act, RSC 1985. The Act assigns exclusive legislative authority to the federal Parliament over 'Indians and lands reserved for Indians'. This also includes Inuit populations. The Supreme Court of Canada unanimously decided in *Re Eskimos*, 5 CNLC 123 [1939] that the term Indians in s.91(24) of the Indian Act 1867 included the Inuit. Inuit are, therefore, within the legislative authority of the federal Parliament.

26   C. Denis, *We Are Not You: First Nations and Canadian Modernity* (Toronto, Broadview Press 1997).

27   See M. Ivanitz, 'Achieving improved health outcomes for urban aboriginal people: Biomedical and ethnomedical models of health', *Australian Journal of Public Administration* 59, 3 (2000): 49–57; T. Rowse, 'Middle Australia and the noble savage: A political romance', in J. Beckett (ed.), *Past and Present – The Construction of Aboriginality* (Canberra, Aboriginal Studies Press, 1988), pp. 161–77.

28 Personal communication, Mary Hager, Nacho Nyak Dun Elder, Yukon Territory, December 1993.

29 Personal communication, Mary Graham, Kombumerri Elder, Southport, Queensland, September 1998.

30 Declines in trust are noted in liberal democracies over recent years. See, for example, J. S. Nye, Jr., P. D. Zelikow and D. C. King (eds), *Why People Don't Trust Government* (Cambridge, MA, Harvard University Press, 1997).

31 I. Shapiro and C. Hacker-Cordón (eds), 'Outer edges and inner edges', in *Democracy's Edges* (Cambridge, Cambridge University Press, 1999), pp. 1–16.

32 N. Pearson *From Campbelltown to Cape York – Rebuilding Community* (Brisbane, Brisbane Institute, 1999).

33 Historically, aboriginal peoples had their own forms of government and socio-economic systems. This recognition led to the signing of treaties between the Crown and aboriginal people. The doctrine of aboriginal title in Canada, and subsequently aboriginal rights, has flowed from this recognition. See J. S. Youngblood Henderson, M. L. Benson and I. S. Findlay, *Aboriginal Tenure in the Constitution of Canada* (Scarborough, Carswell Thomson Professional Publishing, 2000); T. Issac, *Aboriginal Law: Cases, Materials and Commentary* (Saskatoon, Purich Publishers, 1995).

34 The Royal Proclamation of 1763 was issued by King George III and recognizes the rights of Indians to unceded lands in their possession. It further recognizes that Indians may only cede such lands to the Crown.

35 Common law recognition of aboriginal title is found, for example, in *St Catherine's Milling and Lumber Co.* v. *R. 2 C.N.L.C. 541 (J.C.P.C)*, whereby the Privy Council held that Indians possessed a 'personal and usufructory right, dependent upon the good will of the Sovereign' over which Indian title was enjoyed; and in *R.* v. *Calder* [1973] S.C.R. 313, whereby it was noted that aboriginal title was not dependent upon legislative enactments, executive orders or treaties, but was a legal right derived from historic occupation and possession of tribal lands.

36 This section assigns exclusive legislative authority to the federal Parliament over 'Indians and Lands reserved for Indians'.

37 See Issac, *Aboriginal Law*; M. Ivanitz, 'The emperor has no clothes: Canadian comprehensive claims and their relevance to Australia', in M. Edmunds (ed.), *Regional Agreements Key Issues in Australia: Volume 2, Case Studies* (Canberra, Australian Institute of Aboriginal and Torres Strait Islander Studies, 1999), pp. 319–42.

38 The particular sections of the Constitution Act 1882 read as follows: '35(1) The existing aboriginal and treaty rights of the aboriginal peoples of Canada are hereby recognized and affirmed; 35(2) In this Act, 'aboriginal peoples of Canada' includes the Indian, Inuit and

Metis peoples of Canada; 35(3) For greater certainty, in subsection (1) "treaty rights" includes rights that now exist by way of land claims agreements or may be so acquired; 35(4) Notwithstanding any other provision of this Act, the aboriginal and treaty rights referred to in subsection (1) are guaranteed equally to male and female persons' (Constitution Act 1982, Schedule B of the Canada Act 1982 (UK), 1982, c.11).

39   Personal communication, Mayor, Local Government Council, Province of Alberta, December 1999.

40   *Wik Peoples* v. *Queensland* (1996) 187 CLR 1; 141 ALR 129.

41   See The Universal Declaration of Human Rights (Articles 2, 7); The International Covenant on Civil and Political Rights (Articles 2.2, 2.6); The International Covenant on Economic, Social and Cultural Rights (Article 2.2); and The United Nations Charter (Article 1(3); see also Article 55).

42   Parliamentary Joint Committee on Native Title and the Aboriginal and Torres Strait Islander Land Fund, *Commonwealth of Australia Official Committee Hansard*, Reference: Consistency of the Native Title Amendment Act 1998 with Australia's international obligations under the Convention on the Elimination of all Forms of Racial Discrimination, Tuesday, 22 February 2000 (Canberra, Australian Government Publishing Service, 2000).

43   Parliamentary Joint Committee, *Sixteenth Report* (Canberra, Australian Government Publishing Service, 2000).

44   Ivanitz, 'The emperor has no clothes', pp. 321–2.

45   See L. Green, 'Internal minorities and their rights', in W. Kymlicka (ed.), *The Rights of Minority Cultures* (Oxford, Oxford University Press, 1995), pp. 256–74. J. Koshan discusses the application of the charter to the protection of the rights of Aboriginal women, as these rights are individual rights, within self-governing Aboriginal communities, in 'Aboriginal women, justice and the charter: Bridging the divide', *University of British Columbia Law Review* 32, 1 (1998): 23–54.

46   J. Kusugak, 'The tide has shifted: Nunavut works for us, and it offers a lesson to the broader global community', in J. Dahl, J. Hicks and P. Jull (eds), *Inuit Regain Control of Their Lands and Their Lives* (Copenhagen, International Working Group for Indigenous Affairs, 2000), p. 25.

47   The structure of the Nunavut agreement and systems of governance is extremely complex. For further discussion, see essays in Dahl, Hicks and Jull (eds), *Inuit Regain Control of Their Lands and Their Lives*.

48   These provisions pertain to 'Indians and Lands Reserved for Indians' under the Act. It is beyond the scope of this chapter to discuss the reserve system and its impacts on Indian life and culture. For further discussion, see M. Boldt and J. A. Long (eds), *The Quest For Justice* (Toronto, University of Toronto Press, 1988); H. Buckley, *From*

Wooden Ploughs to Welfare: Why Indian Policy Failed in the Prairie Provinces (Montreal, McGill-Queen's University Press, 1992); R. Fumuleau, *As Long As This Land Shall Last* (Toronto, McLelland and Stewart, 1973); L. Little Bear, M. Boldt and J. A. Long, *Pathways to Self-Determination: Canadian Indians and the Canadian State* (Toronto, University of Toronto Press, 1989); A. P. Morrison, *Justice for Natives: Searching for Common Ground* (Montreal, Aboriginal Law Association of McGill University, 1997).

49 The Framework Agreement settled outstanding Treaty Land Entitlement obligations through the provision of money to the PBCN to acquire reserve lands. Reserve creation, however, is not a simple process. The Agreement is 155 pages long, contains 22 articles, and covers land quantum, entitlement monies, land acquisition, minerals, water, provincial roads, third-party interests, urban reserves, procedures for reserve creation, tax loss compensation, taxation, existing and future programmes, arbitration and others. Added to this are seven schedules and three appendices that contain guidelines and parameters for the enactment of particular articles – another 200 pages. By the time the reserve creation process is complete, the PBCN will have acquired 22,466 acres, beyond which the band may acquire more land or engage in a range of development activities.

50 Chesterman and Galligan, *Citizens Without Rights*, p. 213.

51 For discussion on various aspects of these debates, see M. Dillon 'Institutional structures in indigenous affairs: The future of ATSIC', in Patrick Sullivan (ed.), *Shooting the Banker* (Darwin, North Australian Research Unit, 1996), pp. 89–104; T. Rowse, 'Aborigines: Citizens and colonial subjects', in J. Brett, J. Gillespie and M. Goot (eds), *Developments in Australian Politics* (Melbourne, Macmillan, 1994), pp. 182–201; W. Sanders, *Rethinking the Fundamentals of Social Policy Towards Indigenous Australians: Block Grants, Mainstreaming and the Multiplicity of Agencies and Programs*, Discussion Paper No. 46 (Canberra, Centre for Aboriginal Economic Policy Research, 1996); *Reconciling Public Accountability and Aboriginal Self-Determination/Self-Management: Is ATSIC Succeeding?* Discussion Paper no. 51 (Canberra, Centre for Aboriginal Economic Policy Research, 1996).

52 H. C. Coombs, *Aboriginal Autonomy* (Cambridge, Cambridge University Press, 1994), p. 183. See also T. Rowse, *Obliged to be Difficult: Nugget Coombs' Legacy in Indigenous Affairs* (Cambridge, Cambridge University Press, 2000), pp. 198–207.

53 Personal communication, former ATSIC commissioner, Brisbane, November 1996, and confirmed through interviews with other former commissioners, January and October 1997.

54 See Chairperson's Report in *ATSIC Annual Report 1996–1997* (Canberra, Australian Government Publishing Service, 1997).

55 Personal communication, former ATSIC Commissioners and con-

firmed through interviews with other commissioners and officials of government.

56   Personal communication, Senior ATSIC official, Canberra, October 1997. See also D. E. Smith, *The Fiscal Equalisation Model: Options for ATSIC's Future Funding Policy and Practice*, Discussion Paper No. 30 (Canberra, Centre for Aboriginal Economic Policy Research, 1993).

57   See M. Ivanitz, 'Challenges to indigenous service delivery', in G. Davis and P. Weller (eds), *Are You Being Served?* (Sydney, Allen and Unwin, 2001), forthcoming.

58   Based on interview data with members of ATSIC regional councils, past and current ATSIC commissioners, and senior officials of ATSIC over a three-year period (1997–2000).

59   W. Sanders, J. Taylor and K. Ross, 'Participation and representation in ATSIC elections: A 10-year perspective', *Australian Journal of Political Science* 35, 3 (2000): 493–513.

60   See W. Kymlicka, 'Introduction', in W. Kymlicka (ed.), *The Rights of Minority Cultures* (Oxford, Oxford University Press, 1996), pp. 1–30.

6

Democracy and Nationalism

Margaret Canovan

Nationalism and democracy are often connected. Sometimes one seems to reinforce the other, as national autonomy is linked with popular participation in calls for 'self-determination'. To Poles, Hungarians, Estonians and many others, the collapse of Communism in Eastern Europe meant the possibility of self-rule in both senses, while even in the established democracies of the West, pressure for the devolution of power from the state seems to be most urgent where national autonomy as well as democratic participation is at stake. It is true that many forces in the contemporary world are pushing in the opposite direction, towards consolidation rather than devolution of power, but the problems these throw up themselves underline the connection between democracy and nationalism. In a global economy there may, for example, be cogent reasons to increase European economic and political integration. But worries about a 'democratic deficit' inside the EU are connected with widespread objections to being ruled by a foreign 'them' rather than a national 'us'. Meanwhile, the mobility that goes with globalization highlights more disturbing links and tensions between nationalism and democracy. While the long-term presence of non-nationals without citizenship within democratic states raises one set of issues about the relation between democratic rights and national identity, the migrant's claim to inclusion in democratic self-determination is challenged by populist movements that appeal not only to nationalism but to grassroots democracy.

There are a number of ways, then, in which nationalism and democracy, variously connected, crop up on current political and theoretical agendas. The complexity of their connections is scarcely to be wondered at, for each of these two terms is shorthand for a wide range of phenomena and each has generated a vast theoretical literature. Democracy is interpreted even more variously than nationalism. While the focus here is on western-style liberal representative institutions, the chapter will link nationalism with democracy understood in three different ways: as popular sovereignty, as deliberation in the sense of rational discourse (which seeks clarity) and as a process of negotiated compromise (which often requires ambiguity). I shall also consider the use of institutional devices to overcome some of the political threats posed by 'national' issues to stable representative democracy.

The plan of the chapter is as follows. Starting from nationalism, the first half looks at the ways in which some of its features can give support to democratic politics, and then turns the tables to consider the threats nationalism can pose. The second half of the chapter reverses the process by taking democracy as the starting point, considering features that make it ill-fitted to cope with nationalism, and turns, secondly, to aspects of democratic politics that are, on the contrary, particularly *well* fitted to do so. While a number of recent political examples will be used to illustrate key points, the politics of Northern Ireland is an especially fruitful source of salutary insights in exploring the problems and possibilities of both nationalism and democracy. In particular, attempts during the 1990s to resolve the long-standing national/religious conflict by means of the 'peace process' provide a spur to reflections on the contingency of national and democratic politics.

Nationalism as a Help and a Hindrance to Democracy

It is not difficult to make a case on both theoretical and historical grounds for regarding national identity and nationalist mobilization as valuable aids to democratic politics. Although the case can most easily be made if democracy is understood in traditional terms to mean popular sovereignty and a common popular will, it can also accommodate the less voluntaristic and more deliberative understandings of democracy currently favoured by political philosophers.

Nationalism and popular sovereignty

According to clause 3 of the Declaration of the Rights of Man and of Citizens, issued by the French revolutionaries in 1789, 'the Nation is essentially the source of all sovereignty'.[1] Putting the sovereign nation in the place of the sovereign monarch, the French radicals implicitly acknowledged that if a large-scale state is to belong to a 'people' rather than to a king, the population must have a collective identity and be incorporated into what Benedict Anderson calls the 'imagined community' of a nation.[2] Popular sovereignty is a venerable concept, traceable at least as far back as the jurists of the medieval city-states of Italy.[3] But nationhood was required to make plausible the application of that rhetoric of popular sovereignty to an entire realm, thereby opening up a democratic alternative to monarchy in large-scale states.[4] The state could belong to the people rather than the king only if the former were participants in a collective identity capable of lasting over the generations.[5] For the past two centuries, each of the great waves of revolt against established authority in the name of popular self-government has been mobilized through the language of nationalism as well as of democracy. For the liberals of 1848 and 1919, for anti-colonial movements after the Second World War and for those who mobilized against Soviet rule in 1989, self-government meant liberation from empires and the establishment of representative government on a national scale. The history of many of these movements casts doubt on the national as well as the democratic pretensions of those involved. But a vision of 'self-government', in which democracy and national autonomy are linked like two sides of a coin, still retains the apparent plausibility articulated over a century ago by John Stuart Mill, who observed that in most circumstances, 'uniting all the members of the nationality under the same government, and a government to themselves apart . . . is merely saying that the question of government ought to be decided by the governed'.[6]

The mobilizing power of this discourse cannot be doubted, and its key concept of popular, national self-determination continues to find eloquent defenders, albeit defenders more or less chastened by history.[7] In recent years, however, many political theorists have become dissatisfied with the sort of understanding of democracy to which nationalists characteristically appeal. Talk of 'popular sovereignty' or 'self-government' seems to them misleading, dangerously so when it implies that 'the people' can or ought to form a single entity acting as one. Rather than being the exercise of political *will*, democracy in their view means sustained, inclusive engagement in discourse and deliberation.[8] Approached from this angle, democracy has nothing to do with monolithic nationhood and everything to do with recognizing and respecting others' differences.[9] At first sight, this more discursive understanding seems to drive a wedge between democracy and nationalism, particularly since many of the theorists involved are drawn to small-scale participation on the one hand and to schemes for global democracy on the other. But this is by no means the end of the matter. For one thing, deliberative democracy need not mean throwing out the voluntarist conception altogether. Democracy is not just about talking, but about *doing* things, and doing things often requires a mobilization of political will.[10] Nationhood can be a formidable political glue, binding people together into a body politic with the power to take action, for good or ill.[11] But even if we concentrate on deliberation itself, we can argue that democracy is still hard to separate from the nation because it has demanding preconditions. Joshua Cohen observes that the deliberative ideal points towards arrangements required to '*make deliberation possible*',[12] and some of those preconditions are spelled out by Habermas, for whom democracy demands 'all those conditions of communication under which there can come into being a discursive formation of will and opinion on the part of a public composed of the citizens of a state'.[13] What is required, in other words, is effective communication within a shared public space.

Nationhood and communication

Despite the sophistication of the literature on deliberative democracy, an obvious and vital point is rarely made. This is that if people are to engage in political deliberation, they need to be able to understand one another: they need to speak the same language. In fact, they need to speak it rather well, not just well enough to decipher a slogan or understand the plot of a television soap opera, but well enough to follow arguments, appreciate alternative points of view and be persuaded to change their minds. Some democratic countries do, of course, cope more or less effectively with linguistic splits, usually through federal arrangements of some kind.[14] Furthermore, all democracies contain larger or smaller groups of citizens whose mother-tongue is not the language of political communication. But it is nevertheless undeniable that there is a link between ease of linguistic communication and the formation and functioning of the kind of public space democracy requires. This is a space in which issues can be raised and discussed, in which different points of view can be compared and in which representatives can be called to account. The more discussion is expected to open minds to new perspectives and to modify entrenched prejudices, then the more demanding is the requirement of linguistic unity. This limits the public spaces within which deliberation can be carried out. It is striking that despite the steps towards integration taken by the European Union (EU), and despite the recent success of satellite television stations in attracting audiences for entertainment across national and linguistic frontiers, spaces of public debate in newspapers and radio and television news remain quite distinct, separated by national languages and the cultural traditions they carry. Dieter

Grimm observes that 'prospects for Europeanisation of the communication system are absolutely non-existent', and that, in consequence, 'for the foreseeable future there will be neither a European public nor a European political discourse', with linguistic barriers posing insurmountable barriers to effective democracy at the European level.[15]

Some Europhiles nevertheless look forward to the emergence within the EU of a democratic public space that will cross national frontiers and unite all citizens of Europe, while more ambitious democrats imagine a corresponding development at a global level.[16] The former project has a certain plausibility in the sense that it is possible to imagine the existence, perhaps a generation hence, of a substantial Euro-elite of highly educated, multilingual European citizens, sharing a European public space with its own media (probably in English[17]) through which Dutch and Italians, French and Germans, Spanish and Luxembourgers, perhaps Poles and Hungarians might engage in political debate on issues facing the Union as a whole. But the cost of that high-level democracy would be the practical exclusion from such debate of the less linguistically adept citizens of the EU (likely also to be the economically and socially deprived) for whom politics conducted in a foreign language could not be democratic. Such an outcome would not only fail to satisfy the inclusive ideals of deliberative democracy, but would be likely to lead in practice to populist mobilization of the grassroots against the elite, a mobilization that would certainly be national and that could reasonably claim to be democratic.[18]

If we compare the barriers to Europe-wide democracy with the high hopes of supporters of the new Scottish Parliament created in 1999, the link between democracy and nationalism seems strong. Lacking a national people and a national public, the EU suffers notoriously from a 'democratic deficit',[19] whereas a self-consciously national people like the Scots appear to be well placed not only to deliberate but to take collective action and govern themselves. But however persuasive national-democratic self-determination may seem, this is only one side of the story. Equally good reasons can be given for fearing that nationalism is not the natural ally of democracy but its most dangerous enemy. At a later stage in the argument we will consider the plausibility of attempts to distinguish between 'good' and 'bad' versions of nationalism, but for the present let us look at the case for the prosecution.

Them versus us: nationalism as a hindrance to democracy

From the aftermath of the First World War to contemporary troubles in the Balkans, twentieth-century experience has given democrats ample grounds to fear nationalism. Autocratic leaders from Mussolini to Milo-sevic have built their power on the mobilization of nationalist passions, playing the nationalist card to legitimize repression, conquest or ethnic cleansing. While none of the established western democracies with which this book is chiefly concerned seems likely at present to succumb to nationalist dictatorship, it is worth considering the reasons why nation-alism is so often associated with forms of violence that threaten liberal democracy. We need not credit lurid representations of national conflicts as volcanic upsurges of atavistic passions. But whatever the outcome of academic debates on the nature, history and authenticity of 'nations',[20] there are good reasons for democrats to fear nationalist politics. The modern world is one in which (to quote Rogers Brubaker) 'nationhood is pervasively institutionalized in the practice of states and the workings of the state system. It is a world in which nation is widely, if unevenly, available and resonant *as a category of social vision and division.*'[21] Nationhood is associated, in other words, with a phenomenon that is politically fundamental, psychologically touchy and historically associ-ated with violence – the phenomenon of boundaries. Boundaries in the physical sense – the frontiers of states – have rarely been changed with-out war and have often been a *casus belli*. Boundaries in the socio-psychological sense, distinguishing 'us' from 'them', in-group from out-group, regularly mark social faultlines along which hostility and vio-lence erupt. Democrats may have reason to fear nationalist mobilization, not because there is something peculiarly atavistic or irrational about national loyalties in themselves, but because such mobilization cannot help raising questions about boundaries of both kinds. Even in the settled, democratic West, few states have frontiers that are entirely unquestioned, while no society lacks tensions between in-groups and out-groups. Given time and decent obscurity, boundary issues of both kinds can become safely calloused over. The trouble with nationalist mobilization is that its constant rubbing on the sore spots can cause inflammation that strains or subverts democratic politics.

Frontiers of the state and of the nation

This is not to say that any nationalist campaign to change the frontiers of a democratic state must necessarily pose a threat to democracy. Such a change must always be a matter of serious constitutional significance; furthermore, where the threat of secession is constantly present, demo-cratic politics may be disrupted or even destabilized by its use as a lever to secure special favours for one region.[22] But where established western democracies are concerned, the dangers should not be exaggerated,[23] for national secession may, in favourable circumstances, be almost as manageable as political issues that raise less fundamental questions. If the recent restoration of the Scottish Parliament should boost support for the Scottish National Party to the point of success in a referendum on secession, there would be difficult negotiations with the UK government on matters such as control of North Sea oil and gas, perhaps a subsecession by the islanders of Orkney and Shetland, undoubtedly some ill-feeling on all sides, but hardly a threat to democratic politics. Those who support a general right to national self-determination point to cases like this and argue (like their predecessors in 1919) that rectifying frontiers to give each nation its own state spreads democracy.

Unfortunately, experience has repeatedly demonstrated the drawbacks of that general principle. Nations claiming independence rarely come neatly packaged in territory that is indisputably theirs and can easily be split off from just one host state. Areas of nationalist conflict are often areas of mixed populations, ambiguous and disputed identities and rival historic claims to the same territory. In such areas, national mobilization can pose very serious challenges to democratic politics. In fact, the very considerations that can in the right circumstances make the nation such a valuable ally for democracy also make it a dangerous enemy. The ideal of 'self-determination' as national democracy, so helpful where nation and state coincide, becomes subversive in situations like Northern Ireland, where it can be appealed to by both sides in a nationalist conflict, conferring legitimacy on radically opposed claims to territory. Loyalty to the nation is usually taken to justify the use of violence to defend the nation's frontiers; but where a rival nationalist claim disputes those frontiers, the same justification is available to others (such as the Irish Republican Army in its struggle to unite Ireland). Furthermore, because the politics of nationalism concerns frontiers, it is particularly liable to break down the conventional barriers between domestic politics (where violence is not legitimate) and international politics (where it may be justified or necessary).

Introduced into domestic politics, this legitimized violence not only sharpens and embitters boundaries between 'them' and 'us', but exercises a powerful attraction for elements in society marginalized by the general pacification that democratic states have achieved within wide areas of the modern world.[24] This is in itself subversive of democratic politics, and it has knock-on effects on the conduct of democratic government. Nationally legitimized terrorism can make it difficult or impossible for the existing state to govern its territory in accordance with ordinary democratic practices. British imposition of direct rule in Northern Ireland and the long history of the Prevention of Terrorism Act authorizing summary methods illustrate the corrosive effect that such a situation can have even in a well-established liberal democracy such as the United Kingdom.

Cases like this remind us how much a democracy needs agreed frontiers within which its procedures can operate. Popular election can confer authority only if there is general agreement on the boundaries of the relevant constituency – on where 'the people' start and stop, on who is included and who is excluded. And national sentiments and mobilization can cause trouble for democratic politics not only by inflaming disputes over physical frontiers, but also by making it harder to solve problems about the legal and psychological boundaries of 'the people'.

Insiders and outsiders

Because we live in an increasingly global market with more effective communications than ever before, migrants from all over the world are on the move, often towards western democratic countries. No doubt it is economic prosperity that draws most migrants, but part of the attraction is surely democracy itself: the alluring prospect of moving from a life subject to arbitrary and corrupt power-holders to a country in which rulers are accountable and even the ruled have rights. It is therefore a sad irony that western democracies react to the presence of large numbers of migrants in ways that are to a greater or lesser degree inconsistent with their own public political culture. Before the advent of modern democratic commitments to equal citizenship, flourishing civilizations included migrants with distinct cultures and identities, but gave them unequal political statuses within what William McNeill calls 'polyethnic hierarchies'.[25] Alongside that non-*democratic* solution from the past one could set the projected non-*national* solution for the future favoured by some political theorists: the notion of a state that would be democratic but not national, presiding over individual citizens sharing no communal political identity.[26] But whatever the advantages and disadvantages of either of these models, the reality in present political circumstances is that the strongest democratic states are nation-states, belonging to a 'people' who form a particular national political community. The boundaries of that community, how they are defined and how easy it is for migrants to cross them cannot help but become political issues, affected not only by variations in the national traditions of host nations, but also by varying national consciousness among the migrants themselves. Issues of this kind have much more political salience in some places and times than in others (economic growth can, at least in the short term, ease intercommunal tensions) but there can be no doubting the potential here for strains on democratic politics and perhaps for large-scale violence.

The most obvious strain on democracy concerns the treatment of migrants by the democratic states to which they come. Quite apart from the closure of borders against desperate people and the branding of illegal immigrants as criminals, analysts point to the situation of permanent residents, sometimes of several generations' standing, who may have a legal right of residence but who are in some states excluded from democratic citizenship.[27] The presence of such a population, lacking the political rights of citizens because its members are outside the nation, is evidently at odds with some central democratic principles. Tensions of this sort can take different forms depending on different national traditions, for immigrant communities may be excluded from a nation imagined in an 'ethnic' way, as in Germany, or may tend increasingly to exclude themselves from a nation imagined in a different, 'civic' sort of way, as in France. It may be instructive to look briefly at these European cases.

Sorting nations into 'civic' and 'ethnic' varieties is one of the most common strategies pursued by those who attempt to distinguish between 'good' and 'bad' nationalisms. Drawn in different ways for different purposes, this distinction is of dubious coherence.[28] The sphere where it is often thought to be most applicable, however, concerns criteria for the award of citizenship, a matter of crucial significance for migrants. When deciding who is to count initially as a full member of the nation, some traditions stress place of birth, others line of descent.[29] The classic European case of 'ethnic' nationality has been Germany, for reasons to do not only with *völkisch* traditions but also with a history of shifting frontiers and a reluctance to accept that Germany is a country of immigration. Since German law has traditionally conferred citizenship primarily by right of blood, Russian-speaking descendants of German families who moved east two hundred years ago have been accepted as citizens with full democratic rights, while German-speaking descendants of Turkish immigrants, born in Germany into a settled population, have had no such rights unless they chose to undergo an arduous process of naturalization. Moves to reform the law of citizenship in 1998 met predictable resistance from voters prepared to use their own democratic rights to defend their own conception of the nation.[30]

It is easy to suppose that this kind of dilemma of democratic exclusion arises only where the nation is understood in the wrong way, as an ethnic nation based on descent instead of a civic nation based on common citizenship of a territorially defined state. But French experience is instructive here, for questions of inclusion and exclusion are problematic, despite the existence since the Revolution of 1789 of a strong republican tradition of civic nationalism.[31] As recently articulated by Dominique Schnapper, nationhood in this sense is a political project, a matter of drawing individuals out of their communal and ethnic ties and raising them into a new kind of political existence as equal French citizens. This project, which demands a continuous process of integration starting in the school, is at one and the same time national and democratic, intended to forge a self-governing community of citizens.[32] Within contemporary politics, however, it is meeting resistance from opposite quarters, casting doubt on hopes that more 'civic' versions of nationhood can cope easily with the strains of global migration. Unlike earlier waves of immigrants, French Muslims are reluctant to merge their particularity in what Schnapper calls the universality of the nation,[33] seeing civic nationalism as itself a form of oppression. Meanwhile, a strong groundswell of popular opinion, long articulated through the Front National, defends what it sees as its own nation against outsiders, and the mass of the people against a too-cosmopolitan elite.

The dilemmas of immigration underline the complexity of the relations between nationalism and democracy, for it is the presence of the latter as well as the former that makes such situations hard to deal with. Campaigners for the rights of immigrants are inclined to assume that the blame for these tensions lies with nationalism, which is inherently exclusionary and therefore incompatible with democracy. But this is too simple an analysis. It is precisely because states such as France, Germany and the USA *are* democracies that questions of immigration are difficult to deal with. Democratic politicians need to fight elections, and populist movements are in their own way democratic phenomena, articulating genuine grassroots opinions and grievances against the political elite and seeking to make the latter accountable to the mass of the people. We need to recognize, in other words, that democratic politics can itself make nationalist tensions more intractable, or even call them into being. In the second half of this chapter, therefore, let us consider the relationship between democracy and nationalism from the other end, reversing the emphasis and starting this time from democracy.

Democracy as a Hindrance and a Help in Coping with Nationalist Conflict

Democracy as a hindrance: waking sleeping dogs

Sarajevo, symbol of Balkan conflict in the 1990s, was once a mosaic of ethnic and religious communities living as relatively harmonious neighbours under imperial rule. Within the empires that ruled so much of the world until recently, similar patterns of coexistence were common, whereas the breakdown of empires and the move to more democratic politics have been associated with the outbreak of communal tensions, with aggressive nationalism and with what Brubaker calls 'the unmixing of peoples'.[34]

What is the connection between moves towards democracy and towards national hostilities? One explanation (which has the advantage of vivid imagery) is that where a population is ethnically mixed, only a strong hand can keep the lid on the simmering cauldron of ancient hatreds. Looking at the rivalries between Germans, Slavs, Hungarians and Jews in the later Habsburg Empire, or the long-standing grievances (for example) between Armenians and Azerbaijanis in the former Soviet Union, one might certainly have predicted a greater or lesser degree of conflict when authoritarian rule disappeared. Even where such communal divisions have been the deliberate or inadvertent result of imperial policies, such rulers may be best placed to keep them in check, for they have methods of preventing nationalist mobilization and suppressing armed militias that are less easily available to governments with democratic pretensions.

But although in some circumstances democratization may aggravate already existing tensions simply by lifting the lid, democracy also has a closer and more disturbing link with militant nationalism. The advent of more democratic politics may actually encourage such conflicts, by providing a range of political incentives for nationalist mobilization. Within a multinational state, a party contesting elections may find that its most effective strategy is to target a particular section of the population and articulate their grievances. Where this strategy works, the party is likely to reward its ethnic supporters with the spoils of office, thereby exacerbating the grievances of rival groups. Moreover, if democracy implies that the state belongs to the people, to 'us', this inescapably raises questions about who 'we' are and creates the expectation that 'we' will not be ruled by 'them'. Typically, even after disruptive border changes and 'ethnic unmixing', these newly politicized identities do not fit neatly within frontiers, offering opportunities to politicians on all sides to mobilize newly defined discontents.[35]

These opportunities for mobilization are crucial. Whereas traditional autocracies seek to keep their people quiet, and more modern dictatorships mobilize their populations in a rigidly controlled way, democratic politics encourages mobilization of a more open and unpredictable kind, as political entrepreneurs seek out promising lines of cleavage and grievances that might be inflamed to generate bases for power. This does not necessarily produce full-scale nationalist politics, for institutions help to determine what sort of cleavages do become mobilized. A federal state may satisfy some nationalist demands (though it can also provide a base for secession); national confrontation may also be deflected by the electoral system[36] and the historic establishment of a particular system of parties.[37] But there are plenty of cases (including Northern Ireland) to make the point that democratic politics offers incentives to mobilize nationalist constituencies and thereby to conjure up or exacerbate nationalist grievances. Efforts by leaders of mainstream parties to ignore or marginalize such concerns may work up to a point. If the electoral system is responsive to grassroots pressures, however, elite collusion itself offers populist politicians an incentive to articulate popular grievances and mobilize the grassroots against the establishment.

In recent years the politics of immigration has been particularly liable to this treatment, and a familiar dialectic may be seen at work within many western democracies. Under pressure from elite public opinion, leaders of mainstream parties have tried to play down nationalist concerns and to promote a more inclusive conception of democratic citizenship than many of their electorate would support. The resulting gap between politicians and people has not only encouraged the emergence of populist politicians such as Jean-Marie Le Pen in France, Jörg Haider in Austria and Pauline Hanson in Australia, but has allowed them to argue that genuine popular concerns were being ignored. Electoral support for such views has in turn tended to push the mainstream politicians further towards nationalist policies on immigration, the treatment of asylum-seekers and the award of citizenship. This process is certainly democratic in the sense that politicians are being made accountable and forced to respond to their voters' concerns. Nonetheless, it is at odds with liberal democracy in two senses: in its arbitrary treatment of those excluded, and in deepening dangerous cleavages within the electorate by exacerbating tensions between immigrant communities and the rest of the population.

The paradox is that a political system that is democratic in the sense of being accountable to its citizens may find it hard *for that very reason* to deal with nationalist issues. For example, the long intractability of the

Northern Irish problem bears witness not only to the bitterness of the conflict between the majority population of Ulster Protestants of Scottish descent, represented by the Unionists (who want to remain within the UK) and the Catholic 'Nationalist' minority (who have historically favoured union with the Irish Republic). Crucially, accommodation in Northern Ireland has been hindered by the real accountability of leaders to their followers, particularly on the Unionist side. Where a political culture is not deferential, where many at the grassroots are active citizens prepared to act on their own account rather than falling in line behind their leaders, the scope for achieving democratic compromises of nationalist conflicts is greatly reduced because leaders prepared to make such compromises are in danger of being outflanked by hardliners able to mobilize popular opinion.[38] For this reason, the Belfast 1998 Good Friday Agreement, produced by intensive negotiation at elite level, would have been entirely worthless without its accompanying legitimization by popular referendums north and south of the border and within Protestant and Catholic communities.[39] At the time of writing, the successful implementation of that Agreement is far from certain, since there has been no progress in 'decommissioning' the IRA's weapons, and support for the Agreement among Unionists is declining. In the long run it may prove to have been only a respite from full-scale violence rather than the rebirth of Ulster as a 'normal' democratic polity. Nevertheless, it offers an instructive illustration of the *resources* available to democratic politics as well as of democracy's vulnerability to nationalist issues. Let us therefore turn to this somewhat more encouraging side of the matter.

Democracy as a help: talks about talks about talks ...

Only a few weeks before the Good Friday Agreement in Northern Ireland, pessimism about the possibility of any foreseeable resolution for this most intractable of conflicts was being expressed by sober observers as well as professional doom-mongers.[40] Whatever happens in the future, the sheer unpredictability of the events of 1998 not only reminds us of Hannah Arendt's observation that politics is the arena within which (for good and ill) 'miracles' can occur,[41] but should also warn us against convenient simplifications in talking about democracy and nationalism.

The diverse faces of democracy

The features of democracy's best-known face are familiar: popular sovereignty, majority decision, accountability to the electorate. Although theoretical analysis has repeatedly called them into question, these features are indispensable for democratic legitimacy. But democracy has other aspects, less immediately recognizable but equally important. In particular, it denotes a kind of political practice: a manner of conducting politics that plays down 'will' and 'decision', even the will and decision of 'the people', and concentrates instead on *talk*: on negotiation, compromise, accommodation between antagonists.[42]

Democracy identified as 'talking' sounds like the 'deliberative democracy' we encountered earlier. It is important to stress, therefore, that (despite some scope for overlap) these are in principle as distant from one another as they are from the populist democracy of will and decision. Both reject coercion in favour of talking, but their differences are crucial and well illustrated by the 'peace process' in Northern Ireland. Where the one is essentially intellectual, concerned with the meeting of minds, the other is essentially practical, aimed at constructing a document that antagonists can sign. For theorists of deliberative democracy, the implicit model is the (idealized) academic seminar in which participants explore an issue in depth and open their minds to hidden assumptions and to unfamiliar viewpoints. The aim is that the process of deliberation will change the minds of those who take part, allowing them to reach a rational consensus.[43] For this to happen, the greatest possible clarity and transparency of communication is required. But democracy as negotiation is not like that at all. Instead of aiming at a rational consensus achieved by changing minds, it aims to change behaviour by reaching a practical accommodation or modus vivendi – at the extreme, as in Northern Ireland, to substitute a democratic politics of non-violent struggle for the undemocratic politics of the gun and the bomb.

It is characteristic of this kind of democratic talking to avoid the directness beloved of discursive democrats, which would in most cases lead to a walk-out at the first meeting. The issues discussed need to be carefully limited in order to seek areas of possible accommodation; negotiations may be best conducted through mediators, and the talking is a matter of bargaining rather than of being convinced by the force of reason. The sharpest contrast with deliberative democracy lies in the crucial role played by ambiguity – finding a form of words that avoids bringing remaining disagreements into the open. Whereas deliberative democrats aim to clear away confusion and communicate totally, democratic negotiation relies heavily on leaving things unsaid, on finding formulae that all sides can sign up to because they avoid clear positions on particularly sensitive issues.[44] For democracy-as-negotiation is above all a practical business. It is true that certain theoretical commitments are involved in embarking on this practice, and these are what make such negotiation democratic: commitments (at any rate for the duration of the process) to non-violent methods, to acceptance that other interests and points of view have a right to be represented in the negotiations. But acknowledgement of these principles is implicit; explicitly, democracy as negotiation is concerned with achieving acceptance of a set of practical arrangements. The characteristic complexity of such arrangements is itself in part a device to avoid too much clarity, so that a useful cloud of technicalities obscures awkward questions about which party to the negotiations has given ground.[45]

The Belfast Good Friday Agreement was indebted to a tradition of democratic practice and theory that has become increasingly influential in recent decades, and that is often considered to be particularly well fitted to cope with nationalist conflicts. The theory of 'consociational democracy', first elaborated by Arendt Lijphart, who drew on practical examples from a number of (mainly European) countries including the Netherlands, Belgium, Switzerland and Austria, argues that in the many cases where states are split by severe communal divisions, the simple model of democracy as popular sovereignty and majority decision (or indeed the deliberative model of rational consensus) is inappropriate, and that democracy can be achieved and maintained only by means of elaborate devices for power-sharing that institutionalize a politics of accommodation between the elites of the rival groups.[46]

Apart from the difficulty of setting up such arrangements in the first place, a weakness of this kind of democracy is that once it has become established it can provoke a democratic backlash of a more populist kind. The compromises necessary for accommodation may come to be seen as lack of accountability to the electorate, particularly where the same parties share power in a perpetual coalition. Gratitude for the achievement of social peace may give way to suspicion of a system that encourages elite collusion in corruption, and populist politics may flourish in the gap left by absence of an official opposition. In other words, even if political leaders can pull off the difficult feat of establishing consociational democracy in a polity riven by nationalist conflict, this should not be regarded as a panacea.[47] Furthermore, explicit arrangements for power-sharing by representatives of rival national communities may be thought to perpetuate such communities by institutionalizing them. What it may possibly do, however, is to replace a situation in which democratic mobilization itself continually sharpens nationalist differences with one in which there is at least an opportunity for those sharp edges to become softened by time and peace. The crucial point is that where institutional means can be found to induce groups with potentially hostile identities to live together democratically rather than in conditions of violence and repression, shared democratic practices may gradually transform those groups and identities themselves.

More ice than rock: the mutability of nationalism

Talk to a nationalist and he will tell you that he can trace his nation's collective existence and character back into the mists of time. However sceptical of such an account historians or sociologists may be, contemporary politics has to deal with many situations in which national divisions do indeed appear to be solid, immovable features of the political landscape. Accepting that nations are 'imagined communities' does not imply either that they can be dismissed as figments of the imagination or that they can be reimagined to order. But however easy it may be to bruise oneself against the solidity of nations, national identity is more like ice than like rock: it can harden and remain frozen for long periods of time, but it can also become more fluid and may even vaporize. Rather than regarding nations as fixed and uniform entities, in other words, it is important to recognize their variability in space and in time. Some national identities are much more obdurately solid than others, but even the most rock-like have changed their shape in the past and may do so again in the future.[48] Recent developments in Northern Ireland have been eased by unexpected and striking changes in Southern Irish identity that have accompanied the new prosperity and confidence induced by EU membership. The Irish Republic's territorial claim to the whole island of Ireland (regardless of the wishes of the Ulster Unionists) had long been so central to Irish nationhood that no politician could have contemplated giving it up. And yet in their 1998 referendum the people of the Republic overwhelmingly endorsed its renunciation in the Agreement, bearing witness to the fact that (without in any way losing its strong identity) the nation had subtly changed its shape.

While national identities can soften and change shape in ways that favour democratic solutions to political problems, the opposite is unfortunately also the case. Nations that have led a fluid or cloudy existence can also condense and solidify in response to political mobilization, especially under the stress of conflict. Not for nothing are memories of victory or defeat at the heart of national traditions. Times of relative peace in Northern Ireland or Bosnia may allow some thawing around the edges in the form of intermarriage and the growth of links between communities. Times of crisis, violence and 'ethnic cleansing' reverse the process, bearing particularly hard upon those individuals who have ceased to identify themselves solely with one communal group.

Where democratic solutions to nationalist problems are concerned, this malleability makes possible both vicious and virtuous spirals. In the best case, intermingled national communites are induced to accept mutual accommodation in a shared democratic state, an experience which leads over time to thawing identities and greater support for democratic accommodation. In the worst case, conflict so hardens national boundaries and enmities that accommodation is impossible and democracy unsustainable, leading to an intransigent politics that pushes democracy even further away. This is an area in which the sheer contingency of politics is striking, and there are many contemporary trouble spots in which hindsight suggests that a series of particular actions and decisions that could easily have been otherwise led into one spiral or the other, uphill to a negotiated accommodation or downhill to war.

Conclusion

Where do these reflections leave us? Such conclusions as we can draw might perhaps be described as philosophically negative and politically positive, warning us against expecting too much theoretical clarity in this area, but giving some encouragement about the scope for political action. Where democracy is concerned, we need to recognize that its philosophically appealing face of deliberation is flanked by two further aspects that look in different directions, on one side towards the exercise of popular sovereignty and on the other towards negotiation and accommodation of differences, and, crucially, that these two faces supplement *and* challenge one another. Democracy as accommodation needs the legitimating power of popular sovereignty, but is for that very reason vulnerable to populist challenges, not least where national issues are concerned. Nationalism likewise resists attempts at clear definition, which obscure the elusive, fluid, variable character of the phenomena so classified.

Resistance to oversimplification seems particularly important where the relations between democracy and nationalism are concerned. For the boundary problems with which nationalist mobilization so often challenges democratic politics cannot be solved by seeking either to deny or to affirm nationalism. Projected solutions that rely on some democratic but non-national political future underestimate the importance of national identity as a precondition and prop for democratic states.[49] But theories that affirm national self-determination as a democratic right regularly underestimate both the complexities and the perils of the phenomena concerned.[50] Despite the aspiration of many current political theorists to lay down rules that can guide political practice, it may be that in this area the most helpful role for theory is not to provide a route map but to point to thickets of complexity and counsel prudence.

NOTES

I am indebted to April Carter, John Horton and Geoff Stokes for comments on a previous draft.

1   Quoted in R. Postgate (ed.), *Revolution from 1789 to 1906: Documents* (New York, Harper Torchbooks, 1962), p. 30.

2   B. Anderson, *Imagined Communities: Reflections on the Origins and Spread of Nationalism* (London, Verso, 1983).

3   Q. Skinner, *The Foundations of Modern Political Thought*, vol. I (Cambridge, Cambridge University Press, 1978), pp. 62–5.

4   For the claim that this happened first in England, see L. Greenfeld, *Nationalism: Five Roads to Modernity* (Cambridge, MA, Harvard University Press, 1992).

5   On this collective political identity and its significance for democracy, see M. Canovan, *Nationhood and Political Theory* (Cheltenham, Edward Elgar, 1996), chs 3 and 7.

6   J. S. Mill, *Considerations on Representative Government* (Chicago, IL, Henry Regnery, 1962), p. 309.

7   The communist collapse that made possible the establishment of new nation-states in Europe also provoked theoretical defences of self-determination. See, for example, A. Margalit and J. Raz, 'National self-determination', *The Journal of Philosophy* 87, 9 (1990): 439–61; N. MacCormick, 'Is nationalism philosophically credible?', in W. Twining (ed.), *Issues in Self-Determination* (Aberdeen, Aberdeen University Press, 1991), pp. 8–19; K. Nielson, 'Secession: The case of Quebec', *Journal of Applied Philosophy* 10 (1993): 29–43; D. Philpott, 'In defense of self-determination', *Ethics* 105 (1995): 352–85; A. De-Shalit, 'National self-determination: Political, not cultural', *Political Studies* 44 (1996): 906–20; M. Moore, 'On national self-determination', *Political Studies* 45 (1997): 900–13. Later events, notably civil war and 'ethnic cleansing' in the Balkans, are tending to give more recent treatments of the topic a more guarded and less optimistic tone, as in most of the papers collected in M. Moore (ed.), *National Self-Determination and Secession* (Oxford, Oxford University Press, 1998).

8   S. Benhabib, 'Deliberative rationality and models of democratic legitimacy', *Constellations* I (1994): 26–52; J. Cohen, 'Deliberation and democratic legitimacy', in A. Hamlin and P. Pettit (eds), *The Good Polity: Normative Analysis of the State* (Oxford, Basil Blackwell, 1989), pp. 17–34; B. Manin, 'On legitimacy and political delibera-

tion', *Political Theory* 15, 3 (1987): 338–68; J. S. Dryzek, *Discursive Democracy: Politics, Policy and Political Science* (Cambridge, Cambridge University Press, 1990). For critical reflections on this conception of democracy, see J. Elster (ed.), *Deliberative Democracy* (Cambridge, Cambridge University Press, 1998).

9 'To the discourse theory of democracy corresponds . . . the image of a decentered society'; see J. Habermas, 'Three normative models of democracy', *Constellations* I (1994): 1–10, p. 9.

10 David Miller in particular has argued that a democratic state is much more likely to be able to generate the political will necessary for redistributive social policies if that state is a nation in which *we* are taking care of *our* people; see *On Nationality* (Oxford, Oxford University Press, 1995), pp. 24, 83–5, 89.

11 On nationhood and the mobilization and storage of political power, see Canovan, *Nationhood and Political Theory*, pp. 72–4.

12 Cohen, 'Deliberation and democratic legitimacy', p. 26; italics in original.

13 J. Habermas, 'Further reflections on the public sphere', in C. Calhoun (ed.), *Habermas and the Public Sphere* (Cambridge, MA, MIT Press, 1992), p. 446.

14 Switzerland is the most successful example. In Canada and Belgium, strains between the different language communities absorb much of the political system's time and energy.

15 D. Grimm, 'Does Europe need a constitution?', *European Law Journal* I (1995): 282–302, pp. 294–7.

16 D. Held, *Democracy and the Global Order: From the Modern State to Cosmopolitan Governance* (Cambridge, Polity, 1995), ch. 12.

17 In a comment on the essay by Grimm just cited, Jürgen Habermas sees the deliberate fostering of such a public sphere as an urgent task accompanying the building of a European federation, and brushes aside the linguistic problem on the grounds that English is already becoming 'a second first language'; see 'Comment on Grimm', *European Law Journal* I (1995): 303–7, p. 307.

18 Cf. M. Canovan, 'Trust the people! Populism and the two faces of democracy', *Political Studies* 47, 1 (1999): 2–16. The effort to make issues comprehensible in a language only partially familiar to most of the electorate would encourage further vulgarization of political debate, quite the opposite of what theorists of deliberative democracy have in mind.

19 Cf. J. Hayward (ed.), *The Crisis of Representation in Europe* (London, Frank Cass, 1995).

20 On the 'modernist' side of this continuing controversy see E. Gellner, *Nations and Nationalism* (Oxford, Blackwell, 1983); E. J. Hobsbawm, *Nations and Nationalism since 1780: Programme, Myth, Reality* (Cambridge, Cambridge University Press, 1990). Statements of the case for tracing national identities much further back in history

can be found in A. Smith, *The Ethnic Origins of Nations* (Oxford, Blackwell, 1986) and A. Hastings, *The Construction of Nationhood: Ethnicity, Religion and Nationalism* (Cambridge, Cambridge University Press, 1997).

21 R. Brubaker, *Nationalism Reframed: Nationhood and the National Question in the New Europe* (Cambridge, Cambridge University Press, 1996), p. 21; my italics.

22 A. Buchanan, 'Democracy and secession', in Moore, *National Self-Determination*, p. 21.

23 K. Neilsen, 'Liberal nationalism and secession', in Moore, *National Self-Determination*, p. 116.

24 In his encounters with the young warriors of nationalist militias in Ulster and in the Balkans, Michael Ignatieff came across 'lots of young men who loved the ruins, loved the destruction, loved the power that came from the barrels of their guns'. He reflects that '[t]he history of our civilisation is the history of the confiscation of the means of violence by the state. But it is an achievement which an irreducible core of young males has always resented'; see *Blood and Belonging: Journeys into the New Nationalism* (London, Vintage, 1994), p. 187.

25 W. H. McNeill, *Polyethnicity and National Unity in World History* (Toronto, University of Toronto Press, 1986).

26 B. Parekh, 'Politics of nationhood', in K. von Benda-Beckmann and M. Verkuyten (eds), *Nationalism, Ethnicity and Cultural Identity in Europe, Comparative Studies in Migration and Ethnic Relations I* (Utrecht, European Research Centre on Migration and Ethnic Relations, 1995), pp. 139–40. For discussion of this model, and of the difficulties of the idea of a non-national 'constitutional patriotism', see Canovan, *Nationhood and Political Theory*, ch. 8, and M. Canovan, 'Patriotism is not enough', *British Journal of Political Science* 30, 3 (2000): 413–32.

27 Tomas Hammar speaks of 'restoring democracy where it does not function because a permanently settled population of foreign citizens is disenfranchised'; see *Democracy and the Nation State: Aliens, Denizens and Citizens in a World of International Migration* (Aldershot, Avebury, 1990), p. 6.

28 For an account of the distinction, see A. Smith, *National Identity* (Harmondsworth, Penguin Books, 1991), pp. 9–13, though Smith stresses (p. 13) that 'every nationalism contains civic and ethnic elements in varying degrees and different forms'. Cf. B. Yack, 'The myth of the civic nation', and K. Nielsen, 'Cultural nationalism, neither ethnic nor civic', both in R. Beiner (ed.), *Theorizing Nationalism* (Albany, NY, State University of New York Press, 1999); R. Brubaker, 'Myths and misconceptions in the study of nationalism', in Moore, *National Self-Determination*, p. 258.

29 R. Brubaker, *Citizenship and Nationhood in France and Germany* (Cambridge, MA, Harvard University Press, 1992).

30 The government was forced to modify its proposals, though it did pass legislation in 1999 liberalizing the procedure for resident aliens to become citizens.

31 The experience of the USA, thought by many to be the archetypal 'civic' nation, raises different issues. For an analysis that cuts across the 'civic/ethnic' divide, see P. H. Schuck and R. M. Smith, *Citizenship without Consent: Illegal Aliens in the American Polity* (New Haven, Yale University Press, 1985).

32 D. Schnapper, *La Communauté des citoyens: Sur l'idée moderne de la nation* (Paris, Gallimard, 1994).

33 Schnapper, *La Communauté des citoyens*, pp. 49, 92.

34 Brubaker, *Nationalism Reframed*, p. 148.

35 On the mutually reinforcing triangular relationship between 'nationalizing states', 'national minorities' and their 'external national homelands', see Brubaker, *Nationalism Reframed*.

36 On the crucial importance of electoral systems in giving politicians incentives either to exacerbate or to damp down tensions, see D. L. Horowitz, *A Democratic South Africa? Constitutional Engineering in Divided Society* (Berkeley, University of California Press, 1991), pp. 163–203.

37 In British politics, for example, the relative weakness of nationalist mobilization in Scotland and Wales during the long heyday of Old Labour is quite striking.

38 Donald Horowitz's conclusion, based on extensive comparative study of divided societies, is that 'there is frequently an inverse relationship between intra-group democracy and intergroup democracy'; see *A Democratic South Africa?*, p. 120.

39 The Agreement attempted to end the violence by paramilitaries on both sides through a ceasefire and later decommissioning of weapons, to enable Ulster to move from direct rule by Westminster to a degree of self-government under a coalition government and to promote cooperation between the North and South of Ireland, keeping open long-term political options for the province.

40 e.g. 'Boiling point', *The Economist* (14 March 1998), p. 33.

41 H. Arendt, *The Human Condition* (Chicago, University of Chicago Press, 1958), p. 246.

42 Canovan, 'Trust the people!', pp. 9–11. Cf. B. Crick, *In Defence of Politics* (Harmondsworth, Penguin Books, 1969).

43 Cohen, 'Deliberation and democratic legitimacy', p. 23. Shane O'Neill, trying to apply Habermasian principles of democratic deliberation to the case of Northern Ireland, concludes that Unionists must 'engage in a self-critical process of reinterpreting their own identity' – something more likely to come about (if ever) in the wake of a political solution that removed the threat of IRA weapons, which O'Neill does not mention; see *Impartiality in Context: Grounding Justice in a Pluralist World* (Albany, State University of New York Press, 1997),

p. 189. Some theorists of deliberative democracy do extend it to include bargaining (see Mark Warren's chapter in this book) but the primary focus is upon reasoned debate.

44   The Belfast Good Friday Agreement was full of such diplomatic ambiguities, partly to save face on all sides, partly to postpone intractable issues such as decommissioning of weapons. The danger is that since the same document is interpreted differently by different participants, each can later accuse the other of failure to comply, as has indeed happened in Northern Ireland. But, crucially, ambiguities may buy time, allowing the hope that if the parties can begin working together in some areas, the practice of democratic coexistence will itself make it easier later on to tackle the problems that have been put on hold, and harder for the parties to return to open conflict.

45   In the case of the Good Friday Agreement, the elaborate battery of arrangements and institutions for power-sharing inside the province, for cross-border bodies and for contacts between the British and Irish governments blurs explosive issues not only of popular sovereignty and majority decision but of the nature and boundaries of the nation.

46   A. Lijphart, *Democracy in Plural Societies: A Comparative Exploration* (New Haven, Yale University Press, 1977).

47   Donald Horowitz, a critic of the consociational model for its reliance on 'enlightened leadership', advocates the use in divided societies of electoral arrangements (such as use of the Alternative Vote) that would give politicians clear electoral incentives to appeal for votes across communal divides; see *A Democratic South Africa?*, pp. 142, 160, 242.

48   The centuries-long link between militant Protestantism and first English then British national identity now survives only among the Unionists of Ulster. Greenfeld, *Nationalism*, pp. 53, 60–1, 76; L. Colley, *Britons: Forging the Nation 1707–1837* (New Haven, Yale University Press, 1992), p. 18.

49   Cf. Canovan, *Nationhood and Political Theory*, chs 3 and 8.

50   This point is made by many contributors to Margaret Moore's collection, *National Self-Determination*.

Part II

Theoretical Responses

7

Deliberative Democracy

Mark Warren

Democracy consists in two complementary ideals, one involving equal distribution of the power to make collective decisions, the other equal participation in collective judgement. The key power mechanism is voting, which is democratic when every individual affected by a collective decision has an equal and effective right to affect the outcome through their vote. Voting results in a decision. Voting by itself, however, provides no link between the decision and what each individual wants, either for himself or for the collectivity. So ideally, democratic institutions serve not only to distribute power in the form of votes, but also to secure the connection between the power to make decisions and equal participation in collective judgement. Thus, communication – argument, challenge, demonstration, symbolization and bargaining – is as central to democracy as voting. Through communicative processes opinions are cultivated, reasons developed and justifications proffered, so that in one way or another voting as an exercise of power also expresses an act of judgement. Most democrats consider deliberation, as one of many kinds of communication, to be the ideal way of making collective judgements. Deliberation induces individuals to give due consideration to their judgements, so that they know what they want, understand what others want, and can justify their judgements to others as well as to themselves.

Theories of deliberative democracy emphasize this ideal complementarity of deliberative judgement and power. Considered in this very general way, there is little new in theories of deliberative democracy. Both dimensions were eloquently emphasized in Pericles' funeral oration: as ordinary citizens, 'we are able to judge proposals even if we cannot originate them; instead of looking at discussion as a stumbling-block in the way of action, we think of it as an indispensable preliminary to any wise action at all'.[1] Elements of the notion of deliberative political judgement have reappeared in one way or another in most modern democratic theories.[2] Some theorists, like James Madison in *The Federalist*, went to considerable length to show how deliberative capacities can be designed into legislative bodies. Others, like John Stuart Mill, developed theories aimed at encouraging much broader participation in deliberative processes.

What distinguishes emerging theories of deliberative democracy from most of their predecessors is the view that democracy requires not only equality of votes, but also equal and effective opportunity to participate in processes of collective judgement. That is, deliberation about matters of common concern should not be restricted to political representatives, judges, media pundits, technocrats and other elites, but should infuse a society so structured that it underwrites ongoing processes of public opinion-formation and judgement.[3] Theories of deliberative democracy tend to be radically egalitarian in both dimensions.[4] Yesterday's theorists of political deliberation could conceive of these commitments only in small, homogeneous societies of the sort that enable an assembled citizenry. When confronted with the question of where deliberation might be located in large-scale societies, they could only conceive of a division of labour: the mass of citizenry would vote for representatives who would then deliberate. I shall not, then, count theorists as 'deliberative democrats' if they simply emphasize the deliberative functions of representative bodies. Indeed, theories that emphasize deliberations among political elites can even be anti-democratic, as in Edmund Burke's conception of 'virtual representation', as well as in the 1789 US Constitution, which insulated the Senate from direct election with the aim of assuring a higher quality of deliberation. In contrast, deliberative democrats emphasize the interaction between these institutionalized processes of deliberation and those that occur within society.

Nor are republican theories of democracy coextensive with theories of deliberative democracy, despite a shared emphasis on democratic participation, communication, as well as a shared view – contra many liberals – that politics properly and necessarily includes debate about moral matters. What distinguishes republican theories is that they are moral in their construction: they view deliberation as a way of integrating society through shared commitments to the common good.[5] Theories of deliberative democracy differ in at least three ways. First, deliberative theories of democracy place a priority on deliberative processes without supposing that the outcomes can or should be measured according to an ideal of the common good. Not only is theoretical prejudgement presumptuous, but it discredits legitimate compromises among irreconcilable visions of the common good. At the limit, identifying ideal politics with achieving the common good is exclusionary or repressive rather than democratic. Second, many republican accounts of democracy – Hannah Arendt's for example – represent a nostalgia for communities that are integrated by the normative force of deliberation alone. Theories of deliberative democracy, in contrast, take differentiated societies as their point of departure: today's societies are organized by positive law and markets as well as moral identities and other norms, a point to which I shall return. Third, not all goods are common in nature; political conflicts often involve goods that cannot and should not be enjoyed in common – material goods to be divided, intimacy and the like. In contrast to deliberative theories, republican theories typically lack any account of what would make bargains and compromises among non-common goods justifiable.

Over the last three decades liberal democratic societies have been beset by a combination of increasing expectations and exhausted institutional capacities. While the causes are complex, they have much to do with contemporary social developments that have tended to outstrip the conceptual resources of received democratic theories. These include the facts that today's societies are increasingly post-conventional in their culture; pluralized among lifestyle, religious and ethnic groups; differentiated between state, markets and civil society in their structure; subject to globalizing forces that reduce the significance of the state as a locus of democratic collective action; and increasingly complex in ways that tend to undermine the capacities of the state to plan.

The most complete theories of deliberative democracy – Habermas's for example – aim to address the democratic pathologies fomented by these developments, and to identify and deepen the democratic possibilities that have opened as a result. Deliberative democrats hold that democracy can be revived and expanded, piecemeal, by utilizing many of the political forms that already exist or have been found by experimentation such as constitutional procedures, associations, social movements, decentred party structures and public spheres. The aim is not revolutionary – indeed, many claim that the notion has lost its meaning since there is no longer a significant 'centre' to take over as a locus of revolutionary action and organization.[6] Rather, most deliberative democrats are radically reformist. For the most part, they view some form of market-based society as here to stay. They accept the welfare state protections and regulations as one important way, although not the only way, of stemming market excesses while harnessing their powers of economic organization. They value and see as essential the liberal legacy of rights – not so much rights of private property, but rather the rights that attach to individuals, such as rights of security, citizenship, due process, equal protection, political participation, speech and association, as well as rights to the measure of welfare necessary for other rights to be effective.[7] Importantly, deliberative democrats look to the democratic potentials of liberal constitutionalism, which establish political institutions that bind state power to communicative justification.[8] But equally importantly, deliberative democrats focus on non-state forms and venues of democracy that are becoming increasingly prominent as state-centred democratization runs up against limits imposed by market capitalism, scale and increasing complexity.[9]

The Social Theory of Deliberative Democracy

Before looking more closely at how deliberative democrats conceive the challenges and purposes of democracy, it is worth surveying the social theory within which it is embedded. Here I shall rely on Habermas, whose approach is distinguished by the well-developed social theory that supports his theory of deliberative democracy.[10] Modern societies, on Habermas's account, are differentiated according to three distinct media of social coordination: power, money and solidarity, each centred on the institutions of state, markets and civil society.

1. In modern societies, coercive *power* is mostly monopolized by the state; ideally, it is codified and legitimized through laws resulting from democratic processes. Social coordination organized through law is rule-based and bureaucratic in form.
2. *Money* is the medium of exchange institutionalized in markets, which function as quasi-automatic (non-planned, non-intentional) means of aggregating billions of individual decisions.
3. *Solidarity* is the term Habermas uses (following Parsons) to refer to directly social means of coordination – that is, coordination through social norms, traditions and linguistic communication.

Today's developed capitalist liberal democracies are 'steered' mostly by power and money. States develop the administrative routines, expertise and capacities to carry out large-scale projects, and markets coordinate vast numbers of producers and consumers, whose behaviour responds to the motivation and information carried by prices. Both modes of organization are 'systematic' in that they do not respond directly to, nor do they directly reflect, the intentions of the individuals or norms of groups whose actions are oriented towards them.

Two paradoxes of modern social organization

These systematic qualities provide modern societies with enormous capacities for collective action. But they do so at the cost of detaching high-level social coordination from normative means of social coordination. Thus, the political question of what *ought* we to do cannot be asked of markets (which lack any agency of the sort that could respond), nor, directly, of bureaucratized power (which, institutionalized in state routines, has its own organizational imperatives). In contrast, it is only in those forms of social organization where language-based communication is central that it is possible to put the political question, 'What ought we to do?'. As a matter of basic social theory, then, deliberation connects solidaristic means of social organization to collective self-rule.

From this perspective, one paradox of modern social organization is that its differentiated media dramatically increase capacities of collective action, while detaching these capacities from the collective self-rule inherent in democracy. For shorthand, we might say that Marx was the theorist of market detachment from collective self-rule (which he called 'the anarchy of social production') and Weber was the theorist of the detachment of bureaucratically organized power from collective self-rule (which he referred to as the 'iron cage of bureaucracy').

From this perspective, the problem for democrats is to figure out how to reconnect normatively chosen social futures to self-rule within modern societies. It will not do simply to imagine that all social tasks might be coordinated by deliberative means. Imagined as the sole means of getting things done, democracy – especially in its language-based, deliberative form – quickly runs up against the limits of time, scale and expertise. Scarcity of time, for example, can make deliberation prohibitively costly if delays amount to decisions to let causalities pile up, opportunities pass by and economic costs mount. Indeed, organizing society as a democratic association (which Marx imagined) would undermine the considerable advantages of differentiation, including capacities to respond to social needs in timely, effective and efficient ways.

The advantages of differentiation not only include the efficiencies of delegating billions of relatively trivial decisions to semi-automatic mechanisms like markets or bureaucratic routines. They also include the less well-understood effect of insulating solidarity from the burdens of economic and legal/bureaucratic functions. This effect is a key dimension of the modernization (or 'rationalization') of norms. Relieved of the direct economic and political functions, norms of social association such as love and friendship, ethical discourse, science, art and religion can now follow and develop their intrinsic rationales.[11] The importance of this point for democracy is that moral, ethical, and other normative resources can develop 'freely' – that is, according to their intrinsic logics – only when they are not closely integrated into markets and states, and so not overshadowed by the logics of money and power.

Such developments indicate a second irony of modern social organization: collective deliberation that is 'free' in the sense that it can follow the logic of normative commitments is now possible because these commitments are unburdened of any immediate economic and political functions. Norms can develop as motivational forces all their own. And yet these same enabling conditions mean that the normative resources embedded in solidarity may become relatively powerless when compared to the systematic 'steering' media, power and money. When states use their powers to control and even destroy the normative resources of social integration, they are authoritarian and even totalitarian. When markets are dominant, every aspect of life becomes an economic utility, which just as surely corrodes the normative integrity of social relations. In contrast, a defining feature of democratic institutions is that they enable collective judgements to shift from the forces of power and money to the forces of talk, discussion and persuasion – that is, the force of deliberation.

Democracy within the context of differentiation

How, then, is it possible to connect those spheres within which it is possible to ask 'ought' questions to capacities for collective action (thus realizing the substance of collective self-rule), while at the same time retaining the advantages of differentiated societies? Theoretically, the solution is to understand democracy as having two complementary functions in social coordination and organization.

First, and most ambitiously, democratic institutions should be structured so as to protect as well as respond to the communicative forces within society. The most important of these institutions are rights, including the rights that protect political participation, speech, association, privacy and welfare. While rights are often understood as empowering individuals against society, their important *democratic* effect is to assure forms of social organization based on norms, which in turn provide the social infrastructure of communicative forces. Under these conditions public spheres can emerge, enabling political issues to be deliberated, argued, symbolized and advocated. Ideally, the successive and provisional results of these public 'conversations' ought to guide and contain money- and power-based systems.

From an institutional perspective, the normative forces generated by publics can guide and influence these systems only if they are organized in ways sensitive to these influences. Cohen and Arato write of 'sensors' implanted within these systems.[12] Some of these sensors are already common in liberal democratic states: elected legislative bodies, public hearings and provisions for petition are well-known devices. But more innovative forms are also possible. Executive agencies, for example, increasingly use deliberative processes to bring together those affected by their policies – not so much because of a belief in deliberation, but because deliberation can enhance their capacities to develop and administer policies within highly politicized environments.

Designing sensors that can affect markets requires different strategies, since the structural characteristics of markets can often be altered only by high-level collective action. The traditional strategies are, at best, indirectly responsive to the normative influence of publics. These include regulation, tax incentives, providing alternative means of income through welfare provisions and altering labour markets by enabling union organization. But there are more direct means as well: states, unions, community activists and other agents can alter the composition of representation in firms so that firms attend to a broad range of stakeholder interests. States can use law to alter the internal constitution of firms – for example, by requiring firms to set up worker safety committees to monitor the use of labour. Unions can use pension funds to engage in 'socially responsible' investing. Consumers can organize boycotts, directly affecting the markets of products. And when workers purchase firms, then firms can become directly responsive to the externalities borne by their own worker-owners, such as occupational hazards and local environmental damages. Each strategy increases the chances that decisions will be forced, as it were, onto the terrain of deliberation.

The second broad point is that in modern societies it is important to view democracy as a response to *political conflict* and not to social organization more generally. In differentiated societies, political conflict often occurs at the boundaries of spheres – between markets and states, between systems that are insensitive to the harms they produce and those affected by the harms, and among sectors governed by distinctive ethics or purposes. Thus, in differentiated societies politics is pervasive, but not every social relation or decision is 'political' at any point in time. Indeed, most high-level collective decisions and actions will be organized

systematically, by markets and bureaucratic routines. And in the associative structures of civil society, most social interactions will be non-
conflictual, organized by shared norms and routine clarifications of
misunderstandings. Put in the perspective of the massive numbers of
decisions and actions that occur every day, only a relatively few are
'political' at any point in time.[13]

In order to locate democracy in complex and differentiated societies,
then, we shall need to see it as a good way of responding to *politics* (that
is, the domain of contested decisions) as well as the domain of *suppressed
politics* (that is, potential conflicts suppressed by power, cultural or economic organization).[14] From this perspective, democracy is a good way
to repair torn social fabrics and to create new social relations when the
old ones have failed. Democracy is all the more conceivable when we see
that it is not generally desirable as a means of social coordination, but
rather desirable as a response to conflict. Of course it is entirely appropriate to refer to a social organization – a family, a firm, an association
or a legislature – as 'democratically' organized when it has a flat hierarchy and responsive structure. But we do so as a way of calling attention
to the capacities of these kinds of organization to respond democratically to internal conflicts rather than to indicate the process through
which every decision is made.

Communicative power

These two points depend upon conceiving democracy as involved in generating its own distinctive kind of social adhesive – what Habermas terms
'communicative power'. Talcott Parsons, upon whom Habermas relies
in developing the notion, referred to this sense of power as 'influence'.
Influence is

> a generalized symbolic medium of societal interchange, in the same
> general class as money and power. It consists in capacity to bring about
> desired decisions on the part of other social units without directly
> offering them a valued *quid pro quo* as an inducement or threatening
> them with deleterious consequences.[15]

Influence is traceable, in Parsons's terms, to the 'consensual relations'
individuals share to a 'normative order'. But because politics involves
social relations in which goals are *not* understood to be shared, influence must be exercised explicitly – through communication. Accordingly,
democracy involves structuring political conflict so that it might be

settled through the 'force' of communicative influence rather than through the forces of money or coercive power.

The formula for generating influence under the constraints of politics is straightforward, but of crucial importance to the logic of deliberative democracy. Because all political issues occur within the contexts of power and conflict, democratic institutions should structure decision-making ways that block the impact of power and wealth on decision-making. By default, communicative influence is the only remaining resource – forcing, as it were, the parties to convince one another if they are to get their way. Thus, making room for influence requires close attention to the surrounding contexts of money and power, which must be constrained or equalized for influence to do its work. This is why voting, a power mechanism, is crucial to structuring deliberation: it helps to equalize power at the outset. Likewise, rights that secure freedoms of speech, association and conscience tend to equalize power. But it is equally important that economic vulnerabilities be limited. Obviously vote-buying should be barred. Less obviously, economic barriers to political participation should be mitigated through welfare rights and rights to education. More generally, when institutionalized limits on vulnerability can be devised, parties to a conflict will have only their influence to fall back upon. So, ideally, democratic institutions magnify the power of influence by dispersing and checking (coercive) power and the force of money.

Yet while the term 'influence' captures the kind of forcefulness inherent in solidarity, the term does not quite capture its specifically political modality. As defined by Parsons, influence draws on 'consensual relations to a normative order'. But in politics, there are at least three reasons why this normative background cannot be taken for granted. First, owing to differentiation, in modern societies 'normative orders' rarely coincide with units of political or economic organization. Received norms cannot, therefore, serve as the unquestioned ground out of which influence is generated. Second, political issues often involve normative disagreements, and emerge precisely because individuals inhabit different normative orders. Third, political issues often occur because of the insufficiency of normative resources in the face of power or money. For all of these reasons, democratic institutions must somehow create influence that does not depend upon these normative sources.

Influence can be created by convincing others that one's normative positions are right – or, just as often, that normative positions are overlapping, or that issues involve disputes over means rather than ends. Convincing others, however, requires explicit reasoning that is communicated to others, just because background assumptions are not shared.

So 'deliberation' – the give and take of reasons – is more specific than 'communication' (which is in turn more specific than 'influence'). Communication includes a host of other relations that may, in fact, work against deliberation, or have nothing to do with it. For example, threats and bribes may be communicated. Widely shared prejudices may be evoked and then combined with intimidation, effectively silencing disagreement. Ideological symbols may be manipulated, especially in mass situations that provide few opportunities for challenge. Even conceiving communication as 'discussion' is too imprecise: the logic of democratic institutions leads, or ought to lead, to influence generated through deliberative reasoning. Any conception of communication that is more general misses the kinds of resolution that are possible and desirable within political contexts, namely, those that explicitly articulate the reasons for agreement and compromise that are compelling to participants.[16]

But neither should deliberation be construed too narrowly – especially not as the classical, 'gentlemanly' give and take of arguments among people who respect one another, in spite of disagreements.[17] To be sure, the ideal political deliberation might very well look like this, exemplifying, in Seyla Benhabib's terms, commitments to the principles of universal moral respect and egalitarian reciprocity.[18] But we cannot *define* deliberation – as do some deliberative democrats – in terms of individuals' prior commitments to reasonableness, nor to their intentions to seek consensus, nor even to their respect of opponents.[19] Barring the epistemological and political problems of identifying such commitments, it would in effect depoliticize deliberation, limiting it to the easy kinds of politics that can take place once these commitments are secured.

There are at least two kinds of reason why deliberative democrats should avoid the temptation to define deliberation by referring to deliberative commitments. First, there is a psychological issue. Because political conflict arises precisely because commitments are not shared, politics often brings out the worst in people rather than the best. In politics, people want to win, often even if it means wilful misunderstanding of opponents, distorting their claims, questioning their motives and attacking their character.[20] These attributes of politics are pervasive, and a theory of deliberative democracy needs to show that reasoning can make headway even under these circumstances.

Second, although institutions that enable deliberative democracy ideally equalize background relations of power and money – at least sufficiently to bring people to the table – ideal conditions rarely obtain. In politics, getting to the table and getting others to listen is often three-quarters of the battle. But within contexts marked by inequalities and exclusions, demands for reasonable deliberation too often favour the powerful. Without ideal conditions, it is the powerful and economically secure who can afford to extend discussions indefinitely. Demands for 'reasonable discussions' are often used as weapons against those who are not at the table – those who must, in order to be heard, combine influence with disruptions of routines in the hope that the disruptions will become costly enough to produce a strategic situation sufficient to deliberation. Often these include power strategies combined with public justifications, as exemplified in strikes, demonstrations, theatre, symbolic mischief and civil disobedience. To be sure, when deliberative democracy is successfully institutionalized, it should involve respectful reasoning among equals. But if deliberation is *defined* in these terms, the most political of issues will be barred at the outset – as impervious to the influence of reasoning – and theories of deliberative democracy will turn out to be irrelevant to the tough issues.

If the political work of deliberation cannot be premised on good intentions, what can it be premised upon? We shall need to look at the dynamics of interest that drive parties towards deliberation within the context of political conflict. To find deliberative effects, we must assume that there are strategic or institutional background conditions (such as rights, votes or threats of disruption) that make it impossible for dominant parties to impose their wills without incurring costs they deem unacceptable. Assuming such a background, the dynamic is relatively straightforward: if parties want to influence others, their arguments must

- appeal to common or coinciding interests or norms;
- appear credible in terms of factual circumstances; and
- appear to be made sincerely, in good faith.

Arguments that appear to be narrowly partisan or sectarian, or lack credibility on factual matters, or seem insincere will simply lack influence, especially over time, as challenges expose the arguments. Once parties discover that they must at least *appear* to have common interests in view, they are often subsequently held to their arguments, even if initially made in bad faith. To fail to act on publicly displayed reasons is to squander one's future capacity for influence, whereas to follow through is to increase future capacities for influence – an effect to which Jon Elster appropriately refers as *'the civilizing force of hypocrisy'*.[21]

Deliberative influence depends upon the validity of reasons that are proffered, as assessed by participants, within a context that enables challenge. Validity, to follow Habermas, is an attribute of statements assessed according to whether they are factually true, normatively right and expressively sincere (or truthful).[22] Within deliberative contexts, statements have influence – that is, they motivate – when participants judge them as valid in these three dimensions. Borrowing from Habermas, their force is parasitic on the pragmatics of interacting with the three 'worlds' through which we reproduce ourselves:

- the world of empirical conditions about which factual statements are possible;
- the world of social rules about which normative statements are possible; and
- the inner world of feelings, desires and thoughts about which expressive statements are possible.

The motivational force of communication generally depends on the constant, simultaneous referencing of these three kinds of pragmatic relationship.

The occasions for deliberation, or discourse (in Habermas's somewhat more technical terms), develop among people who have cause to interact when the background presumptions necessary for interaction become questionable. From a pragmatic perspective, coordinating actions requires that individuals share interpretations of facts, norms and intentions. In a discursive interchange, individuals challenge the validity of interpretations (of fact, norm or intention), in this way making the interpretation into a topic. Deliberation can motivate when, owing to reasons offered in face of the challenge, a shared understanding is developed or restored. Ideally, the new understanding is resettled into the background understandings that make ongoing, routine communication possible.[23]

The seeking and gaining of understanding should not be confused (as it often is by critics of deliberative democracy) with seeking or gaining consensus. One can understand the reasons why an opponent holds a position, and even respect these reasons without agreeing with them. Neither should we underestimate the political work that understanding can achieve short of consensus, namely, clarification of interests, motivations and factual matters. These clarifications can in turn underwrite three kinds of possible (and democratically legitimate) outcome:

- agreement about procedures that allow for fair bargaining and compromise, as well as deliberation in search of consensus;
- recognition of others and respect for their arguments, in cases of intractable moral disagreement;

- consensus, when it turns out that clarifications expose or develop common or coinciding interests that had not been apparent.

These differing possible outcomes reflect the pluralism inherent in political conflicts, and the desirability of bargaining and compromise when interests are zero-sum or consensus cannot be reached. The (mistaken) view that deliberative democracy is a consensus-based model of politics in effect crowds the model into a preprocedural conception of politics. On the one hand, what allows for deliberation is precisely the differentiation of procedure and substantive consensus such that bargains and compromises can gain the assent of participants even when the outcomes produce winners and losers, or compromises that satisfy no one. On the other hand, what distinguishes deliberative democracy from the kind of liberalism that understands procedure as a neutral framework for peaceful negotiation of conflicts is the view that procedures themselves are influential – they have normatively motivating content – when they are based on reasons generated by deliberative means.[24] Reasons can include, for example, their fairness, their practicality (that is, that they enable decisions in a timely manner) and their efficiency (resource demands are not so onerous as to limit participation by affected parties). These motivational effects no doubt account for the stability of well-designed constitutional procedures.[25]

In short, democratic institutions generate communicative power by enabling multiple sites of discourse – within public spheres, associations, legislatures, juries, public hearings and town meetings, for example. When institutions allow communicative power to be 'converted' into state power, and to limit and guide the reach of markets, then deliberation is institutionalized.[26] When all persons affected have the chance to influence decisions (backed by rights to speak and organize, the power of the vote and petition, and protections against economic blackmail), then deliberation is democratically institutionalized.

This sketch should suggest why some common characterizations of deliberative democracy are misunderstandings or implausible interpretations. These include the views that:

- deliberative theories are naïve about power relations and strategic interactions in politics;
- theories of deliberative democracy seek to characterize all communication in politics as 'deliberation';
- individuals must discuss issues reasonably and respect their opponents as conditions for participating in deliberative processes;
- the purpose of deliberative democracy is to achieve consensus.

What Should Deliberative Democracy Accomplish?

Although the social theory that underwrites theories of deliberative democracy provides some general guidance for what we ought to expect of deliberative democracy, a rather large number of possibilities inhere in the theory. My aim is not to argue the merits of each purpose and function – impossible in any case within the confines of a chapter – but only to indicate the range of issues through which the theory is now being developed. I group these potential purposes and functions into three broad classes: political, ethical and epistemological.

Political functions

By the 'political functions' of deliberative democracy, I simply mean the effects it ought to have on underwriting, enabling and enhancing democratic governance, as distinct from the questions having to do with the ethical or epistemological validity of decisions.

Effects of communicative power on individuals Many of the political effects of deliberative democracy depend on its postulated impact on individuals. Deliberative democracy is often contrasted with theories (such as rational choice) that view democratic institutions as mechanisms for aggregating the preferences of individuals, rather than forming, altering, generating preferences.[27] Likewise, whereas some theories characterize politics as bargaining among interests (such as American pluralist and elite theories of democracy), deliberative democracy emphasizes decision-making through public reasoning (although bargaining can be legitimate if prior deliberation has clarified interests).[28] Deliberative democracy is distinct in focusing on the impact of deliberative experiences on individuals' preferences, opinions, ethical horizons, understanding, information and appreciation of the positions of others.[29] Under the right conditions, reasons should motivate individuals to alter, replace or justify existing preferences or received norms. When deliberative reasoning is public, it may create or reveal common interests. In short, when democratic institutions enable public deliberation, they should be able to generate changes in interests, preferences, opinions and judgements necessary to resolve political disputes, or to clarify and authenticate interests that prove to be conflicting.

But there has been little study of the impact of deliberative institutions on individuals. Certainly there is no theoretical reason to expect that every deliberative exchange will produce the kinds of generative effect that are good for democracy, or, even in those venues that do, that the whole range of democratic effects will be produced.[30] Yet it is enough to support the theory if

- the effects are sometimes produced;
- there are no other means through which these effects can be produced; and
- on balance the effects are good for democracy.

There is, I think, enough intuitive, anecdotal and impressionistic evidence to suggest that these expectations are worth close study.

Post-conventional legitimacy Over the last several decades, contemporary liberal democracies have been struggling with deficits of legitimacy. The deficits are, in part, structural: states respond to imperatives of markets, often overriding the guidance of democratic institutions.[31] But some of the deficits flow from the post-conventional qualities of contemporary political culture. In the not-so-recent past, political units could gain allegiance by evoking values based on nationalism, regionalism, patriotism, religious commandments, shared ethics and ethnicity. While politicians still often attempt to evoke these conventional sources of deference, they are no longer widely shared enough to provide broad legitimacy. Under these circumstances, legitimacy may become more 'rational' – not in Max Weber's sense, which refers rational legitimacy only to the outcomes of positive procedures, but in the sense that legitimacy is generated out of public deliberations which produce reasons with motivational force. Theories of deliberative democracy, in other words, suggest that the kind of legitimacy created by democratic political processes is more desirable than the kinds it replaces.[32]

Identity politics and moral conflict Closely following this point is one that is prominent in Habermas's approach, and which also serves as the basis for Amy Gutmann and Dennis Thompson's account of deliberative democracy. Democratic deliberation is the only ethically compelling means of addressing moral conflict.[33] Post-conventional societies include a pluralism of moral positions, closely attached to moral identities. These identities are in turn embedded within religions, secular moralities and lifestyles which, because they are identity-based, cannot be negotiated in the same way that, say, marginal tax rates are negotiable. Examples are legion, from the human rights implications of foreign policies, to social justice issues embedded in economic distribution, public recognition of sexual preferences, debates over abortion, the role of religion in public education, environmental ethics and the morality of the death penalty. Democratic theories that emphasize voting and bargaining (such as American pluralism and rational choice theory) are helpless to explain how moral conflicts might be contained or resolved, or why the losers in a moral struggle should abide by a majority decision. Republican theories that call for a common ethical source of citizenship fail, in the end, to recognize the reality of today's ethical pluralism – and, indeed, the legitimacy of this reality.[34]

Deliberation is the only resource that can carry the reasons for moral positions into public space. Because they are deeply rooted in identities, it is unlikely that public deliberation about moral reasons will change moral convictions. But deliberation can have two other generative effects important for negotiating moral conflict. First, it can often turn out that incommensurable moral positions have similar policy effects because different reasons produce the same policy conclusions.[35] The legitimacy of a policy may draw from many different moral sources. From a policy perspective, it does not much matter whether an environmental law regulating logging is backed by Christian environmental ethics, enlightened self-interest, New Age paganism, Native American respect for nature or aesthetic taste, as long as there is convergence on the decision. Second, deliberation can demonstrate to participants that positions are, in fact, held as a matter of conviction and not, say, opportunistically or hypocritically. Deliberation can lead to understanding short of agreement, and in this way generate recognition and even respect among those who do not share moral identities.[36] Recognition and respect make it less likely that one party will seek to impose their principles on another by non-discursive means – for example, by seeking laws that regulate religious activities or impose religious commandments. Deliberation can, in this way, reinforce liberty, while at the same time contributing to the integrity of moral identities.

Governability If deliberative democracy can increase capacities for resolving political conflicts by altering preferences, producing legitimacy and generating recognition and respect among those with different moral identities, then it should also enhance governability. Enhanced governability strengthens democracy because it means enhanced capacities for collective action.

Governability should also be strengthened by another aspect of deliberative democracy, namely, that to make deliberative experiences widely available, a deliberative democracy would make use of subsidiarity: that is, collective decisions and actions should be devolved to their lowest possible level of organization. In many cases, subsidiarity may require high-level state organization of lower-level political arenas. Gunther Teubner and Ulrich Beck, for example, have been interested in the many cases in which states push political problems into the domain of relevant actors, while structuring the terms under which the political issues are addressed.[37] Collective bargaining provides one example: the state levels the playing field by enabling workers to withhold their labour, which forces the issues into the realm of bargaining and deliberation. In such cases, governability is enhanced by devolving conflict while enhancing resolutions that are legitimate to the parties to the conflict. More generally, many deliberative democrats have become interested in *associative democracy*, which theorizes that democracy could be enhanced by devolving many political decisions into associational venues.[38]

Proceduralism Habermas characterizes deliberative democracy as a procedural theory based on constitutional law.[39] From the perspective of deliberative democracy, constitutional procedures should be structured in ways that shift decisions from money and power to deliberation, using law to constrain power and money, while equally distributing opportunities to make collective decisions through votes and persuasion. If the procedures enable communicative power by displacing and constraining other powers, then the outcomes should be more legitimate, more rational and more ethical than any other possible political arrangement.[40]

The proceduralism of deliberative democracy differs from the more familiar liberal accounts, which typically seek constraints on the substance of topics. Rawls, for example, stipulates that arguments and intentions be 'reasonable,' while Ackerman proposes that they be morally 'neutral'.[41] In contrast, the proceduralism of deliberative democracy constrains the *medium* rather than the *substance* of political decision-making by using law to block the forces of coercive power and money.

The proceduralism of deliberative democracy has two important consequences. First, by constraining medium rather than topic, the approach sidesteps the problem that there are no prepolitical means of deciding what should count as a 'reasonable' argument, nor any good way of empowering authorities to make such decisions. Second, the approach gets around the common objection to moral neutrality that the line of demarcation between what is and is not a moral or ethical topic is itself a political issue. To the contrary, the proceduralism of deliberative democracy opens political space to moral arguments by ensuring that their force is not trumped by money or coercive power.[42] This logic justifies the constraints that constitute formal decision-making institutions

– legislatures, public meetings and decision-making within states, associations and organizations, for example. Procedural constraints can also structure informal deliberative spaces: with the right rules and blocks, constitutional structures enable public spheres to emerge with their free-flowing and unconstrained deliberations. In neither case are there constraints on topics, but only on the modes of force participants may use to get their way.

Ethical functions

It should be clear from the discussion above that theories of deliberative democracy seek to provide space for the political deliberation of moral issues. But it is not itself a moral or ethical theory, but rather a *political* theory. As I have suggested, this feature distinguishes deliberative democracy from those republican theories that conceive a good society as one integrated on the basis of common moral principles or a common good.[43] In contrast, deliberative democracy is a theory of the procedures that, among other matters, allow moral conflicts to be argued.

There are at least four reasons why this distinction is crucial. First, democratic procedures provide the conditions under which decisions may be justified by means of public reasoning. Not all reasons for political decisions, however, are moral. They may also be pragmatic, focused on material conditions or time constraints, or on alternative means to reach goals. They may also involve justifiable compromises among interests and moral identities. In short, political justification is not coextensive with moral justification.[44] Second, borrowing from Habermas, in large-scale, pluralistic societies, legal rights, protections and procedures compensate for the 'functional weakness' of morality as a source of solidarity.[45] In today's societies, moral integration of the sort that depends on socialization and conscience can only have a narrow compass. Institutionalized rights, protections and procedures can 'stabilize behavioural expectations' among strangers, and thus allow behaviour consistent with moral duties to spread beyond face-to-face relations. Law broadens the functional equivalent of morality, however, only when it can be justified by deliberative processes that elucidate its moral purposes. Ideally, laws that are morally justifiable (those that protect basic rights, for example) reinforce what most would do anyway, motivated by moral reasons. In the absence of knowledge about the motivations of strangers, however, laws ensure that those acting on moral motivations are not disadvantaged by the few who do not. Third, in differentiated societies, moral integration of the whole of society is impossible in any case owing to the semi-autonomous forces of markets and legal rules. A morally integrated society comes at the cost of dedifferentiation, and the consequent loss of capacities of collective action. Finally, even when possible, morally integrated societies are inherently oppressive within the context of moral pluralism. Societies that seek to guarantee social order through moral agreement – often societies that model themselves as religious communities – raise the costs of moral disagreements, since disagreement immediately threatens social order. For this reason, morally integrated societies will tend to be intolerant of any moral discourse that seems to threaten orthodoxy.[46] In contrast, societies that distance political procedures from moral identities can, for this very reason, protect the vitality of moral attachments while enabling moral deliberation.

Nonetheless, at a high enough level of abstraction, principles of morality and principles of democracy have a homologous form. Habermas has provided the most comprehensive account of the relationship between moral theory and democratic theory, articulating the 'discourse principle' that is common to both morality and the laws governing democratic procedure: 'Just those action norms are valid to which all possibly affected persons could agree as participants in rational discourses.'[47] The principle applies to all political justifications, not just moral ones. As a principle of democracy, it can be elaborated as procedure: laws and policies 'may claim legitimacy that can meet with the assent . . . of all citizens in a discursive process of legislation that in turn has been legally constituted'.[48] The discourse principle does not determine what arguments are morally valid. But, clearly, it is possible to provide a moral account of the principle. In addition, it isolates the moral content in laws governing democratic procedures in the form of a side-constraint: we ought to treat humans as ends in themselves. Indeed, without this deontological element, principles of inclusion have no weight except as strategic necessities of governance.

This moral side-constraint is not, however, simply stipulative: it is always already implied within democratic practices. It may, of course, be idealized as an imagined utopia in which individuals are committed to equal respect and reciprocity. The principle of democracy operates at one remove from this idealization, however, expressing institutionalized rights that generate the language through which 'a community can understand itself as a voluntary association of free and equal consociates *under law*'.[49] The moral legitimacy of democracy comes, then, not directly from morality or moral identity, but from its procedurally secured openness to the full range of reasons, including moral reasons, that enter into collective decisions, in this way attesting to the equal moral status of participants.

Epistemological functions

The most famous objection to democracy, immortalized by Plato, is that democratic decisions are likely to be worse than decisions made by those better qualified by virtue of their knowledge.[50] Deliberative democrats hope to put to rest the longstanding war between democratic and expert judgement. Decisions resulting from properly constituted procedures have more validity – that is, they are likely to be truer or more right or more truthfully related to needs – than decisions made by experts acting alone. Deliberative democracy is, in other words, a more *rational* means of making political decisions than any other available method. This claim is epistemological in nature, and is distinct from any other political or ethical advantages deliberative democracy might have.

The claim depends, of course, on an account of how epistemic validity is established. What is at issue, on the Habermasian view that often underwrites these claims, is the process through which individuals become convinced that a statement is factually true, normatively right or expressively sincere, depending upon the topic. Validity is, in other words, given by the knowledge that a statement is authoritative in relation to its referent: facts, norms or subjective desires and experiences. So while a statement may be true (or right or truthful) in some onto-logical sense, epistemological questions have to do with how we can *know* it to be so. We gain such knowledge, or confidence in the validity of the statement, through processes of challenge, reason-giving and verification.

Here is the key point: the rational validity of a statement – its author-ity – cannot be separated from the processes that establish this author-ity in the absence of privileged or objective or independent knowledge. But we never have such knowledge: as suggested above, our confidence in a statement will depend on a consensus that is checked only by the pragmatic conditions of reproducing life. This is quite clear in the case of scientific statements: their validity is established when the results of experiment and observation withstand deliberative challenge within scientific communities. Not just any challenge counts: only those that conform to institutionalized processes that ensure, as it were, that the challenge is directed towards the truth of the statement itself. Scientific deliberations are institutionalized in a negative sense when they are shielded from the direct influence of money, power and criteria that have nothing to do with establishing facts, such as theological or political dogma. They are institutionalized in a positive sense through peer review, discussions among colleagues, scientific meetings and publications.

Under these conditions, when others recognize statements as true, they gain in epistemological authority and hence validity. It is important that validity does not come in any direct sense from the ontological 'objectivity' a statement might claim. There is nothing that could establish such objectivity outside of scrutiny of the statement by others. Indeed, scientists accept that innovative formulations are merely provisional; even those that withstand challenge are likely to be displaced by other accounts as research progresses. This does not, however, make a provisional formulation any less valid or rational, for it serves as a basis for a new consensus upon which scientists can develop further research.

Validity in the case of political issues is parallel in two important ways. First, validity is the product of procedure, suggesting that institutionalized deliberation can establish the epistemic validity of claims and assertions. Second, like science, politics works at the frontiers of validity, although in a different sense. Political issues emerge precisely when epistemic authority is questioned or has yet to be established. But in other ways politics is distinct from science. In politics, factual issues are intermingled with normative and expressive issues, so that the authority deriving from knowledge of facts is not as easily achieved within political contexts as within the relatively insulated institutions of science. This is why experts – scientists, economists and the like – do not have the kind of authority they may be able to take for granted in other contexts. In politics, they must argue and convince. They must enter into deliberations in order to educate, persuade – or be persuaded. Here, expertise has no prepolitical rights.

Disputes over norms and/or expressions of needs and desires are even more clearly dependent upon deliberation for valid resolutions. To know a norm is to understand the rules that constitute it. To be compelled by a norm's rightness is to understand the reasons that would justify the norm. Thus, when norms are contested (that is, received or conventional norms are not shared sufficiently for collective decisions), their authority must be established by the reasoning processes through which participants become convinced of their rightness.

In the case of assertions about needs, desires, preferences and experiences, the primary epistemological relationship is given by the privileged relationship individuals have to their own needs and experiences. In this case, the validity of assertions depends upon convincing others that, in fact, one is representing oneself as truthfully and sincerely as possible. The epistemological contribution to collective decisions is straightforward (and can be traced at least back to Aristotle): since collective decision-making is what *we* want, 'we' can only know what we want by having as much information about the desires, needs, preferences and experiences of individuals as possible – what some refer to as 'private information'.[51] Deliberation reveals the private information necessary to collective decisions.

Private information is also necessary to establish the validity of norms, which are often abstract principles, commands or rules of everyday conduct. Kant's categorical imperative, for example, requires that we imagine a community governed by a proposed maxim, which in turn requires that we know how the maxim would impact on different kinds of individual in different situations. To gain an answer that is valid *as a maxim* we have to ask of others what we may not be able to imagine. A *monological* application of the categorical imperative is likely to be wrong owing to a lack of private information. This is why Habermas, Arendt and others argue that such moral principles have meaning only within *dialogical* contexts.[52] If we propose a maxim under circumstances that enable deliberation, people will tell us what they believe the impact would be upon them. Here, expertise counts for little or nothing, except in the form of skilled facilitators and interpreters who are able to help people articulate their experiences and formulate their needs and positions.

Nonetheless, factual matters loom large in political judgements, and the question of epistemological authority here is somewhat different, namely, how can democratic judgement make use of expertise? Although there are no straightforward formulations, there are several ways democratic deliberation and expertise actually complement one another.

First, because deliberative democracy uses empowerments and protections to enhance deliberation, it also enhances flows of *reliable information*. Hierarchies increase the incentives for subordinate parties to use their information strategically – since this is often the only power they possess. Accordingly, those at the top of a hierarchy will tend to receive partial and distorted information, thus limiting their ability to make good decisions, even if so motivated. They also have incentives to use information to retain power over subordinates. In contrast, flat organizational structures encourage cooperative relations and thus enhance the flow of information. In this way, expertise is less distorted by the strategic use of information.

Second, under these conditions, deliberation helps to *aggregate information*, in this way overcoming problems of bounded rationality – that is, limits to rationality inherent in the fact that individual perspectives cannot encompass complex social problems.[53] Deliberation can serve to pool information, and pooled information should result in better decisions.

Third, the same conditions enhance the *devolution* of decisions, in ways that capture the everyday expertise of individuals who have expertise simply because they know their jobs. High-level planning is increasingly beset by the problem that in a complex environment no single set of rules, laws or policies can encompass all the consequences of their application. By democratizing decisions, deliberative democracy should also enhance social capacities to handle complexity.[54]

Fourth, deliberative democracy can enhance the authority of experts in ways that can lead to what might be called 'epistemic divisions of labour' that are compatible with democracy.[55] In complex societies, no one has the capacities to know all the facts about every collective decision that affects them. Inevitably, we depend upon experts. Ideally, we should also be able to trust experts, and we should be able to know when trust is warranted. Deliberative democracy can make it easier for individuals to determine when trust is warranted by making it more difficult for experts to hide behind their status, power or money.[56] Under these conditions, experts are left to establish their authority – as they should – on *epistemic* grounds, on the basis of which warranted trust in expertise can develop. When trust develops in this way, then epistemic divisions of labour are compatible with democracy.[57]

These points suggest that, when properly structured, deliberative democracy can enhance the validity of democratic judgements even with respect to factual matters. But of course proper structuring is everything. Different kinds of deliberative designs will enable or discourage different dimensions of epistemic validity. Highly adversarial designs that enhance incentives to use language strategically may be good for getting issues onto the table, but less good for exploring the various dimensions of the issue. Thus, no expert will want to think out loud about the risks of a new technology in an open public venue. She will want already to have a defendable position. But this will require the prior opportunity for a different kind and venue of deliberation – one in which experts can explore ideas without fear that their unguarded words will become others' strategic weapons. Likewise, expressive validity is likely to be less constrained in the voluntary associations in civil society than in more adversarial public venues. Consciousness-raising groups, for example, can allow for deeper explorations of needs, ideologies and preferences than can occur in less friendly environments. In addition, smaller groups will be more conducive to epistemic validity than larger groups, simply because numbers limit deliberative interactions. In each case, 'unconstrained deliberation' depends on restricted venues. But at the same time, such restricted venues are likely to be impoverished in terms of combining the several dimensions of epistemic validity necessary for political judgements. Small groups also make for insularity, and so their epistemic benefits are likely to be higher when they are embedded in larger, more pluralistic contexts. Because there are trade-offs, a deliberative democracy will need many different kinds of forum which combine to maximize these democratic effects.[58]

Conclusion

The theory of deliberative democracy is only now emerging as a credible alternative to received liberal, republican-communitarian, pluralist and elitist theories of democracy. It is not yet fully developed, nor do those who think of themselves as 'deliberative democrats' agree about its features. What distinguishes the theory and unites its proponents, however, is a common commitment to the notion that political decisions are better made through deliberation than money or power, as well as to the ideal that participation in deliberative judgements should be as equal and widespread as possible.

The simplicity of deliberative ideals stands in marked contrast to the many conditions and institutions that would encourage them. There are, of course, no sufficient conditions for democratic deliberation: because of the inherent unpredictability of political conflicts and the responses to them, there are no guarantees that the ideals of democratic deliberation will hold sway in any given decision. On the other hand, there are probably no necessary conditions either. Deliberation can be induced simply by situations in which parties to a conflict each have enough power so that none can unilaterally impose its will, and many different conditions can produce this effect. Nonetheless, as I have suggested, there are a number of conditions which, in aggregate, will tend to promote and extend deliberative democracy.

1. Social conditions include differentiation among the media of money, power and social norms (which unburdens deliberation and enables public spheres), as well as the development of post-statist politics (which expands the venues for democracy and thus the opportunities for political participation in large-scale, complex societies).
2. Cultural conditions include the development of post-conventional cultures, which tend to discourage cultural insularity, encourage non-dogmatic kinds of reasoning and self-reflection, reduce deferential and authoritarian attitudes and place a premium on self-government.

3. Economic conditions include political limits on, and justifications of, spheres in which market decisions are dominant; institutional arrangements that counter the blackmail effects of mobile capital (such as firms structured to be accountable to all stakeholders); and economic securities that counter market-induced economic inequalities that translate into political inequalities.

4. Political conditions include security against military threats and other sources of violence, both foreign and domestic; the rule of publicly justified law; rights that secure deliberative spheres including the rights of speech, conscience and association; mechanisms of voting and representation that are appropriate to the domain and scale of issues, to the composition of interests in the electoral unit, and which encourage deliberative coalition-building; mechanisms of opinion-formation that encourage deliberation (such as deliberative polling and dual voting on initiatives); and institutions that insert deliberative 'sensors' into institutions that are structured by power and money.

A few of these conditions are mostly realized in existing liberal democracies, while many other conditions are partially realized or exist only in experimental forms. Thus the theory of deliberative democracy is not a description of a utopia, but rather an articulation of radically democratic ideals already embedded in much of what we already know and do.

NOTES

1 Thucydides, *The Peloponnesian War*, II, 40.
2 Apparent exceptions are theories of rational choice or public choice that view democracy as a mechanism of aggregating individual preferences. See, e.g., W. H. Riker, *Liberalism Against Populism: A Confrontation Between the Theory of Democracy and the Theory of Social Choice* (San Francisco, Freeman, 1982), p. 5: 'Voting . . . is the central act of democracy.' Since these theories exclude communication by stipulation, they have little relevance to received democratic theory. For a critique of Riker, see G. Mackie, 'All men are liars: Is democracy meaningless?', in J. Elster (ed.), *Deliberative Democracy* (Cambridge, Cambridge University Press, 1998), pp. 69–96. Because rational choice accounts of democracy do not issue in democratic theories, I shall not consider them here.
3 Although there are differences in emphasis, this broad conception of deliberative democracy is shared by J. Habermas, *Between Facts and Norms: Contributions to a Discourse Theory of Law and Democracy*

(Cambridge, MA, MIT Press, 1996); A. Gutmann and D. Thompson, *Democracy and Disagreement* (Cambridge, MA, Harvard University Press, 1996); S. Benhabib, 'Toward a deliberative model of democratic legitimacy', in S. Benhabib (ed.), *Democracy and Difference: Contesting the Boundaries of the Political* (Princeton, Princeton University Press, 1996), pp. 67–94; J. Elster, 'Introduction', in Elster (ed.), *Deliberative Democracy*, pp. 1–18; J. Cohen, 'Procedure and substance in deliberative democracy', in Benhabib (ed.), *Democracy and Difference*, pp. 95–119; J. Cohen, 'Democracy and liberty', in Elster (ed.), *Deliberative Democracy*, pp. 185–231; J. Bohman, *Public Deliberation* (Cambridge, MA, MIT Press, 1996); John Dryzek, *Discursive Democracy: Politics, Policy and Political Science* (Cambridge, Cambridge University Press, 1990); B. Manin, 'On legitimacy and political deliberation', *Political Theory* 15, 3 (1987): 338–68; J. Cohen and A. Arato, *Civil Society and Political Theory* (Cambridge, MA, MIT Press, 1992); C. Offe, *Modernity and the State: East, West* (Cambridge, MA, MIT Press, 1996); J. Fishkin, *The Dialogue of Justice: Toward a Self-Reflective Society* (New Haven, Yale University Press, 1992); and I. M. Young, *Inclusion and Democracy* (Oxford, Oxford University Press, 2000). Elements of a deliberative conception of democracy inform Robert Dahl's defence of democratic judgement against 'guardianship' in *Democracy and Its Critics* (New Haven, Yale University Press, 1989), and *On Democracy* (New Haven, Yale University Press, 1998).

4   There are disagreements about scope. Joshua Cohen defines democratic political legitimacy in 'Democracy and liberty', p. 185, as the claim that 'authorization to exercise state power must arise from the *collective decisions* of the equal members of a society who are governed by that power', a definition that implicitly equates politics with the state, and thus circumscribes the domain of democracy to state-centred collective decisions. Contrast J. Dryzek, *Democracy in Capitalist Times: Ideals, Limits, and Struggles* (Oxford, Oxford University Press, 1996) and Young, *Inclusion and Democracy*, chs 5–7. My own view is that democracy is an appropriate response to any political conflict. For analysis, see M. E. Warren, 'What is political?', *Journal of Theoretical Politics* 11 (1999): 207–31.

5   M. Sandel, *Democracy's Discontent: America in Search of A Public Philosophy* (Cambridge, MA, Harvard University Press, 1996); R. N. Bellah, R. Madsen, W. M. Sullivan, A. Swidler and S. M. Tipton, *The Good Society* (New York, Alfred A. Knopf, 1991); C. Taylor et al., *Multiculturalism: Examining the Politics of Recognition* (Princeton, Princeton University Press, 1994). See Jürgen Habermas's distinctions between deliberative democracy and republican theories of democracy in *The Inclusion of the Other: Studies in Political Theory* (Cambridge, MA, MIT Press, 1998), ch. 9. Hannah Arendt's approach to democracy, although often classified as republican because of her

view that society ought to be constituted in its entirety through public deliberation, is nonetheless an important precursor of theories of deliberative democracy, owing to her emphasis on communication (as opposed to moral identity) as *the* distinctive and definitive force of politics. H. Arendt, *Between Past and Future: Eight Exercises in Political Thought* (New York, Viking, 1968).

6   Cf. Cohen and Arato, *Civil Society and Political Theory*, p. 72; Offe, *Modernity and the State*; U. Beck, *The Reinvention of Politics: Rethinking Modernity in the Global Social Order*, trans. M. Ritter (Cambridge, Polity Press, 1997).

7   Habermas, *Between Facts and Norms*, pp. 121–23; Cohen and Arato, *Civil Society and Political Theory*, pp. 439–55. Gutmann and Thompson, *Democracy and Disagreement*, chs 7–9.

8   This point was first developed by J. Habermas, *The Structural Transformation of the Public Sphere: An Inquiry into a Category of Bourgeois Society*, trans. T. Berger (Cambridge, MA, MIT Press, 1989 [1963]), but has become a staple. See, e.g., Gutmann and Thompson, *Democracy and Disagreement*, ch. 3.

9   Dryzek, *Democracy in Capitalist Times*; U. Preuss, *Constitutional Revolution: The Link Between Constitutionalism and Progress*, trans. Deborah Lucas Schneider (Atlantic Highlands, NJ, Humanities Press, 1995); Beck, *The Reinvention of Politics*; J. Cohen and J. Rogers, 'Secondary associations and democratic governance', in E. O. Wright (ed.), *Associations and Democracy* (New York, Verso, 1995), pp. 7–98; Young, *Inclusion and Democracy*.

10 The following account draws loosely on J. Habermas, *The Theory of Communicative Action*, vol. 2, trans. T. McCarthy (Boston, Beacon Press, 1987).

11 Habermas, *The Theory of Communicative Action*, vol. 2, part V.

12 Cohen and Arato, *Civil Society and Political Theory*, pp. 471–87; Habermas, *Between Facts and Norms*, pp. 359–87.

13 For further analysis, see Warren, 'What is political?'.

14 Warren, 'What is political?'. Cf. M. E. Warren, 'Deliberative democracy and authority', *American Political Science Review* 90 (1996): 46–60; M. E. Warren, 'Democratic theory and trust', in M. E. Warren (ed.), *Democracy and Trust* (Cambridge, Cambridge University Press, 1999).

15 T. Parsons, *The System of Modern Societies* (Englewood Cliffs, NJ, Prentice-Hall, 1971), p. 14.

16 These misunderstandings are exemplified in S. Stokes, 'Pathologies of deliberation,' pp. 123–39; A. Przeworski, 'Deliberation and ideological domination,' pp. 140–60; and in J. D. Fearon's otherwise excellent essay, 'Deliberation as discussion', pp. 44–68, all in Elster (ed.), *Deliberative Democracy*.

17 Cf. Young's excellent discussion in *Inclusion and Democracy*, pp. 36–51; N. Fraser, 'Rethinking the public sphere', in C. Calhoun (ed.),

Habermas and the Public Sphere (Cambridge, MA, MIT Press, 1992), pp. 109–42.

18 Benhabib, 'Toward a deliberative model of democracy legitimacy', p. 78.

19 Cf. J. Johnson, 'Arguing for deliberation: Some skeptical considerations', in Elster (ed.), *Deliberative Democracy*, pp. 161–84, pp. 173–4.

20 For a more extensive analysis, see M. E. Warren, 'What should we expect from more democracy? Radically democratic responses to politics', *Political Theory* 24, 2 (1996): 241–70.

21 J. Elster, 'Deliberation and constitution making', in J. Elster (ed.), *Deliberative Democracy*, pp. 97–122, p. 111.

22 I am borrowing, roughly, from Habermas, *The Theory of Communicative Action*, vol. 2.

23 These points allow us to make sense of what seems a rather puzzling claim in Habermas's conception of deliberative democracy, namely, that deliberation gains its force when people seek understanding (engaging in 'communicative action') as opposed to engaging in strategic action, in which individuals seek an instrumental influence over others. In political situations, strategic attitudes are, initially at least, dominant. But strategic influence tends to be unstable by itself, since it does not rest on motivations aligned by understanding. So within political situations that allow challenges by those subject to strategic actions, the dynamics of interest will cause strategic uses of language to bleed over into communicative action. That is, people do not need to be *motivated* to understand others in order to *seek* understanding. The reason is, simply, that seeking understanding and then abiding by the understandings established through deliberation is an effective and durable way of gaining influence. See, e.g., J. Habermas, *The Theory of Communicative Action*, vol. 1, trans. T. McCarthy (Boston, Beacon Press, 1984), pp. 286–94.

24 Demonstrating this point by looking at the ways law mediates between facts and norms is Habermas's central aim in *Between Facts and Norms*.

25 Habermas, *Between Facts and Norms*, pp. 151–68; Elster, 'Deliberation and constitution making'.

26 See especially Habermas, *Between Facts and Norms*, pp. 341–79.

27 Cf. ibid., pp. 289–95; J. Cohen, 'Democracy and liberty', pp. 185–6.

28 Cf. J. Elster, 'Introduction', p. 6; D. Gambetta, 'Claro! An essay on discursive machismo', in Elster (ed.), *Deliberative Democracy*, pp. 19–43, p. 20.

29 For an account and critique of these expectations within democratic theory more generally, see M. E. Warren, 'Democratic theory and self-transformation', *American Political Science Review* 86, 1 (1992): 8–23.

30 See ibid., and my analysis of the effects of different associational venues on individuals' democratic capacities and dispositions in M. E. Warren, *Democracy and Association* (Princeton, Princeton University Press, 2001).

31 Cf. Dryzek, *Democracy in Capitalist Times*; J. Habermas, *Legitimation Crisis*, trans. T. McCarthy (Boston, Beacon Press, 1975).

32 Fishkin, *The Dialogue of Justice*, pp. 123–9.

33 Cohen and Arato, *Civil Society and Political Theory*, ch. 8; Gutmann and Thompson, *Democracy and Disagreement*.

34 E.g., Sandel, *Democracy's Discontent*.

35 See Joshua Cohen's excellent account of the difference between moral and political consensus in 'Democracy and liberty', pp. 189–91.

36 Cf. Axel Honneth's important *The Struggle for Recognition: The Moral Grammar of Social Conflicts* (Cambridge, Polity, 1996).

37 G. Teubner, 'Substantive and reflexive elements in modern law', *Law and Society Review* 17, 2 (1983): 239–85; Beck, *The Reinvention of Politics*.

38 Offe, *Modernity and the State*, chs 1–2; Cohen and Rogers, 'Secondary associations and democratic governance'; Warren, *Democracy and Association*; Young, *Inclusion and Democracy*, pp. 188–95.

39 J. Habermas, 'Three normative models of democracy', in Benhabib (ed.), *Democracy and Difference*, pp. 21–30.

40 Such theorizing about the relation between deliberation and procedural constraints has reinvigorated constitutional studies. See, e.g., Preuss, *Constitutional Revolution*; Elster, 'Deliberation and constitution making'; C. R. Sunstein, *The Partial Constitution* (Cambridge, MA, Harvard University Press, 1993); and Habermas, *Between Facts and Norms*, especially ch. 4.

41 J. Rawls, *Political Liberalism* (New York, Columbia University Press, 1993); B. Ackerman, *Social Justice in the Liberal State* (New Haven, Yale University Press, 1980).

42 Cf. Habermas, *Between Facts and Norms*, p. 110.

43 Ibid., pp. 308–14.

44 Ibid., p. 108.

45 Ibid., p. 118.

46 S. N. Eisenstadt and L. Roniger, *Patrons, Clients, and Friends: Interpersonal Relations and the Structure of Trust in Society* (Cambridge, Cambridge University Press, 1984) suggest why relatively undifferentiated societies – North African Muslim societies, for example – also tend to be intolerant, lack civil liberties and do not afford spaces for public deliberation.

47 Habermas, *Between Facts and Norms*, p. 107.

48 Ibid., p. 110.

49 Ibid., p. 111.

50   This is the key issue in Robert Dahl's defence of democracy against 'guardianship' in *Democracy and Its Critics*.

51   Fearon, 'Deliberation as discussion', pp. 45–9.

52   J. Habermas, *Moral Consciousness and Communicative Action*, trans. C. Lenhardt and S. Weber Nicholsen (Cambridge, MA, MIT Press, 1990); H. Arendt, *Lectures on Kant's Political Philosophy* (Chicago, University of Chicago Press, 1982).

53   Fearon, 'Deliberation as discussion', pp. 49–52.

54   Dryzek, *Discursive Democracy*.

55   I make this case in 'Deliberative democracy and authority'.

56   Warren, 'Democratic theory and trust'.

57   Cf. J. Bohman, 'Democracy as inquiry, inquiry as democratic: Pragmatism, social science, and the cognitive division of labor', *American Journal of Political Science* 43, 2 (1999): 590–607.

58   The question of what kinds and mixes of venue are most conducive to deliberative democracy remains undertheorized. I provide some analysis, however, in *Democracy and Association*, chs 5–6. See also Elster, 'Deliberation and constitution making', and Habermas, *Between Facts and Norms*, ch. 8.

8

Civil Society and Democracy

Baogang He

The idea and practice of civil societies are important for theories of democracy and for democracy itself. Indeed, civil society is a necessary condition for democratization, for parliamentary democracy to be established and for the boundary question to be peacefully settled. This chapter has three key objectives. First, it aims to review briefly the diverse range of theories of civil society that have been put forward by various thinkers, discuss the recent revival of the notion of civil society and address various disputed interpretations of the concept. Second, the chapter aims to discuss the relationship between different models of democracy and civil society. Finally, it seeks to examine the theoretical question of how civil society can define the political boundary within which national democracy can take place.

The chapter adopts a conventional definition of civil society as de facto autonomous organizations that are independent of direct political control by the state. The notion of the national boundary problem refers to the difficulties associated with the boundaries of nation-states. It is particularly concerned with territorial disputes, such as secession or unification, all of which involve the modification of national boundaries. The boundary problem is also defined as a national identity problem, whereby certain sections of peoples, who do not identify with the existing nation-states in which they reside, seek instead their own political identity through the reconstruction of cultural and ethnic identities.

Concepts of Civil Society

Classical and contemporary meanings

The concept of civil society has diverse and complex meanings. The classical notion, according to Adam Ferguson, for example, refers to state institutions, civic law and commercial economy.[1] For Jean Bodin, the sixteenth-century French philosopher, '[t]he State [*république* or *res publica*] is the civil society that can exist on its own without associations and other bodies, but it cannot do so without the family'.[2] In the eyes of Hobbes civilized society was seen essentially as the political order and institution which established a sovereign power in order to prevent the war of all against all. As Hobbes said: 'The Multitude so united in one Person, is called a COMMON-WEALTH, in latine CIVITAS. This is the Generation of the great Leviathan.'[3] Similarly, Locke stated: 'Those who are united into one Body, and have a common establish'd Law and Judicature to appeal to, with Authority to decide Controversies between them, and punish Offenders, *are in Civil Society* one with another: but those who have no such common Appeal, I mean on Earth, are still in the state of Nature.'[4] However, for Locke, absolute monarchy 'is indeed *inconsistent with Civil Society*, and so can be no Form of Civil Government at all'.[5]

Adam Smith, on the other hand, referred to civil society as commercial economy and the division of labour. He pointed out: 'Nobody ever saw a dog make a fair and deliberate exchange of one bone for another with another dog.' By contrast, 'In civilized society [a person] stands at all times in need of the cooperation and assistance of great multitudes.'[6] Hegel conceptualized civil society as a source of inescapable tensions that embraced the sphere of the market and private interests.[7] He believed these tensions hindered moral development and this led him to synthesize his views on family, civil society and the state into a systematic moral theory.[8] Hegel's views on civil society provided a theoretical basis for Karl Marx, who stressed the means of production behind civil society and the dangers of capitalism,[9] emphasizing class conflict and the built-in crises of capitalism. His alternative was a political society that embodied all economic and political powers in a single institutional framework. But when communist states put Marx's theory into practice, civil society was atomized and ultimately destroyed.[10]

Today, there is a diversity of meanings attributed to the notion of civil society and, as a consequence, there are definitional difficulties associated with the concept. Nevertheless, there are a number of concrete contemporary interpretations of civil society that can be cited. Ernest Gellner, for example, holds a macro-view of civil society, seeing it as 'a society in which polity and economy are distinct, where polity is instrumental but can and does check extremes of individual interest, but where the state in turn is checked by institutions with an economic base; it relies on economic growth which, by requiring cognitive growth, makes ideological monopoly impossible.'[11] At a micro-level, by contrast, civil society is sometimes regarded as the sphere of non-governmental organizations (NGOs). Charles Taylor clarifies three senses of civil society. First, a *minimal* sense, according to which civil society exists where there are free associations, such as the family, church and club, which are not under the tutelage of state power. Second, a *stronger* sense, in which civil society is seen as existing where society as a whole is able to structure itself and coordinate its actions through associations, such as the green movement, which are free of state tutelage. According to the third sense, civil society denotes that ensemble of associations (e.g., interest and pressure groups) that can significantly determine the course of state policy.[12] Similarly, in Schmitter's view, an ideal type of civil society refers to a set of self-organized intermediary groups or organizations which: (1) are relatively independent of both the state and private units of production and reproduction (i.e., firms and families); (2) are capable of taking collective action in defence/promotion of the interests or passions of their members; (3) do not seek to replace either state agents or private (re)producers or accept responsibility for governing the polity as a whole; (4) do agree to act in 'a civil fashion' within pre-established rules.[13]

The revival of the idea of civil society

The failure of the communist system shows that attempts to abandon the liberal separation between state and civil society are dangerous. It is this failure that has done most to revive the notion of civil society, and this is especially so in Eastern Europe.[14] The fundamental theme underpinning the revival of civil society in Eastern Europe was 'the rejection of totalitarianism in favour of the idea that individuals and organizations ought to be free to act autonomously rather than be subject to all-pervasive state direction and control'.[15]

The normative distinction between the state and civil society is also being rediscovered in China. The communist hegemony over mainland China has radically reinforced the age-old tradition of unitary, noncompetitive politics, and created a highly centralized, highly dependent society.[16] In a bid to end the invidious and inhuman conflicts, which

Marx saw as characteristic of capitalist societies, the Chinese communist system attempted a deliberate connection between the state and civil society. It was on the grounds that the abolition of civil society would remove the divisions and conflicts which bedevil capitalist societies that the Chinese Communist Party (CCP) suppressed and destroyed civil society in the 1950s, a move that has led to the expansion and aggrandizement of the power of the state.

Indeed, it was the failure of communist practices that contributed most to the revived notion of civil society. Most Chinese critics of the CCP consider the distinction between the state and civil society to provide a useful perspective on economic and political reforms. It is this separation – the main feature of any democratic political order – that is seen as the most important step in the revival of civil society, and as a prerequisite to genuine political freedom and economic prosperity in China. The idea of civil society reflects the desire to curb the power of the overweening state through autonomous organizations.[17]

The concept of 'the reconstruction of civil society' has also been revived in the West. In France, for example, there are three justifications for this revival: the statist political culture of the French left; the expansion of the role of the centralized modern state; and the 'totalitarian' expansion of capitalism, which engulfs all spheres of social activity under the single dimension of economic activity. As Rosanvallon writes, the welfare state disorganizes all social networks, associations and solidarity, replacing them by state-administrative relations. He goes on to propose an alternative based on the concept of civil society: 'The reorientation to civil and political society relocates the locus of democratization from the state to society and understands the latter in terms of groups, associations, and public spaces primarily.'[18]

In the former West Germany, the welfare state is seen as a mechanism by which to repoliticize the economy and dissolve the sharp boundaries between state and society. To promote civil society against the welfare state in Germany, the analysis of new social movements emphasizes a model for politicizing civil society ('non-statist socialism' makes no concessions to economic privatization or to statist authoritarianism). Offe argues that civil society must be politicized and emancipate itself from the state. The revitalization of political society or a political version of civil society lies in the form of citizen initiatives and social movements.[19]

A common feature that unites these theories is the separation of the state from civil society. Also, most have an anti-state tendency. Nevertheless, there are substantial differences in their application, as theories of civil society serve different purposes in different environments. For instance, the theory of civil society held by the left in the West tends to relate to a critique of the welfare state. By contrast, the theory held in Eastern Europe and China is directed more towards an attack on totalitarian rather than welfare states. The ideological mobilization power of civil society discourse developed by the western democratic left, however, is much less influential than its counterpart in Eastern Europe and China. In Eastern Europe and East Asia, the discourse of civil society plays an important role in political mobilization and democratization. By comparison, civil society discourse in the West seems too weak to constitute a political force capable of reforming welfare states. This can largely be understood in an historical and political context: that is, the discourse of civil society has empowered various new social associations that have then challenged the totalitarian or authoritarian societies in Eastern Europe and East Asia. It is no wonder that White, Diamond and Schmitter have theorized the role played by civil society in the process of democratization.[20] They see it providing reservoirs of potential resistance to arbitrary or tyrannical actions by rulers, and contributing to a balanced opposition, thus setting limits on state power. It has also facilitated the development of democratic attributes such as mitigating the principal polarities of political conflicts, enforcing standards of public morality, improving the performance of democratic polities through the articulation, aggregation and representation of interests, and defining the rules of the political game along democratic lines, thereby strengthening the democratic state. Nevertheless, it is suggested that the discourse of civil society will decline in importance when democratization reaches a certain level. This is because social associations will then have become a *normal* part of a new democratic order, and various new problems associated with civil society will have arisen.

Disputes over the notion of civil society

Should markets be included in the notion of civil society? Classic liberals, such as Adam Smith and David Hume, tend to regard markets as crucial institutions of civil society, and contemporary liberals such as Diamond see productive and commercial associations and networks as part of civil society.[21] By contrast, the left emphasizes equality and democratic control over the market economy. Cohen and Arato, for example, stress the dangers of markets and separate them from civil society in their *tripartite* model, which incorporates civil society, the state and the economy.[22] It is also debatable whether multinational firms can be regarded as part of global civil society.

A further dispute concerns whether or not the notion of civil society contains normative elements or moral judgements about civility. Schmitter, for example, does not consider any rightwing nationalist NGO to be part of civil society.[23] There are others, however, who tend to de-emphasize the moral dimension of civil society and take civil society as a residual concept which includes all autonomous organizations independent of the state, even including organized crime.[24]

In the context of the individualist versus communitarian debate, individualists tend to see civil society as a series of civic associations through which individuals pursue their interests and happiness, agreeing to establish rules and laws to regulate their relations. Communitarians, by contrast, stress the basic ingredients of the concept of civil society: the sense of society's separation from the state, the widespread unity among disparate groups, paternal concern for society's members at risk, trust, mutuality, social connection and cooperation, social fabric and social capital.[25] A similar debate has taken place in China. Thus, while Chinese liberals fight against the legacy of Confucianism in introducing the individualist notion of civil society, Confucian communitarian scholars often dismiss individualist elements of civil society and tend to incorporate civic associations into the scope of state control.[26]

Despite such disputes, liberal and left scholars seem to agree that the normative distinction between civil society and the state is necessary. For the democratic left, the democratic socialist alternative has to confirm the fundamental liberal notion that the 'separation' of the state from civil society must be a central feature of any democratic political order. Nevertheless, they maintain a substantially different attitude towards the relationship between the state and civil society. While some scholars use the notion of civil society in their anti-state projects, others draw on the writings of Kant to stress mutual support and interdependence between the state and civil society.[27] Anthony Giddens, allegedly British Prime Minster Tony Blair's favourite intellectual, stresses the important role that governments can and must play in fostering and renewing civil society.[28] But Foucault sees civil society as the 'correlate of a political technology of government', and the 'distinction between civil society and the state is a form of "schematism" for the exercise of political power'.[29]

A sceptical view

A sceptic will offer a critical view of civil society and the organizations that comprise it, suggesting that many so-called civil associations, such as NGOs, lack grassroot support in their own society. For example, some members of NGOs in Cambodia and Eastern European countries speak fluent English and engage in various fund-raising activities. Consequently, they have developed closer links with foreign funding organizations than with their own grassroot supporters. Because they are financially dependent on these foreign organizations, the agendas and activities of NGOs are strongly influenced by their priorities.

A sceptic is likely to venture further, pointing out the illusory nature of civil society discourse.[30] Civil society, it could be suggested, has been interpreted in the West as a type of 'democratic rescue operation', or seen as something that will dictate a new dimension of democratic development in Eastern Europe and East Asia. However, such an idealized view may prove to be illusionary. A lesson from Eastern Europe is that civil society is not an all-purpose political panacea. As Bronislaw Geremek, one of the outstanding proponents of the civil society idea during the heyday of Solidarity and later Speaker of the Polish Parliament, correctly points out, earlier hopes that the struggle for civil society would yield support for a future democratic order have proved to be mere wishful thinking:

> In light of the dangers that have appeared on the horizon for Poland in particular and for Central and Eastern Europe in general, we must ask whether the idea of a civil society – however effective it was in helping to bring down communism – will turn out to be useless in the building of democracy.[31]

Theories of Democracy and Civil Society

Despite these difficulties, it is contended that civil society is a necessary condition for democracy. This can be confirmed with reference to the historical fact that no democracy has existed and developed without the institutions of civil society. Without civil society, communist collectivist 'democracy' is merely one-party dictatorship, as demonstrated by the experience of Eastern Europe and China. Moreover, the development of civil society nurtures a plurality of interest groups, which, when reaching a certain stage in their growth in the economic and other sectors, will in a variety of ways demand to express their interests in the political domain. These aspirations and activities are a powerful impetus towards the creation of democracy. In this sense, then, civil society lays down a solid social foundation for democracy.

Civil society, however, does not constitute a sufficient condition for democracy. This can be demonstrated by the fact that civil society can exist without democracy and that a civil society will not automatically lead to a democratic polity. More importantly, certain types of civil society may distort democratic order, and civil associations may contain many uncivil and undemocratic elements. Even the theory of civil society contains some anti-democratic elements, as, for example, in the Chinese discourse of civil society.[32] Therefore, as Held suggests, civil society needs to be democratized.[33]

Although civil society is an integral part of democratic order, different theorists of democracy prescribe different political roles for civil society. These include maintaining pluralism, assisting democratization, enhancing and providing the basis for associational democracy and furthering global democracy.

Pluralist democracy and civil society

In a model of pluralist democracy, an accountable government is secured by various associations, which are crucial obstacles to the development of excessively powerful factions and an unresponsive state. One of the key features of pluralist democracy is a functioning civil society: 'If men living in democratic countries had no right and no inclination to associate for political purposes, their independence would be in great jeopardy.'[34] Robert Dahl argues that elections and parties alone do not secure the equilibrium of democratic states. Active groups of various types and sizes are fundamental mechanisms that constrain the scope of political leaders. This is an essential difference between democracy by *minorities* and tyranny by *a minority*. For pluralists, the democratic regime is secured by the existence of multiple groups or multiple minorities.[35]

On this view, a highly articulated civil society with cross-cutting cleavages, overlapping memberships of groups and social mobility is a guarantee both for a stable democratic polity, and against permanent domination by any one group. Civil society is, therefore, a necessary condition for a pluralist model of democracy. The dispersion of economic power means that political, economic and legal powers cannot be monopolized, and that checks and safeguards against the abuse of power are able to operate. Thus, liberals see civil society as associations that assist individuals in their pursuit of liberties, interests and happiness and as a key mechanism by which to curb the power of the state. Under this model, civil society has the capacity to check the state, defend the freedom of its institutions from abnormal intervention and infringement by the state and maintain its independence and autonomy.

It is in this sense that civil society is seen as the last bastion for protecting freedom and preventing the reversion of political authority to totalitarianism.

Elitist versus participatory democracy and civil society

An elitist democratic theory does not trust people and diverse associations. It emphasizes the insulation or autonomy of elites from the influence of peoples and their associations and organizations. It even discourages the direct participation of civil associations and sees an over-politicized civil society as a threat to parliamentary democracy.[36]

Unlike the elitist theory of democracy, a participatory theory stresses the direct participation by citizens in the regulation of the key institutions of society, including the workplace and local community.[37] It is widely contended that without active participation on the part of citizens in civil associations and politically relevant organizations, there would be no way to develop and maintain the democratic character of a political culture or social and political institutions. A classical example is a town meeting and a self-governing urban crisis centre where individuals seek to arrive at a consensus through face-to-face encounters and open debate.[38] Under this model, it is through various associations that individuals participate in democratic life. In this sense then, civil society is seen as an institutional instrument for individuals to advance their interests, develop their political skills and contribute to the improvement of democratic life. Nevertheless, it should be pointed out that when the scope of democracy is local and face-to-face, there is little need for this variety of associations. That is why in village elections in China, associations play a very limited role in developing and promoting village democracy.

Advocates of civil society in Eastern Europe and East Asia reconfirm representative democracy as unsurpassable,[39] a view that is challenged by the civil society discourse of the western social democratic left, which espouses the principles and practices of participatory democracy. For proponents of this discourse representative democracy is too elitist and fails to deliver accountability to the popular will. They argue that offices should be rotated, and revocable delegates should be preferred to mandated representatives. According to these advocates of civil society, a genuine democracy depends on the existence of a public sphere for the formation of a rational or enlightened public opinion. The free rational formation of a popular will in the public sphere is a condition of genuine democracy.

Sceptics may doubt whether civil associations and social movements do actually challenge parliamentary or representative democracy in the West. Not only have we witnessed the decline of social movements and civil society's lack of success in popular mobilization, but also social movements seem to have given up their pursuit of democracy, participation and equality.[40] Ironically, while the left in the West has celebrated the emergence and development of civil society in Eastern Europe, it does not seem to have understood that the discourse of civil society has served to create a new myth of a non-coercive and non-hierarchical political order, which in a sense reinvents some fundamental ideas of 'communism' at a deeper level.[41] Moreover, civil society in Eastern Europe has undermined communist rule and strengthened international capitalism and representative democracy. As a result, the West, now deprived of rival communist systems, has become dominated by the principle of neo-liberal economics, while the principles of social justice appear to be in decline.[42]

Cosmopolitan democracy and civil society

While the civil society project at the level of the nation has become problematic, it has re-emerged with new vigour at the global level. In this context, the cosmopolitan model of democracy aims to democratize the global arenas of decision-making that are now dominated by state and market forces.[43]

When democracy extends to the level of international and global politics, it requires an increasing number of social and political associations to deal with the multiplicity of interests that pertain to a global population. The theory of cosmopolitan democracy, therefore, prescribes a large role for civil society: '[e]nhancement of non-state, non-market solutions in the organization of civil society', and '[c]reation of a diversity of self-regulating associations and groups in civil society'.[44] Held's theorizing of cosmopolitan democracy combines globalization with local civil society. He sees 'the recovery of an intensive and participatory democracy at local levels as a complement to the deliberative assemblies of the wider global order'.[45] Peoples' rule is therefore embodied at different levels, through local participation, global representatives and the restructuring of the UN system. Held writes: 'It is possible to conceive of different types of democracy as forming a continuum from the local to the global, with the local marked by direct and participatory processes while larger areas with significant populations are progressively mediated by representative mechanisms.'[46]

Table 8.1 The role of civil society in different models of democracy

Model of democracy	The role of civil society
Pluralist democracy	Curbing the state, constraining the scope of political leaders and securing democratic regime
Participatory democracy	Providing channels for democratic participation, improving people's ability to participate in political life
Elitist democracy	Over-politicized civil society is a threat to a democratic order and therefore should be restricted
Cosmopolitan democracy	Enhancement of non-state, non-market solutions in the organization of civil society, and the increasing role of global civil society

Special attention should be given to transnational or global civic society, which is an integral part of the cosmopolitan model of democracy (for a detailed discussion see the next section). Archibugi, for example, asserts that the members of global civil society who represent the peoples rather than their governments ought to constitute the UN People's Assembly or Citizen Assembly. Institutions of global civil society are likely to challenge nation-states through their global activities.[47]

Table 8.1 summarizes the role played by civil society in different theories of democracy.

Civil Society, Democracy and the Boundary Question

Civil societies play diverse roles in developing and maintaining democracy/democratization, as discussed above; they also perform different functions in addressing the boundary question. A growing literature testifies to the emerging importance of the function of civil society in defining the boundaries of political communities,[48] and the participation of ordinary people and the institutions of civil society in defining these boundaries gives rise to the possibility of a democratic approach to this question.

A democratic approach encompasses not only the use of referenda and the right to self-determination, but also the participation of people and the institutions of civil society in the decision-making process dedicated to the peaceful resolution of the boundary question. Under conditions of democratic management, the general public has the opportunity for meaningful participation in defining national boundaries and in the formation of policies. Civil society is an integral part of the democratic project in the sense that it is the main mechanism, apart from referenda, by which the will of the people is expressed. In contrast to management by elites, democratic management encourages the participation of ordinary people and the institutions of civil society.

It has been a longstanding assumption of democratic theory that democracy is incapable of playing a role in addressing the boundary question. However, such a presupposition is no longer able to withstand the challenges put up by the various urgent boundary problems that continue to proliferate around the world. Given the urgency of such problems, it is of critical importance that contemporary democratic theorists develop a theory dedicated to outlining how the boundary question can be democratically managed.

For this purpose, the notion of civil society can be understood not only to include autonomous organizations, but also to embrace normative elements, or moral judgements about civility. As Schmitter stresses, civil society must act in a civil manner within established rules.[49] In this respect, as noted earlier, rightwing nationalist NGOs, for example, will not be regarded as part of civil society.[50] Moreover, with regard to the boundary question, the notion of civil society as an ideal model stresses a way of coexistence between overlapping associations and communities; and challenges the old idea that a unified polity must have a unified ethnic base.

Connecting the boundary issue and civil society

In the past, national boundaries were largely decided by force, with states claiming their prerogatives and manipulating popular opinions and sentiments. Most nation-states have statutory rights granted by their constitutions to deal with issues concerning national boundaries. Nation-states appear to be the major players in the matter of determining national boundaries. They negotiate with other states, declare wars or sign international agreements to settle certain boundary disputes. The division of the world into states has strengthened claims to state sovereignty and created ongoing pressure for the continuation of the statist approach to the boundary issue. Such an approach tends to deny or exclude civil social groups from the decision-making process, on the grounds that they represent only sectional or private interests, rather than the general interests of bordered nation-states.

The limitations of the statist approach have become increasingly clear in recent decades. The failure to resolve the national identity question in Northern Ireland highlights problems with this approach.[51] The events in Eastern Europe around 1989 demonstrate that civil society has played a crucial role in the struggle against communist states and in the redefinition of national boundaries. Globalization has tended to weaken the power of states and the statist tradition. Global civil society, albeit at a fledgling stage of development, has posed a serious challenge to the arbitrary boundaries of nation-states. States, once seen as the exclusive decision-makers and problem-solvers in boundary disputes, are now seen to contribute to, and even intensify, boundary problems. Faith in the capacity of nation-states to deal with the boundary issue is either completely or at least partially lost, depending on one's view of nation-states. As Freeman points out, the state-centred theories of self-determination neglect the importance of non-state, trans-state and super-state actors. In particular, Freeman argues that there is an inherent contradiction in the theories of self-determination elaborated by Beran, Margalit and Raz, which consider states to be part of the problem and yet offer them as part of the solution.[52] Thus, Freeman calls for a paradigm shift from a state-centred to a society-centred approach.[53]

Given the context outlined above, it is possible to see that the idea of civil society has challenged the state's monopoly of national territory. By competing against nation-states, civil society has become an increasingly important agent in defining national boundaries. The linkage between the boundary issue and civil society is thus established, so much so that civil society is sometimes seen as an alternative or supplement to the statist approach. It is deemed to be one source of legitimacy for the national boundary. Moreover, a state with multiple nationalities requires not only tolerance, but also a public discourse where citizens and civil societies are able and willing to engage in discussion about the social arrangements that hold them together.[54]

A shift in the theoretical paradigm towards civil society can be understood further by an analysis of the strengths of the civil society approach in comparison with the statist approach. First, because their very existence is based on fixed borders, nation-states have a static view of what constitutes the boundary and they are reluctant to make changes. Civil societies, on the other hand, in particular global associations such as human rights organizations, may raise and discuss issues that go beyond the fixed borders of nation-states. Because the organizations or associations of civil societies do not have privileged interests within the nation-state system, they are able to consider issues concerning the justice of national boundaries.

Second, it is argued that the statist approach gives power to a few politicians or representatives, while the civil society approach empowers NGOs and assigns them an important role in the process. In short, the civil society approach enables more people and social organizations to participate in a diversity of spheres, making it much more representative than states in articulating the will of the people.

Third, the statist approach tends to impose a single-state-centred notion of national identity, as demonstrated by the Chinese government's imposition of Chinese national identity on the Chinese diaspora.[55] Nation-states commit themselves to the monopoly of violence: the willingness to use force to manage the boundary problem is a common attribute among nation-states. By contrast, civic associations generally advocate non-violence, new principles of morality and new means for resolving conflicts.

Fourth, nation-states tend to close off the discussion of the national boundary issue. In the eyes of the state, civil society may become a 'troublemaker' and make the boundary issue more complex. When the people are 'sleeping', it is easy for the state to decide the boundary issue, to strike a secret deal and to close off the issue. But if the people are awake, and civil society expresses the diversity of their opinions on the national identity issue, the state is more likely to encounter difficulties in dealing with the boundary issue. From the perspective of civil society, however, civic associations would produce different solutions and proposals, and help create a diversity of political forces. The participation of civil society could knit different ethnic groups together because it promotes the exchange of opinions and mutual understanding between groups, increases overlapping membership and the level of tolerance and provides a public basis for the unity of national identity.

Furthermore, the suppression by the state/party of public discussion on the national identity/boundary problem may lead to trouble and disorder. When a political regime suppresses NGOs, it is likely to face difficulties in solving the boundary problem. Consider, in this context, the breakdown of the former Soviet Union. The state there did not encourage cultural creativity and the free flow of discourse. Only state-sponsored cultural products were used to unify the large and heterogeneous country as a whole. This had enormous negative consequences. As Calhoun points out: 'When the state lost its credibility, so did much of the cultural basis for unity at the largest level.' When discussion and creativity were suppressed in order to maintain ideological conformity, it became difficult to achieve the manifold continuous cultural adjustments that were essential to both legitimization processes and the sense of common membership in a political community. 'So, ironically, the very attempt to maintain complete conformity undermined identification with the whole, left it superficial and easily forgotten.'[56] Nevertheless, the civil society approach cannot presuppose that the more NGOs there are, the easier it is to solve the boundary problem. Nor can it assume that the members of civil society are unitary rational actors who are able to reach consensus and agreement on the boundary issue.

Fifth, governments and NGOs operate differently. NGOs tend to be more loosely organized, more flexible and less costly than governments. For example, international governmental organizations cannot work at the Thai–Burma Border, nor enter Tigray or Eritrea. They are restricted in their work in Cambodia and do little in Vietnam. In these areas, the private agencies carry the burden; and in some places the NGOs do the bulk of the work.[57]

A conceptual framework concerning the role of civil society

How does civil society play its actual and potential roles in defining the boundary of a political community? Consideration of the role of civil societies is largely influenced by our view of civil society – as a set of societal conditions, a means of conflict resolution, political actors or transnational phenomena.

Civil society as a set of societal conditions For the successful operation of civil society, a number of social conditions, including non-segregation, integration and people's contact between divided nations or ethnic groups, are necessary. Such conditions make dialogue and accommodation possible, reduce tension, break down barriers and stereotypes and promote mutual sympathy and mutual understanding. The civil society approach assumes that the more a society is integrated, the more its membership is overlapping or cross-cutting, and therefore the easier the boundary issue is to solve. Conversely, the more a society is segregated, the more difficulty it has managing the boundary issue. Dixon, for example, argues against segregation, which he sees as facilitating fears and suspicions in Northern Ireland. While civil society may not directly solve the boundary problem, it 'appears to at least offer a way out of the current impasses by creating the environment in which accommodation might be possible'.[58] In the context of the two Koreas, Young Whan Kihl also proposes integration and people's contact, including NGOs' involvement in such areas as relief work, environmental protection, religious mission trips and youth exchanges in North Korea.[59]

Civil society as a means of conflict resolution When civil society is used as a model for conflict management, it celebrates plural, overlapping and cross-cutting associations, while rejecting nationalist principles. The civil society approach appeals to civility, non-violence and dialogue, as opposed to the state's monopoly of violence and its use of force to resolve disputes. If nation-states tend to use whatever methods are necessary, including military force, to solve the national boundary problem, the civil society approach insists that the method of dealing with the national boundary problem does matter. Indeed, it is emphatic that it must be civic and non-violent. As such, it aims to break with the human habit of fighting over territories. It rejects the terrorist view that violence, terror and bloodshed are necessary means of dealing with the boundary issue. It envisages that a civilized way to deal with the boundary issue will bring about a more desirable result. Consider, for instance, the bloody disintegration in Yugoslavia. It could be assumed that with a more developed civil society and civic culture, the disintegration could certainly have been more civilized. The war itself could have been avoided, or it could have resulted in far fewer human casualties and destruction, and less cruelty and war crimes.[60] It was the domination by the strongly rightwing nationalist groups (which should not be regarded as a part of civil society according to the working definition of the concept adopted in this chapter) that made compromise and peaceful settlement impossible. Moreover, the tragedy in Kosovo in 1999 shows that without civil society and a civic culture, ethnic conflict and ethnic cleansing are likely to take place. It also demonstrates that the best solution to the boundary conflict must come from within. NATO's intervention in Kosovo played a limited role in protecting Albanians and it did not prevent ethnic conflict after the withdrawal of Serbian forces in 1999. Intervention alone cannot produce peace.

Those advocating the civil society approach argue further that the articulation of the national identity question by violent groups may undermine civil society, and such groups are unlikely to manage the boundary issue successfully. An example of this can be found in Northern Ireland. When 'uncivil' society prevails over 'civil' society, as demonstrated by the Ulster Workers Council strike in 1974, the power-sharing executive was brought down, and the peace process was blocked.[61] Conversely, if members of civil society are rational and committed to compromise and engage in productive and fruitful debates, the articulation of the national identity issue by civil society helps to manage the boundary issue and will not undermine a community on which civil society depends. A good example is the Corrymeela Community, whose aim is to be a symbol in a divided society that Protestant and Catholic can share together in a common witness to Christ, who transcends division. Its members are both Roman Catholic and Protestant and are encouraged to explore the nature of conflict and to establish mediation networks. It gives us a hope that it will be possible to rebuild a civil society in Northern Ireland, although its role is very limited.

Civil society associations as actors Associations in civil societies, understood as political actors, can express a collective voice, adopt certain strategies, take certain collective actions, such as demonstrations and petitions, and influence and change state policy concerning the national boundary issue. The idea of civil society implies the 'capacity of ordinary people to join together in associations' and 'to create a public sphere capable of shaping social and political decisions on the basis of rational-critical discourse'.[62] Bleiker, Bond and Lee, for example, discuss an alternative to conventional political approaches for achieving unification and promoting democratization in the Korean peninsula. They focus on the non-violent direct action of non-governmental actors and the general public and continued grassroots support for alternatives to current unification strategies and engagement in inter-Korean affairs.[63]

Various associations in South Korea and Taiwan have mobilized peoples and organized collective action to challenge and break down the monopoly of the boundary issue by the governments. Today, the state alone cannot decide the national identity question. Nation-states cannot simply deny or ignore the roles of civil society in relation to the boundary issue. If the states do not trust people and do not rely on civil society, they will face a legitimacy crisis. They have to think how to co-opt and manipulate civil associations in a skilful way.

Global civil society Increasing economic and technological globalization has challenged the nation-state system. Global networking and overlapping memberships increasingly make national boundaries unclear and render identities more blurred. Today, minority questions can easily draw international attention and become a global issue and it is becoming increasingly common for minority groups, such as Aboriginal and Torres Strait Islanders in Australia and Tibetans in China, to bring an issue to the international arena.

For some commentators, our awareness of the global village should begin to transform the character of social sciences and influence the structure of our theoretical frameworks.[64] Both state-centred and society-centered approaches are now proving problematic and inadequate. Importantly, the civil society approach is itself problematic if it does not take account of global civil society. It seems that the idea of global civil society combines elements of both anti-state and anti-nation positions. Anti-state because states are seen as part of the boundary problem; anti-nation because nations are deemed to be redundant.

Global civil society includes various international NGOs (INGOs).[65] It is not only subject to international law, but is also an active participant in shaping such law. It is important in shaping opinion and serves as an autonomous actor in competition with states. In other words, global civil society is more concerned with global issues, such as human rights and the global environment, and less concerned with national sovereignty.

Those who are theorists of global civil society see the boundary problem from the aspect of global civil society without adopting the views of states with regard to certain boundary questions. The general consensus is that global civil society plays an increasingly important role in diminishing the sacredness of the national boundary. It challenges the boundaries of nation-states, in that the boundaries and perspectives of global civil society do not coincide with the boundaries of nation-states. It aims to create a global culture, the consciousness of a global village, which overrides the sense of national identity. As Richard Falk puts it:

> [T]he modernist stress on territorial sovereignty as the exclusive basis for political community and identity would be displaced both by more local and distinct groupings and by association with the reality of a global civil society without boundaries. . . . Global civil society treated as the hopeful source of political agency needs to free the minds of persons from an acceptance of state/sovereignty identity, and rethink the contours of community, loyalty, and citizenship.[66]

It should be noted that, although global civil society diminishes the importance of national boundaries, this does not imply that the boundary problem will gradually disappear. Instead the national boundary issue is relocated in local politics with different settings, at least in the case of the European Union. With the increasing importance of local territories and of local associations, the concept of borderlands, in contrast to borderlines, has developed.[67] The idea of the borderline expresses both the dividing line and the sanctuary line, which thus defines nation-states in terms of difference. In other words, the nation-state is defined in terms of what lies on the other side or of what they do not or will not admit. The notion of the borderland, conversely, refers to the border 'that draws all things into it, the place identified with the middle-ground, with the union of opposites, and with mediation'.[68] The idea of the borderland was suggested and championed by a religious studies group which sponsored a series of lectures on regional trade and economic development at Baylor University in Waco, Texas in 1988 and 1989.[69]

Particular attention should be paid to the role of INGOs in managing the boundary issue. Usually, international governmental organizations are averse to, or indifferent towards, boundary issues such as secessionist movements. Before the 1990s, as Heraclides observes: '[T]he UN intervened drastically only once, and in that case decidedly against a secessionist movement (in Katanga in the early 1960s).'[70] The Organization of African Unity is even more firmly committed to the status quo in relation to the existence of national boundaries, and it regards any redrawing of African boundaries as totally unacceptable.[71] By contrast, INGOs have sometimes been involved in secessionist situations, and have even lobbied to support secessionists. Such groups can be outright partisan supporters in a subtle manner, initiators of contacts and then mediators or supportive consultants. They include Amnesty International, the Minority Rights Group, Oxfam and Caritas International (the relief agency of the Roman Catholic Church), the International Commission of Jurists (a quasi-juridical organization), the Roman Catholic Church, the Anglican Church, the World Council of Churches and the World Muslim League.[72]

Laurie Wiseberg summarizes the role of INGOs in secessionist movements in the following way: according legitimacy to the secessionists by dealing with them directly; providing moral support; publicizing the secessionist case through appeals for funds for the starving or displaced or for refugees; providing the secessionist movement, directly or indirectly, with medicine, food, funds, currency or perhaps even fuel or means of transportation or communication; serving as a cover for arms shipments; and providing access to the outside world.[73]

Amnesty International, as a moral agent dedicated to promoting universal human rights, has privileged human rights principles in a way that goes beyond the idea of national sovereignty. It has defended the freedom of speech, which guarantees the right to express dissident views on questions of national identity, such as in South Korea and Taiwan. For many years the annual reports of Amnesty International have challenged the National Security Law (NSL) and its restriction on people's contacts and movements between South and North Korea. On 25 November 1995, the London-based wing of Amnesty International, for example, published a 62-page report urging the South Korean government to amend the NSL.[74] It should be acknowledged that Amnesty does not intend to address the unification question per se. Nevertheless, its primary concern with human rights and its activities against the NSL do have unintended consequences. It has, for instance, facilitated people-to-people contact across borders, reinforced the unification forces from civic groups in South Korea, and provided moral support for NGOs in challenging the government's monopoly of the unification issue.

INGOs are likely to have much more impact on South Korea than on North Korea. This is because, as of the end of 1989, South Korea had 820 INGO memberships, while North Korea had only 141.[75] Moreover, the government of North Korea does not allow Amnesty International to establish branches in its territory, while the government of South Korea does in its. As a democratic regime, the government of South Korea is subjected much more to international pressure than that of North Korea. In North Korea, INGOs only began to operate and exercise influence in the 1990s. The Rockefeller Foundation, for example, funded projects in North Korea, which were initiated by the Asia Society. It is believed that this type of NGO activity will build confidence and facilitate people-to-people exchange before official exchange and co-operation with North Korea.[76]

A sceptical view

A sceptic is likely to argue, however, that states have been, and will continue to be, key players and decisive forces in dealing with the boundary problem. Civil society does not, and cannot, replace the state. Civil society *alone* cannot resolve or manage the boundary problem and will not eliminate all the deep-rooted problems. It is not a panacea, nor a viable alternative to nation-states. Moreover, states now adopt new strategies, using NGOs for their own purposes. In Taiwan, for example, the government increasingly uses NGOs as an alternative channel to win international space and to promote the national identity and political profile of Taiwan.

Furthermore, the view that civic groups and associations should play their part in defining the boundary question not only brings a new perspective on, and a new approach to, the old problem, but also gives rise to new questions and new problems. First, global civil society goes beyond the nation-state only in the sense that its members are not necessarily restrained by their nation-state. Nevertheless, when they come to support certain groups' effort to establish a new state, such activities presuppose and strengthen the centrality of national boundaries and the nation-state system. In this sense, they are not purely global nor beyond the nation-state system. Second, even the concept of civil society itself begs many questions. As has been discussed before, it is very difficult to define the boundary of civil society, draw the line between civil society and the state and avoid the arbitrary judgement of the 'civility' of civic associations.

Conclusion

Civil society is a necessary condition for both established parliamentary democracy and democratization, for it curbs the excessive power of states and enables people to participate in democratic life. It is also a supplement to, and crucial part of, the democratic management of the boundary question. Civil society has played an increasing role in developing and maintaining democracy and in addressing the national boundary issue, not only in western liberal democratic countries, but also in East Asia. The emergence and rapid growth of civil society might be seen as an 'association revolution', which may prove to be significant in both promoting global democratization and in addressing the national boundary issue well into the twenty-first century.

NOTES

The author is grateful for the critical and useful comments and suggestions from Geoff Stokes and April Carter, and assistance from Christine Standish and Yingjie Guo.

1　A. Ferguson, *An Essay on the History of Civil Society* (Edinburgh, Edinburgh University Press, 1966 [1767]).

2　Cited in N. Bobbio, *Democracy and Dictatorship: The Nature and Limits of State Power*, trans. P. Kennealy (Minneapolis, University of Minnesota Press, 1989), p. 35.

3　T. Hobbes, *Leviathan*, ed. C. B. Macpherson (London, Penguin, 1968 [1651]), p. 227.

4　P. Laslett (ed.), *Locke: Two Treatises of Government* (Cambridge, Cambridge University Press, 1960 [1690]), p. 324.

5　Ibid., p. 326.

6　A. Smith, *An Inquiry into the Nature and Causes of the Wealth of Nations*, vol. 1, ed. R. H. Campbell and A. S. Skinner (Oxford, Clarendon Press, 1976), p. 26.

7　Hegel included in civil society elements we would usually think of as part of the state, e.g., commercial law.

8　See Z. A. Pelczynski (ed.), *The State and Civil Society: Studies In Hegel's Political Philosophy* (Cambridge, Cambridge University Press, 1984); and A. B. Seligman, *The Idea of Civil Society* (New York, The Free Press, 1992), pp. 44–51.

9　Seligman, *The Idea of Civil Society*, pp. 51–8.

10   See E. Gellner, 'Islam and Marxism: Some comparisons', *International Affairs* 67, 1 (1991): 1–6.

11   E. Gellner, *Conditions for Liberty: Civil Society and its Rivals* (Hamilton, Penguin Books, 1994), p. 211.

12   C. Taylor, 'Models of civil society', *Public Culture* 3, 1 (1990): 95–118.

13   P. C. Schmitter, 'On civil society and the consolidation of democracy: Ten general propositions and nine speculations about their relation in Asian societies', paper presented at an International Conference on Consolidating the Third Wave Democracies: Trends and Challenges, Taipei, 27–30 August 1995.

14   See Z. Rau (ed.), *The Reemergence of Civil Society in Eastern Europe and the Soviet Union* (Boulder, Westview Press, 1991).

15   R. Rose, 'Toward a civil economy', *Journal of Democracy* 3, 2 (1992): 13–26, p. 20.

16   See E. Vogel, *Canton Under Communism: Programs and Politics in a Provincial Capital, 1949–1968* (Cambridge, MA, Harvard University Press, 1969); Tang Tsou, *The Cultural Revolution and Post-Mao Reforms: A Historical Perspective* (Chicago, University of Chicago Press, 1986); and P. Duara, *Culture, Power and the State: Rural North China, 1900–1942* (Stanford, Stanford University Press, 1988).

17   Baogang He, *The Democratic Implications of Civil Society in China* (London, Macmillan, 1997).

18   Rosanvallon, cited in J. L. Cohen and A. Arato, *Civil Society and Political Theory* (Cambridge, MA, MIT Press, 1992), p. 39.

19   See Cohen and Arato, *Civil Society and Political Theory*.

20   G. White, 'Civil society, democratization and development (I): Clearing the analytical ground', *Democratization* 1, 3 (1994): 382–5; L. Diamond, 'Rethinking civil society: Toward democratic consolidation', *Journal of Democracy* 5, 3 (1994): 4–17, esp. pp. 7–11; Schmitter, 'On civil society and the consolidation of democracy', pp. 13–14.

21   Diamond, 'Rethinking civil society', p. 6.

22   Cohen and Arato, *Civil Society and Political Theory*.

23   Schmitter, 'On civil society and the consolidation of democracy'.

24   See J. H. Mittelman and R. Johnston, 'The globalization of organized crime, the courtesan state, and the corruption of civil society', *Global Governance* 4 (1999): pp. 103–26.

25   E. Cox, *A Truly Civil Society* (Sydney, ABC Books, 1995).

26   Chen Kuide, 'The misleading conception of clan society and the reconstruction of civil society in China', *Chinese Intellectuals* (Summer 1990): 23–30; Jiang Qing, 'Rujia wenhua: Jiangou zhongguodeshe shimin shehui de shenhou ziyuan' ('Confucian culture: The rich source of constructing Chinese type of civil society'), *Zhongguo shehui kexue jikan* (HK) (15 May 1993): 170–5.

27 R. Madsen, 'The public sphere, civil society, and the moral community', *Modern China* 19, 2 (1993): 183–98.

28 A. Giddens, *The Third Way: The Renewal of Social Democracy* (Cambridge, Polity Press, 1998), p. 79.

29 G. Burchell, 'Peculiar interests: Civil society and governing the system of natural liberty', in G. Burchell, C. Gordon and P. Miller (eds), *The Foucault Effect: Studies in Governmentality* (Hemel Hempstead, Harvester Wheatsheaf, 1991), p. 141.

30 See C. Tempest, 'Myths from Eastern Europe and the legend of the West', *Democratization* 4, 1 (1997): 132–44.

31 B. Geremek et al., *The Idea of Civil Society* (Research Triangle Park, NC, The National Humanities, 1992), p. 18.

32 See Baogang He, *The Democratic Implications of Civil Society in China*.

33 D. Held, *Models of Democracy* (Cambridge, Polity, 1987), p. 283.

34 A. de Tocqueville, *Democracy in America* (New York, The New American Library, 1956), p. 199.

35 See R. Dahl, *Polyarchy: Participation and Opposition* (New Haven, Yale University Press, 1971) and *Dilemmas of Pluralist Democracy: Autonomy vs. Control* (New Haven, Yale University Press, 1982).

36 For an elitist theory of democracy, see J. Schumpeter, *Capitalism, Socialism and Democracy* (London, Allen and Unwin, 1976).

37 C. Pateman, *Participation and Democratic Theory* (Cambridge, Cambridge University Press, 1970).

38 J. J. Mansbridge, *Beyond Adversary Democracy* (New York, Basic Books, 1980).

39 Rau (ed.), *The Reemergence of Civil Society in Eastern Europe and the Soviet Union*; and Baogang He, 'The idea of civil society in both China and Taiwan', *Issues and Studies* 31, 6 (1995): 24–64.

40 E. Etzioni-Halevy, 'Have social movements in the West abandoned the quest for equality and democracy?', paper presented at the First Regional Conference on Social Movements, Tel-Aviv, September 1997.

41 As G. M. Tamas argues, 'like communism, the myth of civil society is a tale of a noncoercive political order . . . civil society is nonhierarchical'. In this sense, 'Eastern Europe . . . has reinvented communism'; see 'A Disquisition on civil society', *Social Research* 61, 2 (1994): 205–22, pp. 216–18.

42 One tragic consequence of this is that the universities' relative autonomy is frequently infringed and the very limited democratic elements and consultative collegiality that have existed in the past have been destroyed by bureaucratic and managerialist control of funding.

43 R. Falk, *On Humane Governance: Toward a New Global Politics* (Cambridge, Polity, 1995).

44   D. Held, *Models of Democracy*, 2nd edn (Cambridge, Polity, 1996), p. 358.

45   D. Held, 'Democracy and the new international order', in D. Archibugi and D. Held (eds), *Cosmopolitan Democracy: An Agenda for a New World Order* (Cambridge, Polity, 1995), p. 112.

46   Held, *Democracy and the Global Order*, p. 280, n5.

47   D. Archibugi, 'From the United Nations to cosmopolitan democracy', in Archibugi and Held (eds), *Cosmopolitan Democracy*, pp. 135–55.

48   See A. Heraclides, *The Self-Determination of Minorities in International Politics* (London, Frank Cass and Co, 1991); R. Bleiker, D. Bond and Myung-Soo Lee, 'The role and dynamics of non-governmental actors in contemporary Korea', *Korean Studies* 18 (1994): 103–22; M. Freeman, 'Democrat and dynamite: The peoples' right to self-determination', *Political Studies* 44 (1996): 746–61; Baogang He, *The Democratic Implications of Civil Society in China*; P. Dixon, 'Paths to peace in Northern Ireland (I): Civil society and consociational approaches', *Democratization* 4, 2 (1997): 1–27; and P. Dixon, 'Paths to peace in Northern Ireland (II): The peace processes 1973–74 and 1994–96', *Democratization* 4, 3 (1997): 1–25.

49   Schmitter, 'On civil society and the consolidation of democracy'.

50   It is debatable whether a moderate nationalist NGO can be seen as part of civil society.

51   Dixon, 'Paths to peace in Northern Ireland (II)'.

52   Freeman, 'Democrat and dynamite'; H. Beran, 'A democratic theory of political self-determination for a new world order', in P. B. Lehning (ed.), *Theories of Secession* (London, Routledge, 1998), pp. 32–59. A. Margalit and J. Raz, 'National self-determination', *The Journal of Philosophy* 87, 9 (1990): 439–61.

53   Freeman, 'Democrat and dynamite'.

54   C. Calhoun, *Neither Gods Nor Emperors: Students and the Struggle for Democracy in China* (Berkeley, University of California Press, 1994), pp. 190–3.

55   Ibid., p. 191.

56   C. Calhoun, 'Nationalism and civil society: Democracy, diversity and self-determination', in C. Calhoun (ed.), *Social Theory and the Politics of Identity* (Cambridge, MA, Blackwell, 1994), 304–35.

57   E. G. Ferris, *Beyond Borders: Refugees, Migrants and Human Rights in the Post-Cold War Era* (Geneva, WCC Publications, 1993), p. 35.

58   Dixon, 'Paths to peace in Northern Ireland (II)', p. 22.

59   Young Whan Kihl, 'Epilogue: Korean conundrum in the post-cold war era', in Young Whan Kihl (ed.), *Korea and the World: Beyond the Cold War* (Boulder, Westview Press, 1994), pp. 332–3.

60   V. Pavlovic, 'Ethical conflicts and democracy in the suppressed civil society', paper presented at the 17th World Congress of IPSA, Seoul, 17–21 August 1997.

61 Dixon, 'Paths to peace in Northern Ireland (II)', p. 22.

62 Calhoun, 'Nationalism and civil society', p. 306.

63 Bleiker, Bond and Lee, 'The role and dynamics of non-governmental actors'.

64 B. Turner, *Orientalism, Postmodernism and Globalism* (London, Routledge, 1994).

65 P. Ghils, 'International civil society: International nongovernmental organisations in the international system', *International Social Science Journal* 44, 133 (1992): 417–31.

66 Falk, *On Humane Governance*, pp. 100–1.

67 S. J. Randall, H. Konrad and S. Silverman (eds), *North America Without Borders? Integrating Canada, the United States, and Mexico* (Calgary, University of Calgary Press, 1992), pp. 201–2.

68 Russell Brown, cited in Randall et al., *North America Without Borders*, p. 202.

69 Until independence in 1836, the state was part of Mexico. It has had a strong Mexican heritage and a close relationship with Mexico since the mid-nineteenth century.

70 Heraclides, *The Self-Determination of Minorities in International Politics*, p. 54.

71 Ibid., p. 55.

72 Ibid., pp. 54–7.

73 See ibid., p. 57.

74 D. Cho, 'National security law may be hot issue in general elections', *The Korea Herald* (10 December 1995), p. 2.

75 Samuel S. Kim, 'The two Koreas and world order', in Young (ed.), *Korea and the World*, p. 34.

76 Young, 'Epilogue: Korean conundrum in the post-cold war era', p. 331.

9

Associative Democracy

April Carter

Theorists of associative democracy seek to promote individual freedom, social justice and political participation, which are in their view undermined by excessive reliance either on the state or on the market.[1] Their proposals are of interest because they seek both to bring about economic and social change and to go beyond the central institutions of liberal democracy. So, although their proposals are rooted in an analysis of current realities, such as disillusion with state socialism and the impact of economic globalization on the state, they believe greater equality and genuine democracy are possible. Associationalists would decentralize state power, transfer many existing state functions to citizen bodies and extend democracy to non-political spheres, in particular the workplace. Although there are anarchist precedents, advocates of associative democracy do not seek to abolish the state – only to restrict its scope; nor do they wish to supplant parliamentary representation and legislation, but to supplement it.

Associative proposals have an appeal in varying political contexts. For example, Mark Swilling in South Africa has argued for associative socialism, combining decentralization of state powers with a political role for community groups, non-state forms of collective ownership of industry and democratic controls within companies.[2] John Matthews in Australia sees associative democracy as a new means of realizing social democratic aims, while accepting the challenge from green, feminist and cultural identity movements to purely class-based politics. He also suggests that associationalism is an appropriate response to the disintegration in the 1970s of the 'Fordist' economic system, based on standardized mass production and concomitant mass consumerism, and managed after 1945 through Keynesian policies and the welfare state.[3]

The political theorists considered here are Joshua Cohen and Joel Rogers in the United States, who write jointly on associative democracy, and Paul Hirst in Britain.[4] Cohen and Rogers, who focus particularly on the nature of groups and their relationship to the state, prompted an illuminating range of critical responses to their ideas at a conference in Wisconsin in 1992. Hirst, who has written extensively on the historical sources of associationalism and its present applications, examines in greater detail a possible institutional framework. Their works reflect the different American and British political and intellectual contexts. For example, whereas Cohen and Rogers comment on the relative weakness of the state, Hirst is hoping to combat Thatcherism's legacy of state encroachment on the autonomy of associations such as trade unions and universities. So, although they have influenced each other, there is a danger of oversimplifying when constructing a model of associative democracy from their writings.[5] They do, however, share a good deal of common ground.

The strategy of this chapter is, first, to locate associative ideas in their political and theoretical context, and, second, to set out key arguments by Cohen and Rogers and by Hirst. In the second part of the chapter I initially examine two questions central to associationalism: the definition and role of social groups and how far the state determines their nature and controls their actions. I then explore three issues arising out of the case made for associative democracy: that it is more realistic than republicanism; that it is the best means of realizing social justice; and that it is compatible with the ideal of global democracy.

The Political and Theoretical Background and Context

Associative democracy has antecedents in earlier liberal as well as socialist thought. Some liberal pluralists have focused on defence of the political and legal autonomy of institutions founded for religious, educational or other social purposes against state control.[6] Others, like Alexis de Tocqueville and John Stuart Mill, celebrated the contribution of voluntary associations, which encourage initiative and provide a political education, to parliamentary democracy.[7]

Socialist precursors of associationalism rejected state control of the economy. They include early socialists who looked to experimentation in small-scale communities or model factories as a means of changing society from below, and their heirs who relied on creating autonomous workers' organizations, such as trade unions and producers' and consumers' cooperatives.[8] The movements for worker control of factories and communal direct democracy might also provide some inspiration. But this tradition of revolutionary socialism, with roots in the 1871 Paris Commune and the 1905 and 1917 Russian Soviets,[9] is too exclusively linked to working-class revolution to be a direct precursor of today's associationalism.

The closest approximation is guild socialism, influential early in the twentieth century in Britain. It aimed to avoid the weaknesses of state socialism by stressing decentralization, the importance of functional as well as territorial representation and by endorsing the ideal of worker democracy. Guild socialism also criticized anarcho-syndicalism, which envisaged centralized trade unions holding exclusive power, and argued that all legitimate interests (for example consumers) should have a voice in policy-making.[10]

Associationalist ideas almost disappeared when the conflict between liberalism and communism dominated political debate.[11] They have a new resonance now the Soviet model of a state-controlled economy, and one-party rule, is discredited. But for the western left the problems besetting social democracy and the Keynesian welfare state since the 1970s have been more important. State direction of the economy seemed less feasible because of globalization. The centralized welfare state also seemed less desirable to some on the left. John Keane, for example, commented that 'in the actual experience of many citizens in daily contact with welfare state institutions, it has become widely assumed that socialism means bureaucracy, surveillance, red tape and state control'.[12]

This critique by the left accepted some of the analysis of new right theorists, and also shared their commitment to enhancing individual autonomy and range of choice. Nonetheless, it rejected the new right's focus on the market as the central social mechanism and its often repressive policies such as the attack on trade union rights. Many liberals were also alienated by this extreme version of market liberalism, its dismissal of social justice and the growing inequalities in practice.

Therefore political theorists of varying political persuasions have shown renewed concern for communal ties and voluntary social organization, and have revived debate about the meaning of citizenship and enhancing democracy. Associationalists agree with theorists of civil society that numerous self-governing groups pursuing varying interests and social goals are essential for a flourishing representative democracy. But associative democrats go further in arguing that voluntary associations should take over many local and national government functions and should be seen as central institutions of governance. They also share with the new civic republicans a belief in participatory democracy and a strong concept of citizenship. But they are critical of what they see as republicanism's unrealistic emphasis on a unitary political community and focus upon an agreed public good.[13]

Associationalism claims to transcend the right–left divide by defending individual and minority freedoms, as well as supporting greater social equality and popular control. It seems, therefore, to suggest a third way. But the kind of third way represented by the British Labour Party, which embraces an extension of privatization and market principles in spheres such as welfare and education, but attempts to use the state to encourage employment and promote a very limited redistribution of wealth, is also alien to associative ideals. 'New Labour' relies too much both on market principles and upon centralized state and party power. Associationalists seek instead to reinstate pluralism and the autonomy of social institutions.[14] Although New Labour policies can accommodate a larger role for mutualist associations like friendly societies, the basic approach is different.[15]

The relationship between associationalism and corporatism is more complex. Hirst does see value in corporatist systems, like those in Germany and Japan in the postwar period, which embodied consultation and cooperation at both a national and company level, and introduced the principle of social contracts between trade unions and employers' associations. But associationalists reject the elitism and centralization implied by tripartite bargaining between the state and national representatives of employers and trade unions, and also deplore the exclusion of other interests from this process. Cohen and Rogers vigorously reject the interpretation of their original essay that saw them advocating 'corporatism for America'.[16] But the kind of neo-corporatism advocated by Philippe Schmitter, who urges a stronger democratic input and inclusion of other interests, is much nearer to associative democracy.[17]

One version of pluralism prominent in recent American thought might seem close to associationalism. But this literature, stressing the function of centralized pressure groups in promoting specific interests, to be resolved by a process of bargaining and compromise between the competing groups before being translated into government policy, is a model rejected by the theorists of associative democracy.[18] It favours powerful organized interests, and assumes that the existing political practices and institutions provide the best form of democracy. Moreover, Hirst argues, it assumes democracy can be achieved within a centralized state claiming sovereign power.[19] Cohen and Rogers are even more concerned to distinguish themselves from this inegalitarian version of pluralism. They also reject 'egalitarian pluralism', which seeks fair access for all groups, and is represented by the later writings of Robert Dahl, partly because it lacks a 'substantive view of the common good and the proper terms of political debate'.[20]

Two Theories of Associative Democracy

Cohen and Rogers: how groups promote democracy

Cohen and Rogers summarized their concept of associative democracy in a long article, 'Secondary associations and democratic governance', in 1992, republished in *Associations and Democracy* in 1995.[21] They set out six criteria for the realization of democracy:

- popular sovereignty to be achieved through elected representatives controlling the public agenda;
- political equality in terms of access to political office and influence on policy;
- distributive fairness based on genuine equality of opportunity;
- civic consciousness committed to deliberation on policy in a way which includes recognition of a public interest and supports democratic processes of decision-making;
- good economic performance (needed to provide the resources for social welfare);
- state competence.

They argue that organized groups can contribute to achieving this ideal through providing policy-makers with necessary information on the interests of their members and promoting equal representation of all citizens, for example by voicing differing occupational concerns or the views of political minorities. They also suggest that voluntary bodies can promote civic consciousness through providing a form of political education – here they cite Tocqueville. Finally, and most distinctively, they suggest that voluntary bodies can be instruments of 'alternative governance', playing a role in developing and implementing policies and creating processes of communication and collaboration. They can therefore offer an alternative to both markets and state hierarchies in such areas as consumer protection, occupation safety and the environment.

Nevertheless, Cohen and Rogers are acutely aware that in the American tradition of political thought, despite a strand eulogizing 'pluralism', organized interest groups have often been seen as a threat both to democratic norms and the public welfare. They explicitly recognize that groups can pose a factional threat to popular sovereignty, political equality and state competence. Indeed, they begin their essay by noting Madison's concerns about 'the mischiefs of faction', and accept the validity of current criticism that, where organized interests lobby government, the richest and most powerful groups have disproportionate control over policy. They also agree that there is a tendency for state agencies designed to regulate interest groups to be, in practice, captured by them. But they argue that groups are not necessarily narrowly factional and can adopt a wider social perspective.

They suggest that how groups act politically depends upon how far they include in their membership all those whose interests they claim to represent, the scope of their responsibilities and the nature of their relations to other groups and to the state. How groups operate politically also depends on the degree of internal accountability of leaders to members and whether they have effective authority to represent all interests within the organization and to bargain with other groups. Cohen and Rogers assume that groups which are most genuinely representative and accountable, and with a wider range of functions, will act most responsibly. The 'core idea' therefore is that the state can use legislation, administrative controls, taxes and subsidies to equalize power between unequal groups, and to foster the right kind of group characteristics. Associative democracy is not only the best way to promote their democratic ideal, but also the most effective way to curb factionalism.

There are four 'democracy-enhancing' functions which associations can already perform: providing information to policy-makers; equalizing representation by putting forward the needs of those previously unheard; providing a political education to their members; and by helping to formulate and implement public policies – i.e., providing 'alternative governance'.[22] Associative democracy focuses on expanding this fourth function. Cohen and Rogers envisage organizations representing key economic and social interests openly negotiating with each other and contributing to the formulation of policy at a national level. (These groups would include trade unions and business representatives, but should encompass all sectors of society, such as women and pensioners, and groups promoting key social issues such as the environment.) At a regional level, associations would promote coordination and cooperation – the authors focus here on economic policy. At a local level, groups using their local knowledge could help both in monitoring and in the implementation of state policy. For example, workplace committees could monitor health and safety standards, or green groups could monitor environmental standards. Churches, community groups and specialized voluntary bodies could expand on their present role in delivering social services; parent teacher associations in running schools.

The authors' concern to counterbalance the dominance of business in the USA and reduce the extreme economic inequalities leads them to stress the need for better representation of workers in unions, and more effective central wage bargaining, supplemented by local bargaining on conditions of work. They also argue for other forms of worker representation within companies, such as committees overseeing health and safety or vocational training. Cohen and Rogers slightly reformulated their ideas in 'Solidarity, democracy, association', which concludes their 1995 book *Associations and Democracy*. Here they identify themselves more explicitly with the values of social democracy than they did in their original essay. (Some critics had suggested this essay paid insufficient attention to American experience and aimed to introduce a European-style social democracy 'through the backdoor'.[23]) In their later essay, they conclude that associative democracy should be viewed 'less as an amendment to traditional social democratic strategies than as a synthesis of social democracy and radical democracy'.[24]

Hirst, despite his own socialist roots and earlier linkage of associationalism with socialist aims, tries in the 1990s to lift associative democracy above right–left affiliations.[25]

Hirst: democratizing the economy and society

Hirst's starting point in his 1994 book *Associative Democracy* is that state socialism of both the Soviet and social democratic variety has demonstrably failed, but that western liberal democracies have also proved unable to protect freedom effectively.[26] The liberal democracies have fostered centralized bureaucracies without real democratic checks. Parliamentary elections tend to hand over unfettered power to the winning party for years, and in some cases do not even ensure a regular alternation of ruling parties. Moreover, about a third of the population in liberal states are excluded from the general affluence, are often unemployed or relegated to marginal jobs and are socially alienated. Since members of this group rebel against their fate, there is in consequence a growth of crime and drug abuse. An increasingly repressive, but ultimately ineffective, state apparatus attempts in vain to check this rising disorder. Associative democracy potentially provides a means of maintaining liberal freedoms, developing stronger democratic controls and delivering satisfactory forms of work and welfare.

Although Hirst's aim is to cut back the role and powers of the state, because hierarchical bureaucracy is rigid and inefficient, he does see government bodies playing a crucial role. He argues against the view of some earlier theorists of associationalism that the state is an association like any other, because it is required to maintain the ground rules for the associations within its borders.[27] The state must delimit the powers of associations over their members and also provide public funding for many bodies undertaking administrative or welfare tasks. Therefore, whilst Hirst envisages that existing states should devolve many of their powers on a territorial basis, and transfer others to a range of functionalist and issue-based associations, there remains a legal, judicial and supervisory role for parliaments, courts and state administrative bodies. The state should also be responsible for enforcing certain common values which are at the core of a liberal and just society, such as basic human rights and racial and gender equality.

Hirst agrees with Cohen and Rogers that associations are not 'communities of fate' in which membership is already socially determined, but products of conscious political decisions and individual choice. Where ethnic, religious or class groupings are closed communities, this is due to social and political forces that create 'social closure'. Hirst argues that communities of fate are incompatible with the liberal commitment to escape oppression through individual rights and representative government. Associationalist theorists in the past were therefore mistaken in trying to base their social order on 'churches, classes or unions conceived as communities'.[28] Whilst churches or trade unions may indeed play a role in Hirst's pluralist society, all associations must respect the principles of individual choice and autonomy. This means that people must in general be free to join or leave associations.[29] It is because individuals cannot (normally) choose their gender or race that they must not be penalized for these characteristics, and the state should ensure there is no discrimination.

Hirst is well aware that associations with strongly opposed beliefs – for example, Gay Liberation and the Moral Majority in the USA – can undermine all social cohesion as they seek to vanquish each other: 'Communities of choice and the associations representing them may be no less disruptive for being recent social constructs than are ancient feuds between traditional communities.'[30] But he argues that a centralized state apparatus does not resolve these basic clashes of ideology – each group tries to capture the power of the state to enforce its own set of beliefs, as on the fraught issue of abortion. He suggests that associationalism, by allowing a considerable degree of self-regulation, can make ideological diversity work. The provisos are that groups must be tolerant of those in other associations with antagonistic beliefs and practices, and there must be a minimum common set of standards upheld by law to protect individuals and the associationalist system.

Although much of Hirst's argument in his 1994 book is based on individualistic liberal principles, he is very critical of economic liberals who rely solely on the market to ensure that wealth trickles down to the poor, and to promote economic efficiency: 'Market economies, unless suitably directed and regulated by public agencies, and embedded in appropriate social institutions, cannot be expected to deliver substantive social outcomes like a healthy environment, an acceptable level of employment, a desired composition of output, or the means to reproduce and expand existing levels of economic activity.'[31] He argues, therefore, not only for worker representation but also for fairer representation of the interests of consumers and local communities in economic decisions. One way of achieving these goals would be for companies to create supervisory boards, which give a voice to workers and the local community as well as shareholders, following the German and Japanese models. Hirst also envisages alternative sources of finance: for example, regional investment banks, non-profitmaking investment funds, in which ordinary people could invest their money to finance manufacturing, and industrial credit unions for cooperatives to deposit funds. These new financial bodies would underwrite and encourage the growth of a new cooperative sector.[32]

The strategy for achieving associative democracy is not through winning power by means of an election and legislating it into practice. Instead, such a society must be built from below by a multiplicity of voluntary initiatives: 'The role of legislation must be permissive and gradual, not prescriptive and peremptory.'[33]

Critical Questions about Associative Democracy

Many questions could be raised about both the strategy of moving towards an associative democracy and what it would look like once fully developed. Detailed answers would vary between countries. The focus of this discussion is on some general issues that are central to associative theory and its relationship to other theories of democracy.

The nature and role of groups

How the groups to be given recognized political and social rights are defined has important political implications. Iris Marion Young, an exponent of the 'politics of difference', criticizes Cohen and Rogers for viewing groups as purely voluntary associations. Young emphasizes that social justice requires full recognition of group identities, which are in a significant sense socially given, not consciously chosen – gender, age, sexual preference, disability, ethnicity or aboriginality. She wishes to distinguish between purely voluntary organized associations and groups sharing a common experience or a common culture. Moreover, the prevalence of social discrimination against women, the old, gays, the disabled, ethnic minorities and indigenous peoples requires that they be given special rights of political representation to ensure that they have a voice in policy-making.[34] Her approach challenges the view that these differences are to be seen as marginal to the political process.

Associative theorists could argue that their own approach allows for representation of special interests and that the needs of the old and the disabled – and special needs of women as mothers or carers – can be met by associative proposals to devolve welfare to voluntary groups. But Hirst hopes to deal with major divisions concerning culture and lifestyle by a strategy of liberal tolerance and legislated non-discrimination, excluding such issues as far as possible from the common political agenda. (Young suggests Cohen and Rogers also neglect non-economic issues and hope to exclude from political negotiation matters that cannot – given a clash of values – be resolved by compromise or decisions about distribution of resources.[35]) Young, on the other hand, wishes differing social perspectives to be brought to bear in deliberation on central political decisions to end social and cultural oppression.

It would be possible (as Young suggests) to interpret associative democracy in a way to accommodate a politics of difference, but this would depend upon giving a significant political role to lifestyle or cultural groups clearly regarded as subsidiary by the theorists of associative democracy discussed here.

Associative democracy and the state

The most difficult question when considering how to implement associative democracy is what role the state should play either in fostering group consciousness or in controlling groups. Hirst has criticized Cohen and Rogers for overstating the artificial nature of groups. He also queries the concomitant implication that they can be created or shaped by government policy, and that governments can promote a level playing field for groups representing less powerful interests.[36] Hirst argues that although associations are to some extent consciously created, they do have an autonomous life of their own. He also suggests that the state lacks 'either the legitimacy or the competence' to impose equality between groups, and that there would be major problems in choosing which interests are truly representative and require support.[37] Those that depend upon a supportive state would be vulnerable to changes in government policy. Groups should not be subjected to 'social engineering', but rather the state should decentralize its powers, and associations should strengthen their own institutions from below.

It is, however, hard to see how moves towards associative democracy could avoid a significant role for the state in deciding which bodies were representative and responsible and in providing funding or other support. Government – or independent organs which reported to it – would also necessarily have to monitor the performance of associations undertaking public functions, especially if, as Hirst recommends, they took over responsibility for welfare benefits, since there would be a real danger of misuse of funds or of corruption.

There are, of course, many precedents for organizations representing those with special needs having a voice in policy-making and perhaps receiving funds from the government in liberal democracies. Immigrant organizations in West European countries advise on policy and receive funds for educational and cultural activities. It may be possible for organizations with clear expertise and high professional standards to be accepted by governments without extensive supervision. But the more functions that are devolved to such bodies, and the more public money they receive (whether directly from individuals or from government funding), the greater the case for government controls. Although associative theorists stress the negative aspects of state bureaucracy, they seem to be proposing that independent organizations should become part of a complex bureaucratic system of controls and accountability.

Secondly, as social institutions and voluntary bodies take on more tasks and receive more money, requirements for accountability become more onerous and impose internal changes. This trend was noticeable in Britain during the 1980s and 1990s as Conservative governments encouraged the voluntary (as well as the commercial) sector to extend its scope. As a result, charities required more administrators, and emphasized management training and undertaking cost/benefit analyses.[38] Gains in efficiency may be offset by less individual commitment – for example a career structure between charities develops – and less internal democracy.

Cooperation between government and voluntary groups may work best at a local level, where people know each other and the issues involved. Cohen and Rogers indeed seem to suggest this. Both the degree of monitoring and the internal changes required of the groups may then be minimized. In Britain local councils already liaise with and fund many autonomous bodies – one council in 1999 funded more than thirty, ranging from library associations to groups caring for the disabled.[39] Local authorities and voluntary associations have also cooperated to support groups embodying participatory democracy, such as tenants' housing associations and small-scale community economic initiatives to revive run-down neighbourhoods.[40]

A third problem in delegating central state functions to voluntary associations is that it will become more difficult for them to maintain a critical and campaigning role in relation to governments. If, for example, a pressure group for widows had to allocate state-funded welfare bene-fits to its members, this would change it from an independent pressure group into a primarily administrative body.

Meshing with the state, especially at central government level, could however be a much greater problem for social movements. Andrew Szasz argues that social movements are vital because they protest against the activities of governments and corporations, for instance on environ-mental issues such as siting of hazardous waste. If the government coopted social movements and imposed regulations upon them, they would be pressured to conform to concepts of 'responsible' behaviour. But 'irresponsible' protest by mobilized citizens is often important in drawing attention to problems.[41]

Associationalism and social justice

The role of the state is also crucial to one of the goals of associative democracy, what Cohen and Rogers term 'distributive fairness'. This implies that everyone should have genuinely equal opportunities. The tension between decentralization and autonomy and ensuring everyone has equal opportunities is also illustrated by comparing the role of immi-grant organizations in Britain, where neo-liberal attitudes flourish, and Sweden, where social democracy has been strongly entrenched. The estimated 2,000 migrant organizations in Britain in 1991 have taken responsibility for special education and training, helping the old and handicapped, running housing schemes and community centres. Much of their funding has come from local government, but some has been channelled through the independent Commission for Racial Equality.[42] But this admirable display of communal initiative and care occurs because the central government does not, as in Sweden, take primary responsibility for meeting migrants' needs. It therefore reflects a weaker public commitment to the welfare and just treatment of migrants, and a less uniform distribution of resources.

Hirst confronts the social democratic claim that the state is necessary to ensure both high and equal levels of welfare. He argues that in practice this is a mirage, that even under a state system standards (for example of health care) vary between regions, and some households benefit more than others. Moreover, state welfare fails to grant due respect to those seeking it and may be badly administered. In addition, most voters are today less willing to pay high taxes to maintain high standards for all, so governments cut back on previous benefits. The alternatives of private charity and mutual self-help, which existed before the welfare state, or of market provision of pensions and health care, the neo-liberal solution, are unacceptable. The former allows too many to fall into extreme poverty and the latter is run for profit, not for the real interests of those who sign up. Associationalism, Hirst argues, allows voluntary choice backed by public funding and could be much more responsive to people's needs and wishes.

It is true that in an associationalist system the state could set and monitor minimum common standards, but it could not by definition ensure uniform standards throughout the country. The case for devolution and for involving non-state bodies is that they will adopt differing and perhaps more creative approaches, which may often have better results than a state-controlled policy. But some people, as Hirst readily admits, will gain more than others.

Associative democracy and republicanism

One key question for associationalism is how far it would require a common set of social values, including commitment to social justice. Hirst concludes that there must be a 'thin common core' of liberal values: belief in individual autonomy, in freedom of choice among individuals belonging to various social groups, and in human rights. There would also have to be, as in current liberal democracies, acceptance of due legal process and an obligation to maintain the political system – for example through taxation. Given a constitutional framework embodying these requirements, he explores how far associationalism could be based purely on individuals and groups pursuing rational self-interest, checked by a market-style competition between groups. (Hirst is responding here to the arguments of Mancur Olson about the problem of finding incentives for individuals to contribute to public goods.[43]) He suggests that 'even on very bleak assumptions about human motivation the system would work' and that organizations would be prevented from exploiting a privileged position by the fact that new members would enter and demand the same benefits.[44] Although associations might be run by active elites, members would demand rewards from their association and if it became corrupt they could abandon it. (Whether this would always be possible is not a question he addresses.)

Hirst therefore appears to demonstrate that even though a system based on pure pursuit of self-interest is undesirable, associative democracy can dispense with republican requirements of citizen commitment to a public good and a virtuous willingness to engage in political activity. But he does believe that in practice members of voluntary bodies tend to become involved in running them and that therefore an associative system ought to encourage participatory democracy.

Moreover, he goes on to reject the idea that a market economy can operate in a social and moral vacuum, noting that 'the market can only work in a context of social institutions that supply it with a distinctive morality' and that it depends upon '[h]onesty, fair-dealing and a respect for law'.[45] Most of his thesis assumes that an associative society will set a high value on social justice and democratic participation in controlling both political and economic life.

In fact, associative democracy, as envisaged by its main theorists, has a good deal in common with contemporary republicanism, since its aim is to promote a sense of responsible citizenship and to elevate social justice above the right to pursue individual wealth. It therefore assumes that individuals will have a sense of belonging to a shared society and accept obligations to other members of this society. Thus, associative democracy arguably requires a much 'thicker' common morality than either Cohen and Rogers or Hirst wish to concede. They postulate, for example, consensus on full racial and gender equality, on provision of generous welfare, and on the need to sacrifice economic gain to the maintenance of the environment.

It is true that republicanism requiring a politically active citizenry is difficult to envisage in societies marked by much greater interest in sport and consumerism than in politics, and with increasingly low voter turnout at elections – as in the USA and Britain.[46] But an effective associative democracy would require a significant *minority* of citizens to be active in a range of voluntary bodies as well as in political parties, and would need the *majority* to engage in at least minimum participation to monitor the performance of these voluntary bodies, as well as of the government. It is also true that republicanism, even though its explicit goals are often internationalist rather than nationalist, seems to rest upon the existence of a society united by a shared sense of national identity.

Republicanism does seem utopian in societies where there is not only considerable ethnic diversity, but cultural and religious pluralism and opposing lifestyles. But associative democracy, which as I have argued presupposes quite wide moral agreement, would face similar – if less extreme – difficulties.

Associative democracy and global democracy

Associative theorists argue that their ideas are appropriate to contemporary conditions because they do not envisage (as republicans do) a unitary nation-state claiming full sovereignty within its territorial borders. Precisely because associationalism envisages decentralizing power territorially and functionally, Hirst claims that it 'has no problems about a complex match between territory and authority'.[47] An associative democracy could, therefore, accept more easily than present states that international law determines in part legislation and public policy. The implication of this erosion of the state is that there must be democratic controls at appropriate international levels. Hirst also suggests that just as some state functions could be devolved to organs of civil society inside its borders, so the growing strength of global civil society means that transnational bodies could also take responsibility for forms of governance in economic, professional, legal and charitable spheres. Groups like Amnesty International, which already monitors human rights across the world, could play an important regulatory role.

It is clearly the case that associative ideas do chime with the increasing interest within international relations in the role of a global civil society as means of coordinating interests across national boundaries and promoting global causes.[48] Associations within civil society often have international representation, and some have explicitly global aims – for example to protect the environment or to alleviate hunger and promote economic development. Such organizations already play a role in influencing world opinion, bringing pressure to bear on governments, lobbying for international agreements and monitoring existing agreements. They may be particularly important in providing information to international bodies, for example about unpublicized violations of rights.[49] Many non-governmental organizations (NGOs) have official links to United Nations agencies and have a presence at international conferences.[50]

But global civil society is only one, still weak, facet of globalization. The forces promoting a global economy are very much more powerful and underpin neo-liberal beliefs about politics, society and culture. The possibility of promoting an associative democracy that depends upon political commitment and participation, and calls for social justice, must surely depend upon curbing the dominant economic and cultural forces. Some analysts of the global economy have argued that the state could still reclaim many of its powers to control economic policy. Indeed, Hirst himself has argued this quite vigorously.

Some of the apparent contradictions between Hirst's belief that associationalism fits into a version of global democracy and his insistence that national governments can still influence the global economy are resolved by his argument that national economic controls depend on international organizations – in the past the Bretton Woods system and today regional organizations like the European Union.[51] Hirst does not believe, like advocates of cosmopolitan democracy, that international bodies should be made directly responsible to the peoples of the world.[52] Instead, in *Globalization in Question* (co-authored with Grahame Thompson) he argues that nation-states act as 'pivots between international agencies and sub-national activities' and can therefore up to a point both represent their own people's wishes on international bodies and help to ensure these bodies are accountable. 'Such representation is very indirect,' they write, 'but it is the closest to democracy and accountability that international governance is likely to get.'[53]

Whether international and regional organizations can either control multinationals or operate in an open, accountable and democratic manner are major questions beyond the scope of this chapter. But the effectiveness of global civil society depends in part on the strengthening of international governmental bodies able to set a framework of rules.

Conclusion

Associative democracy is an attractive idea, which attempts to build on the existing strengths of civil society whilst limiting the danger of powerful groups pursuing their partisan interests at the expense of others. The strategy it proposes of partnership between economic, professional, interest or cause-based groups and local or national government, or international bodies, seeks to extend existing practices. It also recognizes political and economic trends whilst retaining a vision of a better society.

Associationalism is intended partly to reform central government, by making representation of interests fairer (as Cohen and Rogers argue) and by making it more genuinely accountable, by giving voluntary associations a right to monitor its operations. These goals do seem achievable in the present context. But greater clarity is required about how groups would relate to parliament, and to other supervisory organs, such as ombudsmen.

Whether associationalism would achieve its more radical goal of strengthening democratic participation would depend on its implementation. If many of the bodies taking over government functions were themselves highly centralized and market oriented they would not promote internal democracy. But if an associationalist strategy encouraged the growth of organizations owned and directed by their members in the economy and in welfare, and linked public funding to democratic procedures within groups, then it would potentially be a move towards greater participation. How far these organizations should be promoted, funded and controlled by the state is, however, clearly contentious and Cohen and Rogers seem to diverge from Hirst on this issue. There is also tension between devolving power, which implies people should have freedom to make their own decisions, and trying to maintain a set of principles which significant sections of the population may not share.

Finally, a major weakness of present associative proposals is that it is doubtful whether they can achieve their stated goal of delivering social justice. Devolving government powers upon voluntary bodies is at present more readily compatible with an ideology favouring economic competition and reduction in state powers. Moreover, voluntary groups may themselves be influenced by a business ethos – as the evolution of charities indicates. The present economic realities and prevailing neo-liberal ideology are fundamentally hostile to significant gains for equality and workers' economic security. As Cohen and Rogers recognize, a form of associationalism is already flourishing within a liberal economy and culture. Using associations as channels to radical democracy and social justice would surely require clear commitment to egalitarianism and extensive state action.

NOTES

1 The term 'associative' rather than 'associational' democracy is used because the authors examined here have all now adopted this label. Paul Hirst switched to the term 'associative democracy' in his book, *Associative Democracy: New Forms of Economic and Social Governance* (Cambridge, Polity, 1994). He explains that as Cohen and Rogers and Matthews use the term he has adopted it for 'convenience and commonality', p. 204.

2 M. Swilling, 'Socialism, democracy and civil society: The case for associational socialism', *Theoria* 79 (May 1992): 75–82. See also

Heinz Klug, 'Extending democracy in South Africa', in J. Cohen and J. Rogers et al., *Associations and Democracy* (London, Verso, 1995), pp. 214–35.

3 J. Matthews, *Age of Democracy: The Politics of Post-Fordism* (Melbourne, Oxford University Press, 1989).

4 All three have addressed other theoretical issues relevant to democracy, economic growth and globalization. See J. Cohen, 'Deliberation and democratic legitimacy', in A. Hamlin and P. Pettit (eds), *The Good Polity: Normative Analysis of the State* (Oxford, Blackwell, 1989), pp. 17–34; J. Rogers, 'The Wisconsin Regional Training Partnership: A national model for regional modernization efforts?', in *Proceedings of the 46th Annual Meeting of the Industrial Relations Research Association* (Madison, Industrial Relations Research Association, 1994), pp. 403–11; P. Q. Hirst, *From Statism to Pluralism: Democracy, Civil Society and Global Politics* (London, University College London Press, 1997), and (with G. Thompson) *Globalization in Question* (Cambridge, Polity, 1996).

5 To give a minor example, Hirst treats Robert Dahl's later work on participatory democracy as a prelude to his own proposals, whereas Cohen and Rogers treat Dahl's pluralism (including his participatory version of it) as an alternative to their model.

6 This school of thought was influenced by the German legal theorist Otto von Gierke. For an analysis of English pluralism and extracts from key theorists, see P. Q. Hirst (ed.), *The Pluralist Theory of the State: Selected Writings of G. D. H. Cole, J. N. Figgis and H. J. Laski* (London, Routledge, 1989).

7 A. de Tocqueville, *Democracy in America*, ed. J. P. Mayer and M. Lerner, trans. G. Lawrence (New York, Harper and Row, 1966); also A. de Tocqueville, *The Old Regime and the French Revolution*, trans. S. Gilbert (Garden City, NY, Doubleday Anchor, 1955).

8 See G. Lichtheim, *The Origins of Socialism* (London, Weidenfeld and Nicolson, 1969). Mill was impressed not so much by the original 'utopian socialists' – Owen, Fourier and Saint-Simon – but by some of their more political and pragmatic followers. (Fourier in particular had some distinctly bizarre ideas.)

9 See R. Gombin, *The Radical Tradition: A Study in Modern Revolutionary Thought*, trans. R. Swyer (London, Methuen, 1978).

10 Guild socialism emerged in Britain just before the First World War and flourished briefly after it, especially in the building industry where building guilds were set up. The movement had its own papers, the *New Age* and the *Guildsman* (later the *Guild Socialist* and then *New Standards*). Its exponents included S. G. Hobson, A. R. Orage and A. J. Penty. But G. D. H. Cole was the most eloquent and consistent exponent of guild socialist ideas, starting with *Self-Government in Industry*, 1917 and recapitulating them in *The Case for Industrial Partnership*, 1957.

11   One exception is the liberal pluralism stimulated by the cold war itself and totalitarianism. Fear in the West in the 1950s of 'mass society', and that individuals isolated from social ties are vulnerable to extremist movements, suggested that a pluralist society helps to guarantee individual freedom. See, for example, W. Kornhauser, *The Politics of Mass Society* (London, Routledge and Kegan Paul, 1960).

12   J. Keane, 'The limits of state action', in *Democracy and Civil Society* (London, Verso, 1988), p. 4. For an expression of rather earlier doubts about the role of the state in social democracy, see E. Luard, *Socialism Without the State* (London, Macmillan, 1979).

13   To complicate discussion of republicanism, Cohen and Rogers focus on a particular American brand of republicanism (they cite C. R. Sunstein, 'Constitutionalism after the New Deal', *Harvard Law Review* 101 (1987): 421–510), which is somewhat different from Hirst's understanding of republicanism, which is closer to the classical model.

14   Despite the Blair Government's creation of elected assemblies for Scotland and Wales, it is generally seen as continuing the authoritarian and centralist policies initiated by Mrs Thatcher over local government and spheres such as education. New Labour ideas are articulated by A. Giddens, *The Third Way – The Renewal of Social Democracy* (Cambridge, Polity, 1999), and were set out in the joint manifesto issued by Tony Blair and Gerhard Schröder on 8 June 1999.

15   Friendly Societies in Britain have a 200-year history in which members have provided each other with health insurance, loans and practical charitable help and organized joint social occasions. They still have six million members. 'Open Eye Supplement', *Independent* (1 June 1999), p. 7.

16   J. Cohen and J. Rogers, 'Solidarity, democracy, association', in Cohen and Rogers et al., *Associations and Democracy*, p. 237.

17   See P. Schmitter and W. Streeck, 'Community, market, state – and associations? The prospective contribution of interest governance to social order', *European Sociological Review* 1 (1985): 119–38. See also their chapter in Cohen and Rogers, *Associations and Democracy*.

18   A classic statement is R. A. Dahl, *A Preface to Democratic Theory* (Chicago, Chicago University Press, 1956).

19   See Hirst, *The Pluralist Theory of the State*, pp. 2–3.

20   Cohen and Rogers, 'Secondary associations and democratic governance', in *Associations and Democracy*, p. 32. For Dahl's later egalitarian emphasis, see R. A. Dahl, *Dilemmas of a Pluralist Democracy* (New Haven, CT, Yale University Press, 1982).

21   See *Politics and Society* 20, 4 (December 1992) for the original paper by Cohen and Rogers, entitled 'Secondary associations and democratic governance', and a number of commentaries. A more extended range of papers and Cohen and Rogers' reply, 'Solidarity,

democracy, association', were published as *Associations and Democracy* in 1995 in the Real Utopias Project edited by Erik Olin Wright. All references here are to the 1995 book.

22 Cohen and Rogers, 'Secondary associations', pp. 42–4.

23 See P. C. Schmitter, 'The irony of modern democracy and the viability of efforts to reform its practice', in Cohen and Rogers, *Associations and Democracy*, p. 171.

24 Cohen and Rogers, 'Solidarity, democracy, association', p. 236.

25 For his earlier work on associational democracy, see P. Hirst, *Law, Socialism and Democracy* (London, Allen and Unwin, 1986) and P. Hirst, 'Associational socialism in a pluralist State', *Journal of Law and Society* 1, 1 (1988): 139–50.

26 See, for example, P. Hirst, 'Associational democracy', in D. Held (ed.), *Prospects for Democracy* (Cambridge, Polity, 1993), pp. 112–35.

27 Hirst, *Associative Democracy*, p. 47.

28 Ibid., p. 55.

29 Some associations may of course by their nature only be open to certain categories of people whose interests they promote.

30 Hirst, *Associative Democracy*, p. 66.

31 Ibid., p. 78.

32 Ibid., p. 147.

33 Ibid., p. 131.

34 See I. M. Young, 'Social groups in associative democracy', in Cohen and Rogers et al., *Associations and Democracy*, pp. 210–11. For a full statement of her views, see I. M. Young, *Justice and the Politics of Difference* (Princeton, NJ, Princeton University Press, 1990).

35 Young, 'Social groups in associative democracy', p. 212.

36 P. Q. Hirst, 'Can secondary associations enhance democratic governance?', in Cohen and Rogers et al., *Associations and Democracy*, pp. 102–3.

37 Hirst, *Associative Democracy*, p. 37.

38 D. Bird, *Never the Same Again: A History of VSO* (Cambridge, Lutterworth Press, 1998), p. 192.

39 'Voluntary groups fear grants will be slashed', *Hertfordshire on Sunday* (12 December 1999), p. 24.

40 See 'Social enterprise needs support', *Independent* (Wednesday Review, 4 July 1999), p. 4.

41 A. Szasz, 'Progress through mischief: The social movement alternative to secondary associations', in Rogers and Cohen et al., *Associations and Democracy*, pp. 521–8.

42 Yasemin Nuhoglu Soysal, *Limits of Citizenship: Migrants and Postnational Membership in Europe* (Chicago, University of Chicago Press, 1994), pp. 102–4.

43 M. Olson, *The Logic of Collective Action* (Cambridge, MA, Harvard University Press, 1965).

44   Hirst, *Associative Democracy*, p. 64.

45   Ibid., p. 64.

46   These trends arguably apply to Australia too, but cannot be simply reflected in voter turnout because voting is legally compulsory there (although penalties for non-voting are not very severe).

47   Hirst, *Associative Democracy*, p. 71.

48   See, for example, M. Shaw, 'Civil society and global politics: Beyond a social movements approach', *Millennium* 23, 3 (1994): 647–67; P. Wapner, *Environmental Activism and World Civic Politics* (Albany, State University of New York Press, 1996).

49   P. van Tuijl, 'NGOs and human rights: Sources of justice and democracy', *Journal of International Affairs* 52, 2 (Spring 1999): 493–512.

50   Theorists of global democracy suggest institutionalizing NGO representation at the UN. See D. Archibugi 'From the United Nations to cosmopolitan democracy', in D. Archibugi and D. Held (eds), *Cosmopolitan Democracy: An Agenda for a New World Order* (Cambridge, Polity, 1995), p. 142. See also R. Falk, 'The world order between inter-state law and the law of humanity: The role of civil society institutions', in Archibugi and Held (eds), *Cosmopolitan Democracy*, pp. 163–79.

51   See P. Hirst, 'The myth of globalization' and 'The international origins of national sovereignty' in *From Statism to Pluralism*.

52   See e.g. David Held, *Democracy and the Global Order* (Cambridge, Polity, 1995).

53   P. Hirst and G. Thompson, *Globalization in Question*, 2nd revised edn (Cambridge, Polity, 1999), p. 276.

10

Social Democracy

Raymond Plant

Social democracy, which has its origins in the latter part of the nineteenth century, embodies two central ideas. The first is that it is possible to extend democratic values into the social and economic domain to ensure that the economy and society actually serve democratic purposes such as greater social and economic equality, social justice and individual security. Social democrats have generally assumed that real civil and political equality can only be secured by greater social and economic equality. Greater equality in these fields is necessary to make citizens' civil and political rights a reality. The second key idea is that it is possible to use the power of government to achieve these goals. In respect of each of these values there is a major difference between social democracy and the political economy of both Marxian forms of socialism and of neo-liberalism. In this chapter these ideas will be considered against the background of some aspects of the history of the development of social democracy, from the revisionist debates at the turn of the nineteenth century in Germany to the rethinking of social democracy in the 1950s. The first wave of revisionism is represented by Eduard Bernstein and his critique of Marx; the second, by C. A. R. Crosland, whose theory consciously refers back to Bernstein, draws on Keynesian economics and has parallels with John Rawls's theory of social justice. The chapter then examines the challenges posed by neo-liberalism to central tenets of social democracy, and concludes with a brief assessment of the ideas of the Third Way.

Political and Social Democracy

First of all, we need to consider the relationship between political democracy and social democracy. In the late nineteenth century the franchise
was being expanded in many European countries and democratic rights
were recognized and protected in the political sphere. The concept of
political equality was thus being extended, at least for males, in such
societies. Ideas about democratic political equality, however, raised questions about the drastic inequalities to be found in the economy and the
wider social order. The social democratic movement therefore adopted
the principle that the economy and society should be constrained to serve
values such as equality and social justice. The democratic transformation of politics was seen as a major step along the road to a similar transformation of the economy and society.

Of course, it was not the view of these early social democrats that this
process was going to be inevitable or easy. The dilemmas inherent in this
process have remained central to social democracy ever since. If it is
assumed that political action in a democratic society can lead to a transformation of economy and society, how is this to be achieved by democratic means? Should the social democratic appeal be to the votes of the
working class, who have the greatest objective interest in such a transformation, or should social democrats create a broader appeal across
society, to try to engage the interests and the votes of the middle classes?
In other words, should social democratic parties be class-based and try
to secure a transformation of society in the interests of the working class?
Or should social democrats attempt a strategy based upon a wider set
of values and interests, particularly through an appeal to values such as
citizenship to help to achieve their goals? The problem with the former
is that the class base may prove to be neither homogeneous nor large
enough to sustain social democratic parties. The difficulty with the latter
is that in order to incorporate a wider group into supporting the politics of social democracy, the more socialistic of its values have to be
compromised. This dilemma is intrinsic to social democracy that uses
parliamentary methods to attempt the general transformation of capitalist societies. This is not just a theoretical issue, but has been a central
practical dilemma for social democratic parties.

Throughout their history social democratic parties have existed
between the horns of this dilemma. In Germany, for example, the
German Social Democratic Party's (SPD) Erfurt programme of 1891
combined elements of class-based analysis together with an appeal to
middle-class values. Its Bad Godesberg statement in 1959 was founded

primarily on a politics of common values rather than sectional class-based politics. As far as the UK is concerned, in 1959 the Leader of the British Labour Party, Hugh Gaitskell, sought to get the party to change its constitution by dropping its Clause IV, which promised the wholesale nationalization of the commanding heights of the economy to ensure that the economy would secure for all workers 'by hand or brain' the full fruits of their labour. Gaitskell wanted to drop a class-based appeal, which he saw as embedded in Clause IV, but this proposal was rejected. It was not until 1995 that the Labour leader, Tony Blair, secured the party's agreement to drop Clause IV in favour of what he saw as a common set of national values. In some ways the predicament could be put in terms of a struggle between class and citizenship and a debate about which should be at the heart of social democracy. We can trace some of these themes in the history of European social democracy.

Contrasting Marxism and Social Democracy

Before proceeding, we need to consider the contrast between social democracy and Marxist forms of socialism. It is in relation to Marxism, particularly in the history of the SPD in Germany, that we can best elucidate the nature of social democracy. Indeed, social democracy really arose out of a debate on the left with Marxism.

For Marx, himself, the whole project of social democracy was fatally flawed, as he made clear in his polemic *The Critique of the Gotha Programme* (1875).[1] This programme was the policy statement produced at the coming together of the Social Democratic Party and the General Association of German Workers. This latter body was under the influence of the legacy of Ferdinand Lasalle and predisposed towards what we would now call a social democratic direction. Social democracy adopts a moral critique of capitalism, focusing upon its inequalities, insecurities and injustices. It also takes a very strong view about the possibility that electoral policies and political will can in fact fundamentally change these injustices. Marx rejected both of these central aspects of social democracy. He considered the social injustices of the capitalist economy to be the inevitable consequences of the private ownership of the means of production and extraction of surplus value. Therefore unequal distribution of wealth and income would not be changed by moral critique, but by transformation and overthrow of the means of production. Secondly, he did not think that political action had the degree of autonomy from capitalist or bourgeois interests that social democrats believed that it did. Right from the time that he was a journalist on the *Rheinische Zeitung* and his early essay *On the Jewish Question*, Marx had rejected the Hegelian idea that the modern state can act as a universal, reconciling and transforming the antagonisms of the market economy and civil society.[2] On the contrary, Marx saw that politics is about power and interests that were embodied in the market and in civil society. Politics cannot be used autonomously to reshape these forms of power and interest embedded in society. The whole doctrine of a social democracy that assumed workers' political parties could move from political equality (which in any case was not fully achieved) to the democratization of the economy and society was fundamentally incoherent.

Marx argued that the distribution of income and wealth would not be changed until the historical contradictions of capitalist society become more and more unmanageable and palpable, and when, as a result of this, the working class become more homogenous and acted upon their common class interest. This is the prerequisite for the transformation of capitalism. When capitalism is transformed into socialism, it will be a revolutionary change, and will only occur when the historical conditions are mature and when the working class has developed a political consciousness that makes this revolution possible.

Hence, for Marx, the social democrats are attempting to treat the symptoms – social injustice and inequality – without treating the disease – the private ownership of the means of production. This underlying cause, however, cannot be tackled without a revolutionary transformation, since the basic pattern of capitalist ownership cannot be changed by parliamentary means precisely because of the strength of the economic interests. So social democracy is fundamentally distinct from Marxism, in part because its diagnosis of the relationship between political and economic and social power is quite different. Based upon this diagnosis, social democracy's understanding of politics and what is politically possible is also different.

One way of articulating a key issue at stake between Marxists and social democrats, which will lead naturally to a discussion of the relationship between social democracy and neo-liberalism, would be to say that the social democrat treats production and distribution as separable. Goods and services get produced in an economy and then distributive questions arise, such as who is to get what? What is a fair or socially just distribution of what has been produced? For Marx, however, production and distribution are inseparable. In the *Critique of the Gotha Programme*, he makes the point somewhat sharply:

Vulgar socialism (and from it in turn a section of democracy) has taken over from the bourgeois economists the consideration and treatment of distribution as independent of the mode of production and hence the presentation of socialism is turning principally on distribution. After the real relation has long been made clear, why retrogress again?[3]

As we have seen, the Marxist regards production and distribution as inseparable: the maldistribution of income and wealth is a reflection of the maldistribution of the ownership of factors and means of production in the economy.

Marx differed from these incipient social democrats on a range of issues: the point of a moral critique of capitalism; the possibility of the autonomy of the state; the question of how far the growth of democratic rights could lead to economic transformation and thus obviate the need for a revolutionary transformation of society; and on the link between production and distribution. These themes were subsequently played out in the history of the SPD. This party, because of its size and intellectual energy, dominated the debate about the nature of social democracy until the First World War, and it is to that we now turn to illustrate the history of social democracy and its complex relationship to Marxism after Marx.

Revisionism: The First Phase

Karl Marx died in 1883, Friedrich Engels in 1895, and by the turn of the century a bitter debate raged in Europe about the relevance of Marxian socialism to contemporary industrial society, a debate which found its most natural outlet in Germany. The debate within this party between revisionists led by Eduard Bernstein (1850–1932), who had been influenced by the British Fabians, and Marxists such as Karl Kautsky (1854–1938) and Rosa Luxemburg (1870–1919) was largely concerned with the issue of reform or revolution. This was the strategic question of whether socialism was to be achieved through a decisive, revolutionary break with the existing capitalist order – its economic relations, its institutions, its politics and its law – or by working from within the system, by appropriating the means of production from the capitalists and socializing them in a democratic manner. The solution to this dilemma had to be an intellectual one, although of course it was quite central to both the political strategy and the tactics of the SPD in Germany. It was an intellectual problem in that the correct view depended upon the analysis of the existing social and economic system. Bernstein and the revisionists challenged the Marxian analysis of capitalism and rejected the consequent predictions about its future. Such a rejection, if persuasive, would clearly affect the political role of the SPD, and indeed Bernstein called on the party to jettison the Marxian elements in its programme and to modify its revolutionary theory.[4] The party's theory was revolutionary, its practice reformist, and it was upon this bifurcation between theory and practice that Bernstein focused his attention in his book *The Working Assumption of Socialism and the Tasks of Social Democracy* (1892).[5]

What impressed Bernstein was that most of Marx's predictions about the development of capitalism had not come true, and he argued that the failure of the predictive part of the theory indicated a weakness in the analysis on which the predictions were based. Since the foundation of the German Reich in 1870, a period of great prosperity had been experienced, a prosperity which, Bernstein argued, had benefited all classes, not just the capitalists and the leading members of the working class. Marxian theory could, of course, accommodate the view that at certain stages in its development capitalism could generate periods of relative prosperity, but such prosperity would always be restricted to the capitalists themselves, and perhaps to the elite of the proletariat whose revolutionary fervour was thus 'bought off'. It is clear in the mature analysis of *Capital* (1867) that Marx certainly did not envisage the possibility of a general and significant upward trend in real wages under the capitalist system.[6] Earlier, in 1848, in *The Communist Manifesto*, he had even predicted a decline in the living standards of the proletariat.[7] In Bernstein's view, no such decline had taken place and he believed that a modest upward trend could be discerned.

It was not only in its account of economic change that Bernstein found Marxian theory lacking. He argued that it could take no account of correlative changes in social structure. Marx had contended that, as capitalism developed, a polarization of classes would take place between the oppressed and exploited proletariat on the one hand, and the exploiters – the capitalists – on the other. Bernstein argued that such class polarization just had not occurred. On the contrary, a greater differentiation in social structure had taken place in trade, industry and commerce, and in the bureaucracies, middle-class or white-collar occupations were on the increase.

The prediction of the polarization of classes and the increasing impoverishment of the working class were taken widely to be the two cornerstones of Marx's theory of revolution. The growth of these two tendencies would exacerbate the tensions in capitalism to such a degree that the system would eventually collapse. As these predictions were not, in Bernstein's view, correct, the emphasis on revolution, he argued, could be dismissed. Furthermore, the failure of the predictive part of the theory undermined the scientific pretensions of the analyses that underpinned the predictive element, and in his influential lecture *How is Scientific Socialism Possible?* (1901), Bernstein broke with *scientific* socialism, which was considered to be the major hallmark of the Marxian system.[8] He argued that socialism was not an inevitable outcome of the development of capitalism, but rather a moral ideal for which those committed to it must struggle. Rosa Luxemburg, Bernstein's severest critic, conceded that Bernstein's position had a certain logic to it, when she wrote that if one were to admit that capitalist development does not move in the direction of its own ruin, then socialism ceases to be objectively necessary. Bernstein accepted the logic of his own position and formulated a conception of socialism based upon Kantian moral philosophy in which he envisaged socialist society to be an ideal like Immanuel Kant's 'Kingdom of Ends'.[9] Bernstein's work became foundational for social democracy.

Bernstein's critique clearly had significant practical consequences. Revolution was not necessary, since the twin bases upon which the need for it had been predicated did not exist. Instead, the struggle for socialism had to be gradualist and reformist. Politically, it would consist in the attempt to achieve full democracy and then of maximizing electoral support. Economically, the strategy was for the workers to appropriate, both through political power and trade union pressure, the means of production in society. The projected socialization of German economic power had, in Bernstein's view, been made easier by the development of cartels in the economy, thereby rendering the ownership of economic power less diffuse. The task was therefore to engage in peaceful political struggle for particular social democratic objectives, not to wait for socialism to emerge fully formed from the womb of history.

The reaction of the party intellectuals, such as Karl Kautsky, was hostile.[10] Rosa Luxemburg was moved to write her *Social Reform or Revolution* (1899), which was at once a superb polemic against the revisionist social democrats and a brilliant attempt to deal with their arguments from a Marxian standpoint.[11] Luxemburg attempted to dismantle each one of Bernstein's theses. In particular, she attacked his denial of the tendency towards impoverishment of the working class and his assertion of greater social differentiation. She was willing to admit that capitalism did not undergo such frequent crises, as had been the case in the past, and that in consequence the lot of the proletariat might superficially seem to improve. Nonetheless, Luxemburg argued that the basic facts of exploitation, the appropriation of surplus value and the growing contradictions between the relations of production and the means of production, were still present. She contended that what the crises had lost in frequency, they would make up for in intensity and severity. She also rejected Bernstein's theory of growing differentiation. In the long run, she argued, with the increasing crises in capitalism, the middle classes would be forced into implicit identification with either the capitalists or the proletarians. They had no *sui generis* stake in the structure of the society in which there was a basic division between those who did and those who did not own the means of production. She also denied the possibility of any significant political reforms from within the structure of capitalism. In the first place the capitalists would allow only those changes, for example in welfare or conditions of labour, which would protect their interest and put off the development of revolutionary consciousness on the part of the proletariat. Reforms that seek to impose 'social control' over capital are 'not a threat to capitalist exploitation, but simply the regulation of this exploitation'.[12] The second reason she gave for rejecting the possibility of social reform as a means of securing a socialist society was that the relationship between the capitalist and the proletarian was not primarily a *legal* relationship, for it was based upon the *economic* fact of exploitation.[13] Only legal relationships could be changed by the exercise of political power; economic exploitation, on the other hand, could only be ended by the expropriation of the capitalist class.

Whereas Bernstein had looked to the trade unions in the hope of seeing them exert pressure for socialist objectives, in Luxemburg's view such a thesis was quite utopian, for all that trade unions could do was to ward off the worst features of capitalist exploitation. She did not think, therefore, that trade unions could be instruments for the transformation of society, and, as the debates in 1905 over the possibility of a politically motivated general strike showed, she was extremely sceptical of the socialist motivation of a great many union leaders.

The dispute between the various factions of the SPD continued until the outbreak of the First World War, when the bitter controversy about its character broke old alignments and healed old wounds. Kautsky and Bernstein, once ideological enemies, took a stand against the war, which had originally been approved by the majority of socialist deputies in the Reichstag. Rosa Luxemburg and Karl Liebknecht too disapproved of the war, as well as the stand on the issue taken by the Social Democrats, and they founded the Spartacus League, the forerunner of the German Communist Party that came to power in East Germany in 1945. In the long term, however, revisionism and reformism were triumphant within the

German Social Democratic Party, a triumph that was crowned by the explicit adoption of gradualist principles at the Bad Godesberg Congress of the party in 1959.

Revisionism: The Second Phase

In the post-Second World War period, the issue of nationalization stimulated the second major period of revisionism in social democracy. European and British social democrats from the turn of the nineteenth century up until the 1950s believed that the common ownership of the means of production was essential to the achievement of social democratic ideals. Social democrats still assumed that a more just and equal society could only be achieved through state planning and nationalization of the 'commanding heights of the economy'. Nevertheless, by the late 1930s, the assumption was being disputed, as for example in Douglas Jay's *The Socialist Case*,[14] which drew upon the economic theories of John Maynard Keynes. The pivotal intellectual influence here was the publication of Keynes's arguments in his *General Theory*. There he provided a critique of the need for nationalization:

> It is not the ownership of the instruments of production, which it is important for the state to assume. If the state is able to determine the aggregate amount of resources devoted to augmenting the instruments and the basic rate of reward to those who own them, it will have accomplished all that is necessary.[15]

Keynes's ideas enabled social democrats to see ways in which social justice and a more just distribution of resources could be achieved without the need for either state planning or wholesale nationalization. Demand management would also enable social democratic governments to manage capitalism, and so avoid crises of the sort that Marx regarded as endemic in the nature of capitalism and which had wrought havoc in Europe and the USA in 1929. The impact of Keynes's ideas in Britain on social democrats such as Hugh Gaitskell, Douglas Jay and Evan Durbin cannot be over-emphasized. As Adam Przeworski says in his classic book, *Capitalism and Social Democracy*:

> The fact is that social democrats everywhere soon discovered in Keynes' ideas, particularly after the appearance of his *General Theory*, something they urgently needed: a distinct policy for administering capitalist economies. The Keynesian revolution – and this is what it was

– provided social democrats with a goal and hence justification of their governmental role, and simultaneously transformed the ideological significance of distributive politics that favoured the working class.

From the passive victim of economic cycles, the state became transformed almost overnight into an institution by which society could regulate crises to maintain full employment.[16]

The espousal of Keynesian theories, amongst other things, led to the German SPD repudiating its Marxist heritage in the Bad Godesberg declaration in 1959. While the British Labour Party continued with a constitution that theoretically committed it to nationalization, its practice was entirely Keynesian and social democratic. It was not until C. A. R. Crosland published *The Future of Socialism* in 1956, however, that these insights were brought together in a new social democratic synthesis.[17]

Crosland broadened the argument into the issue of whether the post-Second World War democratic society, with Keynesian means of demand management and an extensive welfare state, could in fact still be regarded as a capitalist society in any meaningful sense. If it was not, then, Crosland argued, traditional Marxist explanations no longer applied. We need therefore to look in some detail at Crosland's case.

In *The Future of Socialism* Crosland put equality at the heart of the social democratic project and this is fundamental for understanding his own revisionism. As we have seen, Bernstein – the first revisionist – argued that Marx's economic analysis and its political consequences were fundamentally flawed and that it was perfectly possible to pursue the ideal of a just society by political and democratic means. Crosland stood firmly within this tradition, following a three-track argument. First, he argued that Marx's account of capitalism was mistaken, or at least it did not apply to capitalism in the modern world. Second, he claimed that there was a need for a corresponding emphasis on a political strategy for achieving a more just and egalitarian society. Third, as is obvious from this view, he proposed that the project of social democracy could be understood in terms of values such as social justice and equality, rather than a revolutionary emphasis on expropriating those who own the means of production.

Crosland argued in the early part of *The Future of Socialism* that capitalism in the postwar world was fundamentally different from the economic system that Marx had confronted. This was so for a number of reasons, which I shall identify, rather than discuss in detail. First of all, he thought that capitalism had changed because ownership of the means of production had become dispersed and continues to be so. That is, we do not confront a number of individual owners of capital, who form an homogeneous class with common economic and political interests, as Marx had assumed. Indeed, the 1945 Labour Government had taken into public ownership those means of production, such as coal mines and electricity generating facilities, that bore most directly on the infrastructure of the economy. Crosland welcomed this settlement and showed no signs of wanting to change it. Because of the dispersal of ownership, and the common ownership of certain key industries, the question of management rather than ownership was now central. The primary issue became that of how to ensure that the management of private industry could become more socially responsible and incorporate some sense of the public interest. This question was much more important, Crosland believed, than further acts of nationalization.

Second, greater democratization of British society had put severe constraints on the power of private ownership in the modern economy. Not only did dispersed ownership mean that there was no capitalist class with a common interest, but the growth of liberal democracy (again a change from Marx's time) provided a major countervailing power to the interests of private owners. In addition, trade unions now had a central role in politics and the economy and also acted as a strong countervailing force in society to limit the power of private owners.

Furthermore, Keynesian economic techniques meant that government was able to manage the general macroeconomic climate within which firms operated. Therefore, the idea that capitalists (even assuming that we were still in a situation of non-dispersed ownership) could pursue an economic agenda which did not take account of government-managed macroeconomic conditions was false. Keynesian economic management implied, to a degree, the relative autonomy of politics, in that it could no longer be seen as an arena of class interest. Governments, using Keynesian techniques, could pursue macroeconomic policies that would serve their view of the public interest, and that would in turn be shaped by their political values. Equally, class relations had changed: there has not been a polarization of classes, nor had there been the immiseration of the proletariat (a view of Marx that was central to Bernstein's revisionism, which Crosland self-consciously followed).

Finally, the growth of the welfare state and welfare rights after the reforms of the 1945 Labour Government meant that in terms of health, education and welfare, citizens were no longer subject to the vagaries of the market. Instead, they now had a stake in society mediated not only by non-capitalist institutions, but also based on the principle of recognizing need, which was a profoundly anti-capitalist notion.

The basic value for Crosland was that of equality and social justice, and in his last book, *Socialism Now*,[18] he described his own view of equality as being more or less the same as that developed with great philosophical force by John Rawls in *A Theory of Justice*.[19] Rawls's book was once described by the philosopher and socialist Stuart Hampshire as being precisely the deep philosophical theory social democrats had always needed to underpin their values.[20] Crosland's view of equality, like Rawls's democratic equality, lies on a spectrum between equality of opportunity and equality of outcome. While Crosland welcomed the gains that greater equality of opportunity had secured, he made it clear that he did not think that it was a sufficiently rich conception of equality for a recognizably social democratic commitment. It was not, in his own words, 'enough'.

It was not enough for two main reasons, both of which he shared with Rawls. First of all, equality of opportunity does not pay sufficient attention to starting points and unequal endowments. Family background and genetic legacy make an enormous difference to starting points and are morally arbitrary, in that those who benefit from a regime of equal opportunity will be those with fortunate backgrounds and genetic endowments, but an individual bears little or no responsibility for these. Thus a regime of equal opportunity alone may be unjust in its outcomes, since it will offer greater rewards to those people who bear little personal responsibility for their success.

Second, in Crosland's view, there was certainly a case for income inequality, and those positions which carried differential rewards should be subject to the fairest competition under equality of opportunity, but two conditions are important. The first is that differential rewards should not be seen as a matter of personal desert, for the reason given above. Income inequality is rather to be justified by the 'rent of ability' criterion, that higher rewards will motivate and mobilize people with talent to use it for the benefit of the community as a whole. In this sense, Crosland's view of equality of opportunity was close to Rawls's 'difference' principle. The second condition, which was closer to social policy and bears on Crosland's commitment to comprehensive education, was that we have to be concerned with starting points in life. The social democratic strategy is to use education to compensate, so far as possible, for negative features in family and environmental background, so that the starting point in the competition for differentially high rewards is fairer.

So in Crosland's view, we are no longer living in a capitalist society, and social democratic ends can be pursued in non-Marxist ways, even if the Marxist and the social democrat do pursue the same overall goals: economic justice and the democratization of society. In the second third of the twentieth century Crosland's book seemed to be the canonical statement of social democracy, and in many ways it seemed to fit an analysis of the nature not only of British but also European society at the time.

By the 1980s, however, this vision seemed to be impossibly dated and not capable of revival, for two main reasons. First of all, as we have seen, post-Second World War, social democracy had been sustained by its link to Keynesian economic techniques. This kind of economic doctrine, however, became more and more debatable by the 1970s. In the face of the problems of open, competitive markets in a global economy, Keynesian approaches – which sanctioned strong state intervention – looked impossible to sustain. The British Labour Party under James Callaghan effectively adopted a form of monetarism in the last couple of years before his government lost office in 1979. President Mitterrand of France had to reverse his economic policies when his Keynesian-inspired economic expansion collapsed in the early 1980s. Second, there was an alternative approach available, namely supply-side economics linked to a broader neo-liberal, social and political agenda. Given the link between social democracy and Keynesianism, it is not surprising that its partial eclipse at least would provoke a crisis in social democracy. There was also a major growth in the impact of neo-liberal thought and analysis – sometimes referred to as the new right – and we need to understand the essence of this critique of social democracy.

Social Democracy, Neo-liberalism and Globalization

In an odd sort of way, the neo-liberal, for different reasons, reflects Marx's critique of social democracy's attempt to separate production and distribution. The neo-liberal rejection of this separation is based on two arguments that, though independent, can be held together without contradiction. The first argument, the best modern exponent of which is Robert Nozick in *Anarchy, State and Utopia*, is that a market economy, together with the idea that one owns one's own body, creates rights in the product produced by the labour of those involved in the production.[21] In Nozick's view, the social democrat treats goods and services as if they were manna from heaven, with the only interesting question being how such goods are to be distributed, that is, according to which principle of social justice. Nonetheless, such goods and services come with entitlements built into them, so that it is not therefore an open moral question about how they are to be distributed. Thus, production and distribution are bound together.

The other neo-liberal argument concerns incentives. For the neo-liberal, there is a clear link between incentives and economic productivity. Hence, if a regime of social justice diminishes incentives, then production would be likely to decline. Making economic outputs serve social objectives will, on this view, have an effect on economics in terms of productivity and it is therefore important not to neglect the interaction between outputs and inputs: between distribution and production.

Second, the core value of social democracy, social justice – in the form of greater social and economic equality to mirror political equality in democratic societies – has come under attack. Since the end of the Second World War, the nature and meaning of social justice has been contested by neo-liberals. As we have seen, Marxists will not allow an independent and autonomous role for the moral critique of capitalism. Neo-liberals, for different reasons, argue that the outcomes of a market cannot be judged or corrected by an appeal to social justice. In the view of Friedrich Hayek, social justice is a 'mirage'.[22] To explain why this is so will take us into the heart of some of the theoretical assumptions of social democracy and its differences from neo-liberalism.

There are several aspects to the neo-liberal critique of social justice. The first two to be examined are philosophical. In the view of the neo-liberal, injustice can only be caused by intentional action. Hence, if I destroy your crops in the field I have committed an injustice, since it is an intentional act; if the weather does it, it is not an injustice, because the weather is a non-intentional force. In an economic market millions of people buy and sell, and all these economic exchanges will, at any time, produce a set of outcomes in which some will be rich and some will be poor. Social democrats will typically say at this point that this 'distribution' of income and wealth is unjust and needs to be rectified by political action. The neo-liberal, however, will claim that this is not in any way a 'distribution' of income and wealth, because it is, in fact, the unintended and unforeseeable aggregate outcome of millions of acts of economic exchange pursued for specific individual reasons. As an unintended and unforeseen consequence of economic activity, it is neither just nor unjust, or in Fred Hirsch's words, the outcomes of markets are 'in principle unprincipled'.[23] Hence, there is no case for a moral critique of economic outcomes in terms of social justice and no case for a political strategy allegedly to secure social justice.

Second, the neo-liberals argue that modern societies are diverse and pluralistic in their moral and social outlooks. An appeal to social justice will fall foul of this moral pluralism, because we should be unable to agree on what a socially just distribution of economic goods should be. If it is not possible to agree on criteria for just distribution, as it is not in a pluralist society, then distributive politics will take place in an ethical vacuum. Competing groups will struggle for what, from their own subjective point of view, is seen as their legitimate share of social goods, but

there is no way of arbitrating between them. Social democratic governments in these circumstances are likely to fall prey to coalitions of the
most powerful interest groups in society. Politics will be reduced to a
rather bleak zero-sum game, and instead of the needs of the poor being
served by social justice, the most powerful groups will win most of the
criterionless distributive struggle.

At the same time, the lack of a clear and agreed ethical basis for distribution will mean that there will have to be a necessary degree of unaccountable bureaucracy in the distribution of resources. It is not possible
to write rules of law, it is claimed, that can be applied to all complex
distributive circumstances, and public officials and bodies charged with
administering the distributive consequences of political decisions will, of
necessity, have to act in arbitrary and discretionary ways.

This thesis can be combined with a further element of the neo-liberal
critique. It has been argued by the 'public choice' school of economists
that bureaucrats, like everyone else, are motivated by utility maximiza-
tion and that utility in the context of bureaucracy means an extension
of power, resources and responsibilities. So, a necessary degree of dis-
cretion allied to utility maximizing behaviour without the constraint on
such behaviour provided in the market by the possibility of reduced
profits – or worse, bankruptcy – entrenches a large degree of unaccountable and growing bureaucratic power at the heart of the social
democratic state, in the view of the neo-liberal critic.

A somewhat different sociological analysis claims that social democratic approaches to social justice have spawned a culture of dependency,
and a belief in rights and entitlements without a corresponding sense of
responsibility. The claim here is that the social democratic welfare state
has conferred entitlements on individuals as of right, irrespective of the
character and contribution to society of such recipients, and this has led
to an unintended fostering of dependency. No doubt, social democrats
believed that the creation of welfare entitlements would be empowering
for the poor. But in practice it has created dependency and has undermined a willingness to work. If people believe that they can live a life at
the long-term expense of others, they have a strong incentive to do so,
particularly if the alternative is a low-paid job. So, runs the claim, welfare
benefits create moral hazards.

An economic argument that some Marxists as well as neo-liberals
put forward is that globalization and the growing competitiveness of
the world economy means that social democracy is no longer a viable
political programme in the modern world. First of all, it is claimed that
greater social and economic equality in the context of a global market
will severely affect incentives at all levels in respect of risk-taking, moving

jobs, undertaking training and so on. In addition, it is argued that Keynesian economies can no longer work in a global market. It is not possible to pursue traditional social democratic methods of economic management within a particular state, as President Mitterrand of France found to his cost in his first period of office. Furthermore, the degree of social protection usually associated with social democratic states is incompatible with global competitiveness. Such protection increases labour costs compared with competitor countries which do not have such costs.

So social democrats face major challenges, not only to the moral basis of their beliefs, but also, given an evolving global capitalism, to the feasibility of political strategies to realize their policies.

Third Way Social Democracy?

In the UK and Europe the strength of neo-liberalism and the processes of economic globalization have led to an interest amongst social democrats in what in the UK is called the Third Way and in Germany the Neue Mitte. The Third Way is espoused by Prime Minister Tony Blair and the Neue Mitte by Gerhard Schröder, the German Chancellor. What is unclear about these formulations is how they stand in relation to traditional social democracy. As we have seen, social democrats from Bernstein to Crosland have been perfectly willing to rethink the nature of social democracy. So are Third Way/Neue Mitte ideas to be seen as the most recent form of social democratic revisionism, or are these movements rather to be seen as being alternatives to an exhausted social democracy? In many ways the jury is still out on this question.

There are those, such as Anthony Giddens, who has written several authoritative books on the Third Way, who do see it as a rethinking of the social democratic tradition in modern circumstances.[24] The same view is taken by Tony Blair in his Fabian Society pamphlet, *The Third Way*.[25] Nevertheless, some of the political statements about the Third Way treat it not as a revisionist position within social democracy, but rather as a position between social democracy and neo-liberalism. Those in the UK who take this view believe that it is possible to see the post-Second World War history of the UK in three periods. The first period encompassed the post-1945 world and was initially dominated by the Labour Government which implemented policies that included some nationalization and the establishment of the welfare state, along with a Keynesian approach to economic management. To a degree, such policies were also followed by Conservative Governments between 1951 and

1964. The second phase, the intellectual basis of which was developed in the 1970s and reached fruition in the Thatcher Government, was a repudiation of such social democratic approaches in favour of the neo-liberalism whose nature has been described above. What is needed now, it is argued, is a new philosophy of politics which accepts a good deal of the neo-liberal critique of social democratic political economy, while wishing to preserve a good many of the values of social democracy. Probably, the critical issue here is over the place of equality and the extent to which markets should be restrained to produce greater equality of outcome.

The strategy of placing limits on the outcomes of markets has been rejected in the UK by both New Labour and Third Way theorists as being morally objectionable and also unachievable in a global market with its competitive pressures. Furthermore, the goal of greater equality of outcomes has been replaced by that of equality of opportunity. In this context, it is argued that investment in individuals and their skills throughout their lives, while leaving them to make their way in relatively unconstrained markets, is both morally defensible and economically efficient. The relationship between equality of opportunity and of outcomes is clearly a crucial issue given the importance of equality to social democratic ideas of social justice. It was central to Croslandite social democracy that, although differentiated rewards were economically necessary, the relative position of the worst off members of society also mattered. In Crosland's view, the fiscal dividends of growth should be used to maintain the absolute or real living standards of the better off – otherwise they would not vote for social democratic parties – while improving the relative position of the worst off. Hence the concern with greater equality of outcomes. The neo-liberal exactly reverses this argument. On this view the relative position of the better off should be improved (because inequality is important for economic incentives), while the income of the poor can be improved in real terms through the 'trickle-down' effect. This is then a clear and categorical difference between Croslandite social democracy and neo-liberalism. So where does the Third Way stand on the argument?

The emphasis is put on a radical view of equality of opportunity, with investment in skills and knowledge acquisition (since there is low demand for unskilled labour and this is a cause of inequality), together with attempts to improve the social capital of the worst off neighbourhoods and communities. The aim is to make the pursuit of equality more compatible with the market economy, since that economy will need such skills. Such skills will enable the trickle-down process to work much more effectively than it would under neo-liberals whose views of the role of the state would not really allow them to undertake programmes based on the radical form of equality of opportunity to which modern social democrats are committed. At the same time, however, a radical approach to equality of opportunity will not increase equality of outcomes unless there is some attempt to curb the growth of income and wealth, for example via the tax system. Increasing taxes for the rich has not, however, been adopted, because European social democratic governments see high incomes and other rewards as part of the dynamic of a modern economy in a global market place, one that includes a global market for highly skilled labour. A failure to raise taxes does mean, however, that the radical approach to equality of opportunity is not likely to make a marked difference in relative positions.

One thing that a Third Way approach does is to resolve an issue that was noted early in this chapter: the tension within social democracy between a class-based and a citizenship-based strategy. The modern approach to equality, as investment in skills to enhance the effectiveness of the economy in the global market, shows that this kind of social democracy pursues a political programme based upon the perceived requirements of citizenship rather than class. Certainly, presenting social democracy as having a national agenda as opposed to a more universalistic class based one has been central to restatements of social democracy in the late 1980s and 1990s.[26]

It is too early to say whether modern developments should be located within previous social democratic traditions, or understood as a genuinely different form of politics. At the same time, as we have seen, the social democratic tradition has been through many changes since the mid-nineteenth century. There is no undisputed account of social democracy. Hence the question about modern political developments and their relation to social democracy cannot be resolved by comparing them with some alleged essence of social democracy. It is a political issue rather than an academic one, since there are both political costs and benefits associated with claiming that the Third Way and the Neue Mitte are still forms of social democracy.

Conclusion

Social democracy differs from Marxism on the one hand and neo-liberalism on the other in stressing the goal of social justice, the moral case for both a genuine equality of opportunity and greater equality of outcomes. It also accepts the possibility of achieving these aims through gradualist political means within a capitalist society. Contemporary defences of social democracy therefore need to restate its moral vision and the political relevance and feasibility of that vision. Given that social democrats rely on government to secure their goals, reform of political institutions to ensure their effectiveness and accountability is also important. Finally, as social democracy abandons a class-based politics for programmes founded upon citizen entitlements, restatements of social democracy would appear to require a strong concept of citizenship. This is a project that gives renewed emphasis to the links between political and social democracy, and where social and economic rights are accepted as the essential bulwarks of civil and political rights.[27]

NOTES

1   K. Marx, 'Critique of the Gotha programme', in K. Marx and F. Engels, *Selected Works in One Volume* (New York, International Publishers, 1968), pp. 315–35.

2   See e.g., K. Marx, 'On The Jewish Question', in L. D. Easton and K. H. Guddat (eds), *Writings of the Young Marx on Philosophy and Society* (Garden City, NY, Doubleday, 1967), pp. 216–48.

3   Marx, 'Critique of the Gotha programme', p. 325.

4   It should be noted that Engels himself had contributed to a questioning of the assumptions of revolutionary socialism in his 'Introduction' (1895) to the re-issue of Marx's book, *The Class Struggles in France, 1848 to 1850*, in K. Marx and F. Engels, *Selected Works in One Volume* (New York, International Publishers, 1968), pp. 651–68. In that work, he suggested that, since armed struggle was generally no longer a feasible means for achieving socialism in the emerging European democracies, it might be necessary for socialists to concentrate on winning votes and gaining majority support in the parliamentary sphere, at least in the short run.

5   E. Bernstein, translated as *Evolutionary Socialism* (New York, Shocken, 1961).

6   See K. Marx, *Capital*, vol. I (Moscow, Progress Publishers, 1987 [1867]), p. 582.

7   K. Marx and F. Engels, *The Communist Manifesto* (Harmondsworth, Penguin, 1967 [1848]), p. 93.

8   E. Bernstein, *How is Scientific Socialism Possible?* [1901]. See the discussion in P. Gay, *The Dilemma of Democratic Socialism: Eduard Bernstein's Challenge to Marx* (New York, Shocken, 1962), pp. 156–9.

9   Bernstein, *Evolutionary Socialism*, p. 200.

10 See Kautsky's pedestrian but effective *Bernstein and the Programme of the Social Democrats* [1899] published in English as 'The Revi-

sionist Controversy', in *Karl Kautsky: Selected Political Writings*, ed. and trans. Patrick Goode, (London, Macmillan, 1983), pp. 16–31. August Bebel also rejected revisionism largely on pragmatic grounds because in his view the Erfurt programme was the only one to hold the party together.

11   Rosa Luxemburg, *Social Reform or Revolution*, trans. Integer (London, Merlin Press, 1970 [1899]).

12   Ibid., p. 34.

13   Ibid., p. 76.

14   D. Jay, *The Socialist Case* (London, Faber, 1937). For a good analysis of the impact of Keynes, see Elizabeth Durbin, *New Jerusalems: The Labour Party and the Economics of Democratic Socialism* (London, Routledge, 1985).

15   John M. Keynes, *The General Theory of Employment, Interest and Money* (New York, Harvest Books, 1964 [1936]), p. 378.

16   Adam Przeworski, *Capitalism and Social Democracy* (Cambridge, Cambridge University Press, 1985), p. 36.

17   C. A. R. Crosland, *The Future of Socialism* (Cape, London, 1956).

18   C. A. R. Crosland, *Socialism Now*, ed. D. Leonard (London, Cape, 1974), p. 15.

19   John Rawls, *A Theory of Justice* (Oxford, Oxford University Press, 1972).

20   See S. N. Hampshire, 'A new philosophy for the just society', *New York Review of Books* (24 February 1972), pp. 34–9.

21   Robert Nozick, *Anarchy, State and Utopia* (Oxford, Blackwell, 1974).

22   See F. A. Hayek, *The Mirage of Social Justice* (London, Routledge, 1976).

23   Fred Hirsch, *The Social Limits to Growth* (London, Routledge, 1977).

24   See Anthony Giddens, *The Third Way: The Renewal of Social Democracy* (Cambridge, Polity, 1998) and *The Third Way and Its Critics* (Cambridge, Polity, 2000).

25   Tony Blair, *The Third Way* (London, Fabian Society, 1998).

26   See, e.g., R. Plant, *Citizenship, Rights and Socialism* (London, Fabian Society, 1988), Tract 531.

27   For further details on these themes, see R. Plant, 'Social democracy', in D. Marquand and A. Seldon (eds), *The Ideas that Shaped Post-War Britain* (London, Fontana, 1996), pp. 165–94.

11

Transnational Democracy

Anthony McGrew

Democratic theory (and practice), notes Shapiro, has always appeared 'impotent when faced with questions about its own scope'.[1] Binary oppositions between the public and the private, the national and the international have been central to controversies concerning the proper limits to the democratic project. Radical critiques of modern liberal democracy, for instance, have advocated both the widening and deepening of the democratic order to embrace the private spheres of the household and the workplace. Yet, until comparatively recently, democratic theorists rarely ventured beyond the state, since prevailing orthodoxy presumed a categorical difference between the moral realm of the sovereign political community and the amoral realm of the anarchical society between states; the domestic and international arenas respectively.[2] In effect, theorists of modern democracy tended to take no account of the anarchical society, whilst theorists of international relations tended to set aside democracy. It is only in the post-cold war era that the historically estranged literatures of international relations theory and democratic theory have begun to exhibit a shared fascination with the idea of democracy beyond borders, that is, transnational (or global) democracy.[3] This 'transnational turn' articulates a profound shift in thinking about the modern democratic project that deserves serious critical scrutiny.

This chapter commences with a discussion of the factors that have precipitated this 'transnational turn' and establishes the context for taking seriously the literature on transnational democracy. Next, it identifies different accounts of transnational democracy rooted in distinctive traditions of democratic theory. Critical reflection on these four contemporary re-imaginings of democracy – liberal-internationalism, radical democratic pluralism, cosmopolitanism and deliberative democracy – involves exploring fundamental questions about the desirability and possibility of transnational democracy. The following section responds to these sceptical arguments and provides a defence of the idea of transnational democracy. Finally, the chapter considers the prospects for the transnational democratic project and reflects on the plausibility of the four different re-imaginings of democracy.

Globalization and Transnational Democracy

The burgeoning literature on transnational democracy has to be set in the context of several contemporary developments: an intensification of globalization, the third wave of global democratization and the rise of transnational social movements. These interrelated developments – although their exact significance is contested – have encouraged reflection upon the conditions and possibilities for effective democracy. Economic globalization, many argue, has exacerbated the tension between democracy, as a territorially rooted system of rule, and the operation of global markets and transnational networks of corporate power. In a world in which even the most powerful governments appear impotent, when confronted by the gyrations of global markets or the activities of transnational corporations, the efficacy of national democracy is called into question. For if, as Sandel observes, governments have lost the capacity to manage transnational forces in accordance with the expressed preferences of their citizens, the very essence of democracy, namely self-governance, is decidedly compromised.[4] Moreover, in seeking to promote or regulate the forces of globalization, through mechanisms of global and regional governance, states have created new layers of political authority, which have weak democratic credentials and stand in an ambiguous relationship to existing systems of national accountability. Under these conditions, it is no longer clear, to use Dahl's classic formulation, 'who governs?' For instance, in the midst of the South Korean general election in 1997, just following the East Asian crash, both candidates for the presidency were requested by the International Monetary Fund (IMF) to sign a confidential declaration to abide by the conditions of its proposed financial rescue package, irrespective of the election outcome. In an era in which public and private power is manifested and exercised on a transnational, or even global, scale, a serious reappraisal of the prospects for democracy is overdue.

This rethinking of democracy has also been encouraged by the global diffusion of liberal democracy – at least in the formal sense – as a system of political rule at the end of the twentieth century. Of course, for many new democracies the aspiration and political rhetoric far exceeds the realization of effective democracy. While public disenchantment with elected politicians and the capacity of democratic governments to deal with many of the enduring problems – from inequality to pollution – confronted by modern societies suggests that all is not well within the old democracies. Despite such failings, both old and new democracies have become increasingly sensitive to the weak democratic credentials of existing structures of global and regional governance, the more so as the actions of such bodies directly impinge on their citizens. As democratic states have come to constitute a majority within global institutions, the pressures to make such bodies more transparent and accountable have increased.[5] Somewhat ironically, many new democracies, which have been subject to strictures from the IMF and World Bank about the requirements of good governance, are now campaigning for similar principles and practices to be applied in these citadels of global power. But how to combine effective international institutions with democratic practices remains, according to Keohane, amongst the most intractable of contemporary international political problems.[6]

One powerful response to this problem has come from the agencies of civil society. The enormous expansion of non-governmental organization (NGO) activity and of transnational labour, professional, religious and other associations has created the infrastructure of a global civil society.[7] But the democratic credentials of these bodies remain highly questionable. Whether transnational civil society is a significant force for the democratization of world order or simply another arena through which the privileged and powerful maintain their global hegemony remains a matter of contention.[8] NGOs have, however, become instrumental in articulating the concerns of citizens and groups in international forums, even though they do not properly represent all the people of the world.[9]

Transparency, accountability and representation are terms that have become the new mantras of those pressing for the reform of global institutions: from the United Nations to the IMF and World Bank.[10] Such political and diplomatic rhetoric tends to be unspecific. Within the academic literature on globalization and democracy, however, a substantive conversation has been joined concerning the normative and institutional foundations of democracy beyond the state.

Theorizing Transnational Democracy

Within the burgeoning literature on transnational democracy, four distinctive normative theories can be discerned, namely, liberal-internationalism, radical pluralist democracy, cosmopolitan democracy and deliberative democracy. Although a somewhat crude typology, which is open to challenge on a number of grounds, it provides nevertheless a simple mapping of a complex field in so far as it identifies a clustering of arguments. These four clusters can therefore be regarded as ideal types: that is, general syntheses of normative arguments and theories which reflect a shared conception of the fundamental principles which define transnational democracy. As such, this typology provides a basis for systematic analysis of what is at stake in the debate about transnational democracy.

Common to all of these accounts is an attempt to give meaning to the idea of transnational democracy and to clarify the normative principles, ethical ideals and institutional conditions that are necessary for its effective realization. Each account is rooted in a political cosmopolitanism, which seeks to prescribe general principles, structures and practices necessary for a more humane world order, in which people's needs come to take precedence over the interests of states and their geo-political machinations.[11] Cosmopolitanism is therefore to be distinguished from internationalism, which assumes that states constitute the principal moral and political foundations of world order, and aspires to a co-operative society of states rather than peoples. Finally, these four accounts share a belief that, under conditions of contemporary globalization, transnational democracy is a necessary, desirable and politically feasible project: in other words, that democracy is to be valued over alternative systems of authoritative rule.

Liberal-internationalism

In its earliest manifestations liberal-internationalism presented a radical challenge to the prevailing *realpolitik* vision of world order. The goal of liberal theorists from the eighteenth to the twentieth centuries has generally been to construct an international order based on economic interdependence through trade, the rule of law, cooperation between states and arbitration of disputes. Some liberals like Woodrow Wilson have also envisaged a role for international organization. As Long argues, however, contemporary variants of liberal-internationalism have lost this radical edge, promoting the reform, rather than transformation, of world order.[12] Although a liberal radicalism of a kind survives, in the guise of orthodox economic neo-liberalism, it is deeply antagonistic to notions of global governance and transnational democracy, advocating instead a world of unfettered global markets.

Liberal institutionalism within international relations theory is primarily concerned with illuminating the rational calculus of international cooperation, so the question of transnational democracy tends to be conceived principally in procedural terms, such as creating more representative, transparent and accountable international institutions.[13] Keohane, for instance, understands democracy at the international level as a form of 'voluntary pluralism under conditions of maximum transparency'.[14] A more pluralistic world order, in this view, is also a more democratic world order. It involves the reconstruction of aspects of liberal-pluralist democracy at the international level, shorn of the requirements of electoral politics. In place of parties competing for votes, a vibrant transnational civil society channels its demands to the decision-makers, whilst also making them accountable for their actions. International institutions thus become arenas within which the interests of both states and the agencies of civil society are articulated. Furthermore, they function as key political structures through which consensus is negotiated and collective decisions legitimated.

There are other significant contributions to liberal-internationalism, notably the report of the Commission on Global Governance. But they share a common commitment to more representative, responsive and accountable international governance. Such ideas also tend to dominate current thinking about the reform of global institutions, from the IMF to the World Trade Organization (WTO). This is not surprising given that liberal-internationalism reflects the aspirations and values of the western states and elites that dominate the institutions of global governance. But, as Falk argues, it is a philosophy that offers a restricted and somewhat technocratic view of transnational democracy.[15] It also fails to acknowledge that inequalities of power tend to make democracy the captive of powerful vested interests. Critiques of classical pluralism, from those of Dahl to Lindblom, have recognized how corporate power distorts the democratic process.[16] But the insights of neo-pluralism find little expression in the liberal-internationalist literature, which tends to overlook structural inequalities of power in the global system and, in particular, the power imbalances between the agencies of transnational civil society and global capital. Advocating transparency and accountability is insufficient by itself to combat such inequalities of access and influence. Institutional tinkering is unlikely to resolve the democratic deficit that afflicts global governance. Despite acknowledging the significance of transnational civil society, the liberal-internationalist account remains singularly western and state-centric, stressing the transparency and accountability of international institutions to national governments.

Radical democratic pluralism

Radical democratic pluralism eschews the reformism of liberal-internationalism in favour of direct forms of democracy and self-governance. It means, therefore, the creation of alternative forums from the global to the local levels.[17] It rejects vigorously the liberal reformist position, because existing structures of global governance privilege the interests of a wealthy and powerful cosmocracy whilst excluding the needs and interests of much of humanity. Advocates of radical pluralist democracy, who include Burnheim, Connolly, Patamoki and Walker, are therefore concerned with the normative foundations of a 'new politics', which would empower individuals and communities.[18] Its advocates are concerned with the creation of 'good communities' based upon equality, active citizenship, promotion of the public good, humane governance and harmony with the natural environment. Radical pluralist democracy, Hutchings argues, 'represents something of a cocktail of elements of post-modernist, Marxist and civic republican democratic theory'.[19]

Radical democratic pluralism is essentially a 'bottom-up' theory of the democratization of world order, focusing upon environmental, feminist, peace and other social movements. These challenge the authority of states, multinational corporations and international organizations that uphold neo-liberalism. They also challenge liberal conceptions of the 'political' and the conventional divisions between foreign/domestic, public/private, society/nature. Therefore, a radical politics builds on the experiences of critical social movements, which demonstrate that one of the 'great fallacies of political theory is the assumption that a centralized management of power . . . is necessary to assure political order'.[20] 'Real' democracy, therefore, is to be found in the juxtaposition of a multiplicity of self-governing and self-organizing collectivities constituted on diverse spatial scales – from the local to the global.

Radical democratic pluralism reflects a strong attachment to theories of direct democracy and participatory democracy. It also draws upon neo-Marxist critiques of liberal democracy, claiming that effective participation and self-governance require social and economic equality. Furthermore, it connects to the civic republican tradition in so far as its exponents believe that individual freedom can only be realized in the context of a strong sense of political community and an understanding of the common good.[21]

To the extent that radical pluralist democracy requires the construction of alternative forms of global governance, it is a threat to the existing principles of world order. Its critics argue that it is precisely this rejection of the constitution of world order that is problematic. Without, for instance, some conception of sovereignty, it is difficult to envisage how the competing claims of a plurality of communities, even within the same borders, might be reconciled short of force. Furthermore, in the absence of the present rather imperfect liberal world order – embodying (to varying degrees) the principles of the rule of law and normative constraints on the exercise of organized violence – it might be argued there is no secure basis for constructing and nurturing transnational democracy. Territorial democracy, history suggests, has only thrived in circumstances where the rule of law exists and political violence is absent. A compelling critique of the radical pluralist argument might therefore be found in its ambivalence towards the very conditions – the rule of law and sovereignty – which make democracy (at whatever level) possible.

Cosmopolitan democracy

By comparison with the radical pluralist account, cosmopolitan democracy pays particular attention to the institutional and political conditions that are necessary to effective democratic governance within, between and across states. Held develops a sophisticated account of cosmopolitan democracy, which builds upon the existing principles of the liberal international order (e.g. the rule of law and human rights), to construct a new global constitutional settlement.[22] Advocating a 'double democratization' of political life, the advocates of cosmopolitan democracy seek to reinvigorate democracy within states by extending it to the public realm between and across states. Transnational democracy and territorial democracy are conceived as mutually reinforcing, rather than conflicting, principles of political rule. Cosmopolitan democracy seeks 'a political order of democratic associations, cities and nations as well as of regions and global networks'.[23]

Central to this model is the principle of autonomy for both individuals and collectivities, to be upheld through development of a cosmopolitan democratic law. This law establishes 'powers and constraints, and rights and duties, which transcend the claims of nation-states'.[24] Accordingly, the principle of democratic autonomy depends upon 'the establishment of an international community of democratic states and societies committed to upholding a democratic public law both within and across their own boundaries: a cosmopolitan democratic community'.[25] The aim is not to establish a world government, but rather 'a global and divided authority system – a system of diverse and overlapping power centres shaped and delimited by democratic law'.[26] Rather than a hierarchy of political authority, from the local to the global, cosmopolitan democracy involves a heterarchical arrangement. Conceptually, this lies between federalism and the much looser arrangements implied by the notion of confederalism. For it requires 'the subordination of regional, national and local "sovereignties" to an overarching legal framework, but within this framework associations may be self-governing at diverse levels'.[27] The entrenchment of cosmopolitan democracy therefore involves a process of *reconstructing* the existing framework of global governance.

This democratic reconstruction requires that democratic practices be embedded more comprehensively 'within communities and civil associations by elaborating and reinforcing democracy from "outside" through a network of regional and international agencies and assemblies that cut across spatially delimited locales'.[28] Such mechanisms could promote accountability over forms of global power, which at present escape effective democratic control.

Cosmopolitan democracy represents an enormously ambitious agenda for reconfiguring the constitution of global governance and world order. Whilst it draws considerable inspiration from modern theories of liberal democracy, it is also influenced by critical theory, theories of participatory democracy and civic republicanism. It is distinguished from liberal-internationalism by its radical agenda and a scepticism towards the primacy of state-centric and procedural notions of democracy. Whilst accepting the important role of progressive transnational social forces it nevertheless differentiates itself from radical pluralist democracy through its attachment to the centrality of the rule of law and constitutionalism as necessary conditions for the establishment of a more democratic world order.

But the idea of cosmopolitan democracy is not without its critics. Sandel considers the ethic that informs notions of cosmopolitan democracy to be 'flawed, both as a moral ideal and as a public philosophy for self-government in our time'.[29] This, he argues, is because at the core of cosmopolitanism is a liberal conception of the individual, which neglects the ways in which individuals, their interests and values, are 'constructed' by the communities of which they are members. Accordingly, democracy can only thrive by first creating a democratic community with a common civic identity. Whilst globalization does create a sense of universal connectedness, it does not, in Brown's view, generate an equivalent sense of community based upon shared values and beliefs.[30] Nor, it can be argued, do theorists of cosmopolitan democracy deliver a convincing account of how the ethical and cultural resources necessary for its effective realization are to be generated. It can also be criticized for a top-down approach, in which reconstructing the constitution of global governance along more democratic lines is taken as the key to realizing transnational democracy. Such faith in a new constitution for global governance, however, overlooks the inherent tensions that exist between the democratic impulse and the logic of constitutional constraints upon what the demos may do.[31] Nor, as Thompson identifies, is it necessarily clear how, within this multilayered system of global governance, jurisdictional conflicts between different layers of political authority are to be reconciled or adjudicated by democratic means, let alone how accountability in such a system can be made more effective.[32] This raises important issues of consent and legitimacy. The problem, Thompson argues, is one of 'many majorities' such that 'no majority has an exclusive and overarching claim to democratic legitimacy'.[33] Furthermore, he claims that cosmopolitan democracy will only serve to intensify the enduring tensions between democracy and the protection of individual rights, since rights claims may be pursued through international authorities, thus challenging the legitimacy of democratically sanctioned local policies or decisions. Finally, as both Patomaki and Hutchings suggest, in presuming the universal validity of western democratic values, the cosmopolitan democracy project becomes vulnerable to charges of legitimizing a new mode of imperialism.[34]

Deliberative (discursive) democracy[35]

One sympathetic attempt to address some of the criticisms inherent in both the cosmopolitan and radical democratic pluralist projects is to be found in the work on deliberative democracy and related conceptions of stakeholder democracy.[36] Rather than proposing a new constitutional settlement for the global polity, or the creation of alternative structures of global governance, advocates of deliberative democracy are concerned with elucidating 'the possibilities for democratizing the governance that does exist in the international system rather than the government that might'.[37] Deliberative democrats are interested in the discursive sources of existing systems of global governance and the role of transnational civil society 'in establishing deliberative democratic control over the terms of political discourse and so the operation of governance in the international system'.[38] In effect, they are concerned with the principles and necessary conditions for the creation of a genuine transnational public sphere of democratic deliberation. Such principles include non-domination, participation, public deliberation, responsive governance and the right of all-affected to a voice in public decisions that impinge on their welfare or interests.[39] As Dryzek argues, the realization of transnational democracy depends upon a recognition that 'the essence of democratic legitimacy is to be found not in voting or representation . . . but rather in deliberation'.[40]

While advocates of deliberative democracy do not discount totally the value of a liberal attachment to institutional reform of global governance, nor the cosmopolitan requirement for a democratic constitution for world order, both visions are regarded as insufficient in themselves for the grounding of transnational democracy. Instead, the deliberative ideal looks to the creation of 'an association whose affairs are governed by the public deliberation of its members'.[41] This involves, its advocates argue, the cultivation of transnational public spheres in which there can be genuine dialogue between the agencies of public governance and those affected by their decisions and actions. Rational and informed deliberation amongst all those affected, rather than simply those with a declaratory interest in the matter in question, is ultimately tied to realizing the common good. This is to be distinguished from a liberal pluralist conception of democracy, in which the achievement of consensus amongst the expressed interests and preferences of citizens or organized interests is taken to have primacy in public decision-making. Furthermore, public authorities are expected to justify their actions, whilst those affected must have the right to contest these policies, since governance is regarded as democratic only 'to the extent that the people individually and collectively enjoy a permanent possibility of contesting what government decides'.[42] Accordingly, deliberative democracy requires informed and active citizens, as well as the vigorous promotion of those rights and conditions necessary to their empowerment. Given the significance of the all-affected principle, the criteria and procedures for inclusion within the deliberative political process become critical.

Central to the deliberative argument is the principle of stakeholding: that all those affected by, or with a stake in, the decisions of public authorities have the right to a voice in the governance of those matters.[43] Membership of the relevant deliberative community is therefore contingent upon the specific configuration of stakeholders involved on any issue, that is, those whose interests or material conditions are directly or indirectly implicated in the exercise of public power. The process of deliberation itself becomes constitutive of the relevant deliberative community. This reflexivity, argue its advocates, makes deliberative democracy admirably suited to a world in which there are overlapping communities of fate and in which the organization and exercise of power no longer coincide with the bounded territorial political community. Unlike liberal representative democracy, in which the demos is defined in relation to fixed territorial boundaries, deliberative democracy presumes a largely functional or systemic conception of the demos uninhibited by pre-existing territorial, cultural or human boundaries. As Dryzek notes: 'Deliberation . . . can cope with fluid boundaries, and the production of outcomes across boundaries. For we can look for democracy in the character of political interaction . . . without worrying about whether or not it is confined to particular territorial entities.'[44]

Advocates of deliberative democracy argue that it offers a set of principles upon which inclusive, responsive and responsible transnational democracy can be constructed. Its more orthodox variants tend to emphasize its reformist ambitions: deliberation is conceived as a mechanism for enhancing the democratic legitimacy of public decision-making, from the local to the global level.[45] By contrast, more radical manifestations highlight its transformative potential to the extent that it is concerned with the contestation of global institutional agendas, challenging unaccountable sites of transnational power and empowering the progressive forces of transnational civil society.[46] This tension between a procedural, as opposed to substantive, interpretation of deliberative democracy arises from its rather eclectic philosophical origins, which embrace the traditions of critical theory, discourse analysis, republicanism, participatory and direct democracy.

Critics of deliberative democracy argue that it is not a discrete model of democracy so much as a mechanism for resolving and legitimizing public decisions. So it only has value in the context of an established democratic framework. This criticism is valid whether the focus is transnational, local or national democracy. Furthermore, despite its emphasis upon discourse, it tends to overlook the problems which language and cultural diversity present to the construction of a genuine transnational deliberative public sphere. This problem cannot simply be wished away as a technical matter of translation, but raises serious issues about the role of language and culture in defining the conditions of possibility of genuine political deliberation.[47] In arguing too that the deliberative communities are essentially constituted through the all-affected principle, the basis upon which stakeholders are to be incorporated – whether as direct participants or through representatives – is never clearly specified. Indeed, the emphasis upon self-organization tends to ensure that the procedural requirements and institutional conditions of effective deliberation remain somewhat vaguely stipulated. Finally, there is significant silence about how intractable conflicts of interests or values can be resolved deliberatively without recourse to some authoritatively imposed solution. Therefore, deliberative democracy may be of marginal value in dealing with many of the most pressing global distributional or security issues – from debt relief to humanitarian intervention – which figure on the world political agenda. Deliberative democracy, like other theories of transnational democracy, is also vulnerable to a more fundamental critique.

Transnational Democracy: Plausible or Desirable?

Whatever the intellectual merits of any particular design for transnational democracy, serious doubts have been raised about the very plausibility and desirability of the idea. Communitarian, realist and some radical critiques take issue with the advocates of transnational democracy on theoretical, institutional, historical and ethical grounds.

Political communitarians, such as Kymlicka, are unconvinced by the cosmopolitan premises that inform theories of transnational democracy. Democracy, argues Kymlicka, has to be rooted in a shared history, language or political culture: the constitutive features of modern territorial political communities. These features are all more or less absent at the transnational level. Despite the way globalization binds the fate of communities together, the reality is that 'the only forum within which genuine democracy occurs is within national boundaries'.[48] Even within the European Union (EU) transnational democracy is little more than an elite phenomenon. If there is no effective moral community beyond the state, there can be, in this view, no true demos. Of course, advocates of transnational democracy argue that political communities are being transformed by globalization, therefore the idea of the demos as a fixed, territorially delimited unit is no longer tenable.[49] But the sceptics pose the critical question of who or what agency decides how the demos is to be constituted, and upon what basis? Without some unequivocal specification of the principles by which the demos is to be constituted, it is difficult to envisage either how transnational democracy could be institutionalized or how it would necessarily provide the basis for more representative, legitimate and accountable global governance. By failing to respond to this question with a theoretically rigorous or convincing argument, suggest the sceptics, the advocates of transnational democracy fatally undermine the plausibility of their project.[50]

For political realists, state sovereignty and international anarchy present the most insuperable barriers to the realization of democracy beyond borders. Even though elements of an international society of states may exist, in which there is an acceptance of the rule of law and compliance with international norms, order at the global level, suggest realists, remains contingent rather than enduring. Conflict and force are ever present and a daily reality in many regions of the world. These are not the conditions in which any substantive democratic experiment is likely to prosper, since a properly functioning democracy requires the absence of political violence and the rule of law. In relations between sovereign states organized violence is always a possibility and the rule of law largely an expression of *realpolitik*. International order is always order established by and for the most powerful states. Global governance therefore is merely a synonym for western hegemony, whilst international institutions remain the captives of dominant powers. States act strategically to encourage international governance only where it enhances their autonomy, or circumvents domestic scrutiny of sensitive issues, so generating a political imperative prejudicial to the democratization of global governance.[51] Short of a democratic hegemon, or alternatively some form of world federation of democratic states, imposing or cultivating transnational democracy, the conditions for its realization must accordingly appear theoretically and practically implausible. Few sovereign democratic states are likely to trade national self-governance for a more democratic world order, whilst no authoritarian state would ever conceivably entertain the prospect. Transnational democracy remains, for realists, a utopian ideal.

Even if transnational democracy were possible, it remains, many sceptics conclude, a politically and ethically undesirable achievement.[52] At the heart of theories of transnational democracy is an intractable conflict between a normative commitment to effective national democracy and the desire for democracy beyond the state. This dilemma arises from the fact that the democratic practices and decisions of one have enormous potential to override or negate the democratic credentials and requirements of the other. In most mature democracies this dilemma is resolved through constitutional mechanisms, but these are signally absent in the international arena. A telling illustration of this dilemma concerns the EU's 'democratically mandated' intervention in Austrian politics following the electoral success of the far right in early 2000. Collectively, the EU threatened to withhold official recognition of any coalition government in which Mr Haider, the leader of the main far right party, played a role, despite the democratically expressed preferences of the Austrian electorate. Whatever the ethics of this particular case, the general point is that transnational democracy has the potential to extinguish effective self-governance at local or national levels.[53] Without effective safeguards – which, in the absence of a global constitution, cannot be institutionally grounded – the danger of transnational democracy is that it is susceptible to crude majoritarian impulses, which have the potential to negate the legitimate democratic rights and wishes of (national) minorities. Conversely, without the institutional capacity to enforce the democratic will of the majority against the entrenched interests of the Great Powers of the day, transnational democracy simply becomes hostage to the interests of the most powerful geo-political forces. Herein lies what might be referred to as the paradox of transnational democracy. Without a capacity to enforce the transnational democratic will on the most powerful geo-political and transnational social forces, democracy beyond the state is necessarily ineffective, yet the very existence of such a capability creates the real possibility of tyranny.

It is partly for such reasons that even those of a more radical persuasion query the desirability of transnational democracy. Amongst some radical critics the very idea of transnational democracy conceals a new instrument of western hegemony.[54] As with the philosophy of 'good governance' promulgated by G7 governments and multilateral agencies, it is considered primarily a western preoccupation.[55] For most of humanity it is a distraction from global problems such as AIDS, famine, desertification and poverty. As the United Nations Development Programme puts it, the most pressing issue for humankind is whether globalization can be given a human face.[56] In this context transnational democracy may be an entirely inappropriate and irrelevant response, given that the critical problem is how to ensure that global markets and global capital work in the interests of the majority of the world's peoples without destroying the natural environment.[57] Democratizing global governance, even if it were feasible, may be more likely to strengthen and legitimize the hegemony of global capital than it is to challenge its grip on the levers of global power.[58] The historical record of advanced capitalist societies, argue the sceptics, demonstrates how the imperatives of capitalism take precedence over the workings of democracy. Therein lies the prospective fate of transnational democracy. Accelerating global inequality and looming environmental catastrophe simply cannot be resolved by a dose of transnational democracy. On the contrary, as Hirst suggests, what is required are powerful and effective, rather than democratic, global bodies which can override the entrenched interests of global capital by promoting the common welfare – social democracy at the global level.[59] Alternatively, the deconstruction of global governance and the devolution of power to self-governing, sustainable local communities is a strategy favoured by radicals of a green persuasion.[60] The ethical preference of many radical critics is for strengthening existing systems of social democratic governance and new forms of participatory democracy below the state.[61] Real democracy is always local (national) democracy.

What the various sceptical arguments share is a sense that transnational democracy is neither necessarily an appropriate response to globalization nor a project that is as ethically and theoretically persuasive as its advocates suppose. On the contrary, it is fraught with theoretical shortcomings and practical dangers. Not the least amongst these, suggests Dahl, is the danger of popular control in respect of vital matters of economic and military security.[62] Furthermore, the development of national (territorial) democracy has been strongly associated with force and violence, whilst the history of modern democracy illustrates how, even within the context of a shared political culture, it remains a distinctly fragile system of rule. In a world of cultural diversity and growing inequality, the possibility of realizing transnational democracy must therefore be judged to be negligible, unless it is imposed either by a concert of democratic states or a benign democratic hegemon. Not surprisingly, for most sceptics, self-governance within states, whether democratic or not, is considered ethically preferable to the likely tyranny of a more democratic global polity.

Can Transnational Democracy be Dismissed?

In response, advocates of transnational democracy accuse the sceptics of a too hasty dismissal of the theoretical, ethical and empirical arguments that inform their designs for democracy beyond borders. More specifically, they argue that by discounting the significant political transformations being brought about by intensifying globalization and regionalization, the sceptics seriously misread the possibilities for significant political change towards a more democratic world order.[63] These transformations irrevocably alter the conditions which made sovereign, territorial, self-governing political communities possible, for in a world of global flows the local and the global, the domestic and the foreign, are largely indistinguishable.[64]

Modern political communities are historical and social constructions. Their particular form, coinciding with the territorial reach of the 'imagined community' of the nation, is a product of particular conditions and forces. Historically, the state has been the primary incubator of modern democratic life. But, as Linklater observes, political communities have never been static, fixed creations, but have always been in the process of construction and reconstruction.[65] As globalization and regionalization have intensified, modern political communities have begun to experience a significant transformation, whilst new forms of political community are emerging. According to Held, national political communities coexist today alongside 'overlapping communities of fate' defined by the spatial reach of transnational networks, systems, allegiances and problems.[66] In

Walzer's terms these may be conceived as 'thin' communities, as opposed to the 'thick' communities of the locale and nation-state. Nevertheless, they constitute necessary ethical and political preconditions for the cultivation of transnational democracy.[67]

Critics of transnational democracy, as noted, charge that its advocates employ a rather indeterminate conception of the demos. This charge, however, overlooks the indeterminate, constructed nature of the modern (national) demos itself which has always been contested – witness the struggle for the female vote and current controversies about citizenship. The demos therefore is not some preformed entity which is the precursor to democratic development, but, on the contrary, is itself constituted through processes of democratization. Rather than conceiving of the cosmopolitan demos as a singular, determinate and universal entity – a unified world demos – the literature on transnational democracy tends to emphasize its complex, fluid and multilayered construction: articulated in a multiplicity of settings in relation to the plurality of sites of global power and the architecture of global governance.[68] Such a conception, as indicated by the experience of the EU and federal polities, is certainly not without historical precedent.

Moreover, political communities beyond the state are being created by what some argue is the growing constitutionalization of world order.[69] The accumulation of multilateral, regional and transnational arrangements (which have evolved in the last fifty years) has created a tacit global constitution. In seeking to manage and regulate transborder issues, states have codified their respective powers and authority, and institutionalized an elaborate system of rules, rights and responsibilities for the conduct of their joint affairs. This has gone furthest in the EU, where effectively a quasi-federal constitution has emerged. But in other contexts, such as the WTO, the authority of national governments is being redefined, as the management of trade disputes becomes subject to a rule of law.[70]

Associated with this institutionalization has been the elaboration and entrenchment of some significant democratic principles within the society of states.[71] Thus, self-determination, popular sovereignty, democratic legitimacy and the legal equality of states have become orthodox principles of international society. As Mayall comments, there has been an entrenchment of 'democratic values, as the standard of legitimacy within international society'.[72] This democratization of international society also appears to have accelerated in recent years, in response to processes of globalization, the activities of transnational civil society and the socializing dynamic of an expanding community of democratic states. Despite its unevenness and fragility, it represents, combined with the constitutionalization of world order, the forging of the necessary historical conditions – the creation of 'zones of peace' and the rule of law – for the cultivation of transnational democracy.[73]

Further evidence of this process of democratization is to be found in the political response of many governments and agencies of transnational civil society to the consequences of economic globalization.[74] A common aspiration amongst progressive political forces is a system of global governance that is accountable, responsive and transparent. The growing perception that power is leaking away from democratic states and electorates to unelected and effectively unaccountable global bodies, such as the WTO, has prompted increased political pressure, on G8 governments especially, to bring good governance to global governance.[75] Of course, democracy involves more than simply transparent and accountable decision-making. It is interesting to note that the debate about reform draws significantly upon liberal-internationalism and the deliberative, radical and cosmopolitan discourses of transnational democracy discussed above. In the context of the WTO, for instance, the language of stakeholding has been much in evidence, somewhat curiously in both US official government and civil society proposals for its reform.[76]

Of course, for sceptics such as Dahl these developments do not invalidate the normative argument that international institutions cannot be truly democratic.[77] Yet, as advocates of transnational democracy point out, this overlooks completely the significant examples of international or suprastate bodies, from the EU to the International Labour Organization (ILO), whose institutional designs reflect novel combinations of traditional inter-governmental and democratic principles.[78] While the EU represents a remarkable institutionalization of a distinctive form of democracy beyond borders, it is by no means unique. The ILO, for instance, has institutionalized a restricted form of 'stakeholding' through a tripartite system of representation corresponding to states, business and labour organizations respectively. Newer international functional bodies, such as the International Fund for Agricultural Development and the Global Environmental Facility, also embody stakeholding principles as a means to ensure representative decision-making. Furthermore, virtually all major international institutions have opened themselves up to formal or informal participation by the representatives of civil society.[79] Even the WTO has a created a civil society forum. In certain respects, therefore, basic democratic principles are constitutive of existing global and regional systems of governance.

Finally, in questioning the value of transnational democracy, socialists raise the serious issue of whether democracy can be trusted to deliver greater global social justice. In regard to liberal democracy in the national context, the historical record appears somewhat mixed. By contrast, advocates of transnational democracy commence from a rather different reading (historical and conceptual) of the relationship between capitalism – as a primary engine of global inequality and injustice – and democracy. This reading recognizes the inevitable contradictions between the logic of capitalism and the logic of democracy. It departs from the fatalism of many structural Marxist and radical critiques in arguing, on both theoretical and historical grounds, that transnational democracy is a necessary requirement for the realization of global social justice. The history of European social democracy, in mitigating the inequalities of market capitalism, is taken as an important case in point. Accordingly, the case for transnational democracy is inseparable from the argument for global social justice. Indeed, the value of transnational democracy, suggest its most passionate advocates, lies precisely in its capacity to provide legitimate mechanisms and grounds for taming the power of global capital, thereby promoting and realizing the conditions for greater global social justice. That existing institutions of global governance fail in this task should be no surprise, since they are the captives of dominant economic interests.[80] Nonetheless, for the advocates of transnational democracy this is not a valid reason for abandoning the project, but, on the contrary, for advocating it more vigorously.

Towards a Democratic Global Polity?

If the idea of transnational democracy cannot be so easily dismissed, then the prospects for its realization must be addressed. This involves consideration of two issues: the extent to which it is possible to identify immanent tendencies in global politics that provide the conditions for its potential realization; and the extent to which any of the theories of transnational democracy provide a plausible or persuasive account of the conditions of its possibility.

Despite the compelling credentials of the sceptical case, a cautious optimism is warranted. Globalization and regionalization are stimulating powerful political reactions, which in their more progressive manifestations have engendered an unprecedented public debate about the democratic credentials of governance beyond the state.[81] In the wake of the 1990s East Asian crisis and the 'Battle of Seattle' in late 1999, there is evidence of an emerging awareness of the need for more effective regulation of global financial markets and global capital.[82] The Washington consensus, championing unfettered global capitalism, no longer appears so secure.[83] Reform of the major agencies of global governance, as the

UN Millennium Summit indicated, is now firmly on the world political agenda.[84] Transparency, accountability, participation and legitimacy are rapidly becoming the values associated with the dominant discourses of reform. Progressive elements of transnational civil society, such as Charter 99, are organizing and mobilizing to maintain the political pressure on governments and institutions to follow through on the reform agenda. Understood in the broader context of the democratization of international society (discussed above), these recent political developments acquire a much greater political significance. There is always the serious possibility of ultimate failure or cosmetic reform. Nevertheless, the present conjuncture of the dissolution of the hegemony of neo-liberalism, the vitality of transnational civil society, the urgent requirements for effective and legitimate regional and global governance, and the pervasiveness of democratic values and aspirations underwrite Dryzek's sanguine conclusion that the prospects for the transnational democratic project are 'in many ways more positive than ever before'.[85]

Of course, this leaves open the question of the likely trajectory of democratic reform. Rather than ask which, if any, of the four main theories of transnational democracy provides the best blueprint, which presumes the existence of some objective criteria by which such a judgement might be made, a far more appropriate question is whether any of these theories provide a convincing and coherent account, rooted in the existing realities, of the ethical and political conditions for its own realization.

Since it is largely compatible with the existing liberal world order and the values of dominant western states and elites, liberal-internationalism may appear the most plausible route to transnational democracy. Current deliberations on the reform of global governance, as is evidenced in the priority accorded to accountability and transparency, are dominated by the discourse of liberal-internationalism. This is, however, a limited procedural conception of democracy that is statist and universalist in its assumptions. It is for many progressive social forces the prevailing orthodoxy that they seek to transcend. It aspires primarily to a democracy of states – international democracy – rather than a democracy of peoples – transnational democracy. By contrast, the transformative aspirations of radical pluralist democracy, encouraged by the transversal politics of new social movements, appears tarnished by a failure to specify theoretically or historically how, in the absence of any sovereign authority or the rule of law, transnational democracy can be realized or institutionalized. In a highly decentralized world order, in which self-governing communities proliferate, the conditions for developing a genuine transnational public sphere or for democratizing global governance would seem remote. Why such an order would necessarily engender transnational democracy, as opposed to the tyranny of community, is far from obvious. In these respects radical pluralist democracy lacks a convincing narrative of the conditions of its own realization.

Theories of cosmopolitan and deliberative democracy deliver more systematic and persuasive accounts of their own conditions of possibility. Normatively ambitious and radical, in so far as each aspires to a transformation of world order towards a democratic community of states and peoples, yet each is nevertheless profoundly aware of the powerful structural and economic forces that impede the prospects for transnational democracy. Both provide a rigorous account of the necessary preconditions and processes for bringing about the democratization of world order. In these respects they can be considered complementary accounts of transnational democracy. Whereas the primary concerns of deliberative democracy are with the discursive sources of world order and the significance of the communicative power of civil society in democratizing global governance, the primary interest of cosmopolitan democracy is with the specification of appropriate constitutional and institutional orders for the cultivation and entrenchment of democracy beyond the state. Moreover, advocates of cosmopolitan democracy and deliberative democracy consider transnational democracy 'not as an alternative to national democracy but in part as its salvation as well'.[86] Despite an inherent idealism, cosmopolitan and deliberative theories of transnational democracy constitute the most sophisticated and persuasive arguments for democracy beyond borders. Together they represent original and comprehensive attempts at reimagining democracy to accord with a world in which the organization and exercise of power has acquired significant transnational, regional and even global dimensions.

NOTES

1 I. Shapiro, 'Democracy's edges: Introduction', in I. Shapiro and C. Hacker-Cordón (eds), *Democracy's Edges* (Cambridge, Cambridge University Press, 1999), p. 1.
2 W. E. Connolly, 'Democracy and Territoriality', *Millennium* 20, 3 (1991): 463–84; R. B. J. Walker, 'On the spatio-temporal conditions of democratic practice', *Alternatives* 16, 2 (1991): 243–62.
3 I. Clark, *Globalization and International Relations Theory* (Oxford, Oxford University Press, 1999); D. Held, *Democracy and the Global Order* (Cambridge, Polity, 1995).
4 M. Sandel, *Democracy's Discontent* (Harvard University Press, 1996).

5 See, e.g., Commission on Global Governance, *Our Global Neighbourhood* (Oxford, Oxford University Press, 1995).

6 R. O. Keohane, 'International institutions: Can interdependence work?' *Foreign Policy* Spring (1998): 82–96.

7 See J. T. Matthews, 'Power shift', *Foreign Affairs* (January 1997): 50–66; J. Rosenau, *Along the Domestic-Foreign Frontier* (Cambridge, Cambridge University Press, 1997); J. Boli and G. M. Thomas, 'INGOs and the organization of world culture', in J. Boli and G. M. Thomas (eds), *Constructing World Culture: International Nongovernmental Organizations Since 1875* (Stanford, Stanford University, 1999), pp. 13–49. Of course, the idea of global or transnational civil society remains contested. Although taken here to refer to the transnational sphere of voluntary associations, the distinctions between state and non-state, non-profit and corporate sectors are extremely blurred. Moreover, whether the sphere of economic relations is to be excluded from conceptions of civil society remains a point of debate between Marxist and liberal conceptions. See J. Keane, *Civil Society: Old Images, New Visions* (Cambridge, Polity, 1998).

8 See P. Wapner, *Environmental Activism and World Civic Politics* (New York, SUNY, 1996), T. G. Weiss and L. Gordenker (eds), *NGOs, the UN, and Global Governance* (London, Lynne Reinner, 1996); R. Burbach, O. Nunez and B. Kagarlistsky, *Globalization and its Discontents* (London, Pluto Press, 1997).

9 J. Boli, T. A. Loya and T. Loftin, 'National participation in world-polity organization', in J. Boli and G. M. Thomas (eds), *Constructing World Culture* (Stanford, Stanford University Press, 1999), pp. 50–77.

10 See United Nations, *Renewing the United Nations* (New York, United Nations, 2000); L. Summers, 'Statement to the International Monetary and Financial Committee', IMF (16 April 2000).

11 Radical democratic pluralism and deliberative democracy tend to reject a moral cosmopolitanism in so far as they dispute the existence of universal moral principles of action which apply irrespective of cultural or social differences. Thus Hutchings makes an important distinction between moral and political cosmopolitanism which is followed here. On these issues, see K. Hutchings, *International Political Theory* (London, Sage, 1999), pp. 35 and 153; M. Cochran, *Normative Theory in International Relations* (Cambridge, Cambridge University Press, 1999).

12 P. Long, 'The Harvard school of liberal international theory: The case for closure', *Millennium* 24, 3 (1995): 489–505.

13 R. Falk, 'Liberalism at the global level: The last of the independent commissions?', *Millennium* 24, 3 (1995): 563–78.

14 Keohane, 'International institutions'.

15 Falk, 'Liberalism at the global level'.

16 G. McLennan, *Marxism, Pluralism and Beyond* (Cambridge, Polity, 1989).

17 Hutchings, *International Political Theory*, pp. 166ff.
18 See Connolly, 'Democracy and Territoriality'; Walker, 'On the spatio-temporal conditions of democratic practice'; J. Burnheim, *Is Democracy Possible?* (Cambridge, Cambridge University Press, 1985); J. Burnheim, 'Democracy, nation-states, and the world system', in D. Held and C. Pollitt (eds), *New Forms of Democracy* (London, Sage, 1986), pp. 218–39; J. Burnheim, 'Power-trading and the environment', *Environmental Politics* 4, 4 (1995): 49–65; R. B. J. Walker, 'International relations and the concept of the political', in K. Booth and S. Smith (eds), *International Relations Theory Today* (Cambridge, Polity, 1995), pp. 306–27; H. Patomaki, 'Republican public sphere and the governance of globalizing political economy', in M. Lensu and J-S. Fritz (eds), *Value Pluralism, Normative Theory and International Relations* (London, Macmillan, 2000), pp. 160–95.
19 Hutchings, *International Political Theory*, pp. 166–7.
20 Burnheim, 'Democracy, nation-states, and the world system', pp. 220–1.
21 I. Barns, 'Environment, democracy and community', *Environment and Politics* 4, 4 (1995): 101–33.
22 Held, *Democracy and the Global Order*.
23 Held, *Democracy and the Global Order*, p. 234.
24 D. Held et al., *Global Transformations: Politics, Economics and Culture* (Cambridge, Polity Press, 1999), p. 70.
25 Held, *Democracy and the Global Order*, p. 229.
26 Ibid., p. 234.
27 Ibid.
28 Ibid., p. 237.
29 Sandel, *Democracy's Discontent*, p. 342.
30 C. Brown, 'International political theory and the idea of world community', in Booth and Smith (eds), *International Relations Theory Today*, pp. 90–109.
31 M. Saward, *The Terms of Democracy* (Cambridge, Polity, 1998).
32 D. Thompson, 'Democratic theory and global society', *Journal of Political Philosophy* 7, 2 (1999): 111–25.
33 Ibid., p. 112.
34 Hutchings, *International Political Theory*, p. 177; Patomaki, 'Republican public sphere and the governance of globalizing political economy'.
35 Dryzek makes a distinction between deliberative and discursive democracy. The latter represents a more radical conception of deliberative democracy that seeks to move beyond its origins in liberal and critical theory. For simplicity, however, both versions are used interchangeably here. See J. S. Dryzek, *Deliberative Democracy and Beyond* (Oxford, Oxford University Press, 2000), ch. 1.

36 See e.g. J. S. Dryzek, *Discursive Democracy* (Cambridge, Cambridge University Press, 1990); D. Deudney, 'Global village sovereignty', in K. T. Litfin (eds), *The Greening of Sovereignty* (Cambridge, MA, MIT Press, 1998), pp. 299–325; Thompson, 'Democratic theory and global society'; Dryzek, *Deliberative Democracy and Beyond*.

37 Dryzek, *Deliberative Democracy and Beyond*, p. 120.

38 Ibid., p. 138.

39 See Dryzek, *Discursive Democracy*; Saward, *The Terms of Democracy*, pp. 64–5; and P. Pettit, *Republicanism: A Theory of Freedom and Government* (Oxford, Oxford University Press, 1997).

40 J. S. Dryzek, 'Transnational democracy', *Journal of Political Philosophy* 7, 1 (1999): 44.

41 Cohen, quoted in Saward, *The Terms of Democracy*, p. 64.

42 Pettit, *Republicanism*, p. 185.

43 See Burnheim, 'Democracy, nation-states, and the world system'; Deudney, 'Global village sovereignty'; R. Eckersley, 'Deliberative democracy, ecological representation and risk: Towards a democracy of the affected', mimeo (2000); and M. Saward, 'A critique of Held', in B. Holden (ed.), *Global Democracy: Key Debates* (London, Routledge, 2000), pp. 32–46.

44 Dryzek, *Deliberative Democracy and Beyond*, p. 129.

45 E.g., Saward, *The Terms of Democracy*.

46 E.g., Dryzek, 'Transnational democracy'; Eckersley, 'Deliberative democracy, ecological representation and risk'.

47 W. Kymlicka, 'Citizenship in an era of globalization', in Shapiro and Hacker-Cordón (eds), *Democracy's Edges*, pp. 112–26.

48 Ibid., p. 124.

49 A. Linklater, *The Transformation of Political Community* (Cambridge, Polity, 1998).

50 See, e.g., C. Gorg and J. Hirsch, 'Is international democracy possible?', *Review of International Political Economy* 5, 4 (1998): 585–615; R. A. Dahl, 'Can international organizations be democratic?', in Shapiro and Hacker-Cordón (eds), *Democracy's Edges*, pp. 19–36; Kymlicka, 'Citizenship in an era of globalization'; Saward, 'A critique of Held'.

51 K. D. Wolf, 'The new raison d'état as a problem for democracy in world society', *European Journal of International Relations* 5, 3 (1999): 333–63.

52 See e.g. D. Zolo, *Cosmopolis: Prospects for World Government* (Cambridge, Polity, 1997); Gorg and Hirsch, 'Is international democracy possible?'; Dahl, 'Can international organizations be democratic?'; P. Hirst, 'Between the local and the global: Democracy in the twenty-first century', in R. Axtmann (ed.), *Balancing Democracy* (London, Continuum, 2001), pp. 255–75; and J. Mayall, 'Democracy and international society', *International Affairs* 76, 1 (2000): 61–75.

53   Hutchings, *International Political Theory*, p. 166.

54   See Burbach, Nunez and Kagarlistsky, *Globalization and its Discontents*; M. Elmandrjra, 'The need for the deglobalization of globalization', in C. Pierson and S. Tormey (eds), *Politics at the Edge* (London, Macmillan, 2000), pp. 29–40.

55   The seven most advanced industrial countries – the USA, Germany, Japan, the UK, France, Canada and Italy – hold periodical G7 (Group of Seven) summits to review the state of the international economy. When joined by Russia, the G7 becomes the G8.

56   UNDP, *Globalization With a Human Face – UN Human Development Report 1999* (Oxford, UNDP/Oxford University Press, 1999).

57   See R. Cox, 'Globalization, multilateralism and democracy', in R. Cox (ed.), *Approaches to World Order* (Cambridge, Cambridge University Press, 1996), pp. 524–37; Burbach, Nunez and Kagarlistsky, *Globalization and its Discontents*.

58   S. Gill, 'Globalization, market civilization, and disciplinary neo-liberalism', *Millennium* 24, 3 (1995): 399–424; Burbach, Nunez and Kagarlistsky, *Globalization and its Discontents*.

59   P. Hirst and G. Thompson, *Globalization in Question* (Cambridge, Polity, 1999); Hirst, 'Between the local and the global: Democracy in the twenty-first century'.

60   See J. Dryzek, *The Politics of the Earth* (Oxford, Oxford University Press, 1997); E. Laferriere and P. J. Stoett, *International Relations and Ecological Thought* (London, Routledge, 1999).

61   J. H. Mittleman, *The Globalization Syndrome* (Princeton, Princeton University Press, 2000).

62   Dahl, 'Can international organizations be democratic?'.

63   See D. J. Elkins, *Beyond Sovereignty: Territory and Political Economy in the Twenty First Century* (Toronto, University of Toronto Press, 1995); M. Castells, *End of the Millennium* (Oxford, Blackwell, 1998); Clark, *Globalization and International Relations Theory*; Held et al. *Global Transformations: Politics, Economics and Culture*; Mittleman, *The Globalization Syndrome*.

64   See R. Devetak, 'Incomplete states: Theories and practices of statecraft', in J. MacMillan and A. Linklater (eds), *Boundaries in Question* (London, Frances Pinter, 1995), pp. 19–39; Linklater, *The Transformation of Political Community*.

65   Linklater, *The Transformation of Political Community*.

66   D. Held, 'The changing contours of political community', in B. Holden (ed.), *Global Democracy: Key Debates* (London, Routledge, 2000), pp. 17–31.

67   See M. Walzer, *Thick and Thin: Moral Argument at Home and Abroad* (London, University of Notre Dame Press, 1994).

68   See D. Held, 'Democracy, the nation-state, and the global system', in D. Held (ed.), *Political Theory Today* (Cambridge, Polity, 1991), pp.

197–235; Walker, 'On the spatio-temporal conditions of democratic practice'; Linklater, *The Transformation of Political Community*; Dryzek, 'Transnational democracy'; M. Zurn, *Democratic Govern-ance beyond the Nation State?* (Bremen, Institut fur Interkulturelle und Internationale Studien, Universitat Bremen, 1998); M. Albert, 'Complex governance and morality in world society', *Global Society* 13, 1 (1999): 77–93; Thompson, 'Democratic theory and global society'; M. T. Greven, 'Can the European Union finally become a democracy?', in M. T. Greven and L. W. Pauly (eds), *Democracy Beyond the State? The European Dilemma and the Emerging Global Order* (Boston, Rowman and Littlefield, 2000), pp. 35–63; Held, 'The changing contours of political community'; and Mittleman, *The Globalization Syndrome*.

69 See Gill, 'Globalization, market civilization, and disciplinary neo-liberalism'; D. J. Elazar, *Constitutionalizing Globalization* (Boston, Rowman and Littlefield, 1998).

70 G. R. Shell, 'Trade legalism and international relations theory: An analysis of the WTO', *Duke Law Journal* 44, 5 (1995): 829–927.

71 J. Crawford, *Democracy in International Law* (Cambridge, Cambridge University Press, 1994).

72 Mayall, 'Democracy and international society', p. 64.

73 Held, *Democracy and the Global Order*.

74 See R. O'Brien et al., *Contesting Global Governance: Multilateral Economic Institutions and Global Social Movements* (Cambridge, Cambridge University Press, 2000); J. A. Scholte, *Globalization: A Critical Introduction* (London, Macmillan, 2000).

75 N. Woods, 'Good governance in international organization', *Global Governance*, 5 (1999): 39–61.

76 See Shell, 'Trade legalism and international relations theory'; and A. McGrew, 'The WTO: Technocracy or banana republic?', in A. Taylor and C. Thomas (eds), *Global Trade and Global Social Issues* (London, Routledge, 1999), pp. 197–216.

77 Dahl, 'Can international organizations be democratic?'.

78 Woods, 'Good governance in international organization'.

79 Weiss and Gordenker (eds), *NGOs, the UN, and Global Governance*.

80 S. Gill, 'Economic globalization and the internationalization of authority: Limits and contradictions', *GeoForum* 23, 3 (1992): 269–83; and Cox, 'Globalization, multilateralism and democracy'.

81 D. Beetham and C. Lord, *Legitimacy and the European Union* (London, Longman, 1998); Dryzek, 'Transnational democracy'; Woods, 'Good governance in international organization'; Scholte, *Globalization: A Critical Introduction*; Greven, 'Can the European Union finally become a democracy?'; Mayall, 'Democracy and inter-national society'.

82 UNCTAD, *The Least Developed Countries Report 1998* (Geneva, United Nations Conference on Trade and Development, 1998);

UNDP, *Globalization With a Human Face*; and R. J. B. Jones, *The World Turned Upside Down?* (Manchester, Manchester University Press, 2000).

83   A. McGrew, 'Sustainable globalization?', in T. Allen and A. Thomas (eds), *Poverty and Development into the 21st Century* (Oxford, Oxford University Press, 2000), pp. 345–64.

84   United Nations, *Renewing the United Nations*.

85   Dryzek, *Deliberative Democracy and Beyond*, p. 139.

86   Clark, *Globalization and International Relations Theory*, p. 155.

Index

Aborigines and Torres Strait Islanders
  Aboriginal and Torres Strait
    Islander Act (1989) (Cwlth), 137
  Aboriginal and Torres Strait
    Islander Commission (ATSIC),
    137–41
  Mabo v. the State of Queensland,
    1992 (No. 2), 132–3
  citizenship rights, 8, 126
  Corrymeela Community, 218
  dispossession and disadvantage,
    124–5
  land rights, 101
  native title, 18, 132–3
  Native Title Act (1993) (Cwlth),
    133, 140
  Native Title Tribunal, 133
  political autonomy of, 137–40
  and self-determination, 123–4,
    132–3
  and state policy, 125–7
  Wik Peoples v. Queensland, 1996
    (Cwlth), 132–3
active citizenship, 30–1, 33, 34,
  41–2, 44, 274
affirmative action, 102
African National Congress, 108–9

Amnesty International, 221, 242
anarcho-syndicalism, 230
Arendt, Hannah, 31, 94n, 175, 194,
  198–9n
Aristotle, 27, 193
Asia Society, 222
assistance rights, 102
associational democracy, 244n
associationalism
  and corporatism, 231
  and democratic participation, 244
  and social justice, 239–40
associative democracy
  and civil society, 12–13
  and deliberative democracy, 13
  and democratizing the economy
    and society, 234–6
  and global democracy, 229,
    242–3
  and how groups promote
    democracy, 232–4
  and liberal values, 240
  and the market, 228, 231, 232,
    236
  and the nature and role of groups,
    236–7
  and pluralism, 231

associative democracy *cont.*
   political and theoretical
      background and context, 229–32
   and republicanism, 229, 240–2
   and social democracy, 228, 230,
      234
   and social justice, 228, 229,
      239–40, 241, 244
   and the state, 228, 235, 237–9
   theories of, 232–6
Australia
   associative democracy, 228
   global civil society, 219
   multiculturalism, 6
   One Nation movement, 18n, 160
   similarities with Canada, 130
   social and economic inequality, 53,
      55
   voting and citizenship rights, 8,
      248n
   White Australia Policy, 119
   see also Aborigines and Torres
      Strait Islanders
Austria, 281

the Balkan conflict, 153, 159
Barber, B., 31
Barker, Ernest, 35
'Battle of Seattle' (1999), 286
Bernstein, Eduard, 14, 249, 253,
   254–6, 259, 264
   *How is Scientific Socialism
      Possible?*, 255
   *The Working Assumption of
      Socialism and the Tasks of Social
      Democracy*, 254
Blair, Tony, 55, 208, 246n, 251, 264
   The Third Way, 264
bourgeois democratic nationalism, 111
bourgeois liberalism, 111
Britain
   jury service, 3
   monetarism, 261
   social democracy, 258–9
   social and economic inequality, 5
   Thatcherism, 229

and the voluntary sector, 238–9
   voter turnout, 241
British Labour Party, 35, 231, 251,
   258, 259, 261
Burke, Edmund, 174

Canada
   Charter of Rights and Freedoms,
      131
   collective and special rights for
      aboriginal people, 140–1
   Constitution Act (1867), 131
   Constitution Act (1982), 131
   constitutional entrenchment of
      indigenous rights, 131–2
   Framework Agreement, 147n
   group rights, 9
   Gwich'in Tribal Council, 134
   Indian Act (1985), 136, 144n
   indigenous dispossession and
      disadvantage, 124
   indigenous policy, 125–7
   indigenous political autonomy,
      134–6
   indigenous self-determination, 123,
      130
   Inuvialuit Regional Corporation of
      the Beaufort Sea Coast, 134
   Nunavut Territory, 8, 135–6
   Peter Ballatyne Cree Nation
      (PBCN), 136
   regional agreements, 134–5
   Royal Proclamation of 1763, 131,
      145n
   self-governing territories, 8, 135–6
   *Statement of the Government of
      Canada on Indian Policy* (the
      'White Paper'), 127
   treaties, 143n, 145n
   Treaty Lands Entitlements (TLE),
      134, 136
capitalism, 4
   and democracy, 52–5, 282, 286
   Marxian/ist analysis of, 14, 251–4,
      258–9
   moral critique of, 262

and substantive political equality,
60
see also global capitalism
Caritas International, 221
Charter 99, 287
China, 205–6, 207, 211, 216, 219
Chinese Communist Party (CCP), 206
citizenship
  challenges to conventional notions
    of, 3–4
  as a civic identity, 27
  and critique, 26
  and deliberative democracy, 11
  and gender, 73, 74, 75–80
  as a legal or administrative status,
    24
  as a means for extending citizens'
    rights, 26, 230
  as a means for social control and
    assimilation, 24–5, 26, 30
  need for an independent theory of,
    46
  as a normative political concept,
    24
  and participation, 30, 32, 37, 43,
    44
  as a practical and theoretical
    problem, 23–7
  and sexuality, 85–8
  and social democracy, 266, 267
  and the Third Way, 35, 266
  see also active citizenship;
    corporate citizenship; deliberative
    citizenship; democratic
    citizenship; differentiated
    citizenship; global citizenship; the
    good citizen; participation;
    transnational citizenship
citizenship education, 68–9, 81
citizenship rights, 8, 23, 26, 36, 104,
    119, 126, 135
civic deficit, 24
  and civic republicanism, 33–4
  and developmental democracy,
    38–9
  and liberal minimalism, 30–1

civic education, 25, 44
civic equality, 5
civic identity, 24, 110
civic nationalism, 158
civic republicanism, 31–4, 45, 231
civic rights and obligations, 24, 25,
    29, 31, 32
civic virtue, 32
civil rights, 4, 267
civil society
  as an 'association revolution', 223
  and associations as actors, 219
  and associative democracy, 12–13,
    230, 242, 243
  concepts of, 204–9
  and cosmopolitan democracy,
    212–13
  and definition of boundaries of
    political communities, 213–23
  and democracy, 203
  and elitist vs participatory
    democracy, 211–12, 213
  global or transnational, 289n
  and globalization, 219–22
  and group participation, 81–2
  and markets, 207
  Marxist view of, 252
  as a means of conflict resolution,
    218–19
  as a means of democratization, 12
  and non-governmental
    organizations, 205, 208–9
  and pluralist democracy, 210–11,
    213
  role of, 217–22
  as a set of societal conditions, 217
  and 'social capital', 11–12
  and the state, 205–7, 208
  theories of democracy and, 209–
    13
  see also global civil society;
    transnational civil society
class analysis, 97
Cohen, Joshua
  Associations and Democracy, 232,
    234

Cohen, Joshua *cont.*
  on associative democracy, 229,
    231–4, 235, 237, 238, 241, 243,
    244
  and dangers of markets, 207
  and deliberative democracy, 13, 40,
    42, 152, 179
  and democratic political legitimacy,
    198n
  and distributive fairness, 239
Cole, G. D. H., 35, 245n
collective rights, 127, 140
  see also group rights; indigenous
    rights
collectivism, 111
Commission on Global Governance,
  273
Commission for Racial Equality
  (UK), 239
communication and nationhood,
  152–3
communicative action, 41
communism
  Chinese Communist Party, 206
  collapse in Eastern Europe, 149
  German Communist Party, 256
communitarianism, 98, 99, 100
'communities of choice', 235
'communities of fate', 235
Confucianism, 208
consociational democracy, 163, 170n
consumerism, 3, 33
Coombs, H. C., 137
corporate citizenship, 38
cosmopolitan democracy, 212–13,
  275–7, 288
cosmopolitanism, 272, 289n
  see also political cosmopolitanism
critique
  capacity for, 23
  and self-reflection, 42, 43
  and transformation, 26, 27
Crosland, C. A. R., 14, 249, 264,
  265
  The Future of Socialism, 258–9
  Socialism Now, 259–60

cultural difference and identity, 103
cultural heterogeneity, 111
cultural patrimony, 102
cultural rights, 117

Dahl, Robert, 28, 210, 232, 245n, 270
de Tocqueville, Alexis, 229, 232
Declaration of Independence (1776)
  (USA), 122
Declaration of the Rights of Man and
  of Citizens (1789) (France), 122,
  150
deliberative citizenship, 37–8, 40–1
deliberative democracy, 83, 151–2
  and associative democracy, 13
  and bargaining, 170n
  and citizenship, 11
  and civic deficit, 42–4
  and communicative power, 180–5,
    186–7
  conceptions of the good citizen,
    41–2
  criticism of, 279–83
  and defining deliberation, 182
  and developmental democracy, 37
  epistemological functions, 192–6
  ethical functions, 190–1
  and governability, 188–9
  and identity politics, 43, 45, 187–8
  and the importance of debate, 83
  and liberalism, 40
  and moral cosmopolitanism, 289n
  and the need to speak the same
    language, 152–3
  political functions, 186–90
  and populism, 40
  and post-conventional legitimacy,
    187
  and proceduralism, 189–90
  and republicanism, 40
  the social theory of, 176–85
  theories of, 173–6, 196–7
  theory and practice of, 39–44,
    45–6
  and transnational democracy,
    277–80, 289n

vs democracy as negotiation, 162
vs discursive democracy, 290n
democracy
    and capitalism, 52–5, 282, 286
    challenges for, 2–10
    and civil society, 203
    and communication, 173
    and corporations, 16
    direct forms of, 274
    and economic globalization, 15,
        24, 270
    and gender, 78–9, 84
    and group rights, 104–9
    and indigenous self determination,
        121–4
    moral legitimacy of, 191
    nationalism as a hindrance to,
        153–4
    as negotiation, 162–4
    as popular sovereignty, 163
    and sexuality, 91
    the threat of disenchantment, 24–5
    vs liberalism, 101
    and voting, 173
    within the context of
        differentiation, 178–80
democratic autonomy, 275
democratic citizenship, 129, 156–8,
    160
democratic deficit, 149, 153, 273
democratic disenchantment *see* civic
    deficit
democratic equality, 105, 106
democratic legitimacy, 162
democratic participation
    and associationalism, 244
    and a democratic politics of
        inclusion, 109–14
    and gender, 74
    and gender-based inclusion and
        exclusion, 73, 75–80
    and group rights, 102, 106, 108
    and inclusion of the hitherto
        excluded, 82–4
    independence and interdependence,
        74, 80–1

democratic rights
    and immigration, 149
    and national identity, 149
democratization
    and globalization, 270, 284–5
    of international society, 287
    and militant nationalism, 159–61
    politics of, 114
    of the world order, 274
the demos, 75, 280, 284
developmental democracy
    and civic deficit, 38–9
    conceptions of the good citizen,
        37–8
    and deliberative democracy, 37
    and identity politics, 38, 39
    theory and practice of, 34–9, 45
Dewey, John, 35
dialogic democracy, 83
difference, 103, 107–8, 112
    see also identity; identity politics;
        politics of difference
differentiated citizenship, 101, 106,
    112, 113
discursive democracy, 151–2
distributive fairness, 239
Dryzek, John, 43
Durbin, Evan, 257
Dworkin, Ronald, 61–3

East Asia, 207, 209, 211, 223, 270,
    286
Eastern Europe, 205, 207, 209, 211,
    212, 215
economic equality, 4, 14, 249, 274
economic freedom, 59
economic globalization, 2, 13, 228
    and democratic disenchantment, 24
    and democracy, 270
    as a threat to democracy, 15
economic neo-liberalism, 272
economic rights, 38, 267
economic security, 2
    and civil and political rights, 4–5
education, 231
    state funding of, 17

elections
  and campaign funding, 61–2, 64–6,
    68
  indigenous peoples' participation
    in, 129–30
  proportional representation, 67,
    72n
  and reform of electoral system, 67
  see also voting
elitist democracy and civil society,
    211–12, 213
Elster, John, 183
Engels, Friedrich, 253, 267
equality
  ideals of, 75, 98
  and neo-liberalism, 244, 265–6
  and radical democratic pluralism,
    274
  of respect, 53, 55–9, 69
  and social democracy, 249,
    259–60, 266
  vs liberty, 100, 104, 112
  see also civic equality; economic
    equality; political equality; social
    equality
Estlund, David, 64–6
ethnic heterogeneity, 102
ethnic nationality, 157
ethnicity, 102, 103
ethno-nationalism, 119
European Union (EU), 149, 152–3,
    220, 243, 280, 281, 284,
    285–6
expansive democracy, 49

Fabian Society (UK), 253
The Federalist, 174
femininity, 74, 75
feminism, 5
Ferguson, Adam, 204
Fishkin, James, 43
'Fordist' economic system, 228
Foucault, Michel, 10, 208
France, 122, 158, 206, 261, 264
Fraser, Nancy, 107
free market economy, 252, 261

French Revolution (1789), 158
Friedman, Milton, 59–61
Friendly Societies (UK), 246n
Front National (France), 158

Gaitskell, Hugh, 251, 257
Galston, William, 38
gay movement, 6
Gellner, Ernest, 205
gender
  and citizenship, 73, 74, 75–80
  and democracy, 78–9, 84
  and democratic participation, 74
  and inequality, 77–9
gender equality, 235
General Association of German
    Workers, 251
Geremek, Bronislaw, 209
Germany, 13, 72n, 157, 206, 231,
    250–1, 253–4, 256–7, 264
Giddens, Anthony, 208, 264
Gilligan, Carol, 95–6n
global capitalism, 14, 264, 286
global citizenship, 4, 41, 44
global civil society, 41, 42, 215,
    220–2, 242, 243, 271, 289n
  see also transnational civil society
global democracy, 41, 151, 248
  and associative democracy, 242–3
global democratization, 270, 284–5
Global Environmental Facility, 285
global governance, 276, 287
global social democracy, 282
global social justice, 285, 286
globalization
  and global civil society, 242–3,
    276
  and human rights, 31
  and national citizenship, 25
  and neo-liberalism, 242
  and social democracy, 261–4
  and the state, 215, 230
  and the tensions between
    democracy and nationalism, 149
  and transnational democracy,
    270–1, 286

the good citizen
  civic republicanist conceptions of,
    32–3
  deliberative democratic conceptions
    of, 41–2
  developmental democratic
    conceptions of, 37–8
  liberal minimalist conceptions of,
    29–30
Good Friday Agreement (1998)
  (Belfast), 161, 163, 164, 169n,
  170n
Green, T. H., 35
Greenpeace, 13
group rights
  categories of, 117
  and classical liberalism, 7
  and critiques of liberalism, 97,
    98–101
  and democracy, 104–9
  and democratic participation, 102,
    106, 108
  and a democratic politics of
    inclusion, 109–14
  and discrimination, 103
  and ethnicity, 102
  and identity politics, 6
  and indigenous peoples, 7–8
  and political economy, 113–15
  and political equality, 8
  political goals of, 103–4
  and representation rights, 102
  in South Africa, 109
  as a threat to social order, 100–1
  vs individual rights, 123, 130, 135
guild socialism, 35, 230, 245n
Gutmann, Amy, 187

Habermas, Jürgen
  communicative power, 180–5
  conception of deliberative
    democracy, 40–1, 175, 189,
    200n
  and constitutional patriotism, 51n
  deliberative citizenship, 42
  identity politics, 43, 187–8
  relationship between moral theory
    and democratic theory, 191
  social theory, 11, 40–2, 176–7
Haider, Jörge, 160
Hampshire, Stuart, 260
Hanson, Pauline, 160
Hayek, Friedrich, 262
Hegel, G. W. F., 204
Held, David, 27, 210
Hirst, Paul
  associationalism and corporatism,
    231
  Associative Democracy, 234
  associative democracy and global
    democracy, 242–3
  associative democracy and
    republicanism, 240–1
  associative democracy and the
    state, 237–8
  context for his theory of associative
    democracy, 229
  and democratizing the economy
    and society, 234–6
  on global civil society, 13
  Globalization in Question, 243
  on welfare, 240
Hobbes, T., 204
Hobhouse, L. T., 35
human rights, 26, 31, 221, 235, 242
human rights law and self-
    determination, 122
Hume, David, 207

identity, 103, 112, 118
  see also civic identity
identity politics, 97, 107, 114
  challenge to liberal democracy, 6
  and civic republicanism, 33
  dangers of, 108
  and deliberative democracy, 43, 45
  and developmental democracy, 38
  and group rights, 25–6
  and indigenous peoples, 8–9
  and moral conflict, 187–8
  and political autonomy, 25–6
  and the state, 110

immigration, 149, 156–8, 160
imperialism, 98, 277
indigenous peoples
  failures of liberal democracy,
    129–30
  and group rights, 7–8
  and identity politics, 8–9
  land rights, 127–9
  and participation in elections,
    129–30
  state policy on, 125–7
indigenous peoples in Australia *see*
  Aborigines and Torres Strait
  Islanders
indigenous peoples in Canada *see*
  Canada
indigenous political autonomy,
  134–40
indigenous politics and democratic
  process, 138–9
indigenous rights, 7–8, 26, 126,
  127–9, 130–3, 140
indigenous self-determination, 8–9,
  121–4, 132–4, 142
individual freedom/liberty, 1, 59, 75,
  100, 104, 228, 246n, 274
individual rights, 98, 123, 135, 235
individualism, 33, 97
  see also liberal individualism
inequality, 4, 77–9
  see also equality; material
    inequality
interest group politics, 141
International Commission of Jurists,
  221
International Covenant on Civil and
  Political Rights, 122
International Covenant on Economic,
  Social and Cultural Rights,
  122
International Fund for Agricultural
  Development, 285
International Labour Organization
  (ILO), 285
International Monetary Fund (IMF),
  270, 271, 273

international non-governmental
  organizations (INGOs), 220–2
international relations theory, 269,
  273
internationalism vs cosmopolitanism,
  272
Irish Republic, 164
Irish Republican Army, 155

Japan, 231
Jay, Douglas, 257
  The Socialist Case, 257

Kant, I., 194, 208, 255
Kantian moral philosophy, 255
Kautsky, Karl, 253, 255, 256
Keynes, John Maynard, 257
  General Theory, 257
Keynesian economics, 230, 249,
  257–8, 259, 261, 264
Kiss, Elizabeth, 107, 109, 118n
Kymlicka, Will, 38, 99, 100, 104,
  117n

language rights, 102
Lasalle, Ferdinand, 251
Laski, Harold, 35
Le Pen, Jean-Marie, 160
liberal democracy, 1, 4, 10–15
liberal democratic institutions, 2–3
liberal individualism, 98, 111
liberal institutionalism, 273
liberal minimalism, 27–31, 45
liberal pluralism, 246n
liberal values, 1, 3, 31, 240
liberal-internationalism, 272–3,
  287
liberalism
  communitarian critique of, 7, 98
  and deliberative democracy, 40
  and group rights, 6, 97
  modern critiques of, 97,
    98–101
  role of citizens, 1–2, 116–17
  and self-determination, 122
  vs democracy, 101, 111

see also market liberalism;
neo-liberalism; political
liberalism; social liberalism
liberty vs equality, 100, 104
Liebknecht, Karl, 256
Lijphart, Arendt, 163
Lindsay, A. D., 35
Locke, John, 28, 30, 70n, 204
Luxemburg, Rosa, 253, 256
   Social Reform or Revolution,
   255–6

Macpherson, C. B., 27
Madison, James, 174
Mandela, Nelson, 108
market economy, 207, 228, 261
market liberalism, 230
Marshall, T. H., 35, 36, 49n
Marx, Karl
   analysis of capitalism, 204, 251–4,
   258–9
   and the anarchy of social
   production, 177
   Capital, 254
   The Communist Manifesto, 254
   Critique of the Gotha Programme,
   251, 252–3
   on German social democracy,
   251–3
   On the Jewish Question, 252
   theory of revolution, 254–5
Marxian socialism, 249
Marxism vs social democracy,
   251–61, 266
masculinity, 74, 75
'mass society', 3, 246n
material inequality, 53–5
Matthews, John, 228
Mill, John Stuart, 35, 119, 151, 174,
   229
Minority Rights Group, 221
Mitterrand, François, 54, 264
monetarism, 261
moral agency, 63
moral cosmopolitanism, 289n
moral pluralism, 262

multicultural affirmation, 99
multicultural politics, 103
multiculturalism, 6–7, 100, 104, 112,
   113, 114

national frontiers and boundary
   issues, 154–6
national identity, 110, 149, 164, 216,
   241
National Security Law (South Korea),
   221
national self-determination, 151, 153,
   155, 166n
national sovereignty, 121, 122–3,
   133–4, 142, 221
nationalism
   civic vs ethnic, 157–8
   and cultural identity, 110, 111
   as a hindrance to democracy,
   153–4
   and immigration, 156–8
   the mutability of, 164–5
   and popular sovereignty, 150–2
   and right-wing populism, 9–10
   and self-determination, 122
   in the West, 110, 111
nationalist conflict, 155
   democracy as a help, 161
   democracy as a hindrance, 159–61
nationalization, 257–8, 264
nationhood, 152–4
native title (Australia), 18, 132–3
natural rights, 28, 30
neo-liberalism
   challenges to the authority of, 274
   critique of social justice, 262–3
   and equality, 265–6
   and globalization, 242
   and rise in social inequality, 5,
   244
   and social democracy, 261–4, 265
   and the Third Way, 264
Neue Mitte (Germany), 264, 266
non-governmental organizations
   (NGOs), 25, 205, 208–9, 216,
   217, 242, 248, 271

non-governmental organizations
(NGOs) *cont.*
see also international non-
governmental organizations
North Korea, 217, 221–2
Northern Ireland, 10, 150, 155–6,
160, 161, 164, 170n, 217,
218–19
Good Friday Agreement (1998)
(Belfast), 161, 163, 164, 169n,
170n
Nozick, Robert, 98, 261
Anarchy, State and Utopia, 261
Nunavut Territory, 8, 135–6

O'Donohue, Lois, 138
Oldfield, A., 31, 32–3
Olson, Mancur, 240
One Nation movement (Australia),
18n, 160
Organization of African Unity, 221

Pareto, Vilfredo, 71n
Pareto Optimality, 71n
parliament, culture of, 82
Parsons, Talcott, 180
participation *see* democratic
participation; political
participation
participatory democracy, 126,
211–12, 213, 241, 274
Pateman, Carole, 93n
Pericles, 173
Pettit, Phillip, 31
Plato, 192
pluralism, 231–2, 233, 235
see also liberal pluralism; radical
democratic pluralism
pluralist democracy, 28–9, 210–11,
213
political apathy, 3, 16, 25, 30
see also civic deficit
political autonomy and self-
determination, 133–41
political cosmopolitanism, 272
political democracy and social
democracy, 250–1

political economy, 98, 113–15
political equality, 4, 5, 8, 250
and associative democracy, 232,
233
and exclusion of women, 5
formal vs substantive, 52–5, 130
and group rights, 8, 142
and self-determination, 121–4
and social democracy, 250
see also substantive political
equality
political freedom, 59
political liberalism, 100, 101, 105,
106
political participation, 25, 228
political rights, 28, 29, 30, 31, 36,
236, 267
political will, 151–2, 167n
politics of difference, 97, 99, 103,
114, 237
politics of identity *see* identity
politics
politics of multiculturalism, 103,
114
politics of recognition, 97, 99, 101,
103, 107
see also identity politics
polyethnic hierarchies, 156
Popper, Karl, 31
popular sovereignty, 150–2, 161,
232, 233
populism, 9–10, 40, 160
postmodernism, 99
Prevention of Terrorism Act (UK),
156
private vs public realm, 105
privatization, 231
proportional representation, 67, 72n
protective democracy, 28
protective republicanism, 31
protective rights, 103, 118
Przeworski, Adam, 257
Capitalism and Social Democracy,
257
public choice economics, 263
public good, 104, 231, 241
public identity and sexuality, 85–8

public reason, 100
public vs private realm, 105
Putnam, Robert, 3, 12

racial discrimination, 103
racial heterogeneity, 111
radical democracy, 113–15, 234,
    244
radical democratic pluralism, 274–5,
    287, 289n
Rawls, John
    A Theory of Justice, 100, 260
    on the basic liberties, 52–3
    deliberative citizenship, 37–8
    first principle of justice, 70n
    and liberal developmentalism, 35
    liberal view of the individual, 98
    public reason, 37, 117n, 189
    on redistribution of wealth, 64
    theory of social justice, 249
Raz, Joseph, 104
recognition rights, 104, 107
regional nationalism, 9
regionalization, 286
representation rights, 102
republican democracy, 31
republicanism, 1, 40, 240–2, 246n
    see also civic republicanism;
        protective republicanism
revolutionary socialism, 230
right-wing populism and nationalism,
    9–10
rights *see* assistance rights; citizenship
    rights; civic rights and
    obligations; civil rights; collective
    rights; cultural rights; democratic
    rights; economic rights; group
    rights; human rights; indigenous
    rights; individual rights; language
    rights; natural rights; political
    rights; protective rights;
    recognition rights; representation
    rights; sexual rights; social
    rights; special rights; trade union
    rights; women's rights
rights of recognition, 101
Rockefeller Foundation, 222

Rogers, Joel, 13, 245n
    Associations and Democracy, 232,
        234
    on associative democracy, 229,
        231–4, 235, 237, 238, 241, 243,
        244
    distributive fairness, 239
rule of law, 272, 275, 280, 281

Saami parliaments (Scandinavia), 8
Scandinavia, 8
Schmitter, Philippe, 205, 231
Schröder, Gerhard, 264
Schumpeter, Joseph, 28
scientific socialism, 255
Scottish Parliament, 153, 155
secession, 154–5
secessionist movements, 221
self-determination
    and human rights law, 122
    and indigenous peoples, 8–9
    and indigenous rights, 130–3
    and liberalism, 122
    and political autonomy, 133–
        41
    and political equality, 121–4
    state-centered theories of, 215
    see also indigenous self-
        determination; national self-
        determination
sex differences, 74, 77–8
sexual character, 89–90
sexual harassment, 84, 88–9
sexual identity *see* gender
sexual rights, 75
sexuality
    and citizenship, 85–8
    and democracy, 91
    the politicization of, 74, 84–90
    and public identity, 85–8
Shapiro, Ian, 117n, 118–19n
Smith, Adam, 204, 207
Smith, Rogers, 119n
social capital, 3, 12
social citizenship, 13, 36
Social Darwinism, 110
social democratic parties, 250–1

social democracy
  and associative democracy, 228,
    230, 234
  and citizenship, 266, 267
  and electoral politics, 251
  and equality, 13–14, 249, 252,
    257, 258, 259–60, 266
  evolution of, 14, 249
  first phase of revisionism, 249,
    253–7
  and globalization, 261–4
  and Keynesian economics, 249,
    257–8, 259, 261
  moral critique of capitalism, 251
  and nationalization, 257–8, 259
  and neo-liberalism, 249, 261–4
  and political democracy, 250–1
  second phase of revisionism, 249,
    250–1, 257
  and social citizenship, 13
  and social justice, 240, 249, 250,
    252, 257, 258, 259, 261, 262,
    265, 266
  and the Third Way, 264–6
  vs Marxism, 249, 251–61, 266
Social Democratic Party (SPD)
    (Germany), 250–1, 253, 254,
    256–7, 258
social discrimination, 237
social equality, 4, 5, 249, 274
social justice, 36, 126, 228, 230, 237,
    285, 286
  and associationalism, 239–40
  and associative democracy, 239–40
  neo-liberal critique of, 262–3
  and social democracy, 249, 250,
    252, 257, 258, 259, 261, 262,
    265
social liberalism, 4–5
social movements, 25, 77, 239, 270,
    274
social rights, 35, 38, 236, 267
social stability, 2, 100–1
socialism, 60, 253, 255
  see also guild socialism; Marxian
    socialism; revolutionary

socialism; scientific socialism;
    state socialism
South Africa, 108–9, 118n, 228
South Korea, 217, 219, 221–2, 270
sovereignty, 275
  see also national sovereignty
Soviet Union, 216
Spartacus League, 256
special rights, 23, 106, 141, 237
stakeholder democracy, 277
the state
  and associative democracy, 228,
    237–9
  and civic identity, 110
  and civil society, 205–7, 208
  elite domination of, 112–14
  and global civil society, 215
  and globalization, 215
  and group rights, 109–14
  and identity politics, 110
  and national boundaries, 214–17,
    222
  and respect of citizens, 55–9
  and voluntary organizations, 237–9
state socialism, 228, 230, 234
substantive political equality
  the agency objection to, 63–4
  argument for, 55–9
  the feasibility objection to, 59–61
  implications for campaign funding,
    68–9
  implications for education, 68
  the inequality objection to, 61–2
  institutional implications, 66–9
  the maximin objection to, 64–6
  and reform of electoral systems, 67
  and socialism, 60
Sunstein, C. R., 31
Sweden, 13, 14, 239–40
Swilling, Mark, 228
symbolic non-recognition, 118

Taiwan, 219, 221, 222
Taylor, Charles, 99, 205
Thatcher Government (UK), 265
Thatcherism, 229

the Third Way, 35, 61, 264–6
Thompson, Dennis, 187
tolerance, 99, 100, 142
totalitarianism, 246n
trade union rights, 4, 230
trade unions, 230, 231, 233, 234,
   256
transnational citizenship, 41
transnational civil society, 284, 287,
   289n
   see also global civil society
transnational democracy
   and cosmopolitan democracy,
      275–7, 288
   criticisms of, 280–3
   defences of, 283–6
   and deliberative (discursive)
      democracy, 277–80, 289n
   and globalization, 270–1
   and international relations theory,
      269
   and liberal-internationalism,
      272–3, 287
   and radical democratic pluralism,
      274–5, 287, 289n
   theories of, 271–80
   towards a democratic global polity,
      286–8
transnational social movements, 270

Uhr, John, 43
Ulster Workers Council strike (1974),
   218
United Kingdom, 54, 55, 67, 71n,
   76, 251, 264–5
United Nations, 248, 271
United Nations Charter, 122
United Nations Committee on the
   Elimination of All Forms of
   Racial Discrimination (CERD),
   133, 140
United States of America
   affirmative action, 6–7
   'ascriptive Americanism', 119n
   campaign funding, 68

cultural heterogeneity, 111
Declaration of Independence
   (1776), 122
electoral system, 67, 71n, 72n,
   241
group rights, 7
US Constitution (1789), 174
voter demand for tax cuts, 3
wealth and political inequality,
   53–5, 66
universal suffrage, 75

voluntary associations
   and alternative governance, 233
   and associative democratic theory,
      230, 241
   and the monitoring of central
      government, 243
   and the state, 237–9
voting, 8, 28, 29, 35, 76, 173
   see also elections

Weber, Max, 28, 177, 187
welfare, 240
welfare state, 5, 230, 258, 263, 264
Wilson, Woodrow, 122, 272
women
   civic and political equality of, 5, 6,
      7
   and participation in social
      movements, 77
   and unequal participation in
      democratic processes, 75, 76
   and voting, 29, 76
women's rights, 5, 26
worker democracy, 230
World Bank, 217
World Council of Churches, 221
World Muslim League, 221
World Trade Organization (WTO),
   273, 284

Young, I. M., 112, 116n, 119n,
   120n, 236–7
Yugoslavia, 218